S0-BBH-815

Manual for the

SAT®

Version 5.0

© 2013 by TPR Education IP Holdings, LLC. All Rights Reserved.

No part of this manual may be reproduced for distribution to a third party in any form or by any means, electronic or mechanical, including photocopying, recording, or any information retrieval system, without the prior consent of the publisher, The Princeton Review.

Permission to reprint this material does not constitute review or endorsement by the Educational Testing Service or the College Board of this publication as a whole or of any other sample questions or testing information it may contain.

This manual is for the exclusive use of The Princeton Review course students and is not legal for resale.

Educational Testing Service and ETS are registered trademarks of the Educational Testing Service.

SAT is a registered trademark of the College Board.

The Princeton Review is not affiliated with Princeton University or the Educational Testing Service.

1-866-TPR-PREP

PrincetonReview.com

Contributors

Thanks to Brian Becker, John Fulmer, Curtis Retherford, and David Stoll for their contributions to this edition.

Special thanks to Debbie Silvestrini for her work in producing this edition.

I would also like to thank the following for their contributions in previous editions:

Ed Carroll, Dan Coggshall, Mariwyn Curtin, Vinni Drybala, Paul Kanarek, John Katzman, Lisa Mayo, Katie Noone, Adam Redfield, Joy Westdorp, *many* other authors and contributors, and the staff and students of The Princeton Review.

Finally, special thanks to Adam Robinson, who conceived of and perfected the Joe Bloggs approach to standardized testing, as well as many other techniques in this manual.

—Jonathan Chiu
National Content Director
High School Programs

Contents

INTRODUCTION

CLOSE TO HOME © 1997 John McPherson.
Reprinted with permission of UNIVERSAL PRESS SYNDICATE. All rights reserved.

© 1997 John McPherson/Dist. by Universal Press Syndicate

The year the SAT creators decided to mess with students' minds.

THE SAT: EVERYTHING YOU NEVER WANTED TO KNOW

THE SAT:

Stands for

S _____

A _____

T _____

Is made by

E _____

T _____

S _____

How Important Is It?

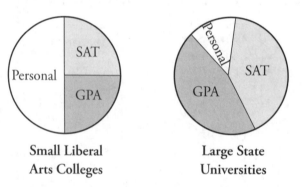

Small Liberal
Arts Colleges

Large State
Universities

What Does It Test?

Math _____

Reading _____

Writing _____

What Does It *REALLY* Test?

The SAT tests: _____

 © TPR Education IP Holdings, LLC

The SAT and YOU

How beatable is the SAT?

_____

When is the SAT administered?

_____

How many times can you take the SAT?

_____

When will YOU take the SAT?

_____

By knowing the layout and style of the SAT and executing the techniques
and strategies you learn in this course, you will
experience much success in your SAT prep journey.

STRUCTURE OF THE SAT

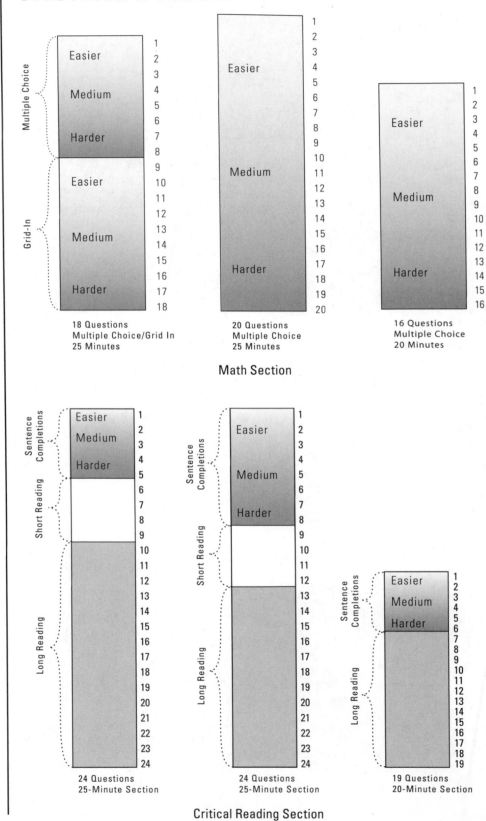

Math Section

18 Questions
Multiple Choice/Grid In
25 Minutes

20 Questions
Multiple Choice
25 Minutes

16 Questions
Multiple Choice
20 Minutes

24 Questions
25-Minute Section

24 Questions
25-Minute Section

19 Questions
20-Minute Section

Critical Reading Section

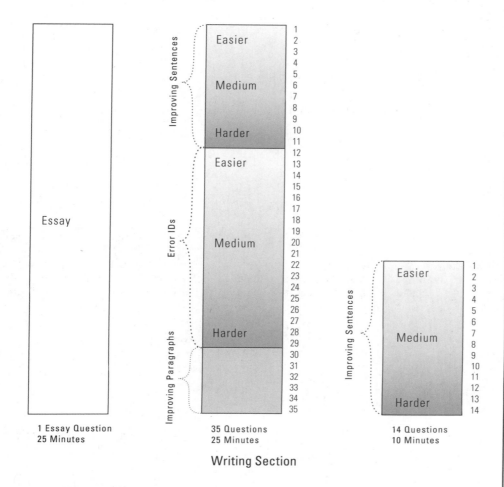

Essay

1 Essay Question
25 Minutes

35 Questions
25 Minutes

14 Questions
10 Minutes

Writing Section

Note the following:

- There are 10 sections, totaling 3 hours, 45 minutes.
- Questions come in three flavors: easy, medium, and hard.
- The Essay is the first section, the 10-minute Grammar section always appears last, and the middle eight sections are mixed.
- The Experimental section can consist of any of the three subjects.

Experimental Section

Time—25 Minutes
Math: 18–20 Q's
Reading: 23–25 Q's
Writing: 35 Q's

Don't assume any particular section is the Experimental. Do your best in every section!

© TPR Education IP Holdings, LLC | **5**

HOW IS THE SAT SCORED?

Correct answer: +1 points

Blank: 0 points

Incorrect Answer: $-\dfrac{1}{4}$ point

Scores taken from a recent SAT test:

Raw Score	Critical Reading Scaled Score	Raw Score	Critical Reading Scaled Score
67	800	31	500
66	800	30	490
65	800	29	490
64	780	28	480
63	760	27	470
62	750	26	470
61	730	25	460
60	720	24	460
59	710	23	450
58	700	22	440
57	690	21	440
56	680	20	430
55	670	19	420
54	660	18	420
53	650	17	410
52	640	16	400
51	630	15	400
50	630	14	390
49	620	13	380
48	610	12	380
47	600	11	370
46	600	10	360
45	590	9	350
44	580	8	340
43	580	7	330
42	570	6	320
41	560	5	310
40	560	4	300
39	550	3	280
38	540	2	270
37	540	1	250
36	530	0	230
35	520	−1	210
34	520	−2	200
33	510	−3	200
32	510	& below	

Raw Score	Math Scaled Score	Raw Score	Math Scaled Score
54	800	25	490
53	790	24	490
52	760	23	480
51	740	22	470
50	720	21	470
49	710	20	460
48	700	19	450
47	690	18	440
46	680	17	430
45	670	16	430
44	660	15	420
43	650	14	410
42	640	13	400
41	630	12	390
40	620	11	390
39	610	10	380
38	600	9	370
37	590	8	360
36	580	7	350
35	570	6	340
34	570	5	330
33	560	4	310
32	550	3	300
31	540	2	290
30	530	1	270
29	520	0	250
28	520	−1	230
27	510	−2	210
26	500	−3	200
		& below	

Raw Score	Writing Multiple Choice Scaled Score	Raw Score	Writing Multiple Choice Scaled Score
49	80	22	47
48	80	21	46
47	77	20	45
46	75	19	44
45	73	18	43
44	71	17	42
43	69	16	42
42	68	15	41
41	66	14	40
40	65	13	39
39	63	12	38
38	62	11	37
37	61	10	36
36	60	9	35
35	59	8	34
34	58	7	33
33	57	6	32
32	56	5	31
31	55	4	30
30	54	3	28
29	53	2	27
28	52	1	25
27	51	0	23
26	50	−1	21
25	49	−2	20
24	49	−3	20
23	48	& below	

SCORING CURVE ON THE SAT

Below is an approximate representation of the SAT scoring curve.

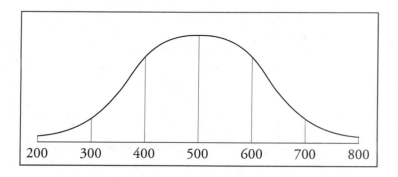

The majority of students score between 400 and 600 on each section of the SAT.

FASCINATING FUN FACTS ABOUT THE SAT

- All questions are worth the same number of points—1 point each.
- Total number of questions: 67 Reading, 54 Math, and 49 Writing.
- Question difficulty is indicated often by the question number, and most sections appear with a set Order Of Difficulty (OOD).
- Two-thirds of the questions are of easy or medium difficulty. This means a student can get about 600 on each section without doing one hard question. (That's an 1800 without having to pull your hair out!)
- Invest your time when and where it will yield the biggest payoff for you—for most students that means the easy and medium problems.
- Unless you're aiming for a 750+ in a section, it doesn't make sense to answer every question in that section.

Slow down; score more.

Drill

Instructions: Write the *first* thing that comes to mind:

First Word: _____

Second Word: _____

Third Word: _____

Your Number: _____

Pretty predictable, eh? ETS thinks so, too. What do they want you to answer on the following question?

> If a store raises the price of an item by 20%, then decreases the new price by 15%, what was the percent change in the price of the item?

Just Your Average Joe

We've come up with a name for the average, predictable student that ETS is expecting: Joe Bloggs. He's your average guy—not too bright, but not too dumb either. We love him, though, because he's completely predictable. Knowing this, we can beat ETS at its own game.

How Does Joe Do?

Easy Questions:	Joe gets over 90% right.
Medium Questions:	Joe gets about 50% right.
Hard Questions:	Joe gets almost none right.

Knowing how Joe Bloggs approaches the test can help you know what to do and what *not* to do.

PACING AND POOD

It would be great if you had all the time in the world to finish the SAT. But you don't, so make sure you use the time available in the most efficient manner. ETS doesn't order all question types by difficulty. For the reading passages, you have to make your own Personal Order of Difficulty (POOD). Just remember to do all the questions you find easiest first, and save the ones you think are the most difficult for last.

DO the questions that you have time for and aim for accuracy.
DON'T waste time with questions that are too hard or too long.

POE & Guessing: Less Work = Higher Score?

Well, the title is not exactly true! What the title does mean is that by spending more time to improve your accuracy on selected problems, you can earn a higher score. For example, suppose the SAT contained only 5 questions. What would these students' raw scores be?

Student A		Student B		Student C	
(1)	✔	(1)	✔	(1)	✔
(2)	✔	(2)	✔	(2)	✔
(3)	✔	(3)	✘	(3)	✔
(4)	✘	(4)	✘	(4)	—
(5)	✘	(5)	✘	(5)	—
Raw score: _____		Raw score: _____		Raw score: _____	

Extrapolated across an entire test, the difference in raw scores between Student A and Student C—and *especially* between Student B and Student C—will result in dramatically different scaled scores. All this because of simply more strategic—and smarter—test-taking! Therefore, what does that mean for you? NO GUESSING! If you can't eliminate any answer choices, you're better off leaving the question blank.

Doing fewer problems to maximize accuracy
can increase your score!

HOW TO USE OUR COURSE TO NAIL THE SAT

Please keep some things in mind as we go through the course.

- This isn't school. We don't give you a grade, but we do expect you to realize that YOUR score improvement reflects the amount of work YOU put into the course.

- Try to do at least half an hour a day on homework/practice. Three hours the night before the class isn't going to work for you. If you are an athlete or a musician, would you practice for three hours the night before a big game or a big concert? Hopefully not! Consistent daily practice is the most effective way to ensure long-term success.

- You must try the techniques. They might be strange at first but you'll get used to them. They work towards accuracy. Do you want to get the question right slower or wrong faster?

- Use a pencil. Not only to fill in an answer sheet, but to write all over the pages, problems, etc.

Setting Goals

Everyone wants to increase his or her score. A big difference between those who succeed and those who don't is whether they set realistic goals and pursue them systematically. Also keep in mind that learning doesn't always happen in a linear fashion or overnight; sometimes it takes a step back to take two forward. Don't be discouraged. Keep working, and you'll see your effort pay off in the long run.

If you are serious about increasing your scores significantly, then you must

1. Come to ALL of the classes.
2. Complete ALL of the homework.
3. Use and practice the techniques on the homework, on the practice tests, and on the real SAT.
4. Take advantage of the extra time available to you to work with your instructor.

Your Present Score: Math _____ Reading _____ Writing _____

Your Target Score: Math _____ Reading _____ Writing _____

Refer back to this page upon after your diagnostic tests to check your status.

What are my biggest SAT strengths from Diagnostic Test A?

_____

What are my biggest areas of improvement from Diagnostic Test A?

_____

After this course is completed, I will have accomplished the following (feel free to add on as necessary!).

1. _____

2. _____

3. _____

SAT MATH:
GLOBAL TECHNIQUES

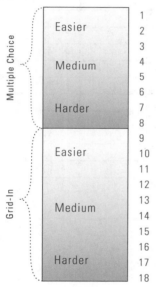

Multiple Choice

Easier
Medium
Harder

1
2
3
4
5
6
7
8

Grid-In

Easier
Medium
Harder

9
10
11
12
13
14
15
16
17
18

18 Questions
Multiple Choice/Grid In
25 Minutes

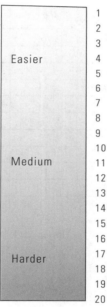

Easier
Medium
Harder

1
2
3
4
5
6
7
8
9
10
11
12
13
14
15
16
17
18
19
20

20 Questions
Multiple Choice
25 Minutes

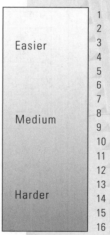

Easier
Medium
Harder

1
2
3
4
5
6
7
8
9
10
11
12
13
14
15
16

16 Questions
Multiple Choice
20 Minutes

SCORING

Believe it or not, you can improve your math score before you even start to learn any SAT Math! The following chart will show you how to use the predictable order of difficulty on the Math section to maximize your score. Refer to this chart after each diagnostic; as your score goes up, increase your target as well.

DIAG Test B GOALS

Diag Test A math score: _____

Diag Test B math goal:_____

Slow down. Maximize the time you spend on each question and read it carefully. Don't give points away by making careless errors.

To get (scaled score)	You need to earn (raw points)	So attempt this many questions				
		20 question MC	8 question MC	Grid-Ins	16 question MC	Total # of questions to attempt
350	8	6	2	2	2	12
400	13	7	3	3	4	17
450	20	9	4	4	6	23
500	27	11	5	5	8	29
550	33	14	6	6	10	36
600	39	16	6	7	13	42
650	45	18	7	8	14	48
700	49	19	7	9	15	50
750	52	all	all	all	all	54
800	54	all	all	all	all	54

How many **you** are going to do: _____   _____   _____   _____   _____

Your Total

Unless you are already scoring a 750 or higher, don't do every question.

GUESSING AND PACING

If you're not supposed to do every question in a section, there will be some questions that you intentionally leave blank. However, if you are a few questions short of your pacing goal, you should definitely guess on some problems that are within your OOD.

Guess on problems ONLY IF you need to answer a few more questions to hit your Pacing Goal.

JOE BLOGGS AND PROCESS OF ELIMINATION (POE)
What Would Joe Bloggs Do?

15. On Tuesday, Jasmine buys an apple pie. She eats $\frac{2}{5}$ of the pie that night. On Thursday, she eats $\frac{2}{5}$ of what is left. How much of the pie still remains uneaten?

(A) $\frac{4}{25}$

(B) $\frac{1}{5}$

(C) $\frac{6}{25}$

(D) $\frac{9}{25}$

(E) $\frac{3}{5}$

Don't pick convenient answers on difficult questions.
That's what Joe does!

16. Paul drives from his apartment to his parents' house and back. On the trip to his parents' house, he travels at an average speed of 60 miles per hour. On the return trip, Paul drives at an average speed of 100 miles per hour. Which of the following is the closest approximation of Paul's average speed, in miles per hour, for the round trip?

(A) 60
(B) 75
(C) 80
(D) 85
(E) 100

For a math question, the question number will indicate the difficulty of the problem.

MATH

WRITING

READING

VOCABULARY

BALLPARKING

Ballparking will also help you eliminate answer choices on multiple-choice questions.

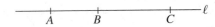

For some questions, you can ballpark the correct answer without actually solving the problem.

8. On line ℓ, the length of $\overline{BC}$ is 1.5 times the length of $\overline{AB}$. If the length of $\overline{AC}$ is 30, what is the length of $\overline{BC}$?

    (A) 10
    (B) 12
    (C) 15
    (D) 18
    (E) 20

YOUR CALCULATOR IS ONLY AS SMART AS YOU ARE

Before using the calculator

1. Read the question.
2. Set up the problem.

Using the calculator is the *last* step.

7. What is the remainder when 22 is divided by 8 ?

    (A)   .75
    (B)   2
    (C)   2.75
    (D)   6
    (E)   14

Be mindful of PEMDAS when using your calculators!

P _____
E _____
M _____
D _____
A _____
S _____

10. $\left(\sqrt{5} + \sqrt{5}\right)^2 =$

    (A)   7
    (B)   10
    (C)   12
    (D)   20
    (E)   50

R.T.F.Q.

ETS will often make seemingly easy problems very tricky and, of course, have trap answers ready for you to select! Individually underline the key words (a.k.a. "hot words") in the problem to make sure that you remember to account for them.

8. What is the least of 3 consecutive even integers if the sum of these integers is 66 ?

   (A) 20
   (B) 21
   (C) 22
   (D) 23
   (E) 24

R _____

T _____

F _____

Q _____

11. If $x + y = 10$ and x and y are distinct positive integers, what is the greatest possible value of xy ?

   (A) 25
   (B) 24
   (C) 21
   (D) 16
   (E) 9

13. At a certain store, shirts sell for $21 each. If a customer buys a pair of shirts, the second shirt costs only $9. How much per shirt does a customer save by buying a pair of shirts instead of two shirts separately?

   (A) $6
   (B) $9
   (C) $12
   (D) $15
   (E) $21

18. The graph above shows the breakdown of Merry's $3,600 monthly expenses. The amount Merry pays for the rent is only part of the total rent for the month because she shares the cost of renting the house equally with her 4 housemates. What is the total monthly rent of the house?

   (A) $30
   (B) $1,080
   (C) $2,520
   (D) $4,320
   (E) $5,400

BITE-SIZED PIECES

Don't be overwhelmed by long word problems. These problems test your reading patience, not your math skills. Do not try to digest an entire question in one big gulp. Take bite-sized pieces and chew one piece at a time.

When there's something to figure out, STOP!
Figure it out and write it down before you move on.

5. Randy bought four rare books that cost $130, $120, $80, and $75, respectively. If he paid $\frac{1}{3}$ of the total cost immediately and the remainder in three equal payments, how much was each of the three equal payments?

    (A) $45
    (B) $55
    (C) $70
    (D) $90
    (E) $135

6. David goes camping with walkie-talkies that can operate within a range of 500 feet from each other. David leaves one walkie-talkie with his friend in his tent and then walks 400 feet due south. From that point he walks due west and stops at the maximum range at which his walkie-talkies can still be in range. In which of the following directions can David walk and still be in range of the other walkie-talkie?

    I.   200 feet due west
    II. 200 feet due southeast
    III. 300 feet due east

    (A) I only
    (B) III only
    (C) I and II only
    (D) I and III only
    (E) II and III only

Summary

- Knowing advanced math is necessary to beat the SAT Math: TRUE / FALSE

- SAT Math isn't tough because it tests difficult concepts; it's tough because the questions are so _____.

- R _____

  T _____

  F _____

  Q _____

- By slowing down, I can _____!

- I have accomplished _____ of my _____ stated goals in the Introduction chapter.

NO MORE ALGEBRA

MATH

WRITING

READING

VOCABULARY

SAT MATH GAME-CHANGER: PLUGGING IN

Algebra or arithmetic? Plugging In numbers for the variables turns an algebra problem into an arithmetic problem.

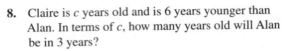

"In terms of" is a needless phrase. If you see it, cross it out, and remember to Plug In.

8. Claire is c years old and is 6 years younger than Alan. In terms of c, how many years old will Alan be in 3 years?

(A) $c - 6$
(B) $c - 3$
(C) $c + 3$
(D) $c + 6$
(E) $c + 9$

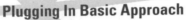

Plugging In Basic Approach

1. Identify the variable.
2. Plug in a number for the variable.
3. Work the steps of the problem.
4. Calculate the Target Value.
5. POE until one answer choice is left.

16. If the sum of three consecutive odd integers is k, then, in terms of k, what is the greatest of the three integers?

(A) $\dfrac{k-6}{3}$

(B) $\dfrac{k-3}{3}$

(C) $\dfrac{k}{3}$

(D) $\dfrac{k+3}{3}$

(E) $\dfrac{k+6}{3}$

WHAT TO PLUG IN
Choose numbers that make the arithmetic as easy as possible.

12. Lou can drive 50 miles in a hours. If he must drive b miles at the same rate, in terms of a and b, how many hours will the trip take?

(A) $\dfrac{a}{50b}$

(B) $\dfrac{50}{ab}$

(C) $50ab$

(D) $\dfrac{ab-b}{25}$

(E) $\dfrac{ab}{50}$

What's a good number to Plug In for b? Why?

Plugging In Tips

- Try numbers that make the math easy; numbers like 2, 3, 5, and 10 work great.

- Plug in numbers that do not appear anywhere else in the question or answer choices.

- Avoid using 0 and 1 whenever possible.

- Spot a **relationship**? Plug In!

- **Check all** five answer choices if they have variables.

16. If $\dfrac{a}{b} = \dfrac{4}{7}$ and $\dfrac{b}{c} = \dfrac{14}{15}$, then what is the value of $\dfrac{a}{c}$?

(A) $\dfrac{4}{15}$

(B) $\dfrac{7}{15}$

(C) $\dfrac{8}{15}$

(D) $\dfrac{4}{7}$

(E) $\dfrac{7}{8}$

When you spot mathematical relationships such as fractions, just Plug In!

MATH

WRITING

READING

VOCABULARY

PLUGGING IN YOUR OWN NUMBER

Even when the question doesn't have any variables, you can still Plug In.

When you don't have a starting number? PLUG IN!

13. The price of a dress is reduced by $\frac{1}{5}$. If the new price is then reduced by $\frac{1}{4}$, the resulting price is what fractional part of the original price?

(A) $\frac{1}{20}$

(B) $\frac{2}{5}$

(C) $\frac{9}{20}$

(D) $\frac{11}{20}$

(E) $\frac{3}{5}$

17. If $3a = b$, $2b = c$, $3c = d$, and $abcd \neq 0$, what is the value of $\frac{d}{a}$?

MATH

WRITING

READING

VOCABULARY

FEEL THE POOD!

16. If $4^x = m$, what does 4^{2x+2} equal in terms of m ?

(A) $4m^2$

(B) $16m^2$

(C) $16m^3$

(D) $m^2 + 4$

(E) $m^2 + 16$

If you only had 1 minute left, would you rather do #16 or #18?

18. At a grain packaging company, sacks of grain are filled by a machine that weighs each sack to be sure that it holds between $24\frac{3}{4}$ and $25\frac{1}{4}$ pounds of grain. Only then will a sack be sealed and shipped. If a sack holding b pounds of grain is shipped, which of the following describes all possible values of b ?

(A) $|b - 25| > \dfrac{1}{4}$

(B) $|b + 25| = \dfrac{1}{4}$

(C) $|b - 25| = \dfrac{1}{4}$

(D) $|b + 25| < \dfrac{1}{4}$

(E) $|b - 25| < \dfrac{1}{4}$

MATH

WRITING

READING

VOCABULARY

PLUGGING IN TIMED DRILL
Time: 10 minutes

Try Plugging In on the following problems. Remember to use POOD! Keep asking yourself: "Can I reach my pacing goal without this question?"

Target score	# of questions to attempt
< 450	3 or 4 questions
460–550	5 or 6 questions
560–650	7 or 8 questions
> 650	All

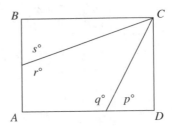

6. If x and y are integers and xy is an even integer, which of the following must be an odd integer?

(A) $xy + 5$
(B) $x + y$
(C) xy
(D) $4x$
(E) $7xy$

8. If d apples cost 5 cents, what is the cost, in cents, of n apples at the same rate?

(A) $\dfrac{5n}{d}$

(B) $5n$

(C) $\dfrac{5d}{n}$

(D) $5d$

(E) $\dfrac{nd}{5}$

12. In the figure above, if $ABCD$ is a quadrilateral, then $r + p =$

(A) $s + q$
(B) $180 + s + q$
(C) $360 + s + q$
(D) $180 - s - q$
(E) $360 - s - q$

13. Lisa, Eric, and Michelle buy a television. Lisa pays half as much as Eric and twice as much as Michelle. If Eric pays x dollars, in terms of x, how much does the television cost?

(A) $\dfrac{3x}{2}$

(B) $\dfrac{7x}{4}$

(C) $2x$

(D) $3x$

(E) $7x$

GO ON TO THE NEXT PAGE

 © TPR Education IP Holdings, LLC

$$A = \{x + 3, x - 4, 3x + 4\}$$

15. If $x > 0$, what is the median of set A shown above?

   (A) $2x - 4$

   (B) $x + 3$

   (C) $3x + 4$

   (D) $3x + \dfrac{3}{2}$

   (E) $x - 4$

15. If $n \neq 0$ and $f(n) = 2n + \dfrac{1}{2n}$, what is the value of $f(3)$?

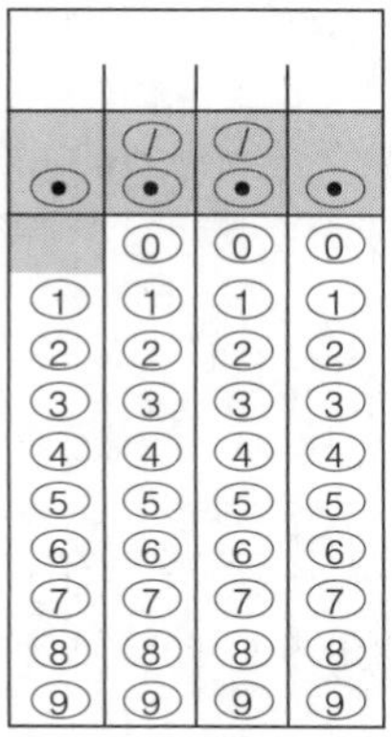

$$a = b + 6$$
$$f = g$$

16. If g is 4 more than b in the equations above, then f is how much less than a ?

   (A)   1
   (B)   2
   (C)   3
   (D)   4
   (E)   6

17. If $x = 3t - 1$ and $y = 12t^2$, what is the value of y in terms of x ?

   (A) $(x + 1)^2$

   (B) $4(x + 1)^2$

   (C) $\dfrac{3(x+1)^2}{4}$

   (D) $\dfrac{4(x+1)^2}{3}$

   (E) $(x - 1)^2$

18. The sum of two consecutive even integers is n. What is the sum of the next two consecutive integers greater than n ?

   (A) $n + 3$
   (B) $n + 5$
   (C) $2n + 2$
   (D) $2n + 3$
   (E) $2n + 6$

19. If the circumference of circle A is twice that of circle B, then $\dfrac{\text{area of circle } A}{\text{area of circle } B} =$

   (A) $\dfrac{1}{2}$

   (B)   2

   (C)   4

   (D) 2π

   (E) 4π

STOP
**If you finish before time is called, you may check your work on this section only.
Do not turn to any other section in the test.**

Summary

- What are the advantages of Plugging In?

  _____

  _____

- Clues to help you recognize a problem on which you can Plug In are
  - Variables in the question or answer choices
  - The phrase "in terms of" in the question
  - Relationships
  - No starting number

- When you Plug In, remember to perform each step

  _____

  _____

  _____

  _____

  _____

- What are examples of good numbers to use to make the math while Plugging In more convenient?

  _____

- I have accomplished _____ of my _____ stated goals in the Introduction chapter.

NO MORE ALGEBRA PRACTICE

PLUGGING IN BASIC APPROACH

1. Identify the variable.
2. Plug in a number for the variable.
3. Work the steps of the problem.
4. Calculate the Target Value.
5. POE until one answer choice is left.

3. If rice costs r cents per kilogram, how many kilograms of rice, in terms of r, may be bought for $5.00 ?

(A) $\dfrac{50}{r}$

(B) $\dfrac{5}{r}$

(C) $\dfrac{r}{500}$

(D) $500r$

(E) $\dfrac{500}{r}$

6. If 6 more than x is two less than y, what is the value of y in terms of x ?

(A) $x + 2$

(B) $\dfrac{x+2}{2}$

(C) $\dfrac{x+8}{2}$

(D) $\dfrac{x+6}{2}$

(E) $x + 8$

6. Beth is two years older than Debbie and four years younger than Marnie. If Debbie is d years old, how old is Marnie in terms of d ?

(A) $d + 2$
(B) $d + 4$
(C) $d + 6$
(D) $2d + 2$
(E) $2d + 4$

7. Susan can stamp x letters per minute. How many letters can she stamp in 3 hours?

(A) $3x$
(B) $30x$
(C) $60x$
(D) $100x$
(E) $180x$

8. Bill is twice as old as Heidi and six years younger than Mel. If Heidi is h years old, how old is Mel in terms of h ?

(A) $h - 4$
(B) $h + 4$
(C) $2h - 4$
(D) $2h$
(E) $2h + 6$

9. If p, q, and r are consecutive odd integers, and $p < q < r$, then in terms of r, $p =$

(A) $r - 4$

(B) $r - 2$

(C) $r + 2$

(D) $r + 4$

(E) $\dfrac{r}{2}$

10. If 4 more than x is 2 times y, what is the value of y in terms of x ?

(A) $2 + \dfrac{x}{2}$

(B) $4 + \dfrac{x}{2}$

(C) $\dfrac{x+2}{2}$

(D) $2(x-2)$

(E) $2x + 4$

10. If x is an odd number, what is the greatest even number less than $4x - 3$?

(A) $x + 1$
(B) $x + 6$
(C) $2x + 4$
(D) $4x - 4$
(E) $4x + 2$

10. If $a \neq 0$, and $a = 2b = 3c$, what is the value of $a + b$ in terms of c ?

(A) $\dfrac{1}{2}c$

(B) $2c$

(C) $\dfrac{9}{2}c$

(D) $5c$

(E) $6c$

11. If $-1 < x < 0$, which of the following has the greatest value?

(A) x

(B) x^3

(C) $-\dfrac{1}{x}$

(D) $\dfrac{1}{x}$

(E) $1 + x$

13. If a light bulb factory can produce 12 light bulbs in x minutes, then, in terms of x, how many light bulbs can it produce in 2 hours?

(A) $2(12)x$

(B) $12(60)x$

(C) $\dfrac{2(12)}{x}$

(D) $\dfrac{2(12)(60)}{x}$

(E) $\dfrac{x}{2(12)(60)}$

14. A three-digit number has hundreds digit h, tens digit zero, and units digit r. If this number is divided by 10, the result is

(A) $\dfrac{h+r}{10}$

(B) $h + \dfrac{r}{10}$

(C) $h + r$

(D) $10h + \dfrac{r}{10}$

(E) $10h + r$

MATH

WRITING

READING

VOCABULARY

15. If $0 < k < 1$, which of the following must also be greater than 0 and less than 1 ?

(A) $\dfrac{3k}{2}$

(B) $k - 1$

(C) $\dfrac{1}{1-k}$

(D) $\dfrac{k}{k+1}$

(E) $\dfrac{k+2}{k}$

17. The product of two positive numbers is k. If each of the numbers is increased by 2, the new product is how much greater than twice the sum of the two original numbers?

(A) $k - 2$
(B) k
(C) $k + 2$
(D) $k + 4$
(E) $2k + 4$

18. Eight years ago, Sylvia was 2 times as old as Adam will be in 3 years. If Adam is a years old now, how old is Sylvia in terms of a ?

(A) $3a - 4$

(B) $2a + 14$

(C) $2a + 6$

(D) $\dfrac{7a+8}{4}$

(E) $\dfrac{a+11}{2}$

19. At the first stop on its route, a bus picks up x passengers. At the second stop, y passengers get on the bus. At the third stop, $\dfrac{2}{3}$ of the passengers exit the bus. At the fourth stop, 2 passengers get on the bus. How many passengers is the bus carrying at this point?

(A) $\dfrac{3x+3y+4}{3}$

(B) $\dfrac{2x-2y-4}{3}$

(C) $\dfrac{6-2x-2y}{3}$

(D) $\dfrac{x+y+6}{3}$

(E) $\dfrac{3x+2y+6}{3}$

20. Pat had a dollars in the bank. She spent $\dfrac{1}{3}$ of her money on a new car. She then deposited b dollars into the same account. Later, Pat withdrew half of the funds to spend on her vacation. How much money, in dollars, was left in Pat's bank account?

(A) $\dfrac{4a-3b}{6}$

(B) $\dfrac{3a-5b}{6}$

(C) $\dfrac{2a+2b-3}{6}$

(D) $\dfrac{3b-a}{6}$

(E) $\dfrac{2a+3b}{6}$

 © TPR Education IP Holdings, LLC

PLUGGING IN YOUR OWN NUMBER

If an algebra question asks you to find a fraction or a percent, Plug In your own number.

10. If m and n are positive integers such that $\frac{2}{3}$ of m is equal to $\frac{1}{2}$ of n, then m is what fractional part of n ?

   (A) $\frac{1}{3}$

   (B) $\frac{3}{5}$

   (C) $\frac{3}{4}$

   (D) $\frac{4}{3}$

   (E) $\frac{5}{3}$

11. On Wednesday, Morris ate half of a pizza pie. On Thursday, he ate one quarter of what was left of the pizza. What fraction of the entire pie did Morris eat on Wednesday and Thursday?

   (A) $\frac{1}{4}$

   (B) $\frac{3}{8}$

   (C) $\frac{1}{2}$

   (D) $\frac{5}{8}$

   (E) $\frac{3}{4}$

18. Over the last 3 months, the output of a shoe factory decreased by a total of 10 percent. If the output continued to decrease at the same rate for the next 3 months, by what percent would the output have decreased over the entire 6-month period?

   (A)   5%
   (B)   10%
   (C)   19%
   (D)   20%
   (E)   21%

© TPR Education IP Holdings, LLC

PLUGGING IN ON GEOMETRY

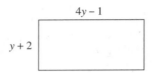

8. What is the perimeter of the rectangle shown above?

(A) $10y + 2$
(B) $10y + 1$
(C) $9y - 1$
(D) $5y - 1$
(E) $4y + 2$

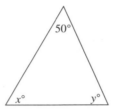

10. In the triangle above, what is the value of x in terms of y ?

(A) $y - 50$
(B) $50 + y$
(C) $180 - y$
(D) $130 + y$
(E) $130 - y$

12. In the figure above, $x + y + z =$

(A) $360 - (w + x + y)$
(B) $360 + (w + x + y)$
(C) $360 - z$
(D) $180 + z$
(E) $360 - (w + y)$

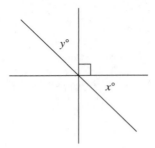

12. In the figure above, what is the value of x in terms of y ?

(A) $\dfrac{y}{2}$

(B) y

(C) $90 - y$

(D) $90 + y$

(E) $180 - y$

13. In a rectangle, the width y is half the length x. What is the area of the rectangle in terms of y ?

(A) $\dfrac{1}{2}y$

(B) $6y$

(C) $2y^2$

(D) y^2

(E) $\dfrac{y^2}{2}$

 © TPR Education IP Holdings, LLC

THE PRINCETON REVIEW GUIDE TO GRIDDING

The Grid-In Questions

Some of the questions on the SAT will not be multiple choice. We call these "grid-ins" because you have to come up with your own answer and enter it into a special grid. You don't lose any points if you get a grid-in question wrong. Getting a grid-in wrong is the same as leaving it blank. Otherwise, these questions are just like the normal five-choice problem solving questions—with the answer choices missing, of course.

ETS's directions for gridding in your answers take up two-thirds of a page, and reading them during the test can eat up some serious time. We'll show you how to grid in your answers so that you'll never have to look at ETS's directions. You can simply fill in your response because you'll know what to do.

Rules for Gridding

1. Write your answer in the top of the grid. Because the answer sheet is scored by a machine, you must fill in the bubbles in order to receive credit for answering the question. However, entering your answer into the spaces at the top of the grid box will keep you from making careless mistakes when you fill in the bubbles.

2. You can use either fractions or decimals. By letting you use fractions or decimals, these questions offer a bit of flexibility. If the correct answer is $\frac{1}{2}$, you can enter it as

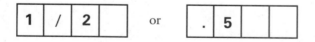

3. Don't grid in mixed numbers. The computer can't recognize mixed numbers. If your answer is $5\frac{3}{4}$, you can either grid in 5.75 or you can convert the mixed number to an improper fraction. In this case, your answer would be marked correct if you gridded in $\frac{23}{4}$. If the improper fraction doesn't fit in the grid, you'll have to use a decimal.

4. Start at the far left and use all four spaces if necessary. Not all your answers will take up all four spaces but it's a good idea to always start at the far left of the grid. Why? Well, suppose that your answer is some long decimal such as .142856, which doesn't fit into the grid. ETS wants the most accurate answer possible. If you just grid in .1 or .14, you'll be marked wrong. Those answers aren't as accurate as possible. If you start at the far left, you can grid in more of the digits from your answer.

Here's what ETS would credit as a correct response:

| . | 1 | 4 | 2 | or | . | 1 | 4 | 3 |

5. Lop, don't round. As you just saw, the answer .142856… can be entered in two different ways. ETS doesn't care whether you round up the last digit of a decimal that doesn't fit in the grid. Save yourself a little time and don't worry about rounding; just enter the digits that fit and ignore the rest. Be aware, though, that strange decimals are very rare on the SAT.

6. Don't bother reducing fractions that already fit. If you get $\frac{4}{28}$ as your answer, you might be tempted to reduce it. Don't waste your time! It already fits in the grid and ETS will give you credit for any answer that's equivalent to $\frac{4}{28}$. Why bother figuring out that you could also grid in $\frac{2}{14}$ or $\frac{1}{7}$? Reducing is just one more place to make a mistake. However, if your answer is $\frac{10}{70}$, that won't fit in the grid. Now, you've either got to reduce or convert your fraction to a decimal.

7. There's no bubble for this!?! The grid box can't handle negative numbers, variables, or square root signs. If any of these appear in your answer, go back and check your work.

If you get an answer that has π in it, you should also check your work. Don't simply multiply your answer by 3.14. ETS would consider it unfair to expect students without calculators to know the value of π and to multiply that value as part of their answer.

Quick, what's $\sqrt{7}$? (Not fair to use your calculator.) If you didn't know, then you're like most people. If you get a weird square root as an answer, you should also check your work. Something's wrong.

8. Just drop the percent sign. If you get 75% as your answer, just drop off the percent sign and grid in 75. Don't convert it to a decimal. Don't convert it to a fraction. If you grid in .75, the machine will think that you mean .75 *percent* and mark you wrong.

Here's what your answer should look like:

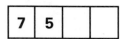

If any of this information is unclear, be sure to ask your instructor about it at the next class.

Now that you've seen how to work with the grid box, try a few grid-in questions. Be sure to practice filling in the grid boxes!

9. The ratio of 4 to 100 is equivalent to what number?

11. If $x = \dfrac{2}{3}$ and $y = \dfrac{1}{2}$, what is the value of $2x + 2y$?

10. In a group of 30 boys and girls, $\dfrac{1}{6}$ are girls. How many boys are in the group?

12. A full water jug has 20 ounces poured out of it and is now $\dfrac{3}{5}$ full. How many ounces did the jug contain?

13. If x is an integer and $5x + 4 > 24$ and $x - 3 < 5$, what is one possible value of x ?

15. If the sum of four consecutive integers is 86, what is the least of these integers?

14. How many integers between 6 and 60 (inclusive) are divisible by 7 ?

16. A class consists of 11 boys and 13 girls. If 1 of the boys and 2 of the girls are absent, what fraction of the entire class is absent?

MATH

WRITING

READING

VOCABULARY

FUNDAMENTALS I

Here are some questions to help you remember math vocabulary. Be sure to review the explanations that follow these questions when you are done.

2. If n is the difference between two positive integers, and $n = 4$, then the two positive integers could be

    (A) 4 and 6
    (B) 5 and 6
    (C) 3 and 3
    (D) 1 and 4
    (E) 2 and 6

3. If $a + b$ is a negative number, and $a = 5$, which of the following could be the value of b ?

    (A) −2
    (B) −3
    (C) −4
    (D) −5
    (E) −6

4. If $x = 6$, then $6 - \left(\dfrac{x}{3} \cdot 2\right)^2 + 1 =$

    (A) −248
    (B)   −9
    (C)   4
    (D)   6
    (E)   16

5. If r is the remainder when 45 is divided by 6, what is the remainder when 17 is divided by r ?

    (A) 1
    (B) 2
    (C) 3
    (D) 4
    (E) 5

6. What is the sum of the distinct prime factors of 60 ?

    (A)   9
    (B) 10
    (C) 11
    (D) 12
    (E) 30

7. If $\dfrac{p}{4}$ is an integer, which of the following CANNOT be the value of p ?

    (A) 12
    (B) 16
    (C) 18
    (D) 20
    (E) 24

    List Q: 2, 2, 3, 3, 4, 4, 6

11. Which of the following is the sum of three distinct even numbers shown in list Q above?

    (A)   7
    (B) 10
    (C) 12
    (D) 13
    (E) 14

FUNDAMENTALS II

Here are some more questions to help you remember math vocabulary. Be sure to review the explanations that follow these questions when you are done.

1. Which of the following is greater than $\frac{2}{5}$ but less than $\frac{3}{5}$?

   (A) 0.20
   (B) 0.25
   (C) 0.30
   (D) 0.35
   (E) 0.45

2. $0.461 =$

   (A) $\frac{6}{1,000} + \frac{4}{100} + \frac{1}{10}$

   (B) $\frac{4}{1,000} + \frac{6}{100} + \frac{1}{10}$

   (C) $\frac{1}{1,000} + \frac{4}{100} + \frac{6}{10}$

   (D) $\frac{4}{1,000} + \frac{1}{100} + \frac{6}{10}$

   (E) $\frac{1}{1,000} + \frac{6}{100} + \frac{4}{10}$

3. Which of the following expressions is the greatest?

   (A) $2 + \frac{1}{5}$

   (B) $2 \div \frac{1}{5}$

   (C) $2 \times \frac{1}{5}$

   (D) $2 - \frac{1}{5}$

   (E) $\frac{1}{5} - 2$

4. If $|x - 3| = 7$, what is one possible value of x ?

   (A) −10
   (B) − 4
   (C) −3
   (D) 4
   (E) 7

5. What is the first positive integer multiple of 16 ?

   (A) 0
   (B) 2
   (C) 8
   (D) 16
   (E) 32

6. Of the following numbers, which is the greatest?

   (A) 0.1002
   (B) 0.099
   (C) 0.08
   (D) 0.103
   (E) 0.11

10. If $-9m - 12 > 11 - 3m$, which of the following must be true?

   (A) $m < -\frac{23}{6}$

   (B) $m < -\frac{1}{6}$

   (C) $m > -\frac{23}{12}$

   (D) $m > -\frac{1}{6}$

   (E) $m > -\frac{23}{6}$

12. Which of the following represents the set of all the digits that are either even or prime in the number 1,032,897 ?

   (A) {0, 2, 3, 7, 8}
   (B) {0, 1, 2, 3, 7, 8}
   (C) {1, 2, 3, 7, 8}
   (D) {1, 2, 3, 7, 8, 9}
   (E) {2, 3, 7, 8}

ANSWERS AND EXPLANATIONS TO FUNDAMENTALS I

2. **E**   A *difference* is the result of subtracting. Subtract the numbers in the answer choices until you find one that has a difference of 4. Since 6 – 2 = 4, the correct answer is (E).

3. **E**   A *negative* number is a number that is less than zero. Plug In the answer choices until you get a negative sum. Answer choices (A), (B), and (C) all produce positive sums when added to 5. *Positive* numbers are numbers greater than zero. Answer choice (D) produces a sum of zero when added to 5 and zero is neither positive nor negative. Using POE, the correct answer is (E).

4. **B**   Here ETS gives you a number to Plug In. Remember to follow the order of operations, PEMDAS (parentheses, exponents, multiplication and division, addition and subtraction). This tells you to do any arithmetic in parentheses first, then apply exponents, then do multiplication and division from left to right, and finally do any addition and subtraction from left to right. In this question, remember that the fraction bar means divide. Plug In 6 for x to get
    $$6 - \left(\frac{6}{3} \cdot 2\right)^2 + 1 = \ = 6 - (2 \cdot 2)^2 + 1 = 6 - (4)^2 + 1 = 6 - 16 + 1 = -9.$$

5. **B**   A *remainder* is the integer that's left over after dividing. The first step of this problem is to find the remainder when 45 is divided by 6. First, find the number of "full times" that 6 goes into 45, which is 7. Now, multiply the 7 by 6 to get 42. Finally, subtract 42 from 45 to find that the remainder is 3. Now, find the remainder when 17 is divided by 3. The remainder of that operation is 2.

6. **B**   Use bite-sized pieces to handle the math vocab. *Prime* numbers are numbers that are only divisible by themselves and one. Examples of primes are 2, 3, 5, and 7. Notice that one is not on the list. That's a dead mathematician rule. Some long dead mathematician said that **one is not prime** so it's not prime! A *factor* of a number divides evenly into that number. Factors are also called *divisors*. To find prime factors, use a factor tree. Break 60 down to 2 × 30. Now, break 30 down to 2 × 15. Since 15 is not prime, break it down to 3 × 5. Your factor tree should be showing only primes now. The prime factors of 60 are 2, 2, 3, and 5. Since this problem wants the sum of the distinct prime factors, we get 2 + 3 + 5 = 10.

7. **C**   An *integer* is a number that does not contain a decimal or a fraction. Plug In the answer choices until you find one that is not evenly divisible by 4. Since 4 does not divide into 18 evenly, the correct answer is (C).

11. **C**   ETS tries to make problems harder by stringing together lots of math vocab terms. Use bite-sized pieces to break the problem down. This problem wants a *sum,* so you'll need to add. The word *distinct* means different, so only add different numbers on the list together. *Even* means that the number is evenly divisible by two. Examples of even numbers are 0, 2, 4, and 6 (it's important to remember on the SAT that 0 is *even*). Here the sum is 2 + 4 + 6 = 12.

ANSWERS AND EXPLANATIONS TO FUNDAMENTALS II

1. **E** Convert the fractions to decimals so that it is easier to work with the answer choices. Remember that the fraction bar means divided by. So, $\frac{2}{5} = 2 \div 5 = 0.4$ and $\frac{3}{5} = 0.6$. Now, it's easy to see that only 0.45 is in between the two fractions.

2. **E** This problem requires knowledge of place values. In the number 0.461, 0 is in the ones or units place, 4 is in the tenths place, 6 is in the hundredths place, and 1 is in the thousandths place. Now, do some POE. The first thing you need is a 4 in the tenths place. Look for answers that have $\frac{4}{10}$ in them. Only answer choice (E) works.

3. **B** Don't forget to Ballpark on this problem. Answer (E) is negative and answer (D) is clearly smaller than answer (A). Eliminate (D) and (E). Now, start working out the remaining answers. Answer (A) is 2.2, (B) is 10, and (C) is $\frac{2}{5}$. To find the value of answer (B), remember that when dividing by a fraction, you flip and then multiply. So, $2 \div \frac{1}{5} = 2 \times 5 = 10$.

4. **B** The vertical lines around the expression mean to take the *absolute value*. The absolute value of a number is simply its distance from zero on the number line. Absolute values are always nonnegative (positive or zero) because distances can't be negative. To find the possible values for *x*, remember that $x - 3$ could equal 7 or 7. So, if $x - 3 = 7$, then $x = 10$. If $x - 3 = -7$, then $x = -4$.

5. **D** A *multiple* of a number is divisible by that number. It's just like making a times table or counting by a number. Thus, the first positive integer multiple of 16 is just $1 \times 16 = 16$.

6. **E** To compare the size of decimals, compare the numbers place value by place value. First, look at the tenths place. Answers (A), (D), and (E) have a 1 in the tenths place, while answers (B) and (C) have a 0 there. Eliminate (B) and (C). Now, compare the hundredths place for the remaining answers. Answer (E) has a one in the hundredths place, and answers (A) and (D) have a zero there. Eliminate (A) and (D).

10. **A** Inequalities work like normal equations unless you multiply or divide by a negative number. If you do either of those operations, you need to flip the inequality sign. To solve this inequality, follow these steps:

$-9m - 12 > 11 - 3m$

$-9m > 23 - 3m$ (add 12 to both sides)

$-6m > 23$ (add $3m$ to both sides)

$m < -\dfrac{23}{6}$ (divide both sides by -6 and flip the sign)

12. **A** First, find the even digits in the number. The even digits are 0, 2, and 8. ETS expects you to know a few rules about zero such as zero is even. Zero is even because there is no remainder when you divide zero by two. The other rules of zero are as follows:

- Zero is an integer.
- Zero is neither positive nor negative.
- You can't divide by zero.

Since 0 needs to be in the correct answer, eliminate (C), (D), and (E). Now, find the prime digits. The prime digits are 3 and 7 (remember that 1 is *not* prime and that 2 *is* prime!). Eliminate (B) because it contains 1.

MATH FUNDAMENTALS: THE BASICS

REVIEW EXERCISE

Use the concepts from the homework to answer these questions.

5. 16 has how many distinct prime factors?

(A) 1
(B) 2
(C) 4
(D) 8
(E) 16

11. A is a set of prime one-digit integers, and B is a set of odd integers. Which one of the following CANNOT be the product of a member of set A and a member of set B ?

(A) 6
(B) 10
(C) 12
(D) 45
(E) 49

3. If $\frac{1}{4} + \frac{1}{6} = \frac{x}{48}$, then $x =$

(A) $\frac{1}{2}$

(B) 2

(C) $\frac{24}{5}$

(D) 20

(E) 48

8. If $\frac{1}{xy}(x + y) = \frac{3}{4}$, and $\frac{1}{y} = \frac{1}{2}$, what is the value of $\frac{1}{x}$?

(A) $\frac{1}{4}$

(B) $\frac{1}{2}$

(C) $\frac{3}{2}$

(D) 2

(E) 4

7. If $3x - 8 < 12 + 5x$, then

(A) $x > 10$

(B) $x < 10$

(C) $x > -10$

(D) $x < -10$

(E) $x > 0$

Underline all math "hot words" in the problem.

MATH HOT WORDS: KNOW THEM!

Often a problem will require you to know one or more "hot words," or math vocabulary, in order to answer it.

6. The remainder when positive integer z is divided by 6 is 5. If $z + 21$ is divided by 6, what is the remainder?

(A) 1
(B) 2
(C) 3
(D) 4
(E) 5

8. If set A consists of all the nonnegative even integers less than 12, then how many elements are in set A ?

(A) 5
(B) 6
(C) 7
(D) 11
(E) 12

9. If d is the sum of 4 consecutive prime numbers, what is the smallest possible value of d ?

(A) 6
(B) 11
(C) 16
(D) 17
(E) 26

10. Which of the following is the product of two consecutive odd integers?

(A) 12
(B) 13
(C) 14
(D) 15
(E) 16

14. When $\dfrac{1}{a}$ is expressed as a decimal, the thousandths digit is 4. What is the greatest possible value of a ?

(A)   0.00025
(B)   0.004004...
(C)   0.994999...
(D) 250
(E) 1000

MORE MATH VOCABULARY!

2. How many integers from 42 to 72, inclusive, are multiples of 6 ?

(A) 3
(B) 4
(C) 5
(D) 6
(E) 7

What if the question did not contain the word "inclusive"?

12. If x and y are negative numbers, which of the following must be true of xy ?

   I. xy is negative
  II. xy is positive
 III. xy is an integer

(A) I only
(B) II only
(C) I and II only
(D) II and III only
(E) I, II, and III

13. If $\dfrac{x-5}{3}$ is a positive even integer, then x must be

(A) prime
(B) a positive even integer
(C) a positive odd integer
(D) a multiple of 6
(E) a multiple of 11

2. If $|p| - 4 = |q|$, which of the following could be the values of p and q ?

(A) $p = 2$ and $q = -6$
(B) $p = -2$ and $q = -6$
(C) $p = -6$ and $q = -2$
(D) $p = -3$ and $q = 7$
(E) $p = 3$ and $q = 7$

> The difference between m and 9 is greater than the cube of one-third m but less than the cube of the sum of m and 9.

16. Which of the following is equivalent to the statement above?

(A) $\dfrac{1}{3}m^3 < m - 9 < (m+9)^3$

(B) $\dfrac{1}{3}m^3 < m - 9 < m^3 + 9$

(C) $\dfrac{1}{3}m^3 < m^3 + 9 < m^3 - 9$

(D) $\dfrac{1}{27}m^3 < m - 9 < (m+9)^3$

(E) $\dfrac{1}{27}m^3 < m - 9 < m^3 + 9$

MATH

WRITING

READING

VOCABULARY

Term	Definition	Examples
Number		
Integer		
Digit		
Units Digit		
Negative		
Positive		
Non-negative		
Non-zero		
Not positive		
Even		
Odd		
Difference		
Sum		
Product		
Quotient		
Divisible		
Ratio		
Prime		
Factor/Divisor		
Prime factor		
Multiple		
Remainder		
Distinct		
Consecutive		
Absolute Value		
The square of...		
The square root of...		
The cube of...		
The cube root of...		
Rules of zero		
Mean		
Median		
Mode		
Percent		
Quadratic		
Inclusive		
Range		

 © TPR Education IP Holdings, LLC

MATH FUNDAMENTALS
PRACTICE

PROPERTIES OF NUMBERS

1. A number is always divisible by its

   (A) exponents
   (B) multiples
   (C) digits
   (D) remainder
   (E) factors

2. How many prime factors does 10 have?

   (A) 1
   (B) 2
   (C) 3
   (D) 4
   (E) 5

3. $\left|-7+3\right|+4 =$

   (A) −4
   (B) 0
   (C) 4
   (D) 8
   (E) 14

4. The product of the even integers from 1 to 7 inclusive is how much greater than the sum of the integers from 2 to 6 inclusive?

   (A) 8
   (B) 11
   (C) 23
   (D) 28
   (E) 34

4. Which of the following expressions represents an odd integer if b is an odd integer?

   (A) $b - 3$
   (B) $2b - 3$
   (C) $2b - 4$
   (D) $3b - 1$
   (E) $3b + 1$

4. How many distinct prime factors does 12 have?

   (A) 1
   (B) 2
   (C) 3
   (D) 4
   (E) 5

4. How many factors do 12 and 16 have in common?

   (A) 7
   (B) 6
   (C) 5
   (D) 4
   (E) 3

4. Which of the following sets contains only factors of the number 75 ?

   (A) {1, 4, 5, 20}
   (B) {1, 3, 5, 25}
   (C) {0, 75, 100, 125}
   (D) {3, 15, 17, 25}
   (E) {2, 3, 5, 15}

   > "All even numbers have at least 4 factors."

5. Which of the following numbers can be used to show that the statement above is FALSE?

   (A) 2
   (B) 6
   (C) 10
   (D) 13
   (E) 20

6. If the remainders when three consecutive integers are each divided by 5 are 2, 3, and 4 respectively, which of the following could be the three integers?

   (A) 3, 4, 5
   (B) 5, 6, 7
   (C) 6, 7, 8
   (D) 7, 8, 9
   (E) 8, 9, 10

6:26	9:27	9:13	6:19	9:16

9. Meredith ran a mile and a half five times last week. The time of each run in minutes and seconds is shown in the table above. For example, the time 6:26 equals 6 minutes and 26 seconds. What is the range, in seconds, of Meredith's five runs' times?

   (A) 167
   (B) 170
   (C) 181
   (D) 188
   (E) 198

9. If $x = |{-5} - 2|$, then what is the sum of x and the next odd integer greater than x ?

   (A)   −16
   (B)   −7
   (C)   15
   (D)   16
   (E)   63

11. C, D, and E are positive, single-digit integers. Which of the following is equal to $(C \times 10^4) + (D \times 10^3) + (E \times 10^1)$?

   (A) $CD0,0E0$
   (B) $CD0,00E$
   (C) $CD,0E0$
   (D) $CD,00E$
   (E) $C0,DE0$

14. The sum of a set of consecutive even integers is 12. If the least integer is −10, how many elements are in this set?

   (A)   6
   (B)   11
   (C)   12
   (D)   23
   (E)   24

15. The elements of set F are all the integers less than 20 that are the product of exactly two different prime numbers. Which of the following is set F ?

   (A)   {2, 3, 5, 7}
   (B)   {2, 3, 4, 5, 7, 9}
   (C)   {6, 10, 14}
   (D)   {6, 10, 14, 15}
   (E)   {4, 6, 9, 10, 14, 15}

15. When the two digit number p is divided by 5, the remainder is 1, and when p is divided by 11, the remainder is 0. What is one possible value of p ?

18. If the sum of five consecutive odd integers is k, which of the following could be a value of k ?

   I.   0
   II. −1
   III. −5

   (A)   I only
   (B)   II only
   (C)   III only
   (D)   I and III only
   (E)   II and III only

19. When the positive integers j and m are divided by 8, the remainders are 4 and 3, respectively. What is the remainder when the product jm is divided by 8?

   (A)   0
   (B)   1
   (C)   2
   (D)   3
   (E)   4

MATH

WRITING

READING

VOCABULARY

FRACTIONS AND DECIMALS

3. A rope is cut into fourths. Each piece is then cut into fifths. How many pieces of rope are there?

(A)   4
(B)   5
(C)   9
(D)   15
(E)   20

4. Kevin transferred $\frac{1}{6}$ of the songs on his computer to his portable music player. If he transferred 36 songs, how many songs did he have on his computer?

(A)   6
(B)   36
(C)   72
(D)   216
(E)   288

$$\frac{s}{60}, \frac{s}{77}, \frac{s}{80}$$

5. Each of the fractions above must be in its simplest reduced form. Which of the following could be a value of *s* ?

(A)   7
(B)   9
(C)   11
(D)   13
(E)   15

6. If $\frac{1}{3x} < \frac{1}{14}$ and *x* is a positive integer, all of the following are possible values of *x* EXCEPT

(A)   8
(B)   7
(C)   6
(D)   5
(E)   4

7. A fish tank is $\frac{2}{9}$ full. If the tank holds 117 gallons of water when filled to the top, how many gallons are presently needed to completely fill the tank?

(A)   26
(B)   65
(C)   91
(D)   97
(E)   115

12. Which of the following is NOT equal to $\frac{1}{5}$ of an integer?

(A)   −1

(B) $-\frac{1}{5}$

(C)   1

(D) $\frac{3}{2}$

(E)   5

EQUATIONS AND INEQUALITIES

2. If $\dfrac{rs}{t} = 10$, for which of the following triples (r, s, t) is the equation NOT satisfied?

(A) (10, 10, 10)
(B) (4, 5, 5)
(C) (40, 2, 8)
(D) (15, 4, 6)
(E) (12.5, 4, 5)

3. If $4x + 6 = 30$, then $2x$ equals

(A) 2
(B) 4
(C) 6
(D) 8
(E) 12

4. If $u > 0$ and $v > 0$ and u and v are both integers, what are all the solutions (u, v) of the equation $3u + 4v = 19$?

(A) (1, 4) only
(B) (5, 1) only
(C) (1, 4) and (1, 5)
(D) (4, 1) and (5, 1)
(E) (1, 4) and (5, 1)

5. If $7x - 5 < 13 + 4x$, then

(A) $x > 18$

(B) $x > 6$

(C) $x < 6$

(D) $x < \dfrac{17}{2}$

(E) $x < 18$

7. If $2 - 4x \le 10$, all of the following are possible values of x EXCEPT

(A) −3
(B) −2
(C) 0
(D) 2
(E) 3

9. If $|3 - x| > 5$, which of the following is NOT a possible value of x ?

(A) −10
(B) −5
(C) −3
(D) 5
(E) 10

10. If $-5 < m < 10$ and $2 < n < 4$, which of the following must be true for $(m + n)$?

(A) $-3 < (m + n) < 14$
(B) $-7 < (m + n) < 6$
(C) $-5 < (m + n) < 12$
(D) $8 < (m + n) < 14$
(E) $12 < (m + n) < 14$

10. If $\dfrac{7 - 2y}{3} < -5$, then

(A) $y < -4$
(B) $y < 11$
(C) $y > -4$
(D) $y > 4$
(E) $y > 11$

11. If $a > 5$ and $b > 4$, then which of the following must be true?

   I. $a > b$
   II. $a + b > 9$
   III. $a + b > 11$

(A) I only
(B) II only
(C) I and II only
(D) II and III only
(E) I, II, and III

11. If $\dfrac{4}{x} = \dfrac{6}{7}$ and $\dfrac{3x}{a} = \dfrac{7}{2}$, then a equals

(A) $2\dfrac{1}{3}$

(B) 3

(C) $3\dfrac{1}{2}$

(D) 4

(E) $4\dfrac{2}{3}$

$$|s - 5| = 8$$
$$|t + 2| = 10$$

11. Which of the following is a possible value of $s + t$?

(A) −4
(B) −3
(C) 1
(D) 13
(E) 25

12. If q, r, s, t, and u are consecutive positive integers such that $q > r > s > t > u$, what is $(q - r)(r - s) - (s - t)(t - u)$?

(A) −2
(B) −1
(C) 0
(D) 1
(E) It cannot be determined from the information given.

13. If $13 \le 31 - 2x \le 39$, which of the following represents all possible values of x?

(A) $-9 \le x \le 4$
(B) $-4 \le x \le 4$
(C) $-4 \le x \le 9$
(D) $9 \le x \le 22$
(E) $22 \le x \le 35$

18. Which of the following accurately defines all possible values of $p - q$ if $15 \le p \le 30$ and $7 \le q \le 19$?

(A) $-4 \le (p - q) \le 23$
(B) $-4 \le (p - q) \le 30$
(C) $8 \le (p - q) \le 11$
(D) $15 \le (p - q) \le 23$
(E) $22 \le (p - q) \le 49$

GEOMETRY I

Here are some problems to help you review some basic geometry facts and formulas that you'll need to know for the SAT. Be sure to review the explanations that follow these questions when you are done.

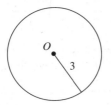

2. In the figure above, what is the circumference of the circle with center O ?

(A) 3π

(B) $\dfrac{9}{2}\pi$

(C) 6π

(D) 9π

(E) 12π

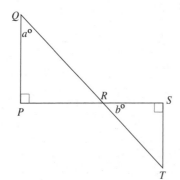

3. In the figure above, if $\overline{QT}$ and $\overline{PS}$ intersect at point R, what is the value of $a + b$?

(A)   30
(B)   45
(C)   60
(D)   90
(E)   180

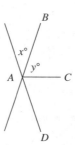

4. In the figure above, if $\overline{AC}$ bisects $\angle BAD$, and $x = 30$, then $y =$

(A)   40
(B)   60
(C)   75
(D)   80
(E)   150

5. If a square has a perimeter of 32 feet, what is its area in square feet?

(A)   8
(B)   16
(C)   32
(D)   64
(E)   1,024

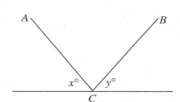

8. In the figure above, if $\overline{AC} \perp \overline{BC}$, what is the value of x in terms of y ?

(A) $180 + y$
(B) $180 - y$
(C) $90 + y$
(D) $90 - y$
(E) $45 + y$

MATH

WRITING

READING

VOCABULARY

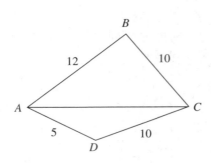

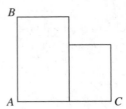

Note: Figure not drawn to scale.

12. In the figure above, the perimeter of △*ABC* is how much greater than the perimeter of △*ADC* ?

(A) $\sqrt{2}$

(B) 7

(C) $5\sqrt{5}$

(D) 14

(E) 22

14. The figure above is composed of two rectangles. If *AB* = 8 and *AC* = 9, what is the perimeter of the figure?

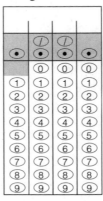

GEOMETRY II

Here are some more problems to help you review some basic geometry facts and formulas that you'll need to know for the SAT. Be sure to review the explanations that follow these questions when you are done.

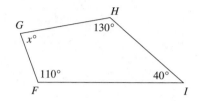

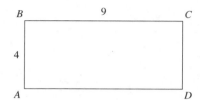

4. Quadrilateral *FGHI* is shown in the figure above. What is the value of *x* ?

(A) 40
(B) 60
(C) 70
(D) 80
(E) 90

6. In the figure above, *ABCD* is a rectangle. If point *X* (not shown) is on $\overline{BC}$, then what is the area of $\triangle AXD$?

(A) 6
(B) 12
(C) 18
(D) 36
(E) It cannot be determined from the information given.

7. What is the area of a circle with circumference 10π ?

(A) 5
(B) 10
(C) 5π
(D) 10π
(E) 25π

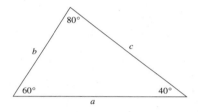

5. In the figure above, which of the following must be true?

(A) $a < b < c$
(B) $b < a < c$
(C) $c < b < a$
(D) $b < c < a$
(E) $c < a < b$

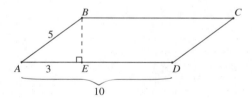

8. In the figure above, $\overline{AB}$ is parallel to $\overline{CD}$, and $\overline{AD}$ is parallel to $\overline{BC}$. If *AE* = 3, what is the area of *ABCD* ?

(A) 30
(B) 40
(C) 50
(D) 60
(E) 70

MATH

WRITING

READING

VOCABULARY

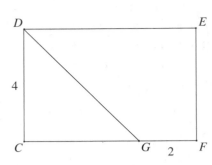

Note: Figure not drawn to scale.

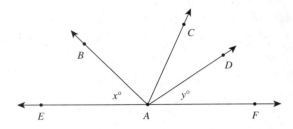

Note: Figure not drawn to scale.

12. In the figure above, *CDEF* is a rectangle. If the area of $\triangle CDG$ is 10, what is the area of *CDEF* ?

(A)   5
(B)   7
(C)   10
(D)   20
(E)   28

14. In the figure above, the angle between $\overline{AB}$ and $\overline{AC}$ is 40°. If the angle between $\overline{AC}$ and $\overline{AD}$ is 50°, then the average (arithmetic mean) of *x* and *y* is

(A)   10
(B)   40
(C)   45
(D)   50
(E)   90

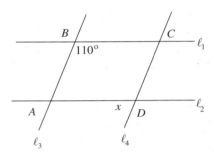

13. In the figure above, if $\ell_1 \| \ell_2$ and $\ell_3 \| \ell_4$, then what is the value of *x* ?

ANSWERS AND EXPLANATIONS TO GEOMETRY I

2. **C**   Write down the formula for the circumference of a circle, $C = \pi d = 2\pi r$. Now, substitute what you already know into the formula. For this circle, the radius is 3. Remember that the radius of a circle is the distance from the center of the circle to any point on the edge of the circle. So, $C = 2\pi r = 2\pi(3) = 6\pi$.

3. **D**   You'll need to know two big facts about angles to solve this problem. First, when two straight lines intersect, the opposite angles are equal. So, the measure of $PRQ = b°$. Be sure to mark that the measure of $PRQ = b°$ on the figure. Second, the angles in a triangle sum to 180°. So, $a + b = 90°$.

4. **C**   You should always show information from the problem on the figure, so go ahead and write 30 for the angle marked $x°$. Bisect means to cut exactly in half. So, the measure of $CAD = y°$. Show that, too. Using the rule of 180 for straight lines, you know that $30 + y + y = 180$. Hence, $y = 75$.

5. **D**   In a square, all the sides are equal. So, for a square, perimeter is given by $P = 4s$. Always start by writing down any formulas that you need because that will help you to see what you already know and what you need to find. Now, use the formula to find the side of this square. $P = 32 = 4s$, so $s = 8$. For a square, the area is given by $A = s^2$. So, $A = s^2 = (8)^2 = 64$.

8. **D**   The symbol $\perp$ stands for perpendicular, which means that $\overline{AC}$ and $\overline{BC}$ form a 90° angle when they meet. Be sure to show the right angle on the provided figure. You'll need one other big fact to solve this problem. There are 180° in a straight line. Now, Plug In (you can do that on geometry questions, too). Don't forget to write your numbers on the figure. If $x = 40°$, then $y = 180° - 90° - 40° = 50°$. Answer choice (D) is 40 when $y = 50$.

12. **B**   You don't need to know the length of $\overline{AC}$ to solve this problem. That's good, because there's no way to calculate it anyway! Since $\overline{AC}$ is common to both triangles, it doesn't affect the difference in their perimeters. Also, both triangles have a side of 10, so you can ignore that when computing the difference in the perimeters as well. So, the difference in the perimeter will be $12 - 5 = 7$.

14. **34**   To find the perimeter, you need to add up all the sides. The problem here is that you don't know the values of all the sides and you can't find them. However, the two sides parallel to $\overline{AB}$ must add up to the length of $\overline{AB}$. The two sides parallel to $\overline{BC}$ must add up to the length of $\overline{BC}$. So, $P = 8 + 8 + 9 + 9 = 34$.

ANSWERS AND EXPLANATIONS TO GEOMETRY II

4. **D**   This problem requires you to remember an important fact about quadrilaterals. In any four-sided figure, the sum of the angles is 360°. So, 110 + 130 + 40 + x = 360 and x = 80.

5. **D**   Here's another big fact about triangles. There's a relationship between the sides and the angles: **the shortest side is opposite the smallest angle and the biggest side is opposite the largest angle.** The smallest angle in this triangle is 40°, so b is the shortest side. Use POE and eliminate (A), (C), and (E). The largest angle is 80°, so a is the largest side. The correct order for the sides is $b < c < a$.

6. **C**   Don't worry about the fact that you don't know exactly where point X is; it doesn't matter. So don't be Joe Bloggs and pick (E). Remember the formula for a triangle is $A = \frac{1}{2}bh$. We know the height is 4 and the base is 9, so therefore $\frac{9 \times 4}{2} = 18$, or answer choice (C).

7. **E**   The formula for the circumference of a circle is $C = \pi d = 2\pi r$ so be sure to write that down. Now, $C = 10\pi = 2\pi r$ and r = 5. You should have also written down the formula for the area of a circle, which is $A = \pi r^2$. So, for this circle, the area is $A = \pi r^2 = \pi(5)^2 = 25\pi$.

8. **B**   Start by writing down the formula. To find the area of a parallelogram, the formula is $A = bh$, where b is the base and h is the height. Now, you can see that you already know the base, but you need to find the height of the parallelogram. The height of the parallelogram is represented by $\overline{BE}$. The triangle containing the height, $\triangle ABE$, is a 3:4:5 right triangle. So, $\overline{BE}$ = 4. The area of the $ABCD$ is therefore $A = bh = (10)(4) = 40$.

12. **E**   Write down the two formulas that you'll need. The formula for the area of a triangle is given by $A = \frac{1}{2}bh$. Once you substitute in what you already know, $10 = \frac{1}{2}(4)b$, you'll see that you need to find the length of $\overline{CG}$, which, after solving, is 5. The formula for the area of a rectangle is $A = lw$, where l is the length and w is the width. So, the area of $CDEF$ is $A = (7)(4) = 28$.

13. **70**   The question says that the lines are parallel and that means that you can use Fred's theorem. Fred said that when you have two parallel lines that are intersected by a third line you get two kinds of angles: big angles and small angles. Fred went on to say that all the big angles are equal, all the small angles are equal and that any big angle plus any small angle is equal to 180 degrees. In this problem, 110 is a big angle and x is a small angle. Therefore, $x = 180 - 110 = 70$.

14. **C** $\overrightarrow{AB}$, $\overrightarrow{AC}$, and $\overrightarrow{AD}$ are all rays, as the arrow above each one indicates. A ray starts at the first point under the arrow, and goes on forever in the direction of the second point under the arrow, unlike a line, which continues in both directions forever. Be sure to mark the information provided on the figure. In this question, adding up the two given angles tells you that $\angle BAD$ measures 90°. Since there are 180° in a straight line, the total degree measure of the leftover angles $(x + y)$ must be 90. So the average of x and y is $\dfrac{x + y}{2} = \dfrac{90}{2} = 45$.

MATH

WRITING

READING

VOCABULARY

MASTER LIST OF GEOMETRY FACTS

Put an "x" next to any rule that you don't know.

Angle Facts

- There are _____ degrees in a right angle.
- When two straight lines intersect, angles _____ each other are equal.
- There are _____ degrees in a triangle.
- Two lines are called _____ when they meet at a 90° angle.
- The sign for perpendicular is _____.
- There are _____ degrees in a straight line.
- _____ means to cut exactly in half.
- The angles of any four-sided figure add up to _____ degrees.

Four-Sider Facts

In a square:

- All 4 sides are _____.
- All 4 angles are each equal to _____ degrees.
- Area = _____
- Perimeter = _____

In a rectangle:

- Opposite sides are _____.
- All 4 angles are each equal to _____ degrees.
- Area = _____
- Perimeter = _____

In a parallelogram:

- Opposite sides are _____ and equal.
- Area = _____

In a quadrilateral:

- Angles add up to _____.

Triangle Facts

In any triangle:

- The _____ side is opposite the largest angle.
- The _____ side is opposite the smallest angle.
- Equal sides that are opposite equal _____.
- Angles add up to 180°.
- Area = _____
- The _____ is a perpendicular distance from the base to the opposite vertex.
- _____ is the sum of the sides.
- Any side of a triangle must be greater than the _____ but less than the _____ of the other two sides.

In an isosceles triangle:

- Two _____ and _____ are equal.
- _____ opposite the equal sides are equal.

In an equilateral triangle:

- _____ sides are equal.
- All angles are each equal to _____ degrees.

Circle Facts

- There are _____ degrees in a circle.

Radius

- A radius is the distance from the _____ to any point on the edge of the circle.
- All _____ in a circle are equal.

Diameter

- The straight line distance from one point on the circle to another, passing through the _____.
- The longest _____ in the circle
- Equals twice the _____

Chord

- Any line segment from one point on the circle to another.
- The _____ is the longest chord.

Circumference

- The distance around the outside of the circle.
- The formula for circumference is _____or _____.

Arc

- Any part of the circumference.
- Arc measure is _____ to the size of the interior angle.

Area

- The amount of space within the boundaries of the circle.
- The formula for area is _____.

Line Facts

Line

- A line has no width and extends infinitely in both directions.
- On the SAT, if something looks like a straight line (rather than a big angle), it is a straight line. Actually, a line is just an angle that measures 180°.
- On the SAT, if a line looks like it passes through a point, it does.
- A line that contains points A and B is called $\overleftrightarrow{AB}$.

Line Segment

- A line segment is a part of a line, and has two endpoints.
- The degree measure of a line segment is _____.
- A line segment which has endpoints of A and B is expressed as $\overleftrightarrow{AB}$.

Tangent

- Tangent means touching at one point. For example, a line, line segment, or ray can intersect the circumference of a circle at exactly one point. Two circles that touch at one point are also tangent.
- A tangent line is always _____ to a radius.
- If $\overleftrightarrow{AB}$ intersects a circle at point T, then you would say "$\overline{AB}$ is tangent to the circle at point T."

Perpendicular

- Two lines that intersect in a 90° angle are perpendicular and their _____ are negative reciprocals.

MATH

WRITING

READING

VOCABULARY

Transformation Facts

Rotation

- Rotation means turning an object around a point, which is called the _____.

Reflection

- To reflect an object means to create its mirror image across a _____.
- Lines reflected across the *x*-axis have slopes that are _____ of each other and also *y*-intercepts that are _____ of each other. In the figure below, line *m* is the reflection of line *n* across the *x*-axis.

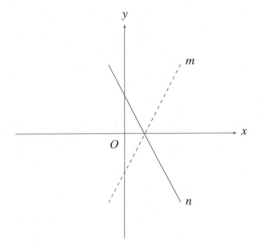

- Lines reflected across the *y*-axis have _____ *y*-intercept and slopes that are _____ of each other. In the figure below, line *n* is the reflection of line *m* across the *y*-axis.

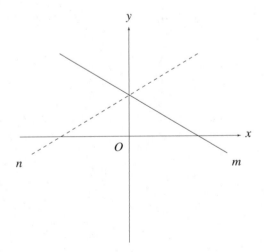

Symmetry

- A figure has _____ symmetry if it looks the same after a reflection. Such a figure reflects across a *line of symmetry*.
- A figure has _____ symmetry if it can be rotated and still look the same. Such a figure is rotated around a *point of symmetry*.

Translation

A translation moves a figure without rotation or reflection. Start with the graph of $f(x) = x^2$. What happens to this graph if you apply different operations to parts of the expression?

- If the number is INSIDE the parentheses, the graph moves right or left. So, in relation to the graph of $f(x) = x^2$, the graph of $f(x - 4)$ moves four units to the right.

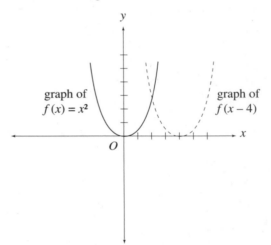

- If the number is OUTSIDE the parentheses, the graph moves up or down. So, in relation to the $f(x) = x^2$, the graph of $f(x) - 4$ moves down four units.

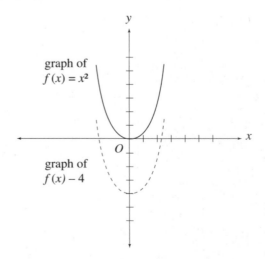

MATH

WRITING

READING

VOCABULARY

ANSWERS

Angle Facts

- There are *90* degrees in a right angle.
- When two lines intersect, the *opposite* angles are equal.
- There are *180* degrees in a triangle.
- Two lines are called *perpendicular* when they meet at 90° angle.
- The sign for perpindicular is ⊥
- There are *180* degrees in a straight line.
- *Bisect* means to cut exactly in half.
- The angles of any four-sided figure add up to *360* degrees.

Four-Sider Facts

In a square:

- All four sides are *equal*.
- Each of the 4 angles is *90°*.
- Area = s^2
- Perimeter = *4s*

In a rectangle:

- Opposide sides are *equal*.
- Each of the 4 angles is *90°*.
- Area = *lw*
- Perimeter = *2l + 2w*

In a parallelogram:

- Opposite sides are *parallel* and equal.
- Area = *bh*

In a quadrilateral:

- Angles add up to *360°*.

MATH

WRITING

READING

VOCABULARY

Triangle Facts

In any triangle:

- The *largest side or hypotenuse* is opposite the largest angle.

- The *smallest side* is opposite the smallest angle.

- Equal sides are opposite equal *angles*.

- $A = \dfrac{1}{2}bh$

- The *height* is perpendicular to the base.

- *Perimeter* is the sum of the sides.

- Any side of a triangle must be greater than the *difference* but less than the *sum* of the other two sides.

In an isosceles triangle:

- Two *angles* and *sides* are equal.
- *Angles* opposite the equal sides are equal.

In an equilateral triangle:

- *All* sides are equal.
- All angles each equal *60°*.

 © TPR Education IP Holdings, LLC

Circle Facts

- There are *360°* in a circle.

Radius

- A radius is the distance from the *center* to any point on the edge of the circle.
- All *radii* in a circle are equal.

Diameter

- The straight line distance from one point on the circle to another, passing through the *center*.
- The longest *line or chord* inside the circle.
- It equals twice the *radius*.

Chord

- The *diameter* is the longest chord.

Circumference

- πd, $2\pi r$

Arc

- Arc measure is proportional to the size of the interior angle.

Area

- πr^2

Line Facts

Line Segment

- The degree measure of a line segment is *180°*.

Tangent

- A tangent line is always *perpendicular* to the radius.

Perpendicular

- Perpendicular lines have *slopes* that are negative reciprocals.

MATH

WRITING

READING

VOCABULARY

MATH

WRITING

READING

VOCABULARY

Transformation Facts

Rotation

- Rotation means turning an object around a point, which is called the *center of rotation*.

Reflection

- Reflecting an object or lines means to create its mirror image acorss a *line of reflection*.
- Lines reflected across the *x*-axis have slopes that are *negatives* of each other and *y*-intercepts that are *negatives* of each other.
- Lines reflected across the *y*-axis have *the same y*-intercept and slopes that are *negatives* of each other.

Symmetry

- A figure has *reflective* symmetry if it looks the same after a reflection.
- A figure has *rotational* symmetry if it can be rotated and still look the same.

SAT GEOMETRY: SHAPE UP OR SHIP OUT!

File Under: Questions We'd Like To See On The SAT

3. Find *x*.

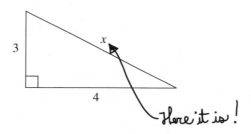

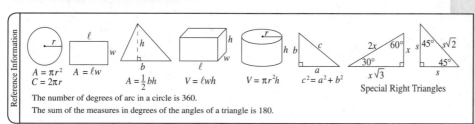

Here it is!

Reference Information

Reference Information

$A = \pi r^2$
$C = 2\pi r$

$A = \ell w$

$A = \frac{1}{2} bh$

$V = \ell w h$

$V = \pi r^2 h$

$c^2 = a^2 + b^2$

Special Right Triangles

The number of degrees of arc in a circle is 360.

The sum of the measures in degrees of the angles of a triangle is 180.

MATH

WRITING

READING

VOCABULARY

Geometry Basic Approach

DRAW YOUR OWN FIGURE

For Geometry problems that don't provide figures, you will need to draw your own figure so that you can work the problem more efficiently and carefully. Draw the shapes for the descriptions below.

An equilateral triangle

An isosceles right triangle

A line tangent to a circle

Two tangential circles

A rectangular solid

A right triangle inscribed in a cylinder

A circle inscribed in a square

A square inscribed in a circle

(for both of the above: also draw a diameter that will relate to the square)

LABEL ALL INFO

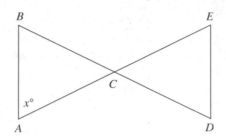

6. In the figure above, C is the midpoint of both $\overline{AE}$ and $\overline{BD}$. If $AE = BD$, and $\angle BCE = 120°$, then $x =$

(A) 30
(B) 45
(C) 50
(D) 60
(E) 75

Add all info to the picture. Draw on it with your pencil.

WRITE COMPLETE FORMULAS

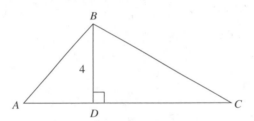

11. In the figure above, the area of $\triangle ABC$ is 20. If $AD = BD$, then what is the length of DC ?

(A) 2

(B) $2\sqrt{2}$

(C) $4\sqrt{2}$

(D) 6

(E) 10

What formula do you need for this problem?

© TPR Education IP Holdings, LLC

MATH

WRITING

READING

VOCABULARY

ALL TOGETHER NOW

12. If a square has an area of x, then, in terms of x, what is the circumference of the largest circle that can be inscribed in the square?

(A) $\pi\sqrt{x}$

(B) $\dfrac{\pi\sqrt{x}}{2}$

(C) πx^2

(D) $\dfrac{\pi x}{4}$

(E) $2\pi\sqrt{x}$

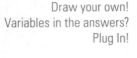

No figure?
Draw your own!
Variables in the answers?
Plug In!

For all geometry questions:

1. **Draw** your own figure if one is not provided.

2. **Label** all information from the problem on the figure.

3. **Write** complete formulas.

You will be able to apply the Geometry Basic Approach to all Geometry problems. However, if you get **STUCK...**

GEOMETRY BALLPARKING

When figures *are* drawn to scale, you can Ballpark to eliminate incorrect answers. Answers that don't agree with a figure drawn to scale *cannot* be correct!

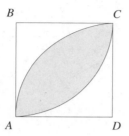

18. In square *ABCD* above, the shaded region is the intersection of two circular regions centered at *B* and *D*, respectively. If $AB = 10$, then the area of the shaded region is

(A) $25(\pi - 2)$

(B) $50(\pi - 2)$

(C) 25π

(D) 50π

(E) $40\pi(5 - \sqrt{2})$

When you Ballpark, remember:

$\pi \approx 3^{+}$

$\sqrt{2} \approx 1.4$

$\sqrt{3} \approx 1.7$

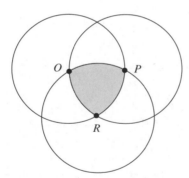

19. In the figure above, *O*, *P*, and *R* are the centers of three circles, each with radius 2. What is the perimeter of the shaded region?

(A) $\dfrac{2\pi}{3}$

(B) π

(C) $\dfrac{4\pi}{3}$

(D) 2π

(E) $\dfrac{8\pi}{3}$

MATH

WRITING

READING

VOCABULARY

DARN THAT ETS!

When ETS folks want to have fun, they find unusual ways of asking about basic geometry rules. Even really hard problems can be cracked by using the same rules that you use to solve straightforward problems.

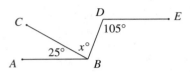

Got parallel lines? Use your pencil and make them look more familiar by extending them out.

6. In the figure above, if $\overline{AB}$ is parallel to $\overline{DE}$, then $x =$

(A) 105
(B) 90
(C) 85
(D) 80
(E) 75

Stuck? Look for basic shapes that ETS has hidden in the figure.

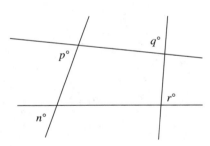

Note: Figure not drawn to scale.

What answer would Joe Bloggs choose?

16. In the figure shown above, four lines intersect as shown. If $n = 60$, what is the value of $p + q + r$?

(A) 180
(B) 240
(C) 300
(D) 420
(E) It cannot be determined from the information given.

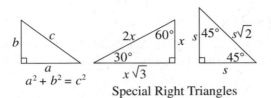

Special Right Triangles

When looking for basic shapes, look for 3:4:5, 6:8:10, and 5:12:13 right triangles as well as 45°-45°-90° and 30°-60°-90° triangles.

ETS l-o-v-e-s these special right triangles. Learn them. Master them. Own them.

14. If the diagonal of square A is twice that of square B, then the area of square A is how many times that of B ?

(A) 1

(B) $\sqrt{2}$

(C) 2

(D) 3

(E) 4

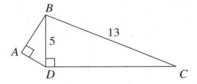

17. In the figure above, if $AD = \frac{1}{4} DC$, then what is the area of quadrilateral $ABCD$?

(A) 12

(B) 30

(C) 36

(D) 40

(E) 65

Not a classic shape of a triangle, circle, or square? Carve it up.

MATH

WRITING

READING

VOCABULARY

Similar Triangles

Two triangles are similar if the three angles in one triangle are the same as the three angles in the other triangle. Similar means "same shape, different size."

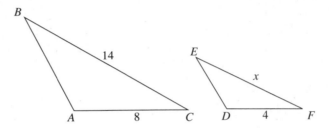

The corresponding sides of two similar triangles are proportional in length.

For example:

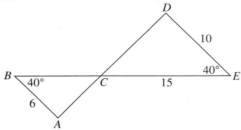

If the two triangles above are similar, what is the value of x?

Now try this question:

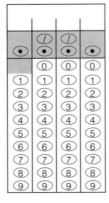

Re-draw similar triangles to orient them the same way.

16. In the figure above, if $\overline{BE}$ and $\overline{AD}$ intersect at point C, what is the length of BC?

Third Side Rule

Sometimes the SAT will give us a non-right triangle in which we know the lengths of two sides, but not the third.

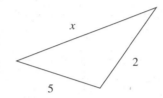

The length of any side of a triangle is greater than the difference—but less than the sum—of the other two sides of the triangle.

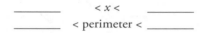

Note: Figure not drawn to scale.

_____ < x < _____
_____ < perimeter < _____

12. In $\triangle ABC$ (not shown), if $AB = 7$ and $BC = 5$, which of the following is a possible value for the perimeter of $\triangle ABC$?

  (A) 35
  (B) 24
  (C) 15
  (D) 12
  (E)   2

14. The lengths of two sides of a triangle are 7 and 24, and the length of the third side is an integer. What is the greatest possible perimeter of the triangle?

  (A) 23
  (B) 39
  (C) 55
  (D) 61
  (E) 62

© TPR Education IP Holdings, LLC

MATH

WRITING

READING

VOCABULARY

C-A-r-d is
a-w-e-s-o-m-e.

CIRCLES

The thing to remember about circles on the SAT is that if you know the radius, diameter, circumference, or area, then you can solve for all of them. Just organize the information in a CArd chart.

Circumference	Area	radius	diameter
πd	πr^2	$\dfrac{d}{2}$	$2r$

C	A	r	d
		4	
	25π		
12π			
			18
		1	
π			
	π		
			π

Is a semicircle *ALWAYS*
exactly half a circle?

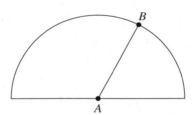

10. Semicircle A above has an area of 36π. What is the length of line segment $\overline{AB}$?

(A) $3\sqrt{2}$
(B) 6
(C) $6\sqrt{2}$
(D) 12
(E) $12\sqrt{2}$

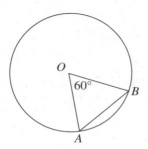

18. Points *A* and *B* lie on a circle with center *O*. If the perimeter of triangle *AOB* is 18, what is the circumference of circle *O*?

(A)   4π
(B)   6π
(C)   12π
(D)   18π
(E)   36π

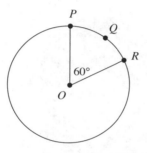

14. The radius of circle *O*, shown above, is 9. What is the length of arc *PQR* ?

(A)   2π
(B)   3π
(C)   6π
(D)   9π
(E)   12π

- An arc is any part of the circumference.
- Arc measure is proportional to the size of the interior angle and to the sector area.

MATH

WRITING

READING

VOCABULARY

A line tangent to a circle

- Intersects the circle at only one point.
- Is perpendicular to the radius of the circle at the point of intersection.

?

What does your POOD tell you to do with this question?

17. Side $\overline{AC}$ of $\triangle AOC$ (not shown) is tangent to the circle with center O and radius 3 at point B. If the measure of $\angle AOB$ is 45° and $\angle AOB = \angle BOC$, what is the perimeter of $\triangle AOC$?

(A) 3

(B) 6

(C) $3+3\sqrt{2}$

(D) 12

(E) $6+6\sqrt{2}$

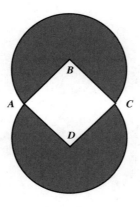

20. In the figure above, B and D are the centers of the circles, and the perimeter of square $ABCD$ is 24. What is the total area of the shaded regions?

(A) $12\pi - 24$

(B) 27π

(C) 54π

(D) $72\pi - 36$

(E) 72π

 © TPR Education IP Holdings, LLC

COORDINATE GEOMETRY

Some problems will ask about the distance between two points that lie on a plane. You can always solve these problems by drawing a right triangle and using the Pythagorean theorem.

8. In the *xy*-coordinate plane, what is the distance from (5, 3) to (2, 7) ?

(A)   3
(B)   4
(C)   5
(D)   6
(E)   7

Look for 3:4:5, 6:8:10, and 5:12:13 triangles.

15. *AB* is the diameter of a circle that lies in the rectangular coordinate system. If the coordinates of point *A* are (5, 9) and those of *B* are (17, 17), what is the sum of the *x* and *y* coordinates of the center of the circle?

(A)   11
(B)   12
(C)   13
(D)   24
(E)   156

Do we need to know the midpoint formula or just...?

17. In the *xy*-coordinate plane, line *m* passes through the origin and is perpendicular to the line $8x - 3y = n$, where *n* is a constant. If the two lines intersect at the point $(r, r - 2)$, what is the value of *r* ?

(A) $-\dfrac{16}{11}$

(B) $-\dfrac{11}{16}$

(C) $\dfrac{3}{11}$

(D) $\dfrac{11}{16}$

(E) $\dfrac{16}{11}$

Remember that the standard form of the linear equation is $y = mx + b$.

WEIRD COORDINATE GEOMETRY

12. In the xy-plane, line m passes through the points $(-9, 8)$ and $(-2, 6)$. What is the x-intercept of line m ?

(A) $-\dfrac{2}{7}$

(B) 6

(C) $\dfrac{38}{4}$

(D) 19

(E) 23

16. In the xy-coordinate plane, A and B are different points that have the same y-coordinate and are on the parabola given by $y = x^2 - 5x - 14$. What is the x-coordinate of the midpoint of AB ?

(A) $-\dfrac{2}{5}$

(B) $\dfrac{2}{5}$

(C) 1

(D) $\dfrac{5}{2}$

(E) $\dfrac{9}{2}$

20. In the xy-coordinate plane, point Q is the reflection of the point with coordinates $(2, 9)$ across the line $y = x$. Point R is the reflection of point Q across the x-axis. What are the coordinates of point R ?

(A) $(-9, 2)$
(B) $(-9, -2)$
(C) $(2, -9)$
(D) $(9, 2)$
(E) $(9, -2)$

 © TPR Education IP Holdings, LLC

MATH

WRITING

READING

VOCABULARY

GEOMETRY TIMED DRILL

Time: 10 minutes.

Target score	# of questions to attempt
< 450	3 or 4 questions
460–550	5 or 6 questions
560–650	7 or 8 questions
> 650	All

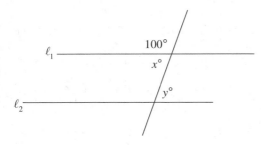

4. In the figure above, if ℓ_1 is parallel to ℓ_2, then the value of $x + y =$

(A)   50
(B)   80
(C)   100
(D)   160
(E)   180

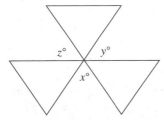

6. In the figure above, if three equilateral triangles have a common vertex, then the value of $x + y + z =$

(A)   90
(B)   120
(C)   150
(D)   180
(E)   270

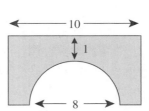

7. In the figure above, a rectangle is intersected by a semicircle. What is the perimeter of the shaded region?

(A) $22 + 4\pi$
(B) $20 + 8\pi$
(C) $40 + 4\pi$
(D) $50 + 8\pi$
(E) $100 + 16\pi$

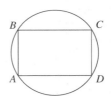

9. Rectangle *ABCD* has length 6 and width 8. What is the area of the circle?

(A) 10π
(B) 20π
(C) 25π
(D) 64π
(E) 100π

GO ON TO THE NEXT PAGE

MATH

WRITING

READING

VOCABULARY

10. In rectangle *PQRS* above, $\dfrac{PQ}{QR} = \dfrac{2}{3}$. The sum of

PQ, *QR*, and *RS* is what fraction of the perimeter

of the rectangle?

(A) $\dfrac{5}{9}$

(B) $\dfrac{2}{3}$

(C) $\dfrac{7}{10}$

(D) $\dfrac{3}{4}$

(E) $\dfrac{5}{7}$

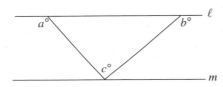

11. In the figure above, if $\ell \parallel m$, what is the value of
$a + b$ in terms of c ?

(A) $360 - c$
(B) $360 - 2c$
(C) $180 + 2c$
(D) $180 + c$
(E) $180 - c$

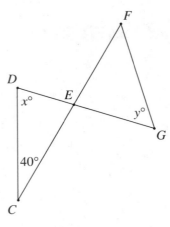

12. In the figure above, $EF = EG$. What is the value
of *y* in terms of *x* ?

(A) $x - 35$

(B) $x - 20$

(C) $\dfrac{x}{2}$

(D) $\dfrac{x}{2} + 20$

(E) $\dfrac{x}{2} + 40$

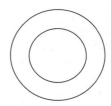

<u>Note:</u> Figure not drawn to scale.

13. In the figure above, the area of the larger circular
region is twice the area of the smaller circular
region. If the diameter of the larger circular
region is *x*, then in terms of *x*, what is the area of
the smaller circular region?

(A) $\dfrac{\pi x^2}{2}$

(B) $\dfrac{\pi x^2}{4}$

(C) $\dfrac{\pi x^2}{8}$

(D) $\dfrac{\pi x}{2}$

(E) $\dfrac{\pi x}{4}$

GO ON TO THE NEXT PAGE

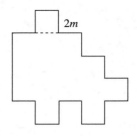

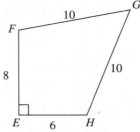

14. In the figure above, if each short segment has length $2m$, and all segments intersect at right angles, then what is the area of the figure?

(A) $6m$

(B) $6m^2$

(C) $15m^2$

(D) $18m^2$

(E) $60m^2$

18. What is the area of quadrilateral *EFGH* shown above?

(A) $24 + 25\sqrt{3}$

(B) $24 + 50\sqrt{3}$

(C) $48 + 50\sqrt{3}$

(D) 72

(E) It cannot be determined from the information given.

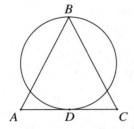

15. In the figure above, point *D* lies on $\overline{AC}$. Points *B* and *D* lie on the circle such that there is no segment longer than $\overline{BD}$ (not shown) in the interior of the circle. If the area of the circle is 36π, and $BD = AC$, what is the area of $\triangle ABC$?

(A) 18

(B) 36

(C) 48

(D) 72

(E) 144

STOP

**If you finish before time is called, you may check your work on this section only.
Do not turn to any other section in the test.**

MATH

WRITING

READING

VOCABULARY

Summary

- TPR's basic advice for solving any geometry question:

    1) _____
    2) _____
    3) _____

- If a figure is drawn to scale, _____ can be useful to POE some answer choices by approximating the answer.

- When a figure is not drawn to scale, believe what you _____ in the problem and not what you _____ in the figure.

- Triangles that have the same angle measurements but not the same side lengths are called _____ triangles.

- Any side of a triangle must be greater than the _____ and less than the _____ of the other two sides of the triangle.

- Anytime a "wedge" problem in a circle is given, you can use the relationship of _____ over _____.

- When asked to find the length of a line in the *xy*-coordinate plane, make a _____ to use _____ Theorem.

- I have accomplished _____ of my _____ stated goals in the Introduction chapter.

 © TPR Education IP Holdings, LLC

SAT GEOMETRY PRACTICE

GEOMETRY VOCABULARY

Term	Definition	Examples/Draw It
Perpendicular		
Parallel		
Intersection (of lines)		
Bisect		
Midpoint		
Vertex / Vertices		
Number Line		
Venn Diagram		
Hypotenuse		
Area		
Perimeter		
Diagonal		
Quadrilateral		
Polygon		
Plane		
Similar		
Radius		
Chord		
Diameter		
Arc		

Term	Definition	Examples/Draw It
Tangent		
Circumference		
Semicircle		
Right triangle		
Isosceles triangle		
Equilateral triangle		
Equilateral polygon		
Inscribed		
Circumscribed		
Cube		
Edge (of 3-D figure)		
Face (of 3-D figure)		
Altitude		
Cylinder		
Sphere		
Volume		
Surface Area		
Origin		
x-axis		
y-axis		
Slope		
x-intercept		
y-intercept		
Constant		
Function		
$y = f(x)$		
Interval		
Increasing (as a function)		
Decreasing (as a function)		
Symmetric		
Reflection		
Rotation		

GEOMETRY BASICS

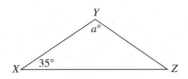

2. In △XYZ above, if XY = YZ, then a =

(A) 125
(B) 115
(C) 110
(D) 70
(E) 55

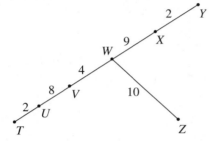

Note: Figure not drawn to scale.

2. In the figure above, $\overline{ZW}$ is perpendicular to $\overline{TY}$. Of the following line segments (not shown) which has the least length?

(A) $\overline{ZT}$
(B) $\overline{ZU}$
(C) $\overline{ZV}$
(D) $\overline{ZX}$
(E) $\overline{ZY}$

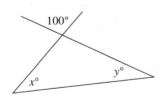

3. In the triangle above, the value of x + y =

(A) 40
(B) 65
(C) 80
(D) 90
(E) 100

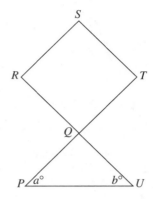

3. In the figure above, if QRST is a square, what is the value of a + b ?

(A) 30
(B) 45
(C) 60
(D) 80
(E) 90

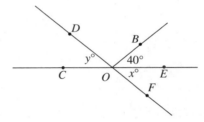

5. In the figure above, if x + y = 60, what is the measure of ∠COF ?

(A) 40°
(B) 60°
(C) 90°
(D) 100°
(E) 150°

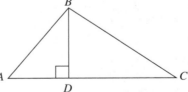

6. In the figure above, the area of △ABC is 30. If AD = 4 and DB = 5, then what is the area of △BDC ?

(A) 5
(B) 10
(C) 15
(D) 20
(E) 40

MATH

WRITING

READING

VOCABULARY

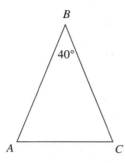

Note: Figure not drawn to scale.

7. If △ABC is isosceles, the measure of ∠BAC could be which of the following?

    (A) 40°
    (B) 50°
    (C) 60°
    (D) 65°
    (E) 80°

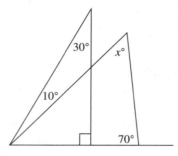

7. In the figure above, the value of $x =$

    (A) 70
    (B) 60
    (C) 50
    (D) 40
    (E) 30

8. If the area of a square is $9a^2$, what is the length of a side of the square?

    (A) $9a^2$
    (B) $3a^2$
    (C) $2a^2$
    (D) $9a$
    (E) $3a$

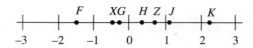

8. Which of the lettered points on the number line above could represent the result when the coordinate of point Z is divided by the coordinate of point X ?

    (A) F
    (B) G
    (C) H
    (D) J
    (E) K

9. If the radius of a certain circle is the same as the length of the side of a square that has an area of 36, what is the area of the circle?

    (A) 6π
    (B) 12π
    (C) 18π
    (D) 36π
    (E) 81π

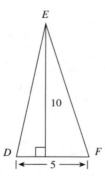

10. If the area of triangle DEF above is equal to the area of square M (not shown), what is the length of a side of the square?

    (A) $2\sqrt{5}$

    (B) 5

    (C) $5\sqrt{2}$

    (D) 20

    (E) 25

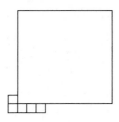

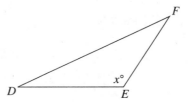

Note: Figure not drawn to scale.

10. In the figure above, a square with a side of 10 feet is to be surrounded by square tiles, each with a side of one foot. The completed border will contain how many smaller squares?

(A)   36
(B)   40
(C)   44
(D)   100
(E)   104

14. In the figure above, $DE = 5$ and $EF = 12$. If $x < 90$, what is one possible length of DF ?

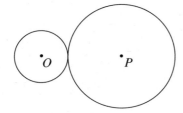

12. In the figure above, points O and P are the centers of the two circles. If the area of the circle with center P is 25π, and the diameter of the circle with center O is equal to the radius of the circle with center P, what is the sum of the circumferences of the two circles?

(A) 5π
(B) 10π
(C) 15π
(D) 50π
(E) 125π

18. What is the area of a square with sides of lengths $2x + 1$ and $x + 2$?

(A)   1
(B)   9
(C)   16
(D)   25
(E)   It cannot be determined from the information given.

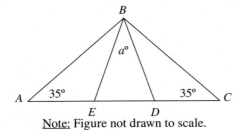

Note: Figure not drawn to scale.

14. In the figure above, if $AE = EB = BD = DC$, then what is the value of a ?

(A)   35
(B)   40
(C)   55
(D)   70
(E)   110

20. The lengths of the sides of an isosceles triangle are c, c, and 16. If c is an integer, what is the smallest possible perimeter of the triangle?

(A)   30
(B)   32
(C)   33
(D)   34
(E)   48

PARALLEL LINES

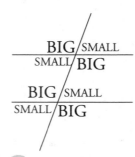

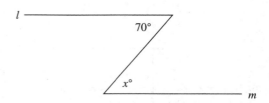

5. In the figure above, if $l \parallel m$, what is the value of x ?

(A) 30
(B) 70
(C) 90
(D) 110
(E) 130

When parallel lines are intersected by the same line:

1) BIG angles = BIG angles

2) small angles = small angles

3) BIG + small = 180 degrees

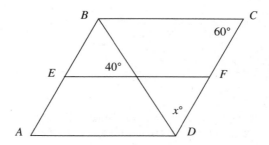

10. In the figure above, if quadrilaterals *EBCF* and *ABCD* are both parallelograms, what is the value of x ?

(A) 100
(B) 80
(C) 60
(D) 40
(E) 20

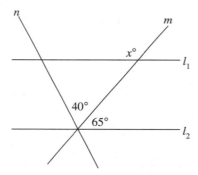

4. In the figure above, l_1 is parallel to l_2 . What is the value of x ?

(A) 60
(B) 75
(C) 105
(D) 115
(E) 140

CIRCLES

10. If the length of a minor arc formed by two radii of a circle is $\frac{1}{20}$ of the circumference, what is the measurement of the arc in degrees?

(A) 30
(B) 24
(C) 18
(D) 12
(E)   6

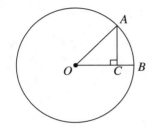

13. In the figure above, the length of the minor arc AB is $\frac{1}{12}$ of the circumference of the circle with center O. What is the measure of $\angle OAC$?

(A) 30°
(B) 40°
(C) 45°
(D) 50°
(E) 60°

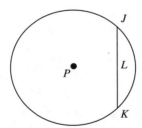

14. In the figure above, the circle has center P and circumference of 52π. The midpoint of $\overline{JK}$ is L, and $\overline{JK} = 20$. What is the length of PL?

(A)   5
(B) 10
(C) 12
(D) 24
(E) 26

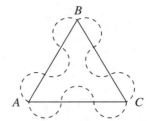

14. The diameters of the 9 dashed curves above all lie on equilateral triangle ABC. If the perimeter of triangle ABC is equal to 63, what is the length along the curved line from A to B to C to A ?

(A) $\frac{21\pi}{2}$

(B) 21π

(C) $\frac{63\pi}{2}$

(D) 63π

(E) 126π

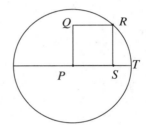

16. In the figure above, point P is the center of the circle and $PQRS$ is a square. If $\overline{PR}$ is a diagonal of square $PQRS$, then the length of minor arc RT is what fractional part of the circumference of the circle?

COORDINATE GEOMETRY

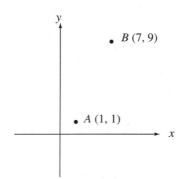

7. What is the distance between points *A* and *B* in the *xy*-coordinate plane above?

(A)   5
(B)   10
(C)   12
(D)   14
(E)   16

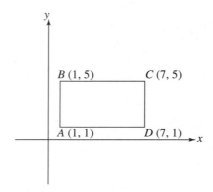

8. In the rectangle shown above, what are the coordinates of the point of intersection of $\overline{BD}$ and $\overline{AC}$ (not shown) ?

(A)   (3, 2)
(B)   (3, 4)
(C)   (3, 8)
(D)   (4, 3)
(E)   (8, 6)

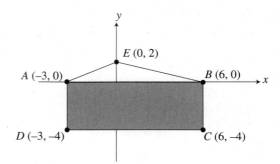

11. In the *xy*-coordinate plane above, what is the ratio of the area of the shaded region to the area of triangle *AEB* ?

(A)   1 to 5
(B)   1 to 4
(C)   2 to 1
(D)   4 to 1
(E)   5 to 1

13. In the *xy*-plane, line *d* passes through the origin and point (–3, 8). Which of the following is an equation of a line that is perpendicular to line *d* ?

(A) $y = -\dfrac{8}{3}x - 5$

(B) $y = -\dfrac{3}{8}x + 4$

(C) $y = \dfrac{3}{8}x + 7$

(D) $y = \dfrac{8}{3}x - 4$

(E) $y = 3x + 5$

16. In a rectangular coordinate system, the coordinates of point *A* are (2, 3) and those of point *B* are (8, 11). What is the distance from the midpoint of $\overline{AB}$ to point *C* (6, 9) ?

(A) $\sqrt{2}$
(B) $\sqrt{5}$
(C) $\sqrt{7}$
(D) $\sqrt{17}$
(E) $\sqrt{21}$

16. Points X and Y are the endpoints of a line segment at $(3, 5)$ and $(3, -7)$, respectively. Point Z lies on $\overline{XY}$ such that the distance from Z to X is $\frac{1}{3}$ the distance from Z to Y. What is the y-coordinate of Point Z ?

(A) 3
(B) 2
(C) −1
(D) −2
(E) −3

17. Points S and U are the endpoints of a line segment. Point R is the midpoint of $\overline{SU}$ and point T lies on the same line such that $TR = 6$ and $TU = 14$. What is one possible value of ST ?

OVERLAPPING FIGURES

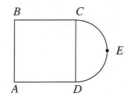

9. In the figure above, if square *ABCD* has sides of length 2, what is the area of semicircle *CED* ?

(A) 4π

(B) 2π

(C) π

(D) $\dfrac{\pi}{2}$

(E) $\dfrac{\pi}{4}$

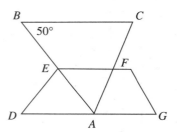

12. In the figure above, if $\overline{BC} \parallel \overline{EF} \parallel \overline{DG}$ and $ED = EA$, what is the measure of $\angle DEA$?

(A) 40°
(B) 50°
(C) 60°
(D) 65°
(E) 80°

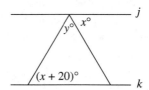

Note: Figure not drawn to scale.

14. In the figure above, line *j* is parallel to line *k*. If $y - x = 10$, what is the value of *x* ?

(A) 50
(B) 60
(C) 70
(D) 80
(E) 150

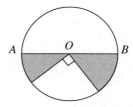

15. In the figure above, the circle with center *O* has a radius of 2. If *AB* is the diameter of *O*, what is the area of the shaded region?

(A) $\dfrac{\pi}{8}$

(B) $\dfrac{\pi}{4}$

(C) $\dfrac{\pi}{2}$

(D) π

(E) 4π

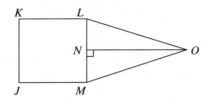

16. In the figure above, *JKLM* is a square and *LOM* is a triangle with area 12. If *NO* = 6, what is the area of *JKLOM* ?

(A) 32
(B) 28
(C) 24
(D) 16
(E) 12

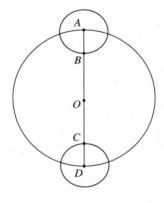

Note: Figure not drawn to scale.

16. In the figure above, points *B* and *C* lie on segment $\overline{AD}$ that passes through the center of circle *O*. The area of each of the two congruent circles with centers *A* and *D* is 9π, and the area of circle *O* is 121π. What is the length of segment $\overline{BC}$?

(A) 19
(B) 16
(C) 11
(D) 8
(E) 5

19. A square and a circle have equal areas. What is the ratio of the side of the square to the radius of the circle?

(A) 1 to 2
(B) $\sqrt{\pi}$ to 1
(C) 2 to 1
(D) π to 1
(E) π² to 1

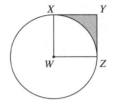

19. In the figure above, side *XY* of square *WXYZ* has length 8. If *W* is the center of the circle, what is the area of the shaded region?

(A) 64 − 32π
(B) 64 − 16π
(C) 64 − 4π
(D) 32 − 4π
(E) 32 − 16π

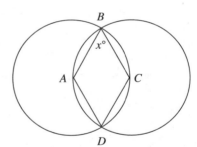

20. In the figure above, if *A* and *C* are the centers of the two circles, then *x* =

(A) 30
(B) 40
(C) 45
(D) 60
(E) 90

MATH

WRITING

READING

VOCABULARY

GEOMETRY ET CETERA

Here are a few other geometry concepts that ETS likes to test. Be sure to review the explanations that follow these questions when you are done.

2. What is the distance from the origin to (0, 4) ?

(A) 0
(B) 2
(C) 4
(D) 6
(E) 8

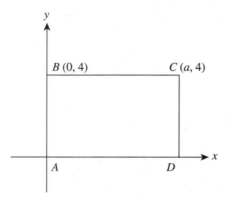

4. In the figure above, if the area of rectangle *ABCD* is 28, what is the value of *a* ?

(A) 4
(B) 7
(C) 8
(D) 12
(E) 24

7. What is the volume of a cylinder with a height of 1 inch and a radius of 3 inches?

(A) 3π
(B) 6π
(C) 9π
(D) 27π
(E) 36π

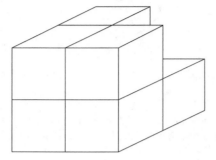

8. In the figure above, a cube is made up of 8 smaller cubes that have edges of length 4. If one of the smaller cubes is removed as shown, what is the surface area of the resulting solid?

(A) 64
(B) 128
(C) 336
(D) 384
(E) 512

9. What is the volume, in terms of *a*, of a cube with side 2*a* ?

(A) a^3
(B) $2a^3$
(C) $4a^3$
(D) $8a^3$
(E) $12a$

10. What is the total surface area of a rectangular solid with a length of 6 feet, a width of 4 feet, and a height of 2 feet?

(A) 12
(B) 24
(C) 44
(D) 48
(E) 88

16. If the points E (−3, 2), F (4, 2), G (4, −1), and D (−3, −1) are the vertices of a rectangle (not shown), what is the area of rectangle $DEFG$?

17. In the rectangular coordinate plane, a circle shares exactly one point with the y-axis. If the circle has its center at (8, 6), what is the radius of the circle?

ANSWERS AND EXPLANATIONS TO GEOMETRY ET CETERA

2. **C**   You'll need to draw your own picture. Start by drawing the coordinate axes. The *x*-axis is horizontal and the *y*-axis is vertical. The *origin*, the point where the axes cross, is (0, 0). Now, plot the point given in the problem. Point (0, 4) is on the *y*-axis, 4 places above the origin. So, the distance is 4.

4. **B**   Since point *B* has a *y*-coordinate of 4, the distance from *A* to *B* is 4. So the rectangle has a width of 4. The area is 28, so: $A = lw$; $28 = (l)(4)$; $l = 7$. Since the width of the rectangle is 7, the distance on the coordinate plane from *B* to *C* is 7. So the *x*-coordinate of *C* is 7.

7. **C**   The formula for the volume of a cylinder is $V = \pi r^2 h$. Since ETS provides this formula, you can always look it up if you forget it. Now, plug in the numbers from the problem.
$V = \pi r^2 h = \pi(3)^2(1) = 9\pi$.

8. **D**   The surface area of the entire cube (if it were complete) would be 384, the total of the areas of all 6 faces of the cube. When one cube is removed, three "faces" of the solid are taken away (a total area of 48), leaving us with a total surface area of 336. However, when the small cube is removed, three faces from the adjacent small cubes become exposed, giving us back a surface area of 48. Thus, the surface area of the resulting solid is the same as that of the original, whole cube, or 384.

9. **D**   The formula for the volume of a cube is $V = s^3$. So, $V = (2a)^3 = 8a^3$. Don't forget that you could have also plugged in!

10. **E**   To find the surface area of a rectangular solid, add up the areas of all the faces. The area of the top of this figure is $6 \times 4 = 24$. The area of the front of the figure is $2 \times 6 = 12$. The area of one of the sides is $2 \times 4 = 8$. Now, add up the areas and multiply by 2 since the solid also has a bottom, a back, and another side. So, *Surface Area* $= 2(24 + 12 + 8) = 88$.

16. **21**   If ETS doesn't give you a figure, you should draw your own. *E* has an *x*-coordinate of –3 and *F* has a *x*-coordinate of 4. So, the distance from *E* to *F* is 7. Therefore, the rectangle has a length of 7. *F* has a *y*-coordinate of 2 and *G* has a *y*-coordinate of –1. So, the distance from *F* to *G* is 3. Therefore, the rectangle has a width of 3. The area of the rectangle *DEFG* $= 3 \times 7 = 21$.

17. **8**   If ETS describes the shape but doesn't draw it, they're trying to fool you into making a silly mistake. Draw the figure! Sketch the coordinate axes and the point (8, 6). If the circle shares exactly one point with the *y*-axis, the radius (going straight out to the left) must be 8, the horizontal distance from the center to the *y*-axis.

SAT MATH:
MORE WAYS TO PLUG IN

MATH

WRITING

READING

VOCABULARY

REVIEW EXERCISE

Use the concepts from the homework to answer these questions.

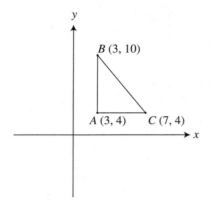

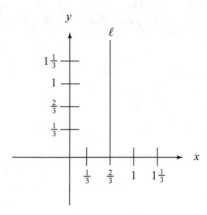

3. What is the area of $\triangle ABC$?

(A)   6
(B)   12
(C)   16
(D)   20
(E)   24

7. The volume of a rectangular solid with a length of 3, a width of 4, and a height of h is 24. What is the volume of a rectangular solid with a length of 4, a width of 5, and a height of h ?

(A)   20
(B)   28
(C)   32
(D)   40
(E)   52

10. What is the maximum number of points of intersection of 4 distinct lines?

(A)   3
(B)   4
(C)   5
(D)   6
(E)   7

11. In the figure above, line ℓ is parallel to the y-axis. All of the following points lie on line ℓ EXCEPT

(A) $\left(\dfrac{2}{3}, -10\right)$

(B) $\left(1, \dfrac{2}{3}\right)$

(C) $\left(\dfrac{2}{3}, \dfrac{1}{3}\right)$

(D) $\left(\dfrac{2}{3}, \dfrac{2}{3}\right)$

(E) $\left(\dfrac{2}{3}, 1\right)$

 © TPR Education IP Holdings, LLC

PLUGGING IN THE ANSWERS (PITA)

For certain Plug-In questions, you can Plug In the numbers that ETS gives you.

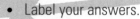

- Label your answers.
- Starting with answer choice (C), work the steps of the problem (a.k.a. Bite-Sized Pieces).
- If (C) doesn't answer the question, determine whether it is too big or too small.
- Getting warmer or colder? When you find the correct answer, STOP.

10. In a group of students, there are 22 more girls than boys. If there are 80 students in the group, how many girls are there?

   (A) 36
   (B) 44
   (C) 48
   (D) 51
   (E) 58

11. Adam is half as old as Bob and three times as old as Cindy. If the sum of their ages is 40, what is Bob's age?

   (A)   3
   (B)   6
   (C) 12
   (D) 18
   (E) 24

If the question asks for a specific amount, PITA!

11. If $|6x - 26| < 6$, which of the following is the greatest possible value of x ?

   (A) 6
   (B) 5
   (C) 4
   (D) 3
   (E) 2

If the question asks for the *greatest* value, start with the biggest number. Similarly, for *least* value problems, start with the smallest number.

MATH

WRITING

READING

VOCABULARY

When plugging in
numbers for Must Be /
Could Be problems, use

Zero
One
Negative
Extreme
Fraction

POE is very important
when you're Plugging In
more than once.

MUST BE/COULD BE

5. If y is an integer, which of the following must be an odd integer?

(A) y^2

(B) $3y$

(C) $2y + 1$

(D) $y + 3$

(E) $\dfrac{y}{2}$

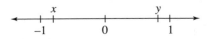

If a question uses the phrase "must be" or "could be,"
be ready to Plug In as much as needed.

$$x \quad\quad\quad\quad\quad y$$

```
   |---+---|---+---|---+---|--->
      -1      0       1
```

15. In the above number line, points x, y, and z (not shown) are defined by the equation $x < z < y$. Which of the following could be true?

   I. $xz > 0$

  II. $\dfrac{z}{x} \geq 1$

  III. $xy < z$

(A) I only
(B) II only
(C) III only
(D) I and III only
(E) I, II and III

$$(2x - 7)(3x + 2) < 0$$

18. For how many integers x is the above inequality true?

(A) Zero
(B) One
(C) Two
(D) Three
(E) Four

THE GREAT PLUGGING IN CHALLENGE

You can Plug In on each of these problems. See if you can figure out how. (Don't forget your POOD!)

2. Vicken, Roger, and Adam buy a radio. Roger pays twice as much as Adam, and Vicken pays three times as much as Roger. If the radio costs $90, how much did Roger pay?

   (A) $10
   (B) $20
   (C) $30
   (D) $45
   (E) $65

5. If p is subtracted from 80 and the result is divided by p, the result is 3. What is the value of p ?

   (A)   4
   (B)   10
   (C)   20
   (D)   24
   (E)   34

$$\frac{1}{2}, \frac{1}{3}, \frac{2}{9}, \frac{4}{27}, \frac{8}{81}$$

7. The first term in the sequence above is $\frac{1}{2}$.

   Each term after the first is determined by

   multiplying the preceding term by a constant k.

   What is the value of k ?

   (A) $\frac{1}{3}$

   (B) $\frac{1}{2}$

   (C) $\frac{2}{3}$

   (D) $\frac{3}{2}$

   (E) 3

8. If $\left|\dfrac{(x+3)}{2}\right| = 5$, what are the possible values for x ?

   (A) 7
   (B) −13
   (C) −13 and −7
   (D) −7 and 13
   (E) −13 and 7

9. If R and S are two sets of numbers and T is the set of numbers that contains only the elements that are in both R and S, which of the following CANNOT be true?

   (A) 6 is in R but not in T.
   (B) If 3 is not in T, then 3 is not in S.
   (C) 5 is in both S and T.
   (D) 4 is in T but not in S.
   (E) There are no numbers in T.

$$m, n, 29, \ldots$$

9. The first term in the sequence above is m, and each term after the first is obtained by subtracting 4 from 3 times the preceding term. What is the value of m ?

   (A)   5
   (B)   6
   (C)   7
   (D)   8
   (E)   9

10. If $x(x + \dfrac{16}{x}) = 25$, which of the following is a possible value for x ?

(A)   −4
(B)   −3
(C)   4
(D)   5
(E)   9

12. The average (arithmetic mean) of a list of seven real numbers is 10. If the least and greatest numbers on the list are 4 and 30 respectively, and the number 7 appears most frequently on the list, which of the following could be the median of the numbers on the list?

    I. 6
    II. 6.5
    III. 7

(A)   I only
(B)   III only
(C)   I and II only
(D)   I and III only
(E)   I, II, and III

14. If $70x + 33y = 4233$ and x and y are positive integers, x could be which of the following values?

(A)   42
(B)   47
(C)   55
(D)   60
(E)   63

15. The average of 2 numbers is x. If the average of x and y is z, which of the following is y in terms of x and z ?

(A) $\dfrac{x + z}{2}$

(B) $\dfrac{x + z}{3}$

(C) $2z - x$

(D) $\dfrac{z}{3} - \dfrac{x}{2}$

(E) $3z - 2x$

15. In the equation $w = \dfrac{2}{z^3}$, if the value of w is multiplied by $\dfrac{1}{8}$, then the value of z is multiplied by what number?

(A) $\dfrac{1}{6}$

(B) $\dfrac{1}{3}$

(C)   2

(D)   3

(E)   6

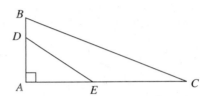

18. In right triangle ABC shown above, $AD = \dfrac{4}{5} AB$ and $AE = \dfrac{1}{3} AC$. If the area of triangle $ADE = 8$, what is the area of triangle ABC ?

18. What is the greatest four-digit integer *ABCD* that meets the following three requirements?

    1.   All of the digits are distinct.

    2. $A + D = B + C$

    3.   The product of the four digits is divisible by 5 but not divisible by 10.

19. If *g* and *q* are positive integers such that

$g = \left(\dfrac{6}{5}\right)x$ and $x = \dfrac{q^2}{4}$, what is the <u>least</u> possible

value of *q* ?

(A) 12
(B) 18
(C) 24
(D) 30
(E) 36

18. If the base of a triangle is increased by 20% and the height of the same triangle is decreased by 20%, what is the effect on the area of the triangle?

(A) It is increased by 40%.
(B) It is increased by 20%.
(C) It remains unchanged.
(D) It is decreased by 10%.
(E) It is decreased by 4%.

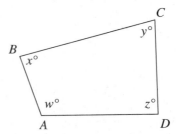

20. In quadrilateral *ABCD* shown above, *y* is an integer, and $w + x > 180$. If $z = y - 10$, what is the greatest possible value of *z* ?

(A)   84
(B)   85
(C)   94
(D)   95
(E) 179

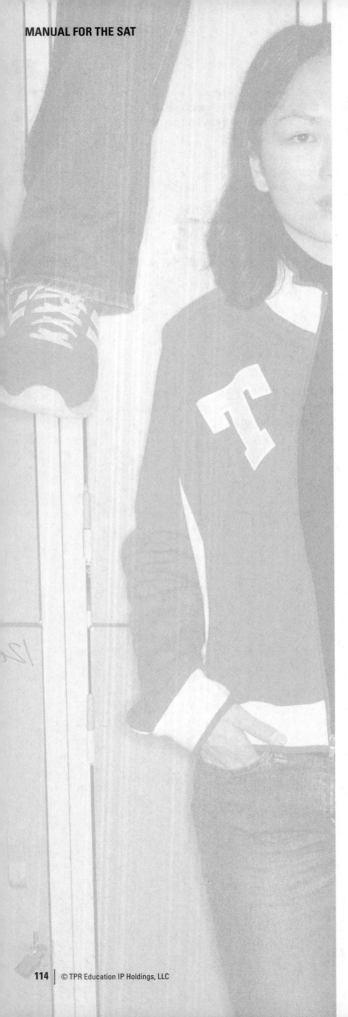

Summary

- You should look to Plug In The Answer (PITA) on problems if:

  - _____

  - _____

  - _____

- The steps to using PITA are as follows:

  1. _____

  2. _____

  3. _____

  4. _____

- On Must Be / Could Be problems, plug in at least a couple times using

  Z _____

  O _____

  N _____

  E _____

  F _____

- I have accomplished _____ of my _____ stated goals in the Introduction chapter.

 © TPR Education IP Holdings, LLC

MORE WAYS TO PLUG IN PRACTICE

PLUGGING IN THE ANSWERS (PITA)

2. Two less than a certain number is one-third of that number. What is the number?

(A) 1
(B) 3
(C) 6
(D) 8
(E) 9

5. Elvis gives his chauffeur a gold lamé suit and gives his cook a diamond ring. If the suit is worth one-fifth of what the ring is worth, and if the two items together are worth $4,800, then how much is the ring worth?

(A) $800
(B) $960
(C) $3,840
(D) $4,000
(E) $4,250

6. The sum of three positive integers is 9 and their product is 24. If the smallest of the integers is 2, what is the largest?

(A) 4
(B) 6
(C) 8
(D) 9
(E) 12

6. If $\frac{1}{d} + \frac{1}{d} = 8$, then $d =$

(A) $\frac{1}{8}$

(B) $\frac{1}{4}$

(C) 1

(D) 4

(E) 8

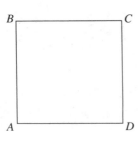

7. If the length of the side of square *ABCD* shown above were 50% greater, the diagonal of the square would be $9\sqrt{2}$. What is the length of the side of square *ABCD* ?

(A) 5
(B) 6
(C) 7
(D) 8
(E) 9

7. Marlene has twice as many gumballs as Carla. If Marlene were to give Carla three gumballs, Marlene would then have one gumball fewer than Carla. How many gumballs does Marlene currently have?

(A)   4
(B)   5
(C)   7
(D)   8
(E)   10

8. Lori is 15 years older than Carol. In 10 years, Lori will be twice as old as Carol. How old is Lori now?

(A)   5
(B)   12
(C)   20
(D)   25
(E)   30

9. If $x^2 - 4y^2 = 5$ and x and y are positive integers, what is the value of x ?

(A)   1
(B)   2
(C)   3
(D)   4
(E)   5

9. Mel owes money to Elizabeth, Rob, and Ken. Mel owes Elizabeth half the amount he owes Rob and owes Ken three times the amount he owes Elizabeth. If Mel owes the three a total of $18, then how much does he owe Elizabeth?

(A) $3
(B) $5
(C) $10
(D) $12
(E) $13

9. Judy is 26 years old and Diane is 5 years old. In how many years will Judy be twice as old as Diane?

(A)   16
(B)   19
(C)   21
(D)   24
(E)   26

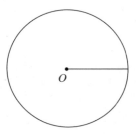

10. If the area of the circle shown above with center *O* is more than 250% of its circumference, which of the following could be its radius?

(A)   2
(B)   3
(C)   4
(D)   5
(E)   6

12. Mike has twice as many stamps as Jean. After he gives Jean 6 stamps, he still has 8 more stamps than Jean. How many stamps did Mike have before he gave Jean the 6 stamps?

(A) 28
(B) 32
(C) 36
(D) 40
(E) 42

12. A pirate captain sails his ship for two days. The distance he sailed on the first day was 150 miles less than twice the distance he sailed on the second day. If he sailed a total of 600 miles, what was the distance, in miles, that he sailed on the second day?

(A) 250
(B) 275
(C) 350
(D) 375
(E) 450

13. If $(x-6)(x+6) = 13$, then one possible value for x is

(A) $\sqrt{7}$
(B) $\sqrt{13}$
(C) 7
(D) 19
(E) 49

14. A group of people are sharing equally the $30 cost of renting a car. If an additional person joined the group, each person would owe $1 less. How many people are in the group currently?

(A) 5
(B) 6
(C) 10
(D) 12
(E) 15

15. If $\dfrac{5}{6}x + \dfrac{1}{3}x - \dfrac{1}{4} = \dfrac{27}{4}$, then what is the value of x ?

(A) $\dfrac{1}{6}$
(B) 3
(C) $\dfrac{39}{7}$
(D) 6
(E) 12

17. Farmer Jones had equal amounts of wheat, oats, and corn. He made horse feed by mixing $\dfrac{1}{3}$ of the wheat, $\dfrac{1}{2}$ of the oats, and $\dfrac{1}{4}$ of the corn. If he made 52 pounds of horse feed, how many pounds of oats did he have originally?

(A) 45
(B) 48
(C) 50
(D) 52
(E) 66

20. Rudy and Michael are trading used CDs. If Rudy were to give three of his CDs to Michael, Michael would have four times as many CDs as Rudy. But if Michael were to give five of his CDs to Rudy instead, Rudy would then have one fewer CD than Michael had before they traded. How many CDs does Rudy have to begin with?

(A) 5
(B) 7
(C) 9
(D) 12
(E) 15

MATH

WRITING

READING

VOCABULARY

MUST BE

With Must Be and Could Be problems, you will have to plug in more than once.

4. If x and y are odd integers, then which of the following must be an odd integer?

(A) $2xy$

(B) $\dfrac{x}{y}$

(C) $x + y + 1$

(D) $x - y$

(E) $3x + 5y$

5. If $x + 1$ is an even integer, which of the following must be an odd integer?

(A) $x - 1$

(B) $x^2 + 1$

(C) $\dfrac{x+1}{2}$

(D) $x + 3$

(E) $x + 4$

10. If d, e, and f are positive integers and $d < e < f$, which of the following must be true?

(A) $d + e > f$

(B) $def > 0$

(C) $d + 2 = e + 1 = f$

(D) $\dfrac{f}{d} = e$

(E) $f - e > d$

12. If p and q are integers, such that $p < 0 < q$, which of the following must be true?

   I. $2p < 2q$
   II. $p^2 < q^2$
   III. $p + q = 0$

(A) I only
(B) II only
(C) I and II only
(D) I and III only
(E) I, II, and III

16. If $x - y$ is a multiple of 3, then which of the following must also be a multiple of 3 ?

(A) $y - x$

(B) $\dfrac{y-x}{2}$

(C) $\dfrac{x+y}{2}$

(D) $x + y$

(E) xy

18. If $y > 0$ and $\dfrac{y+8}{4}$ is an integer, which of the following must be true?

   I. y is a multiple of 4

   II. $\dfrac{y}{8}$ is an integer

   III. $12 + \dfrac{y}{4}$ is an integer

(A) I only
(B) II only
(C) I and II only
(D) I and III only
(E) II and III only

ET CETERA

Here are some other topics that ETS likes to use occasionally. Be sure to review the explanations that follow these questions when you are done.

3. Amy, Ben, Carlos, and Dave are playing a game. Each one pulls a card from a deck and, without looking at it, shows it to the other three. The cards are red, green, or blue. Ben sees two red cards and a green card. Amy sees a red card, a blue card, and a green card. Which of the following must be true?

(A) Ben has a green card.
(B) Amy has a red card.
(C) Dave has a blue card.
(D) Carlos and Dave both have red cards.
(E) Carlos has a green card.

7. A letter has rotational symmetry if it looks identical when rotated 180° around its center point. For example, the letter S has rotational symmetry, as shown above. Which of the following letters does NOT have rotational symmetry?

(A) H
(B) M
(C) N
(D) X
(E) Z

$$36$$
$$\times\ BB$$
$$\overline{79B}$$

8. In the correctly worked multiplication problem shown above, if B represents a digit, then $B =$

(A) 8
(B) 6
(C) 4
(D) 2
(E) 1

9. In the summertime, Joanne will go to Candice's house and swim in the pool only when either there is no rain or the temperature is greater than 85° F. However, Joanne will not go to Candice's house and swim if Candice's dog is outside by the pool. Which of the following statements must be true?

(A) If Joanne did not swim in Candice's pool today, then the temperature was not greater than 85° F.
(B) If Candice's dog is not outside by the pool today, then Joanne will go swim in Candice's pool.
(C) If Candice's dog is outside by the pool today, then it is not raining.
(D) If Joanne did swim in Candice's pool today, then Candice's dog was not outside by the pool.
(E) If it is not raining today, Joanne will go swimming in Candice's pool.

10. Each of the 15 professional athletes who regularly play at the local gym live in Metairie, Kenner, or Uptown. If more of these athletes live in Metairie than in Kenner, and more of these athletes live in Kenner than in Uptown, what is the fewest number of these athletes who could live in Metairie?

(A) 4
(B) 5
(C) 6
(D) 7
(E) 8

11. In a neighborhood with 60 households, 32 households have VCRs and 18 have cable. If 12 have both a VCR and cable, how many of the households have neither?

(A) 20
(B) 22
(C) 30
(D) 44
(E) 50

MATH

WRITING

READING

VOCABULARY

12. Of all the cars on a certain lot, $\frac{3}{4}$ are red, $\frac{1}{5}$ are blue, and the remainder are black. What percent of the cars on the lot are black? (Disregard the percent sign when recording your answer.)

13. The number of Elvis sightings per year in any city varies inversely with that city's distance from Graceland. Last year, there were 88 Elvis sightings in Washington, D.C. If Washington, D.C. is 875 miles from Graceland, then how many Elvis sightings were there last year in Philadelphia, which is 1,000 miles from Graceland?

(A) 12
(B) 77
(C) 82
(D) 88
(E) 100

13. In the three-digit number 3*H*8, *H* represents a digit. If 3*H*7 is divisible by 9, what is the remainder when the three-digit number 3*H*3 is divided by 9?

(A) 5
(B) 6
(C) 7
(D) 8
(E) 9

14. In a club of 40 boys and girls, $\frac{3}{4}$ of the members are older than seventeen and 22 of the members are girls. If 6 of the girls are seventeen years old or younger, how many of the boys are older than seventeen?

(A) 8
(B) 12
(C) 14
(D) 21
(E) 28

15. Five children, Pedro, Quentin, Rena, Sue, and Tasha, are to be seated in five chairs in a row numbered 1 through 5. If Pedro must sit next to Rena, and Quentin must sit next to Sue, in which of the following chairs could Tasha sit?

(A) 1 only
(B) 5 only
(C) 1 and 3 only
(D) 1 and 5 only
(E) 1, 3, and 5 only

16. If four distinct points lie in a plane, what is the greatest possible number of distinct straight lines that can be determined by any two of these points?

(A) 3
(B) 4
(C) 5
(D) 6
(E) 8

 © TPR Education IP Holdings, LLC

ANSWERS AND EXPLANATIONS TO ET CETERA

3. **B** Write down everything you know. Ben sees 2 red cards and a green card. Amy sees a red card, a blue card, and a green card. What's different? Amy sees a blue card that Ben isn't seeing, so Ben must have the blue card. POE (A). Ben sees one more red card than Amy does, so Amy must have a red card, which is answer (B). Carlos and Dave must have the red and green cards, but we can't figure out who has which one. Of course, it doesn't really matter since we already answered the question.

7. **B** This question just wants to know which letters look the same when you look at them upside down as when you look at them right-side up. The less you have to visualize in your head, the better for this type of question. So, flip your book upside down. See how the M turns into a W but everything else looks the same?

8. **D** *Digits* are the integers from 0 through 9. On the SAT, uppercase letters are almost always used for digits, although ETS will tell you when something that looks like a variable is actually a digit. Plugging In The Answers (PITA) is often a great approach to digit questions. For this problem, start with answer choice (C) and multiply: $36 \times 44 = 1,584$. Since answer (C) is too big, try answer (D). Since $36 \times 22 = 792$, (D) is the correct answer.

9. **D** If it is either not raining or greater than 85° F AND Candice's dog also is not outside by the pool, then Joanne will go swimming in Candice's pool. Only D satisfies the rules given in the problem.

10. **C** PITA! Start with the smallest number since this is a "least" problem. If 4 people live in Metairie, the maximum number of people in Kenner must be 3 and, in Uptown, must be 2. Collectively, that's only 9 athletes overall, so that's too small. Moving down to C gives us 6 people in Metairie, 5 people in Kenner, and 4 people in Uptown. This satisfies the total of 15 professional athletes, so (C) is the correct answer choice.

11. **B** Use the group formula. *Total = Group 1 + Group 2 – Both + Neither*. So, $60 = 32 + 18 – 12 + N$. After solving, $N = 22$.

12. **5** Use the Plug In Your Own Number technique to make the problem easier to work. If there are 100 cars on the lot, then $\frac{3}{4} \times 100 = 75$ red and $\frac{1}{5} \times 100 = 20$ blue. Therefore, the five remaining cars are black. Since we started with 100 cars and percent means something out of 100, the answer is 5%. (Drop the percent sign when you grid in your answer and don't grid it in as .05— ETS will think you mean .05% and mark you wrong!)

Suppose you had started with a different number. You would have needed to translate the question "What percent of the cars on the lot are black?" Here's how. The chart shows the math equivalent of words that ETS uses in percent questions.

English	Math Equivalent
percent (%)	$\overline{} \over 100$
of	× (multiply)
what	x, y, z (use a variable)
is, are, were, did, does	= (equals)
out of	÷ (divide by)

For this problem, the sentence "What percent of the cars on the lot are black?" translates as

$\dfrac{x}{100} \times 100 = 5$. Of course, you would have put in your numbers. For example, if you had started

with 200 cars, your equation would have been $\dfrac{x}{100} \times 200 = 10$.

13. **B**   Elvis lives! When two things vary inversely with each other, it means that one gets smaller as the other gets bigger. To solve problems that involve inverse variation, use the formula $x_1 y_1 = x_2 y_2$. For this problem, we plug the numbers given into the formula, then solve for the missing value.

$$(88 \text{ sightings})(875 \text{ miles}) = (x \text{ sightings})(1{,}000 \text{ miles})$$

$$88 \cdot 875 = x \cdot 1000$$

$$x = 77$$

13. **A**   Use your calculator! Again, since capital letters stand for digits on the SAT, begin at 307, 317, 327, etc. until you find a three-digit number that is divisible by 9. 387 is divisible by 9, so $H = 8$. Therefore, when 383 is divided by 9, the remainder (or what's left over after long division) is 5.

14. **C**   Use bite-sized pieces to break this one down since you can't apply the group formula to it. There are 40 members and $\frac{3}{4}$ are older than 17, so 30 members are older than 17. There are 22 girls, and 6 girls are 17 or younger, so 16 girls are older than 17. There are 30 members older than 17, and 16 girls older than 17, so there are 14 boys older than 17. You'll find it helpful to set up a chart to show the information on these types of questions. Put girls, boys, and total across the top. The rows are older than 17, younger than 17, and total. Now, fill in the information given. Add across the rows to get totals and add down the columns to get totals.

15. **E**   Draw a diagram with 1 through 5 across the top because it's better to see what's happening. There are three possibilities for Tasha. Tasha can go in seat #1 and then PR in seats #2 and #3 followed by QS in seats #4 and #5. You can reverse the order of PR and QS but that doesn't change where Tasha sits, so who cares! Next, put T in seat #3. Put PR to her left in seats #1 and #2 and QS to her right in seats #4 and #5. Finally, put T in seat #5. Pick a pair, PR or QS, to go in seats #2 and #3 and the other pair to go in seats #4 and #5. So, T can only go in seats #1, #3, or #5 without breaking up one of the pairs that must be together.

16. **D**   Draw this one out to see what's going on. Draw four points so that they form the vertices of a square. Now, it's time to connect the dots. First, draw the square. Next, draw the diagonals of the square. That's six lines that can be formed. If you were stuck, you could get rid of answer choice (B). It can't be 4. That's too easy. Since it could be 4, however, you can cross off (A) as well. Joe Bloggs might like choice (E), since he might think $4 \times 2 = 8$.

ARITHMETIC:
THE HOT TOPICS

Hoping to impress the ladies, Daryl had his
SAT scores tattooed on his right arm.

MATH

WRITING

READING

VOCABULARY

GIMME SOME AVERAGE PIE!

SAT problems that ask you for the average will almost always include a trick or twist. Don't try to do everything at once—just take it piece by piece and use the Average Pie.

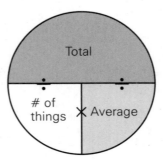

?

How does the average pie help you organize all the information in the problem?

14. If the average (arithmetic mean) of the 4 numbers f, g, h, and m is 40 and the average of the 3 numbers f, g, and h is 20, what is the value of m ?

(A) 20
(B) 25
(C) 30
(D) 80
(E) 100

11. On her first four tests, Anita received an average (arithmetic mean) score of n. If on her fifth test she exceeds that average by 20 points, what is her average score for all five tests?

(A) n
(B) $n + 4$
(C) $n + 5$
(D) $n + 10$
(E) $n + 20$

 © TPR Education IP Holdings, LLC

MEDIAN = MIDDLE

The median is the number in the middle of an ordered group of numbers.

10. A list consists of 10 consecutive even integers. What is the difference between the average (arithmetic mean) of the list and the median of the list?

   (A)   0
   (B)   0.5
   (C)   1
   (D)   1.25
   (E)   1.5

MODE = MOST

The mode is the number that appears the most often in a group of numbers.

List Y : 2, 3, 5, 8, 9, 10, 20

19. List Y above consists of seven integers. List Z is formed by using one of the integers twice and five of the remaining integers once. If 8 is the mean, median, and mode of list Z, which integer from list Y is NOT used?

   (A)   2
   (B)   3
   (C)   5
   (D)   9
   (E)   10

PERCENTS: HAVE NO FEAR

Percents are also fractions. (Percent means "out of 100.") For example:

$$20\% = \frac{20}{100} = \frac{1}{5} \qquad 250\% = \frac{250}{100} = \frac{25}{10} = \frac{5}{2} \qquad 0.5\% = \frac{.5}{100}$$

Translate percent problems into fraction problems.

English	Math Equivalents
% (percent)	
of	
what	
is, are, were, did, does	
out of	

Try it:

8. 25% of a certain number is equal to 75% of 400. What is the certain number?

   (A) 100
   (B) 200
   (C) 600
   (D) 1,200
   (E) 1,500

10. If x percent of 60 is equal to 10 percent of y, and $x > 0$, what is the value of $\dfrac{x}{y}$?

   (A) $\dfrac{1}{6}$

   (B) $\dfrac{2}{3}$

   (C) $\dfrac{3}{2}$

   (D) 6

   (E) 600

 © TPR Education IP Holdings, LLC

PERCENT INCREASE/DECREASE

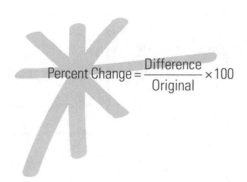

$$\text{Percent Change} = \frac{\text{Difference}}{\text{Original}} \times 100$$

11. A dress that originally sold for $120 is now selling for $96. By what percent was the original price of the dress discounted?

(A)   8%

(B)   12%

(C)   20%

(D)   24%

(E) $33\frac{1}{3}\%$

17. Which of the following is equivalent to the percent increase from 3 to 4 ?

   I. The percent decrease from 4 to 3.
  II. The percent decrease from 12 to 8.
 III. The percent increase from 6 to 8.

(A) I only
(B) I and III only
(C) II and III only
(D) III only
(E) I, II, and III

RATIO BOX: ORGANIZATIONAL POWER

In a club of 35 members, there is a 2-to-3 ratio of boys to girls among the members.

Boys	Girls	Total
	+	=
×——	——×——	——×
=	=	=
=	=	=
	+	=

← Ratio

← Multiply by

← Actual number

1) Girls make up what fractional part of the group? _____

2) Boys make up what percent of the group? _____

3) What is the total number of girls? _____

R.T.F.Q!

11. If a bed of 56 flowers consists of tulips, roses, and daffodils and the ratio of tulips to roses to daffodils is 3:5:6, then how many of the flowers are roses?

(A)   5
(B) 12
(C) 20
(D) 24
(E) 36

16. At a chicken egg farm, a farmer sells brown eggs and white eggs. At the end of one day, he has 750 total eggs that are in a ratio of 2 brown eggs to 3 white eggs. A customer, though, requests a ratio of 6 brown eggs to 5 white eggs. How many more brown eggs must the farmer add to the 750 total eggs to fulfill his customer's request?

(A) 240
(B) 300
(C) 450
(D) 540
(E) 610

 © TPR Education IP Holdings, LLC

DIRECT VARIATION

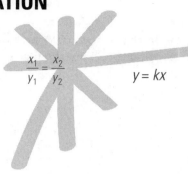

$$\frac{x_1}{y_1} = \frac{x_2}{y_2} \qquad y = kx$$

14. In 1976, Elvis consumed three times his body weight in peanut butter and banana sandwiches. If Elvis's body weight in 1976 was 250 pounds, and if a peanut butter and banana sandwich weighs four ounces, then how many such sandwiches did Elvis consume during 1976 ? (1 pound = 16 ounces)

(A) 750
(B) 1,000
(C) 1,500
(D) 3,000
(E) 4,000

For direct variation, as x increases, y increases.

INVERSE VARIATION

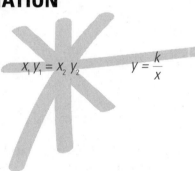

$$x_1 y_1 = x_2 y_2 \qquad y = \frac{k}{x}$$

14. If a indirectly varies with b^3, and $a = 1$ when $b = 3$, then what is the value of b when $a = 8$?

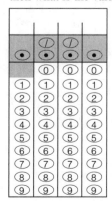

For inverse variation, as x increases, y decreases.

MATH

WRITING

READING

VOCABULARY

PROBABILITY

Probability is the likelihood that something will happen. The probability of an event can never be less than 0 or greater than 1. A probability of 0 means that something is impossible. A probability of 1 means that something has a 100% chance of happening.

$$\text{Probability} = \frac{\text{successful outcomes}}{\text{total outcomes}}$$

9. James owns x Star Trek T-shirts. If he selects a shirt at random, the probability that it will <u>not</u> be long-sleeved is $\frac{7}{10}$. In terms of x, how many of the shirts are long-sleeved?

(A) $\dfrac{3x}{10}$

(B) $\dfrac{7x}{10}$

(C) $\dfrac{10x}{3}$

(D) $\dfrac{17x}{10}$

(E) $10x$

15. If x is chosen at random from the set $\{3, 4, 10\}$ and y is chosen at random from the set $\{6, 7, 8\}$, what is the probability that the sum of x and y is even?

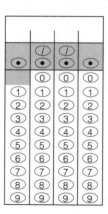

HOW MANY DIFFERENT...

Sometimes ETS will ask you to count how many different ways it's possible to arrange a group of items. Draw the blanks and label them!

12. Five chefs are available to cook three different meals. Each chef will only cook one meal. In how many different ways could the five chefs be assigned to the three meals?

(A) 5
(B) 8
(C) 20
(D) 60
(E) 120

Any time the question asks, "How many different ways..." or "How many different arrangements...", DRAW and LABEL BLANKS!

____ × ____ × ____ = ____

Meal 1   Meal 2   Meal 3   Total

16. One boy and five girls must stand in a line for a school picture. If the boy cannot stand first or last in line, how many different ways could the children be arranged?

(A) 720
(B) 480
(C) 360
(D) 240
(E) 120

Start with the most restricted position.

16. The letters *A, B, C, D, E,* and *F* are to be arranged with the following restrictions:

1. *B, C,* and *D* must be grouped together, in order, as *BCD.*
2. *E* and *F* cannot be next to each other.
3. *A* cannot be in either the first or last position.

How many different arrangements of these letters are possible?

(A)   4
(B)   8
(C) 16
(D) 24
(E) 36

Sometimes you'll have to just list out the possibilities.

MATH

WRITING

READING

VOCABULARY

PATTERNS AND SEQUENCES

For pattern questions, don't let the SAT trick you into doing unnecessary work. Write everything out until you find the pattern.

List patterns out and count them out!

9. A craftsman creates necklaces out of beads. He uses colored beads in a repeating pattern of gray, lime, opal, ruby, clear, white, black; gray, lime, opal, ruby, clear, white, black and so on. If the first bead on a necklace is gray, what is the color of the 86th bead?

(A) Gray
(B) Lime
(C) Opal
(D) White
(E) Black

$$9^{13}, 9^{13} + 9^{13}, 9^{13} + 9^{13} + 9^{13}, \ldots$$

18. In the sequence above, the first term is 9^{13} and each term after the first is 9^{13} more than the preceding term. Which term in the sequence is equal to 9^{15} ?

(A) The 2nd term
(B) The 15th term
(C) The 81st term
(D) The 117th term
(E) The 135th term

$$4, 7, -7, \ldots$$

Write out terms until you spot the pattern.

15. In the sequence of numbers shown above, the first term is 4. Each even-numbered term is 3 more than the previous term. Each odd-numbered term, after the first, is −1 times the previous term. What is the sum of the first 22 terms?

(A) −7
(B) 0
(C) 4
(D) 7
(E) 11

16. Ruwanthi paid $5,000 for her car when she bought it. Over the next several years, the car's value decreases by 10 percent per year. Which of the following functions gives the value, v, in dollars, of the car after n years at this rate?

(A) $v(n) = 5,000 - 0.9n$

(B) $v(n) = 5,000(0.9)^n$

(C) $v(n) = 5,000(0.1)^n$

(D) $v(n) = 5,000(n)^{0.9}$

(E) $v(n) = 5,000(1.1)^n$

What technique can you use with this problem?

Look for ways to Plug In on sequence questions.

14. In a sequence of positive numbers, the ratio of each term to the term immediately following it is 1 to 3. What is the ratio of the 4th term in this sequence to the 7th term?

(A) 1 to 3
(B) 1 to 6
(C) 1 to 9
(D) 1 to 27
(E) 1 to 243

MATH

WRITING

READING

VOCABULARY

ARITHMETIC TIMED DRILL

Time: 5 minutes

6. Which of the following tables shows a relationship in which *a* is inversely proportional to *b* ?

(A)

a	b
2	16
5	40
10	80

(B)

a	b
5	0
10	5
15	10

(C)

a	b
4	2
9	3
16	4

(D)

a	b
2	12
3	8
4	6

(E)

a	b
10	2
20	4
30	6

8. Magda has 6 different prints that she wants to hang on her bedroom wall, but she has room to hang only 2 of them. In how many different ways can she display the prints on her wall?

(A)   8
(B)   12
(C)   18
(D)   24
(E)   30

9. A stereo that normally sells for $200 is on sale for $160. Ben purchased the stereo at the normal price, and Trey purchased the stereo during the sale. By what percent was the price that Ben paid more than the price that Trey paid?

(A)   20%

(B)   25%

(C) $33\frac{1}{3}\%$

(D)   40%

(E)   50%

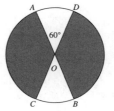

14. In the figure above, *AB* and *CD* are diameters of the circle with center *O*. If a dart thrown at the circle has an equal chance of landing on any point in the circle, what is the probability that the dart will land in the <u>unshaded</u> region?

(A) $\frac{1}{3}$

(B) $\frac{1}{2}$

(C) $\frac{2}{3}$

(D)   1

(E)   It cannot be determined from the information given.

16. If the average (arithmetic mean) of six numbers is 28 and the average of two of these numbers is 18, what is the average of the other four numbers?

(A)   29
(B)   30
(C)   31
(D)   32
(E)   33

Summary

- Any time you see the word *average* in a question, draw _____.

- The _____ is the middle number of an ordered group of numbers.

- The _____ is the number that appears most often in a group of numbers.

- The formula for percent increase/decrease is:

    Percent Change = ───────────────

- Use the _____ to help you on tricky ratio questions.

- The formula for direct variation is

    _____.

- The formula for inverse variation is

    _____.

- Probability = ───────────────

- For "How many different..." problems, draw _____!

- Write out terms and sequences until you _____.

- I have accomplished _____ of my _____ stated goals in the Introduction chapter.

ARITHMETIC PRACTICE

AVERAGE, MEDIAN, & MODE

$$a < b < c < d < e$$

3. If a, b, c, d, and e are consecutive integers, and $a = 13$, what is the average (arithmetic mean) of the five numbers?

(A) 13
(B) 14
(C) 15
(D) 16
(E) 17

4. Three tankers each carry 10,000 tons of oil and a fourth tanker carries 12,000 tons of oil. What is the average (arithmetic mean) number of tons of oil carried by each of the four tankers?

(A) 10,000
(B) 10,050
(C) 10,500
(D) 11,500
(E) 12,000

5. What is the median of the first 5 positive even integers?

(A) 4
(B) 5
(C) 6
(D) 8
(E) 30

$$6n, 6, 6n + 6$$

6. For the three quantities in the list above, what is the average (arithmetic mean)?

(A) $3(n + 1)$
(B) $4(n + 1)$
(C) $6(n + 1)$
(D) $4n$
(E) $6n$

7. The average (arithmetic mean) of two positive numbers, x and y, is 10. If the smaller number is subtracted from twice the larger number, the result is 14. If $y > x$, which of the following pairs of equations could correctly express the information above?

(A) $x + y = 20$
    $y - x = 14$

(B) $x + y = 20$
    $2x - y = 14$

(C) $x + y = 20$
    $2y - x = 14$

(D) $x + y = 10$
    $y - x = 14$

(E) $x + y = 10$
    $2y - x = 14$

8. If the average (arithmetic mean) of x and y is 10, then the average of $(x + 7)$ and $(y + 17)$ is

(A) 11
(B) 12
(C) 20
(D) 22
(E) 26

9. If the average (arithmetic mean) of $2r$ and $2r - 5$ is x and if the average of $2r$ and $2r + 9$ is y, what is the average of x and y ?

(A) 4

(B) $\dfrac{r}{4}$

(C) $2r + \dfrac{1}{2}$

(D) $2r + 1$

(E) $4r + 2$

10. Curtis earns $600 every month except December and January, when he vacations and earns no income. What is his average (arithmetic mean) monthly income for the entire year?

(A) $600
(B) $500
(C) $484
(D) $300
(E) $275

10. The average (arithmetic mean) grade of ten students on a test is 64. What would an eleventh student have to score on the test to bring the class average to 65 ?

(A) 100
(B) 90
(C) 85
(D) 75
(E) 66

11. A certain elevator has a maximum weight capacity of 1,500 pounds. If four boxes with an average weight of 150 pounds and a man weighing 200 pounds are in the elevator, how many additional pounds can the elevator hold?

11. The average (arithmetic mean) of 6, 21, x, and y is 13, where x and y are integers with a product of 100. Which of the following could be x ?

(A) 50
(B) 20
(C) 10
(D) 4
(E) 1

$$S = \{5, 0, -7, -4, 3, -5\}$$

12. Which of the following sets has a median equal to that of set S ?

(A) $\{-\dfrac{1}{2}, -2, 3, 6, -4\}$

(B) $\{0, -2, 6, \dfrac{3}{2}, -8, -5\}$

(C) $\{3, 6, 2, 9, 1\}$

(D) $\{-4, 0, -1, 3, -2, 5\}$

(E) $\{7, -5, 4, 1, -6, -9\}$

13. A basketball team's coach reported that the team scored an average (arithmetic mean) of 82 points in its last 10 games. However, it was later found that the coach entered two of the point totals incorrectly. The number 45 was entered as 65 and the number 86 was entered as 76. What is the correct average for the points the team scored in its last 10 games?

(A) 85
(B) 83
(C) 81
(D) 80
(E) 79

15. Over a three-month period, the average monthly output for a shoe factory was 120 pairs of shoes, and for the next five months the average monthly output was 80 pairs of shoes. What was the average monthly output of pairs of shoes for the entire eight-month period?

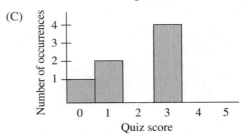

20. Quiz scores in Ms. Carson's class can range from 0 to 5 points, inclusive. If the scores from Tuesday's quiz have an average (arithmetic mean) of 3, a median of 3, and a mode of 2, which of the following graphs could represent those quiz scores?

(A)

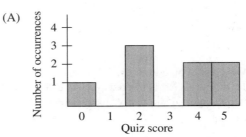

(B)

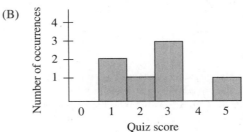

(C)

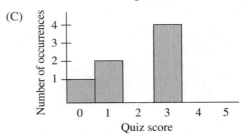

(D)

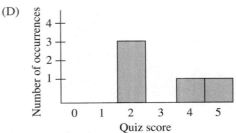

(E)

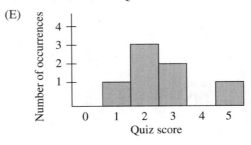

ALL ABOUT PERCENTS

2. 10 is 20% of what number?

- (A)   0.5
- (B)   5
- (C)   50
- (D)   500
- (E)   5,000

5. On a test of 50 questions, Gert answered 47 correctly. If Gert answered every question, what percentage did she answer incorrectly?

- (A)   97%
- (B)   94%
- (C)   47%
- (D)   6%
- (E)   3%

8. A student takes a test with 60 questions. If she answers 14 questions incorrectly and leaves 4 questions blank, what percent of the questions does she answer correctly?

- (A)   18%
- (B)   30%
- (C)   42%
- (D)   70%
- (E)   82%

9. 50% of 25% of what is 96 ?

- (A)   12
- (B)   76
- (C)   120
- (D)   768
- (E)   1,200

10. 40% of 20% of 800 is what?

11. Norton is picking a book to read on vacation. Of the books on his shelf, 14 are science fiction. He will pick one book at random. If the probability that the selected book is science fiction is 35%, how many books are on his shelf?

11. What percent of the integer solutions for n in the inequality $4 < n < 21$ are prime?

(A) 20%
(B) 31.25%
(C) 37.5%
(D) 40%
(E) 43.75%

12. In a bag of lollipops, 35 percent of the lollipops are lemon, 15 percent are cherry, 20 percent are grape, 5 percent are watermelon, and the other 15 lollipops are orange. How many lollipops are in the bag?

(A) 24
(B) 30
(C) 36
(D) 45
(E) 60

13. In a crate of 300 apples, there are 12 more green apples than red apples. What percent of the 300 apples are green?

(A) 46%
(B) 48%
(C) 51%
(D) 52%
(E) 54%

14. If x percent of 500 is y, what is y percent of $10x$?

(A) $50x$

(B) $\dfrac{x^2}{2}$

(C) $\dfrac{2}{5x}$

(D) $5x^2$

(E) $\dfrac{x^2}{50}$

16. Three students are running for class president. Of the 50 students eligible to vote, 26% vote for Sean and 28% vote for Aaron. The rest of the students vote for Jennifer. How many votes does Jennifer receive?

16. A merchant raises the price of a $100 item by 20 percent. After finding that he cannot sell the item at the higher price, however, he discounts it by 20 percent. What is the final price of the item?

(A) $96
(B) $97
(C) $98
(D) $99
(E) $100

RATIOS AND VARIATION

2. The ratio of two numbers is 3 to 4. If the smaller number is 6, what is the larger number?

(A) 8
(B) 7
(C) 6
(D) 4
(E) 3

4. A disc jockey plays only hip-hop songs and country songs. If the disc jockey plays four country songs for every seven hip-hop songs that he plays, then what fraction of the songs he plays are country songs?

(A) $\dfrac{4}{5}$

(B) $\dfrac{7}{11}$

(C) $\dfrac{4}{7}$

(D) $\dfrac{4}{11}$

(E) $\dfrac{1}{28}$

6. If the ratio of boys to girls in a classroom is 1 to 3, what percent of the class is girls?

(A) 10%

(B) 25%

(C) $33\dfrac{1}{3}$ %

(D) 50%

(E) 75%

8. The volume of hydrogen in a balloon varies inversely with the applied pressure. At an applied pressure of 200 torrs, the volume of hydrogen in the balloon is 3 cubic feet. What is the applied pressure, in torrs, when the volume of hydrogen in the balloon is 40 cubic feet?

(A)   0.6
(B)   13.3
(C)   15
(D)   163
(E)   237

9. If there are 16 ounces in a pound, then 152 ounces equals how many pounds?

10. A paint mixture contains yellow, blue, and red in a 3:2:1 ratio, respectively. If the mixture contains 9 pints of yellow paint, what is the total number of pints in the mixture?

   (A) 9
   (B) 12
   (C) 15
   (D) 16
   (E) 18

11. Kate travels d miles to get from New Canaan to Brooklyn. If she travels at 8 miles per hour, the trip takes 6 hours. How many hours does the trip take if she travels at 12 miles per hour?

   (A)   1
   (B)   2
   (C)   4
   (D) 10
   (E) 16

12. If x varies directly as y^2, and $x = 4$ when $y = 3$, then what is the value of x when $y = 12$?

   (A)   8
   (B) 16
   (C) 36
   (D) 48
   (E) 64

13. At a certain factory, all workers either drive their own cars to work or take the bus. The ratio of workers who take the bus to those who drive their own cars is 2:5. If 120 workers drive their own cars, how many workers are there at the factory?

14. The amount of a real estate broker's commission varies directly as the sale price of a home. If the sale of a $200,000 home yields a commission of $14,000, what is the broker's commission on the sale of a $150,000 home?

   (A) $7,000
   (B) $10,500
   (C) $14,000
   (D) $15,000
   (E) $21,000

17. A cafeteria sells Chicken Puck meals for $3.00 and Meatloaf Nugget meals for $4.00. If the cafeteria sold 120 meals for a total of $450, what was the ratio of the number of Chicken Puck meals sold to the number of Meatloaf Nugget meals sold?

(A) 1 to 3
(B) 3 to 4
(C) 3 to 1
(D) 3 to 7
(E) 4 to 3

18. Classroom A and classroom B have an equal number of students. If a total of 3 students move from classroom A class to classroom B, the ratio of students in classroom A to students in classroom B is 3:5. How many students were in each of the classrooms originally?

18. If y varies inversely with the cube root of x, and $y = 9$ when $x = \dfrac{1}{27}$, then what is the value of y when $x = \dfrac{1}{64}$?

19. At Buzz Aldrin High, the total number of girls in the combined junior and senior classes is equal to the total number of boys in those two classes. If the senior class has 400 students and the junior class has 300 students, and if the ratio of boys to girls in the senior class is 5 to 3, what is the ratio of boys to girls in the junior class?

(A) 2:5
(B) 1:2
(C) 5:9
(D) 5:7
(E) 7:9

 © TPR Education IP Holdings, LLC

PROBABILITY

TOTAL SALES BY ACME CO. STAFF

Salesperson	Total Sales
Andrew	$4,000
Becky	$7,000
Chris	$3,500
David	$5,500
Erin	$8,000

10. The table above shows the total sales for five members of the Acme Co. sales staff. Acme Co. is running a lottery. For every $500 in sales, a salesperson receives one lottery ticket. What is the probability that Chris will win the lottery?

(A) $\frac{1}{10}$

(B) $\frac{1}{8}$

(C) $\frac{7}{50}$

(D) $\frac{1}{4}$

(E) $\frac{29}{100}$

13. Sue sells $\frac{1}{4}$ of the tickets for the school lottery to Andrew. Sue then sells $\frac{2}{3}$ of the remaining tickets to Bob. Of the tickets Sue has left, Cathy buys $\frac{3}{5}$. Sue then purchases all of the remaining unsold tickets herself. What is the probability that Cathy will win the school lottery?

(A) 10%

(B) 15%

(C) 25%

(D) 50%

(E) $66\frac{2}{3}$ %

13. A bowl contains six plastic balls, numbered 12, 31, 16, 19, 26, and 5. If one ball is drawn randomly from the bowl, what is the probability that the number written on the ball is less than 20 ?

16. A candy dish contains 6 orange and 4 lime gumdrops. If two gumdrops are drawn from the dish at random, what is the probability that both gumdrops will be orange?

(A) $\frac{2}{15}$

(B) $\frac{1}{3}$

(C) $\frac{9}{25}$

(D) $\frac{3}{5}$

(E) $\frac{2}{3}$

MATH

WRITING

READING

VOCABULARY

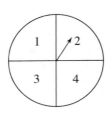

17. A certain game is played by spinning the spinner above. If the number from the first spin is multiplied by the number from the second spin, what is the probability that the square root of the resulting number will be an integer?

(A) $\dfrac{1}{16}$

(B) $\dfrac{3}{16}$

(C) $\dfrac{1}{4}$

(D) $\dfrac{3}{8}$

(E) $\dfrac{1}{2}$

18. A two-sided coin is tossed three times. What is the probability that "heads" will be the result exactly two times?

(A) $\dfrac{3}{4}$

(B) $\dfrac{2}{3}$

(C) $\dfrac{1}{2}$

(D) $\dfrac{3}{8}$

(E) $\dfrac{1}{4}$

19. A single die with six faces numbered 1 through 6 is thrown twice. If the numeral that faces upward as the result of each throw is recorded, what is the probability that the sum of the two numbers is less than 10 ?

(A) $\dfrac{5}{6}$

(B) $\dfrac{2}{3}$

(C) $\dfrac{1}{2}$

(D) $\dfrac{1}{3}$

(E) $\dfrac{1}{6}$

GEOMETRIC PROBABILITY

For Geometric Probability questions, find the <u>areas</u> of the respective shapes.

9. Points A and C lie on the circle (not shown) with center O such that AOC is equilateral. What is the probability that a randomly selected point on the circle lies on minor arc AC ?

(A) $\dfrac{1}{360}$

(B) $\dfrac{1}{60}$

(C) $\dfrac{1}{6}$

(D) $\dfrac{1}{8}$

(E) It cannot be determined from the information given.

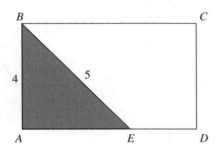

Note: Figure not drawn to scale.

13. In the figure above, $ABCD$ is a rectangle. If $BC = 15$, what is the probability that a randomly chosen point that lies in $ABCD$ lies inside the shaded region?

(A) $\dfrac{1}{15}$

(B) $\dfrac{1}{10}$

(C) $\dfrac{1}{5}$

(D) $\dfrac{1}{3}$

(E) $\dfrac{9}{10}$

14. A square is inscribed in a circle. If a point is selected at random from the interior of the circle, what is the probability that the point lies outside the square?

(A) $\dfrac{\sqrt{2}}{\pi}$

(B) $\dfrac{2}{\pi}$

(C) $\dfrac{\pi}{2}$

(D) $\dfrac{\pi}{\pi - 2}$

(E) $\dfrac{\pi - 2}{\pi}$

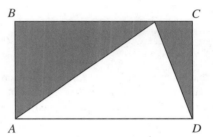

15. If rectangle $ABCD$ shown above has an area of 24, what is the probability that a randomly chosen point that lies in $ABCD$ will lie in the shaded region?

(A) $\dfrac{1}{3}$

(B) $\dfrac{1}{2}$

(C) $\dfrac{2}{3}$

(D) 1

(E) It cannot be determined from the information given.

HOW MANY DIFFERENT...

8. Karen is ordering a hamburger. The restaurant offers 2 different kinds of bread, 3 different condiments, and 2 different kinds of cheese. If Karen selects one type of bread, one condiment, and one type of cheese, how many ways can she order her burger?

(A)   6
(B)   7
(C)   9
(D) 12
(E) 24

9. Kate is choosing DVDs to bring over to her friend's house for movie night. She has 8 comedies, 6 dramas, and 4 musicals in her collection. If she chooses one of each type, how many different selections of DVDs can she make?

(A)   18
(B)   24
(C)   32
(D)   64
(E) 192

14. A snack stand sells 5 different flavors of Italian ice. How many combinations of 4 different flavors of Italian ice can Sharon buy from this stand?

(A)   5
(B)   16
(C)   24
(D)   60
(E) 120

17. The yearbook staff must assign four distinct photographs, one photograph per page, to four different pages. How many different assignments of photographs to pages are possible?

(A)   4
(B)   12
(C)   16
(D)   24
(E) 256

18. At the salad bar, Nicole can choose from 4 different lettuce mixes, 8 different vegetables, 3 different cheeses, and 5 different dressings. She must choose one item from each category. She must also decide whether or not to have croutons. How many different combinations are possible?

PATTERNS AND SEQUENCES

5. A dog breeder discovers that the number of dogs she has bred so far is $2^n + 4$, where n is the number of years that she has been breeding dogs. If she has bred 20 dogs so far, then for how many years has she been breeding dogs?

(A) 3
(B) 4
(C) 5
(D) 6
(E) 7

$$x, x + 1, x, x - 1, x, x + 1, x, x - 1 \ldots$$

8. The sequence shown above repeats indefinitely, and the value of x is 6. What is the value of the 39th term of the sequence?

(A) 4
(B) 5
(C) 6
(D) 7
(E) 8

11. If Griggs deposits $100 in a bank account that will double his money every 10 years, after how many years will his bank account be worth $6,400 ?

(A)   6
(B)   60
(C)   630
(D)   640
(E) 6,300

$$3, 9, 27 \ldots$$

13. The first term in the above sequence is 3, and each term after the first is three times the preceding term. Which of the following expression represents the nth term in the sequence?

(A) 3^{n-1}
(B) 3^n
(C) $3n$
(D) n^3
(E) $(n - 1)^3$

16. In a certain sequence of numbers, each term after the first term is found by multiplying the preceding term by a constant. If the fourth and fifth terms are 8.8 and 17.6 respectively, what is the seventh term in the sequence?

(A)   26.4
(B)   35.2
(C)   61.6
(D)   70.4
(E)   140.8

18. If the first term of a sequence is 3, and each of the following terms is found by multiplying the preceding term by 2, what is the units digit of the 32nd term in the sequence?

(A) 2
(B) 3
(C) 4
(D) 6
(E) 8

19. The amount of memory required to run the MegaSoft Corporation's popular word processing program, Syllable, doubles every three months. If the program currently requires 128 megabytes of memory, which of the following is an expression, in terms of x, for the amount of memory in megabytes that the program will require in x years?

(A) 128×2^x

(B) $128 \times 2^{\frac{x}{3}}$

(C) $128 \times 2^{\frac{x}{4}}$

(D) 128×2^{4x}

(E) $128 \times x^2$

19. After the first term, each term in a sequence is k greater than $\frac{1}{k}$ of the preceding term. If the first term in the sequence is 8 and the ratio of the second term to the first term is $\frac{3}{4}$, what is one possible value of k ?

(A) −4
(B) −2
(C) 1
(D) 2
(E) 8

MORE WORKING WITH EQUATIONS AND EXPRESSIONS

Here are some questions to help you remember a few basics when solving more complicated equations. Be sure to review the explanations that follow these questions when you are done.

4. If $y\sqrt{3} = 12$, what is the value of y ?

(A) 3

(B) $3\sqrt{2}$

(C) $4\sqrt{3}$

(D) 9

(E) 432

5. If $\dfrac{3}{4}x^2 = 3x$, what is one possible value of x ?

(A) -4

(B) $\dfrac{4}{3}$

(C) 3

(D) 4

(E) 12

6. If $x^2 + x - 6 = 0$, which of the following could be the value of x ?

(A) -6

(B) -3

(C) -2

(D) 3

(E) 6

7. If $\dfrac{x^3 + x^2}{x^4 + x^3} = 8$, what is the value of x ?

(A) $\dfrac{1}{16}$

(B) $\dfrac{1}{8}$

(C) 4

(D) 8

(E) 16

8. If $x + y = 9$, what is the value of $x^2 + 2xy + y^2$?

(A) 81

(B) 27

(C) 18

(D) 3

(E) -3

9. If $|x - 8| > 10$, which of the following represents all possible values of x ?

(A) $x > 18$

(B) $x < -2$

(C) $x < -8$ or $x > 10$

(D) $x < -2$ or $x > 18$

(E) $-2 < x < 18$

11. What is the sum of the distinct possible values of x for the equation $x^2 + 3x - 10 = 0$?

(A) -3
(B) -2
(C) 3
(D) 5
(E) 8

12. If $x^5 + 2 = 34$, what is the value of x ?

(A) -4
(B) -2
(C) 2
(D) 4
(E) 32

16. $\dfrac{\left(x^{\frac{1}{3}}\right)^2}{x^{\frac{1}{6}}} =$

(A) $x^{\frac{1}{6}}$

(B) $x^{\frac{1}{3}}$

(C) $x^{\frac{1}{2}}$

(D) $x^{\frac{2}{3}}$

(E) $x^{\frac{13}{6}}$

© TPR Education IP Holdings, LLC

PROPERTIES OF GRAPHS

Here are a few questions to help you remember a few basics about the graphs of linear and quadratic functions. Be sure to review the explanations that follow these questions when you are done.

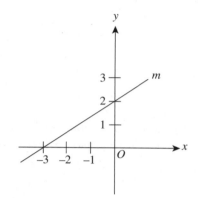

11. In the figure above, what is the slope of line m ?

(A) $-\dfrac{3}{2}$

(B) $-\dfrac{2}{3}$

(C) 0

(D) $\dfrac{2}{3}$

(E) $\dfrac{3}{2}$

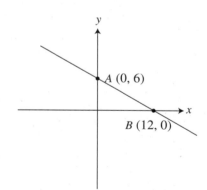

12. Which of the following is the equation of the line passing through points A and B shown above?

(A) $y = -6x^2 + 2$

(B) $y = -2x + 6$

(C) $y = -\dfrac{1}{2}x + 6$

(D) $y = -\dfrac{1}{6}x + 2$

(E) $y = 2x + 6$

13. If the graph of $ax + 2y = 10$ is parallel to that of $2x + y = 6$ in the rectangular coordinate system, what is the value of a ?

	/	/	
⊙	⊙	⊙	⊙
	⓪	⓪	⓪
①	①	①	①
②	②	②	②
③	③	③	③
④	④	④	④
⑤	⑤	⑤	⑤
⑥	⑥	⑥	⑥
⑦	⑦	⑦	⑦
⑧	⑧	⑧	⑧
⑨	⑨	⑨	⑨

14. In the xy-plane, the equation of line b is $y = 4x - 7$. If line a is the reflection of line b across the x-axis, what is the equation of line a ?

(A) $y = -\dfrac{1}{4}x - 7$

(B) $y = \dfrac{1}{4}x + 7$

(C) $y = -\dfrac{1}{4}x + 7$

(D) $y = -4x - 7$

(E) $y = -4x + 7$

© TPR Education IP Holdings, LLC

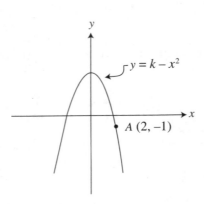

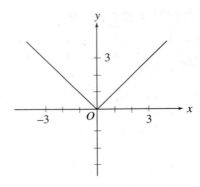

17. Point A lies on the graph of $y = k - x^2$, as shown above, for some constant k. What is the greatest possible value of y ?

(A) −6
(B) −1
(C) 0
(D) 2
(E) 3

19. If the graph of $y = f(x)$ is shown above, which of the following could be the graph of $y = f(x - 2) + 3$?

(A)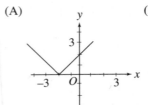

(B)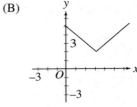

(C)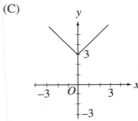

(D)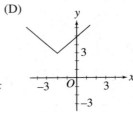

(E)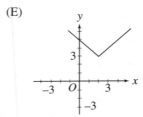

ANSWERS AND EXPLANATIONS TO MORE WORKING WITH EQUATIONS AND EXPRESSIONS

4. **C**   Don't be fooled by the weird coefficient. You do the same algebra steps. To get y by itself, divide

both sides by $\sqrt{3}$. Since you can't leave a square root in the denominator of a fraction, however,

you'll need to normalize. So, $y = \dfrac{12}{\sqrt{3}}$ and $\dfrac{12}{\sqrt{3}} = \left(\dfrac{12}{\sqrt{3}}\right)\left(\dfrac{\sqrt{3}}{\sqrt{3}}\right) = \dfrac{12\sqrt{3}}{3} = 4\sqrt{3}$.

5. **D**   Start by multiplying both sides by 4 to get rid of the fraction. So, $3x^2 = 12x$. Now, divide both sides by 3 to get $x^2 = 4x$. Now, the solution gets a little more interesting. To find all the possible solutions, rewrite the equation as $x^2 - 4x = 0$ and factor. So, $x^2 - 4x = x(x - 4) = 0$. Set each term equal to 0 and solve. So, $x = 0$ or $x = 4$.

6. **B**   This is a quadratic equation. Quadratic equations have an x^2 term as the highest power. When you see a quadratic equation, you'll need to think about FOIL. FOIL stands for First, Outer, Inner, Last, and it's the way to multiply factors to get a quadratic. For this question, you'll need to do FOIL in reverse. The factors are $(x + 3)$ and $(x - 2)$. Notice that if you FOIL the factors, you get the original equation. So, you have $(x + 3)(x - 2) = 0$. Now, set each factor equal to 0. So, $(x + 3) = 0$ and $(x - 2) = 0$. Now, solve each of those equations to find that $x = -3$ or $x = 2$.

7. **B**   When working with rational expressions, you'll often find it helpful to factor. Start by factoring

out x's to make it as easy as possible to reduce or cancel the variables on the top and bottom of

the expression. So, $\dfrac{x^3 + x^2}{x^4 + x^3} = \dfrac{x^3 + x^2}{x(x^3 + x^2)} = \dfrac{1}{x}$. You can't start this problem by canceling some

of the variables on the top with some of the variables on the bottom because you can only do

that in the case of multiplication. Also, don't forget that you can solve problems such as this one

by Plugging In The Answers.

8. **A**   ETS has three favorite quadratic equations. When you see a quadratic equation that has two different variables, you should think about using one of these equations. The equations are

$(x + y)(x - y) = x^2 - y^2$
$(x + y)^2 = x^2 + 2xy + y^2$
$(x - y)^2 = x^2 - 2xy + y^2$

Memorize these equations! ETS uses them all the time. For this question, you know that $(x + y)^2 = x^2 + 2xy + y^2$. Since the question also tells you that $x + y = 9$, you can substitute 9 into the expression. So, $x^2 + 2xy + y^2 = (x + y)^2 = 9^2 = 81$.

© TPR Education IP Holdings, LLC

9. **D**   To solve an inequality involving an absolute value, you start by remembering that the expression inside the absolute value bars can, in this case, be either greater than 10 or less than −10. The first part is easy to write—just remove the absolute value bars to get $x - 8 > 10$. To find the values of x that make the expression inside the absolute value bars less than −10, multiply $(x - 8)$ by −1 and then remove the bars. You get $8 - x > 10$. Now, solve both inequalities. Add 8 to both sides of $x - 8 > 10$ to get $x > 18$. Subtract 8 from both sides of $8 - x > 10$ to first get $-x > 2$. Then, divide both sides by −1, and don't forget to flip the sign. You'll get $x < -2$. Since the inequality signs point in different directions for the two parts of the answer, the correct expression is $x < -2$ or $x > 18$.

11. **A**   Root is another term for the solution to an equation. Start by factoring the equation by doing the FOIL process in reverse. So, $x^2 + 3x - 10 = (x + 5)(x - 2) = 0$. Set each of the factors equal to 0 to find that the roots are −5 and 2. Finally, $-5 + 2 = -3$. Be careful not to choose any of the partial answers.

12. **C**   Start by simplifying to get $x^5 = 32$. To solve for x, you need to undo the power and that's where roots come in. To get rid of a fifth power, take a fifth root of both sides of the equation. A fifth root tells you what number multiplied by itself five times equals the number under the radical sign. So, $\sqrt[5]{x^5} = \sqrt[5]{32} = 2$. Of course, it's often easier to Plug In the answer choices on these questions.

16. **C**   Don't let the funny exponents throw you. The same exponent rules always apply, no matter how funky the exponents. MADSPM (which stands for Multiply-Add, Divide-Subtract, Power-Multiply) will help you to remember the exponent rules. For this problem, work with the top first. Something with a power is being raised to another power, so you need the Power-Multiply rule. Multiply the exponents to get $\left(x^{\frac{1}{3}} \right)^2 = x^{\frac{2}{3}}$. Now, the expression is $\dfrac{x^{\frac{2}{3}}}{x^{\frac{1}{6}}}$, so you need the Divide-Subtract rule. Subtract the exponents to get: $x^{\frac{2}{3} - \frac{1}{6}} = x^{\frac{1}{2}}$.

ANSWERS AND EXPLANATIONS TO PROPERTIES OF GRAPHS

11. **D**   There are two ways to find the slope of a line. If you have the points, use the equation:

slope = $\dfrac{y_2 - y_1}{x_2 - x_1}$. For this problem, you could use the graph to determine the x and y coordinates

for two points on the line. However, if the graph is provided, you can get the same result with

less work by remembering that slope also equals $\dfrac{rise}{run}$. To use that formula, go to the leftmost

point for which you know the coordinates. In this case, use the point (–3, 0). Now, you want to

get to the rightmost point for which you know the coordinates. In this case, use the point (0, 2).

Did you notice that we used the intercepts? Starting at the leftmost point, you need to rise up 2

units and then run over 3 units to get to the rightmost point. If you need to rise up, the slope is

positive. If you need to sink down to get the rightmost point, the slope is negative. In this case,

the slope is positive since you rose up. That makes the slope $\dfrac{2}{3}$.

12. **C**   First, do a little POE. The slope of the line must be negative, so cross off answer choice (E).

Next, remember that the equation of a line is given by $y = mx + b$, where m is the slope and b is

the y-intercept of the y-coordinate of the point where the line crosses the y-axis. Answer choice

(A) doesn't look the equation of a line because of the squared term, so cross it off. Next, the

y-intercept of the line is 6, so cross off answer choice (D) because that line has a y-intercept of

2. Now, just work out the slope. Slope = $\dfrac{y_2 - y_1}{x_2 - x_1} = \dfrac{6-0}{0-12} = -\dfrac{1}{2}$. You could also have picked

answer choice (C) if you'd noticed that the x values are changing faster than the y values and

that makes the slope a fraction.

13. **4**   Both equations will produce the graph of a line. If the two lines are parallel, then their slopes

will be the same. So, start by rearranging the equation $2x + y = 6$ so that it looks like $y = mx + b$.

After some manipulation, the equation becomes $y = -2x + 6$. So, the slope of both lines is –2.

Next, rearrange $ax + 2y = 10$ so that it too looks like $y = mx + b$. After some manipulation, this

equation becomes $y = -\dfrac{a}{2}x + 5$. So, $-\dfrac{a}{2} = -2$. Cross multiply to get $a = 4$. (By the way, the slopes

of perpendicular lines are negative reciprocals. ETS asks about that too.)

14. **E** Use POE! Lines that are reflected across the x-axis have slopes that are negatives of each other. In this case, the original line had a slope of 4, so the new line will have a slope of -4. Cross off answer choices (A), (B), and (C) because they all have the wrong slope. Lines that are reflected across the x-axis have y-intercepts that are also negatives of each others. The original line had a y-intercept of -7, so the new line will have a y-intercept of 7 as in answer (E). You could also solve this question by graphing the original line on your calculator and then graphing each of the answers to see which one is the correct reflection.

17. **E** Since point A is on the graph of $y = k - x^2$, you can use the coordinates of point A to solve for the value of k. Since $-1 = k - (2)^2$, $k = 3$. To finish answering the question, you need to know something about the graphs of quadratic equations. First, the equation $y = k - x^2$ is quadratic because the highest power is 2. Quadratic equations have the general form $ax^2 + bx + c = 0$ and graphs that are parabolas. In this case, $a = -1$, $b = 0$, and $c = 3$. If you plug those values into the general form, you get $y = 3 - x^2$. Each of the constants a, b, and c tells you something about the shape of the graph. For example, since $a = -1$ in this equation, the parabola opens down. The b value shifts the parabola to the right or the left. Since $b = 0$ in this equation, the graph is symmetrical about the y-axis. The c value shifts the graph up or down the y-axis and when the equation looks like $y = c - x^2$, the c value is also the maximum value of y. That makes sense because the way to make y as big as possible is to take nothing away from c. So, when $x = 0$, $y = c$ and that's as big as y can get. Therefore, for the equation $y = 3 - x^2$, the greatest possible value of y is 3.

19. **E** You'll need to know some transformation rules to do effective POE on this question. Just remember that if the number is inside the parentheses, the graph moves left or right. If the number is outside the parentheses, the graph moves up or down. In this question, you have a number inside the parentheses and a number outside the parentheses, so take it one step at a time. The $+3$ is outside the parentheses and the sign tells you that the graph moves up 3. Cross off (A) because the graph didn't move up at all and cross off (B) because the graph only moved up 2. Next, there's a number inside the parentheses, so the graph must move to either the right or left. That's enough to cross off (C) because the graph didn't move to either the right or the left. Now, comes the tricky part. The number inside the parentheses is -2 and you might be tempted to move the graph to the left. Hold on! When the number is inside the parentheses, you actually move the graph *opposite* of the way suggested by the sign. If you add a number, the graph moves to the left and if you subtract a number, the graph moves to the right. So, this graph will move to the right, which is shown in answer choice (E).

FUNCTIONS & GRAPHS: HOW TO BEAT THEM

REVIEW

10. If $x\sqrt{2} = 4\sqrt{x}$ and $x > 0$, what is the value of x ?

(A) 2
(B) 4
(C) 6
(D) 8
(E) 9

14. Which of the following expressions is equivalent

to $\dfrac{\left(3x^3y^2\right)^3}{9x^6y^9}$?

(A) $\dfrac{1}{3}x^{-3}y^{-7}$

(B) y^{-4}

(C) x^3y^{-3}

(D) $3x^3y^{-3}$

(E) $9x^3y^{-3}$

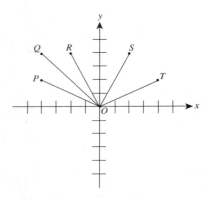

14. In the rectangular coordinate system above, which of the following lines has a slope of 2 ?

(A) $\overrightarrow{OP}$

(B) $\overrightarrow{OQ}$

(C) $\overrightarrow{OR}$

(D) $\overrightarrow{OS}$

(E) $\overrightarrow{OT}$

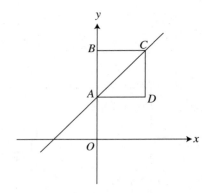

17. In the figure above, $ABCD$ is a square and the equation of line AC is $y = x + 2$. If the coordinates of point C are $(3, 5)$, what is the area of square $ABCD$?

(A) 3
(B) 4
(C) 9
(D) 18
(E) 25

FUNCTION BASICS

A function is a machine for producing ordered pairs. You put an x value into the function and get a y value out of the function. This y value is usually referred to as $f(x)$. The f in $f(x)$ is not a variable; you don't need to solve for it since f is just the name of the function.

10. If $f(x) = x^2 + 8x + 2$, then $f(3) =$

    (A) 11
    (B) 29
    (C) 33
    (D) 35
    (E) 53

14. The function w is defined by $w(x) = 6 + 3x$. If $4 \cdot w(z) = 96$, what is the value of z ?

    (A)   3
    (B)   6
    (C)   10
    (D)   78
    (E) 126

ETS could also ask you to find the number that you put into the function to get another number out.

15. If $f(x) = \left(\dfrac{1}{x}\right)^3$, what is one possible value of x for which $\dfrac{1}{216} < f(x) < \dfrac{1}{64}$?

    (A) 2
    (B) 3
    (C) 4
    (D) 5
    (E) 6

What should you do when you see numbers in the answer choices?

MATH

WRITING

READING

VOCABULARY

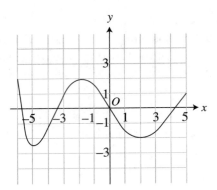

(?)

If *x* goes in and *y* comes out, what does *f*(*x*) mean? See the Content Review section if you don't know.

6. The figure above shows the graph of the function *f*. Which of the following is closest to *f*(−2) ?

(A) −2
(B) −1
(C) 1
(D) 2
(E) 3

If the question gives you a number inside the *f*(*x*) parentheses, such as *f*(3), it means *x* = 3. From there you can see what y-value intersects the line *x* = 3.

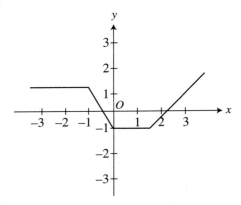

8. The graph of *y* = *h*(*x*) is shown above. If *h*(*x*) = −1, which of the following is a possible value of *x* ?

(A) −2
(B) −0.5
(C) 0.5
(D) 2
(E) 3

Think of *h*(*x*) = −1 as *y* = −1. Replace *h*(*x*) with *y*, and the question becomes much clearer.

Funky Functions

Sometimes, ETS will try to confuse you by using crazy symbols rather than $f(x)$, but you solve these function questions in the same way.

For any integer x, define $\langle\!\langle x \rangle\!\rangle$ by the equation

$$\langle\!\langle x \rangle\!\rangle = 2x + x(x + 3)$$

15. $\langle\!\langle 10 \rangle\!\rangle - \langle\!\langle 3 \rangle\!\rangle =$

    (A) $\langle\!\langle 3 \rangle\!\rangle$

    (B) $\langle\!\langle 4 \rangle\!\rangle$

    (C) $\langle\!\langle 7 \rangle\!\rangle$

    (D) $\langle\!\langle 9 \rangle\!\rangle$

    (E) $\langle\!\langle 11 \rangle\!\rangle$

? What would Joe Bloggs choose?

10. Let $\boxed{a \ \blacksquare\ b\ \blacksquare\ c}$ be defined as $a^2 - \dfrac{b^c}{a}$ for all nonzero numbers a, b, and c. What is the value of $\boxed{4 \ \blacksquare\ 2\ \blacksquare\ 3}$?

    (A)   5
    (B)   9
    (C) 10
    (D) 12
    (E) 14

15. For all positive integers k, let ♠k♠ be defined as the sum of the squares of the integers from 1 through k. Which of the following is equal to $17^2 + 16^2 + 15^2 + \ldots + 4^2$?

    (A) ♠3♠
    (B) ♠13♠
    (C) ♠16♠ – ♠3♠
    (D) ♠17♠ – ♠2♠
    (E) ♠17♠ – ♠3♠

MATH

WRITING

READING

VOCABULARY

LET'S GET FUNCTIONAL!

Functions can be used in many ways on the SAT. Not to fear! There are lots of ways to deal with function questions.

PITA and use your calculator!

11. Jack's band charges by the performance. Jack's share P, in dollars, for x performances is given by the function $P(x) = 1200x - 60$. If Jack earned \$4,740 one month playing with his band, how many performances did the band give?

(A) 3
(B) 4
(C) 5
(D) 6
(E) 7

What is the slope formula?

15. If $f(x)$ is a linear function such that $f(0) = 3$ and $f(1) = 6$, what is the slope of the graph of $y = f(x)$?

(A) -3

(B) $-\dfrac{1}{3}$

(C) 1

(D) $\dfrac{1}{3}$

(E) 3

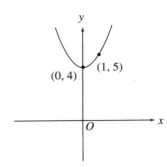

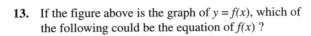

Try plugging points from the graph into the functions.

13. If the figure above is the graph of $y = f(x)$, which of the following could be the equation of $f(x)$?

(A) $f(x) = (x + 2)^2$
(B) $f(x) = (x - 2)^2$
(C) $f(x) = (x + 4)^2$
(D) $f(x) = x - 4$
(E) $f(x) = x^2 + 4$

11. Which of the following is a graph of a function g such that $g(x) = 1$ for exactly 3 values of x between -3 and 3 ?

(A)
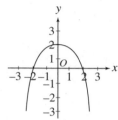

(B)
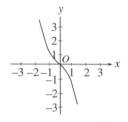

(C)
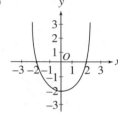

(D)
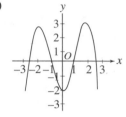

(E)
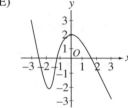

Remember, $g(x) = 1$ means $y = 1$. Start drawing some lines!

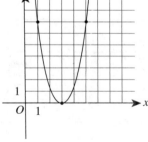

17. If $g(x) = f\left(\dfrac{x}{3} - 1\right)$ and the graph of $f(x)$ is shown in the figure above, then what is the value of $g(6)$?

GET THE FUNC OUT

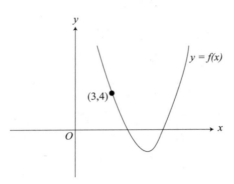

Plug in!

17. The figure above shows the graph of the quadratic function $f(x) = p(x - 5)^2 + q$, where p and q are constants. Which of the following number lines represents the range of all values of x that satisfy the equation $p(x - 5)^2 + q \leq 4$?

(A)
       3   7

(B)
       5   8

(C)
       5   7

(D)
       3   7

(E)
       5   7

m	f(m)
−4	−3
−1	−2
0	−4
2	10
5	7

20. The table above defines the function f. If the function h is defined as $h(m) = f(m) - 3$, what is the value of n when $h(n) = 7$?

(A) −4
(B) −1
(C) 0
(D) 2
(E) 5

 © TPR Education IP Holdings, LLC

MATH

WRITING

READING

VOCABULARY

FUNCTIONS DRILL

Time: 10 minutes

2. If f is a function and $f(-2) = 6$, which of the
following CANNOT be the definition of f?

(A) $f(x) = -3x$
(B) $f(x) = 2x + 10$
(C) $f(x) = 4 - x$
(D) $f(x) = x + 8$
(E) $f(x) = -2x - 2$

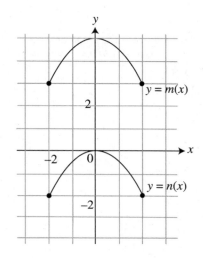

6. The complete graphs of the functions m and n
are shown in the xy-plane above. Which of the
following could be equal to $n(x)$?

(A) $5 \cdot m(x)$
(B) $m(x + 5)$
(C) $m(x - 5)$
(D) $m(x) + 5$
(E) $m(x) - 5$

10. If $f(x)$ is a linear function, $f(2) = 4$, and $f(4) = 8$,
what is the slope of the graph of $y = f(x)$ in the
rectangular coordinate system?

(A) $\dfrac{1}{4}$

(B) $\dfrac{1}{2}$

(C) 1

(D) 2

(E) 4

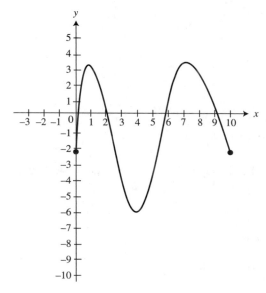

10. The graph of the function f is shown above.
Which of the following are true?

I. $f(3) > f(1)$
II. $f(5) > f(4)$
III. $f(8) > f(2)$

(A) II only
(B) I and II only
(C) II and III only
(D) I and III only
(E) I, II, and III

GO ON TO THE NEXT PAGE

MATH

WRITING

READING

VOCABULARY

15. In the xy-plane, line l passes through the point $(-9, 13)$ and the origin. Which of the following is an equation of a line that is perpendicular to line l ?

(A) $y = -\dfrac{13}{9} x + 13$

(B) $y = -\dfrac{9}{13} x - 9$

(C) $y = \dfrac{9}{13} x + 9$

(D) $y = \dfrac{13}{9} x - 13$

(E) $y = 9x + 13$

18. For all numbers x, if the function f is defined as $f(x) = \dfrac{x}{2}$, then $f(2a - 4b) =$

(A) $a + 2b$

(B) $\dfrac{a - b}{4}$

(C) $a - 4b$

(D) $a - 2b$

(E) $-4ab$

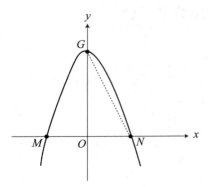

18. The parabola above is the graph of $y = -x^2 + k$, where k is a constant. If $MN = 8$, what is the slope of $\overline{GN}$?

(A) -2

(B) -3

(C) -4

(D) -8

(E) -16

STOP
If you finish before time is called, you may check your work on this section only.
Do not turn to any other section in the test.

 © TPR Education IP Holdings, LLC

Summary

- $f(x) = y$ is just a different way of writing the ordered pair (x, y).

- What is the slope formula?

  _____

- _____ and _____ are two techniques that can make difficult function problems VERY manageable.

- For more on functions, check the Content Review chapter.

- I have accomplished ____ of my _____ stated goals in the Introduction chapter.

FUNCTIONS & GRAPHS PRACTICE

MATH

WRITING

READING

VOCABULARY

Funky Roots and Exponents

6. $9^{\frac{1}{2}} + 9^{\frac{1}{2}} =$

  (A) 3
  (B) 6
  (C) 9
  (D) 18
  (E) 81

8. $(x^{-2})(x^3) =$

  (A) x^{-5}
  (B) x^{-6}
  (C) x^{-8}
  (D) x
  (E) x^6

9. $\left(\sqrt[3]{x}\right)^2 =$

  (A) $\sqrt[3]{x^2}$
  (B) $\sqrt{x^3}$
  (C) $\sqrt[6]{x}$
  (D) $\sqrt[6]{x^2}$
  (E) $\sqrt[9]{x}$

13. $\dfrac{(16x^4 y^6)^{\frac{1}{2}}}{x^5 y} =$

  (A) $x^3 y^2$

  (B) $4x^{-3} y^2$

  (C) $106x^{-3} y^2$

  (D) $4x^{-1} y^5$

  (E) $4x^{-\frac{1}{2}} y^{\frac{5}{2}}$

14. $(x^{\frac{1}{2}})(x^2) =$

  (A) x

  (B) $\sqrt{x^5}$

  (C) $\sqrt[5]{x^2}$

  (D) $\dfrac{1}{\sqrt{x^3}}$

  (E) $x\sqrt{x}$

17. If x is a positive number, then $\left(\sqrt{x^3}\right)^{\frac{1}{3}} =$

  (A) $\sqrt{x}$
  (B) $\sqrt[3]{x^2}$
  (C) x
  (D) x^2
  (E) x^3

Quadratics

4. If $x^2 - 16 = 0$, which of the following could be the value of x ?

(A) 8
(B) 4
(C) 2
(D) −2
(E) −8

6. If $\dfrac{x+y}{3} = \dfrac{4}{x-y}$, what is the value of $x^2 - y^2$?

(A) 0
(B) 1
(C) 7
(D) 12
(E) It cannot be determined from the information provided.

7. If $x^2 + 6x - 7 = 0$, which of the following could be the value of x ?

(A) −7
(B) −6
(C) −1
(D) 6
(E) 7

8. If $x + y = 9$, what is the value of $x^2 + 2xy + y^2$?

(A) 81
(B) 27
(C) 18
(D) 3
(E) −3

9. If $x^2 - 2x = 15$, what is one possible value of x ?

(A) −2
(B) 0
(C) 3
(D) 5
(E) 15

14. If $\dfrac{x^2 - 1}{x - 1} = 4$, what is the value of x ?

19. If $\dfrac{\left(x^2 - y^2\right)^2}{x^2 + 2xy + y^2} = 6$, what is the value of $x^2 - 2xy + y^2$?

(A) −6
(B) $\dfrac{1}{6}$
(C) 2
(D) 6
(E) It cannot be determined from the information provided.

MATH

WRITING

READING

VOCABULARY

Rational and Radical Equations

3. If $\sqrt[3]{8x} = 8$, what is the value of x ?

(A) $\dfrac{1}{8}$

(B) $\dfrac{1}{4}$

(C) $\quad 8$

(D) $\quad 16$

(E) $\quad 64$

6. If $\left| x^3 \right| - 1 = 7$, which of the following is a possible value of x ?

(A) -8
(B) -2
(C) $\quad 3$
(D) $\quad 7$
(E) $\quad 8$

7. If $5x^3 = 3x^3 + 128$, then what is the value of x ?

(A) $\quad 2$
(B) $\quad 4$
(C) $\quad 8$
(D) $\quad 64$
(E) $\quad 128$

9. If $\dfrac{3\sqrt{x}}{3} = \dfrac{12 - \sqrt{x}}{2}$, what is the value of x ?

(A) $\quad 2$
(B) $\quad 3$
(C) $\quad 4$
(D) $\quad 16$
(E) $\quad 36$

10. If $\sqrt[3]{x^2 + 2} = 3$, then what is one possible value of x ?

(A) -25
(B) $\quad -5$
(C) $\quad -1$
(D) $\quad 1$
(E) $\quad 3$

11. If $\dfrac{a^2 - 5a + 6}{a - 3} > 6$, which of the following expresses all of the possible values of a ?

(A) $\quad a < 4$
(B) $\quad a < 8$
(C) $\quad a > 2$
(D) $\quad a > 4$
(E) $\quad a > 8$

13. If $\dfrac{2x^5 + 4x^3}{x^4 + 2x^2} = 8$, then what is the value of x ?

(A) 2
(B) 4
(C) 5
(D) 8
(E) 16

14. If $b^4 - 56 = 25$, what is one possible value of b ?

15. If $\sqrt{x^2 + 6x + 9} = 7$, what is the value of x ?

18. If $\dfrac{\sqrt[3]{x^2}}{x} = \dfrac{1}{2}$, what is the value of x ?

(A) $\dfrac{1}{8}$

(B) $\dfrac{1}{2}$

(C) 2

(D) 8

(E) 64

20. If $\dfrac{x^2 + x - 2}{x^2 - 3x + 2} = \dfrac{x^2 - 5x + 6}{x^2 - 7x + 12}$, what is the value of x ?

(A) −3
(B) −2
(C) 2
(D) 3
(E) 6

Functions and Expressions

7. When Floyd goes cycling, the number of full pedal revolutions is given by $C(m) = 90m - 10$, where m is the number of minutes he rides. How many minutes must Floyd ride for the pedals to go through 1,790 full revolutions?

(A)　　10
(B)　　20
(C)　　90
(D)　　900
(E)　1,800

11. Let $\sim x$ be defined as $\sim x = 3x - 4$. If $\sim a = 59$, what is the value of a ?

(A)　181
(B)　　79
(C)　　63
(D)　　21
(E)　　17

15. Max wrestles in a weight division that requires all wrestlers to weigh between 140 and 150 pounds. Which of the following inequalities can be used to determine whether or not Max's current weight w satisfies the weight requirement?

(A)　　$|w - 130| < 20$

(B)　　$|w - 135| < 15$

(C)　　$|w - 140| < 10$

(D)　　$|w - 145| < 5$

(E)　　$|w - 150| < 2.5$

16. If the function f is defined by $f(x) = x^2 + 5$ and $f(b - 2) = 2b$, what is the value of b ?

20. For all real numbers, let the operation $x \ddagger y$ be defined by $x \ddagger y = x - 2y$. If a and b are real numbers, what is the result when $a \ddagger (b \ddagger a)$ is subtracted from $(a \ddagger b) \ddagger a$?

(A)　　$6a$
(B)　　　a
(C)　　　0
(D)　$-3a$
(E)　$-6a$

Slope

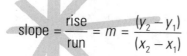

$$\text{slope} = \frac{\text{rise}}{\text{run}} = m = \frac{(y_2 - y_1)}{(x_2 - x_1)}$$

8. What is the slope of a line passing through the origin and the point $(-2, -3)$?

(A) $-\dfrac{3}{2}$

(B) $\dfrac{3}{2}$

(C) $\dfrac{2}{3}$

(D) $-\dfrac{2}{3}$

(E) 1

9. What is the slope of a line that contains points $A\left(\dfrac{1}{2}, -5\right)$ and $B\left(6, -\dfrac{1}{2}\right)$?

(A) -1

(B) 0

(C) $\dfrac{9}{11}$

(D) $\dfrac{11}{2}$

(E) 11

10. If two lines in the xy-coordinate plane do not intersect, and the equation of the first line is $2x + 7y = 5$, what is the slope of the other line?

(A) $-\dfrac{7}{2}$

(B) $-\dfrac{2}{7}$

(C) $\dfrac{2}{7}$

(D) 2

(E) 7

12. If a line contains three points with coordinates $(5, -3)$, $(8, 3)$, and $(z, 7)$, what is the value of z ?

(A) 13
(B) 10
(C) 3
(D) 1
(E) -5

14. Line l contains the point $(2, 3)$ and has a slope of $\dfrac{3}{4}$. Which of the following points must also lie on line l ?

(A) $(0, 6)$
(B) $(3, 4)$
(C) $(10, 9)$
(D) $(5, 7)$
(E) $(0, 0)$

18. If l has a slope of $-\dfrac{4}{5}$ and points $(1, 6)$ and $(a, -2)$ lie on line l, what is the value of a ?

(A) -2

(B) $-\dfrac{1}{3}$

(C) $\dfrac{37}{5}$

(D) 6

(E) 11

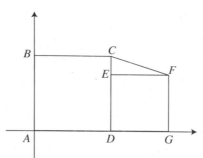

20. In the figure above, $ABCD$ and $DEFG$ are both squares. The coordinates of point A are $(0, 0)$. If the area of square $ABCD$ is 25 and the area of square $DEFG$ is 16, what is the slope of line segment CF ?

(A) -4

(B) $-\dfrac{1}{4}$

(C) $\dfrac{1}{4}$

(D) 4

(E) 5

© TPR Education IP Holdings, LLC

Linear and Quadratic Functions

13. If f is a linear function, the slope of the graph of f in the xy-plane is 2, and $f(0) = 3$, what is $f(10)$?

   (A)   7
   (B) 13
   (C) 17
   (D) 23
   (E) 26

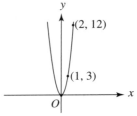

13. If the figure above is the graph of $y = f(x)$, which of the following could be the equation for $f(x)$?

   (A) $f(x) = x^2 + 3$
   (B) $f(x) = (x + 3)^2$
   (C) $f(x) = 3x^2$
   (D) $f(x) = 3x$
   (E) $f(x) = 3x + 6$

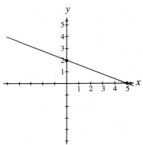

13. If the graph shown above is that of $y = f(x)$, which of the following is the equation for $f(x)$?

   (A) $f(x) = -\dfrac{5}{2}x + 2$

   (B) $f(x) = -\dfrac{2}{5}x + 2$

   (C) $f(x) = \dfrac{2}{5}x + 2$

   (D) $f(x) = \dfrac{5}{2}x + 2$

   (E) $f(x) = 2x - \dfrac{2}{5}$

14. Which of the following is the equation of a line parallel to the line with equation $4x - 3y = 12$?

   (A) $12x - 9y = -15$
   (B) $4x - 4y = 16$
   (C) $4x + 3y = 12$
   (D) $3x + 4y = 15$
   (E) $12x + 9y = 3$

 © TPR Education IP Holdings, LLC

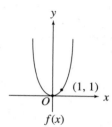

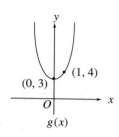

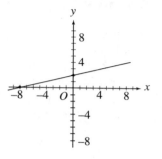

16. In the figure above, $f(x) = x^2$. Which of the following could be the equation for $g(x)$?

(A) $g(x) = (x + 3)^2$

(B) $g(x) = x^2 + 3$

(C) $g(x) = x^2 - 3$

(D) $g(x) = (x - 3)^2$

(E) $g(x) = \dfrac{x^2}{3}$

16. If $f(x)$ is a linear function, $f(2) = 11$, and $f(4) = 12$, then $f(7) =$

(A) $\dfrac{1}{2}$

(B) 10

(C) 13

(D) $\dfrac{27}{2}$

(E) 18

17. The above graph is that of $y = g(x)$. Which of the following is perpendicular to $g(x)$?

(A) $f(x) = -8x + 4$

(B) $f(x) = -4x + 3$

(C) $f(x) = \dfrac{1}{4}x - 2$

(D) $f(x) = \dfrac{1}{4}x + 2$

(E) $f(x) = 2x + 4$

MATH

WRITING

READING

VOCABULARY

Behavior of Graphs

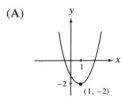

$f(x) + y$ moves the graph up y units
$f(x) - y$ moves the graph down y units
$f(x + y)$ moves the graph left y units
$f(x - y)$ moves the graph right y units

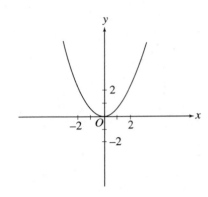

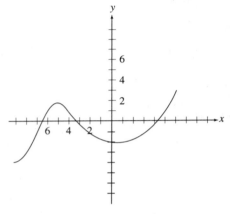

3. For how many points on the portion of the graph of $y = f(x)$ shown above does $f(x) = 1$?

(A) None
(B) One
(C) Two
(D) Three
(E) Four

11. If $f(x) = |x|$, which of the following changes to the graph of $f(x)$ would result in the graph of $y = f(x + 5)$?

(A) It moves to the left 5.
(B) It moves to the right 5.
(C) It moves up 5.
(D) It moves down 5.
(E) There is no such change.

13. The graph of $y = f(x)$ is shown above. Which of the following is the graph of $y = f(x - 1) - 2$?

(A)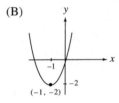

(B)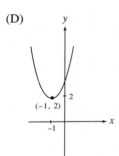

(C)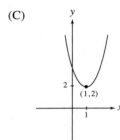

(D)

(E)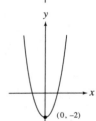

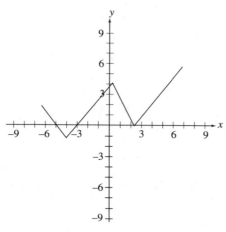

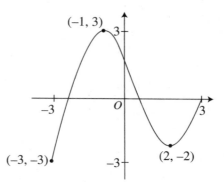

15. For the portion of $y = g(x)$ shown above, for which values of x is $g(x)$ negative?

(A) $0 < x$
(B) $0 \leq x$
(C) $-3 < x$
(D) $-5 < x$
(E) $-5 < x < -3$

18. The graph of $y = f(x)$ is shown above. If $g(x) = f(x) + 5$, for how many values of x does $g(x) = 0$ between -3 and 3 ?

	⊘	⊘	
⊙	⊙	⊙	⊙
	⓪	⓪	⓪
①	①	①	①
②	②	②	②
③	③	③	③
④	④	④	④
⑤	⑤	⑤	⑤
⑥	⑥	⑥	⑥
⑦	⑦	⑦	⑦
⑧	⑧	⑧	⑧
⑨	⑨	⑨	⑨

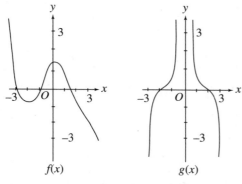

16. Portions of the graphs of $f(x)$ and $g(x)$ are shown above. For which of the following values of a is the number of points for which $f(x) = a$ greater than the number of points where $g(x) = a$?

   I. 0
   II. 1
   III. 2

(A) None of these
(B) I only
(C) II only
(D) I and II only
(E) I, II, and III

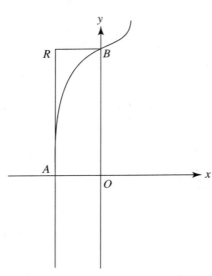

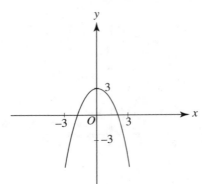

18. In the figure above, the graph of $y = x^3 + 8$ intersects the x-axis at A and the y-axis at B. What is the area of rectangle $ARBO$?

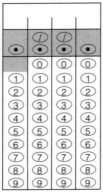

19. If $f(x) = x^2$, which of the following could be the equation of the graph above?

(A) $y = -f(x) + 3$
(B) $y = -f(x) - 3$
(C) $y = f(x + 3)$
(D) $y = f(x - 3)$
(E) $y = f(x) + 3$

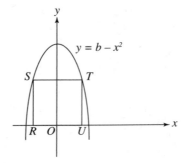

20. In the figure above, $RSTU$ is a square. Points S and T lie on the graph of $y = b - x^2$ for some constant b. If the length of the diagonal of $RSTU$ is $8\sqrt{2}$, what is the value of b ?

(A) 4
(B) 8
(C) 12
(D) 24
(E) 72

POOD REVIEW

EMBRACE YOUR POOD

Remember your Personal Order of Difficulty (POOD). After all, good pacing and careful problem selection have a huge impact on your score. Try these problems. If you can't figure out how to solve it, can you eliminate answer choices by Ballparking? Are there Joe Bloggs answers? Did you try Plugging In or PITA? Good test takers are flexible in their approach.

Drill

4, 5, 5, 6, 7, 7, x

Do it ☐
Skip it ☐

14. The average (arithmetic mean) of the numbers shown above is equal to their median. If $x > 3$, which of the following could be the value of x ?

(A) 8
(B) 7
(C) 6
(D) 5
(E) 4

Do it ☐
Skip it ☐

11. $2A$ is divisible by both 3 and 6. If A is a digit, what is the value of A ?

(A) 1
(B) 2
(C) 3
(D) 4
(E) 6

Do it ☐
Skip it ☐

14. A square is inscribed in a circle. If the area of the square is 36, what is the total area outside the square but inside the circle?

(A) $36 - 6\pi$
(B) $18\pi - 36$
(C) $18\pi - 18$
(D) 18π
(E) $36\pi - 36$

Do it ☐
Skip it ☐

9. How many distinct positive 4-digit <u>odd</u> integers are there in which the digits are 1, 2, 3, and 4 ?

(A) 1
(B) 4
(C) 6
(D) 12
(E) 24

Do it ☐
Skip it ☐

17. If $3^x + 3^x + 3^x = 3^3$, then $x =$

(A) 1
(B) 2
(C) 3
(D) 9
(E) 27

Do it ☐
Skip it ☐

15. If $c = b - 10a$, then for which of the following pairs (a, b) is the value of c <u>greatest</u>?

(A) $(0, 0)$
(B) $(1, 0)$
(C) $(5, 1)$
(D) $(4, 5)$
(E) $(10, 7)$

 © TPR Education IP Holdings, LLC

16. If h is $\frac{4}{5}$ the sum of g and h, then which of the following is equal to h ?

Do it ☐
Skip it ☐

(A) $\frac{1}{4}g$

(B) $\frac{4}{5}g$

(C) $\frac{5}{4}g$

(D) $4g$

(E) $5g$

18. Lea drives from Manayunk to Wilmington at $\frac{2}{3}$ of the average speed at which she returned from Wilmington to Manayunk. What percent of her total driving time did it take Lea to drive from Manayunk to Wilmington?

Do it ☐
Skip it ☐

(A) $33\frac{1}{3}\%$

(B) 40%

(C) 50%

(D) 60%

(E) $66\frac{2}{3}\%$

19. In the xy-plane, what is an equation of $\overleftrightarrow{CD}$ if points $A(-3, -1)$, $B(1, 7)$, C, and D can be connected to form six distinct line segments, all of which have the same slope?

Do it ☐
Skip it ☐

(A) $x = -3$

(B) $y = 7$

(C) $y = -x - 4$

(D) $y = \frac{1}{2}x + \frac{1}{2}$

(E) $y = 2x + 5$

20. If J is the set of all values of x for which $\sqrt{2x - 3} = 3 - x$, then which of the following is set J ?

Do it ☐
Skip it ☐

(A) $\{-2\}$

(B) $\{-2, -6\}$

(C) $\{-8, 12\}$

(D) $\{2\}$

(E) $\{2, 6\}$

CONTENT REVIEW

20. Bandolfo has a series of intersections of sets, each one of which is non-orthagonal to the number of Marsenne primes, but confabulatory with his collar, which has been starched satisfactorily. If the year is currently 1964 in the Current Era (CE), at what point is the conformity of Euclidian space discontinuous?

(A) 42
(B) It cannot be determined from the information given.
(C) It can be determined from the information given.
(D) Both C & D are correct, but not as correct as A.
(E) None of this will ever, ever appear on an SAT.

MATH BASICS ET CETERA

It may have been a while since you've seen many of the following math concepts in school. Here is a brief refresher on the math you need to know to get a good score on the SAT.

Find all <u>factors</u> of the following integers:

| 8 | 47 | 93 | 144 | 205 |

Find all <u>prime</u> factors of the following integers:

| 12 | 68 | 78 | 120 | 156 |

Conversion Chart

Fraction	Decimal	Percent
$\dfrac{1}{2}$	0.5	50%
		$33\dfrac{1}{3}\%$
$\dfrac{2}{3}$		
	0.25	
		75%
	0.2	
$\dfrac{2}{5}$		
	0.6	
		80%
	0.16	
$\dfrac{5}{6}$		
	0.1	
		5%
$\dfrac{1}{50}$		
		1%

WORKING WITH EQUATIONS

Some SAT questions ask you to work with an equation. You can approach these by solving or Plugging In.

Find the value of the variable in each question below.

1. $4x = x + 9$

2. $\dfrac{4x}{3} = 12$

3. $\dfrac{2}{13x + 6} = \dfrac{1}{25 + x}$

4. $\dfrac{\dfrac{x}{5}}{\dfrac{x}{10}} = 17 - x$

5. $\dfrac{x}{3} + 4x = 38 - 2x$

6. $x^2 + 16 = 97$

7. $\dfrac{x^2 + 11}{6} = 31 - x^2$

8. $\dfrac{3\sqrt{x}}{5} = \dfrac{21}{5}$

9. $\dfrac{(3\sqrt{x})^2}{x} = 27x$

10. $\dfrac{(2x^7 + 4x^5)}{4x^5} = 33$

11. $3x^5 = 5x^3$

© TPR Education IP Holdings, LLC

Solving

To solve an equation, you need to isolate the variable. Get the variables on one side of the equal sign and the numbers on the other side. If you do something on one side of the equal sign, you must also do it on the other side.

2. If $10 - 3y = 4$, then $y =$

(A) $-\dfrac{14}{3}$

(B) -2

(C) -1

(D) 2

(E) $\dfrac{14}{3}$

7. If $\dfrac{2m}{5} = \dfrac{m+3}{12}$, what is the value of m?

(A) $\dfrac{3}{19}$

(B) $\dfrac{1}{3}$

(C) $\dfrac{15}{19}$

(D) 5

(E) 15

For many questions, you won't actually have to solve for the variable. Pay attention to what the question asks you to find.

3. If $3(5p - 6q) = 12$, then $5p - 6q =$

(A) 36
(B) 30
(C) 15
(D) 12
(E) 4

 © TPR Education IP Holdings, LLC

TRANSLATING ENGLISH TO MATH

If the question doesn't give you an equation, you may have to make your own. Translate the words in the question into an equation.

3. If $\frac{1}{4}$ of a certain number is 15 less than the number, what is the number?

(A) −20
(B) 5
(C) 15
(D) 20
(E) 60

4. Which of the following represents the statement "The sum of one-half of m and the square of n is equal to the square of the difference between m and n" ?

(A) $\dfrac{mn^2}{2} = (m-n)^2$

(B) $\dfrac{mn^2}{2} = (m+n)^2$

(C) $\dfrac{m}{2} + n^2 = (m-n)^2$

(D) $\dfrac{m}{2} + n^2 = \sqrt{m-n}$

(E) $\dfrac{m}{2} + \sqrt{n} = (m-n)^2$

7. A coin bank contains 23 coins of only two different types. The total value of all of the coins in the bank is $2.75. Of the coins in the bank, m coins are worth $0.25 each, and n coins are worth $0.05 each. Which of the following pairs of equations could correctly convey the information above?

(A) $m + n = 2.75$
$.25m + .05n = 23$

(B) $m + n = 23$
$.3(m + n) = 2.75$

(C) $.25m + .05n = 2.75$
$mn = 23$

(D) $.25m = .05n$
$m + n = 23$

(E) $m + n = 23$
$.25m + .05n = 2.75$

Math Equivalents
- *is* means =
- *of* means multiply
- *what* is the variable

MATH

WRITING

READING

VOCABULARY

SIMULTANEOUS EQUATIONS

Simultaneous equations on the SAT are much easier than they look—just stack them and add or subtract.

11. If $4x - 5y = 15$ and $2x - y = 9$, then $6x - 6y =$

(A) 5
(B) 9
(C) 15
(D) 24
(E) 30

Sometimes you can't get the expression that you need by simply adding or subtracting the equations. Try multiplying or dividing the resulting equation by a number to get what ETS is asking for.

12. If $7x + 35y = 13$ and $23x - 5y = 67$, then what is the value of $3x + 3y$?

(A) $\dfrac{3}{8}$

(B) $\dfrac{9}{5}$

(C) 8

(D) 30

(E) 80

© TPR Education IP Holdings, LLC

EXPONENTS AND ROOTS

Exponents just mean multiplication. Instead of writing 5 × 5 × 5 × 5, write 5^4.

When in doubt, expand it out.

You can use the exponent rules to multiply or divide expressions with exponents. Just make sure that the bases are the same.

1) $x \times x =$ **2)** $\dfrac{y^6}{y^2} =$ **3)** $(z^2)^3 =$

Try these examples:

$n^2 \times n^3 =$ $10^5 \times 10^{15} =$ $2x^4 \times 3x =$

$\dfrac{n^8}{n^2} =$ $\dfrac{6^4}{6^3} =$ $\dfrac{30x^{10}}{15x^5} =$

$(n^2)^3 =$ $(7^4)^6 =$ $(4x^2 y^5)^3 =$

8. If $\left(x^a\right)^6 = x^{18}$ and $\dfrac{x^b}{x^2} = x^8$, then $b - a =$

(A) −7
(B) −2
(C)   4
(D)   7
(E)   13

M _____
A _____
D _____
S _____
P _____
M _____

MATH · WRITING · READING · VOCABULARY

MATH

WRITING

READING

VOCABULARY

SPECIAL EXPONENT RULES: 1 AND 0

Since 3^2 means to multiply two 3s together, if you raise anything to the first power, it means to just leave that one number all by itself.

Anything raised to the first power is itself: $x^1 = x$

Anything to the 0 power is 1: $x^0 = 1$

14. If $a^b = 3$, $a^c = 1$, and $a^d = 27$, what is a^{b+c+d} ?

(A) $\dfrac{1}{81}$

(B) $\dfrac{1}{9}$

(C) 1

(D) 9

(E) 81

NEGATIVE EXPONENTS

What's $\dfrac{y^3}{y^5}$? Well, if you follow the MADSPM rules, it would be $y^{3-5} = y^{-2}$. So what is a negative exponent? It just means you've got variables left over on the bottom, instead of on the top.

$$3^{-2} = \frac{1}{3^2} = \frac{1}{9} \qquad 4^{-3} = \frac{1}{4^3} = \frac{1}{64} \qquad n^{-1} = \frac{1}{n}$$

Negative exponents mean reciprocal: Flip it over, and get rid of the negative sign in the exponent.

$$x^{-1} = \frac{1}{x}$$

12. If $j = 2$, which of the following is equivalent to $j(k^{-1}) + j^{-2}(k^{-1})$?

(A) $\dfrac{2k^2}{3}$

(B) $\dfrac{5}{k}$

(C) $\dfrac{4}{k^2}$

(D) $\dfrac{9}{4k}$

(E) $-5k$

FRACTIONAL EXPONENTS, AKA ROOTS:

Raising something to a fractional exponent means to raise it to the power of the top number, then take the root of the bottom number. In other words, $64^{\frac{1}{2}}$ means "take the square root of 64," which is 8. $125^{\frac{1}{3}}$ means "take the cube root of 125," which is 5.

Most calculators have built-in buttons for square and cube roots. The SAT doesn't really use anything more complicated than cube roots that often, so don't worry about finding the 128th root of a number.

9. If $(3p)^{\frac{1}{2}} = 6$, what is the value of p ?

(A) 1
(B) 3
(C) 12
(D) 18
(E) 36

EXPONENTS AND ROOTS FOR WEIRD NUMBERS

0 to any power is 0 ($0^3 = 0 \times 0 \times 0 = 0$), and 1 to any power is 1 ($1^2 = 1 \times 1 = 1$).

For negative numbers, the sign depends on what power to which the number is raised. $(-2)^2 = 4$, $(-2)^3 = -8$, $(-2)^4 = 16$, $(-2)^5 = -32$, and $(-2)^6 = 64$. Because of this, $x^2 = 25$ actually has two solutions: $x = 5$ and $x = -5$.

If you raise a fraction to a power, or take the root of a fraction, simply apply the power or root to the top and the bottom of the fraction.

$$\left(\frac{2}{3}\right)^2 = \frac{2^2}{3^2} = \frac{4}{9} \qquad \sqrt{\frac{16}{25}} = \frac{\sqrt{16}}{\sqrt{25}} = \frac{4}{5}$$

- If you square a positive fraction less than 1, it gets smaller.
- If you "square root" a positive fraction less than 1, it gets bigger.
- A negative number raised to an even power becomes positive.
- A negative number raised to an odd power stays negative.

If $x^2 = 9$, then $x = +3$ or -3. However, the square root of a number is defined as its positive root only. Thus, $\sqrt{9} = +3$.

You can add and subtract square roots when the numbers under the square root sign ($\sqrt{\ }$) are the same.

Try these:

$$3\sqrt{2} + 4\sqrt{2} = \qquad\qquad 8\sqrt{5} - 2\sqrt{5} =$$

If you take the square root of a fraction less than 1, it gets bigger.

12. If $0 < x < 1$, which of the following inequalities is correct?

(A) $\sqrt{x} < x < x^2$

(B) $x^2 < x < \sqrt{x}$

(C) $x < x^2 < \sqrt{x}$

(D) $\sqrt{x} < x^2 < x$

(E) $x < \sqrt{x} < x^2$

SETS

Sets are collections of distinct objects that get treated as a whole. The items that belong to a set are called the *elements* or *members*. They can sometimes involve knowing the mean, median, or mode.

11. *A* is a set of prime one-digit integers, and *B* is a set of odd integers. Which one of the following CANNOT be the product of a member of set *A* and a member of set *B* ?

(A) 6
(B) 10
(C) 12
(D) 45
(E) 49

17. Set *C* is the set of all positive integer factors of prime number *p*. The elements of set *D* are the positive single-digit integers. If set *F* contains only elements that are in both set *C* and set *D*, which of the following must be a member of set *F* ?

(A) 1
(B) 2
(C) 5
(D) 7
(E) 9

MATH

WRITING

READING

VOCABULARY

In Right Triangles:
- Two sides intersect to form a 90° angle.
- The longest side is opposite the right angle and is called the hypotenuse.
- 3:4:5, 6:8:10, and 5:12:13 triples appear very frequently on the SAT.

Right Triangles

If you know two sides of a right triangle, you can find the third side using the Pythagorean theorem (it's in the formula box at the beginning of each Math section).

Pythagorean theorem: $a^2 + b^2 = c^2$ (where c is the hypotenuse)

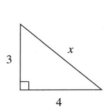

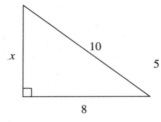

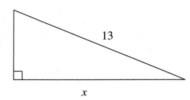

$x =$ _____ $x =$ _____ $x =$ _____

Remember these and you will save time because you won't have to do the math.

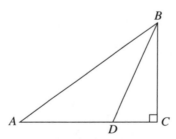

Note: Figure not drawn to scale.

7. In triangle *ABC* above, *DC* = 3, *AD* = 5, and *BC* = 4. What is the area of triangle *ABD* ?

   (A) 16
   (B) 10
   (C)   9
   (D)   8
   (E)   6

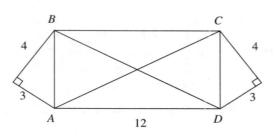

10. In rectangle *ABCD* above, what is the sum of *AC* and *BD* ?

(A) 34
(B) 26
(C) 13
(D) 10
(E) 5

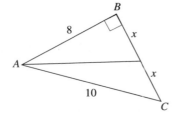

Note: Figure not drawn to scale.

17. In triangle *ABC* shown above, what is the value of *x* ?

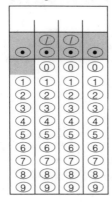

MATH
WRITING
READING
VOCABULARY

ETS loves to hide
Pythagorean triples.

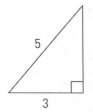

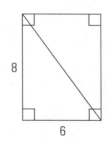

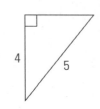

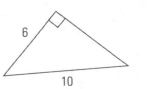

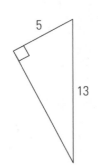

Trig? Who Needs It!

There are no problems on the SAT that require trigonometry. If you like doing things the hard way, you could use trig to solve some problems. These problems just test right triangles that have special angle measures. The ratios of the lengths of the sides are provided at the beginning of every Math section.

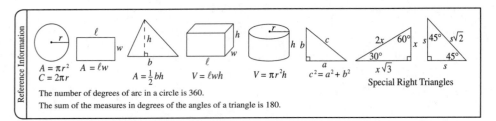

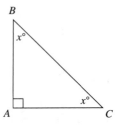

10. In $\triangle ABC$ above, if $AB = 5$, what is the length of side BC ?

(A) $\dfrac{5\sqrt{2}}{2}$

(B) 5

(C) $5\sqrt{2}$

(D) $5\sqrt{3}$

(E) It cannot be determined from the information given.

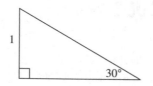

13. What is the perimeter of the triangle above?

(A) $\dfrac{3+\sqrt{3}}{2}$

(B)   3

(C) $2+\sqrt{2}$

(D) $3+\sqrt{3}$

(E) $3+\sqrt{5}$

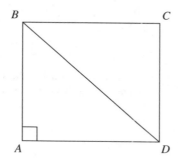

12. *ABCD* is a square. If *BD* = 5, what is the area of the square?

(A) $\dfrac{25}{4}$

(B) $\dfrac{25}{2}$

(C)   25

(D) $25\sqrt{2}$

(E)   50

15. An equilateral triangle has a side of length 10. What is the area of the triangle?

(A) $5\sqrt{3}$

(B) $25\sqrt{2}$

(C) $25\sqrt{3}$

(D) $50\sqrt{3}$

(E) $100\sqrt{2}$

A 45°-45°-90° triangle makes up half a square.

A 30°-60°-90° triangle is half of an equilateral triangle.

MATH

WRITING

READING

VOCABULARY

FOUR OR MORE SIDES?

The angle sum of a triangle is 180 degrees. The angle sum of a quadrilateral is 360 degrees. To find the angle sum of other polygons, add 180 degrees for each additional side.

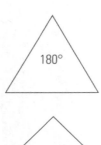

180°

360°

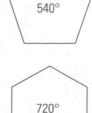

540°

720°

7 sides = 900°
8 sides = 1080°
9 sides = 1260°
10 sides = 1440°

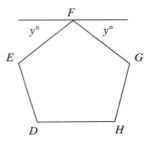

15. In the figure above, pentagon *DEFGH* has equal sides and equal angles. What is the value of *y* ?

   (A)   30
   (B)   36
   (C)   45
   (D)   60
   (E)   72

16. A six-sided polygon has five equal angles. If the measure of one of the angles in the polygon is 100°, what is the degree measure of each of the other five angles?

   (A)   88
   (B)   100
   (C)   124
   (D)   540
   (E)   720

GET THE FUNC OUT—PART DEUX

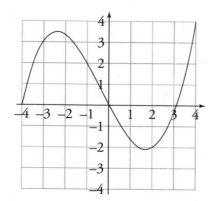

The graph of $y = f(x)$ is shown above. If $-4 \le x \le 4$, then what is the value of each of the following?

$f(0) =$ _____ $\qquad\qquad$ $f(2) =$ _____

$f(-3) =$ _____ $\qquad\qquad$ $f(-1) =$ _____

For how many values of x does $f(x) = 1$? _____

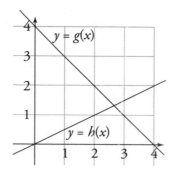

The graphs of $y = g(x)$ and $y = h(x)$ are shown above. What is the value of each of the following?

$g(1) =$ _____ $\qquad\qquad$ $h(2) =$ _____

$g(3) =$ _____ $\qquad\qquad$ $h(4) =$ _____

$g(2) + h(0) =$ _____ $\qquad\qquad$ $h(4) - g(0) =$ _____

MATH

WRITING

READING

VOCABULARY

MATH

WRITING

READING

VOCABULARY

x	f(x)	g(x)
–2	3	–1
–1	1	2
0	–2	–1
1	0	0
2	–1	3
3	0	–2

According to the table above,

What is $f(3)$?_____   What is $g(3)$?_____

What is $f(-1) + 5$?_____   What is $f(2) + g(3)$?_____

What is $f(g(0))$?_____   What is $f(f(f(0)))$?_____

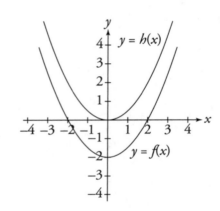

The graphs of the functions f and h are shown above for the interval from $x = -3$ to $x = 3$.

What is $f(-2)$? _____   What is $h(-2)$?_____

What is $f(0)$? _____   What is $h(0)$? _____

What is $f(2)$? _____   What is $h(2)$?_____

16. In the above graphs of function f and h, which of the following could express h in terms of f?

(A) $h(x) = f(x)$
(B) $h(x) = f(x) - 2$
(C) $h(x) = f(x) + 2$
(D) $h(x) = 2f(x)$
(E) $h(x) = f(x + 2)$

 © TPR Education IP Holdings, LLC

RATES

5. An automobile traveling 55 miles per hour will travel 1,100 miles in how many hours?

    (A)   2
    (B)   5
    (C) 20
    (D) 22
    (E) 55

15. A radio advertisement script contains 480 words. The advertisement needs to be exactly one minute in length. What is the average rate in words per second at which the announcer must read the script?

    (A)   6
    (B)   8
    (C) 12
    (D) 24
    (E) 48

17. Machine *A* produces pencils at a constant rate of 3 pencils per minute, and machine *B* produces pencils at a constant rate of 6 pencils per minute. If the two machines work together, then in how many minutes will they produce 1,269 pencils?

18. Rosalita rode her bicycle to the repair shop and rode the bus home by the same route. Excluding the time she spent at the shop, she spent a total of 1 hour traveling from her home to the shop and back again. If she rode her bicycle at an average speed of 5 miles per hour, and the bus traveled at an average speed of 20 miles per hour, then for how many miles did she ride her bicycle?

    (A)   2
    (B)   4
    (C)   5
    (D)   8
    (E) 10

Distance (or work) = rate × time

MATH

WRITING

READING

VOCABULARY

USING DATA

For some questions, a chart will be used to display data. You'll have to look up some information and use it. Make sure that you read the chart carefully.

EARTHQUAKE FREQUENCY BY ZONE

Earthquake Fault Zones	Average Annual Frequency of Earthquakes 1986–1993
Zone One	x
Zone Two	8.7
Zone Three	5.3
Zone Four	5.7
Zone Five	y

20. In the chart above, if the mean frequency of earthquakes in Zones One, Two, and Three is 8.0 and the mean frequency of earthquakes in Zones Four and Five is 5.5, how much less than the mean of the five annual earthquake frequencies is the mode of the five annual earthquake frequencies?

(A) 1.7
(B) 5.3
(C) 5.5
(D) 7.0
(E) 8.0

COST OF ELECTRICITY FOR FIVE COMPANIES

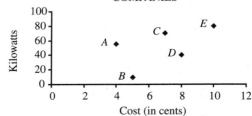

13. A consumer compares five electric companies by graphing the cost, in cents, each charges against the kilowatts of electricity used. If each company charges a constant rate per kilowatt, which company charges the <u>least</u> per kilowatt of electricity?

(A) *A*
(B) *B*
(C) *C*
(D) *D*
(E) *E*

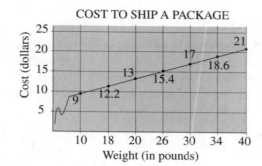

COST TO SHIP A PACKAGE

10. The chart above shows the shipping costs for packages of various weights. A shipping company wants to model the cost to ship a package as a function, $f(x)$, of its weight. If the weight of the package is x, which of the following functions best approximates the cost of shipping a package?

(A) $f(x) = \dfrac{2}{5}x$

(B) $f(x) = \dfrac{5}{2}x + 5$

(C) $f(x) = x - 1$

(D) $f(x) = \dfrac{2}{5}x + 5$

(E) $f(x) = \dfrac{1}{4}x + 6.5$

MULTIPLE CHARTS

Sometimes, ETS displays information on more than one chart. You'll need to look up the information on both charts and do some simple arithmetic with the numbers such as adding or multiplying. Treat these like any other chart question. Read the charts carefully and make sure that you write down your work.

Ticket Sales and Prices at The Film-O-Rama Movie Theater			
Day	Adult	Child	Senior Citizen
Monday	10	4	8
Tuesday	8	4	7
Wednesday	20	9	5

Ticket Type	Price per ticket
Adult	$5
Child	$3
Senior Citizen	$4

8. The tables above show ticket sales and prices at the Film-O-Rama movie theater during a certain week in 2003. What was the dollar amount of the difference between the total value of ticket sales on Wednesday and the total value of ticket sales on Monday that week?

(A) 14
(B) 53
(C) 67
(D) 94
(E) 147

CONTENT REVIEW PRACTICE

WORKING WITH EQUATIONS

Don't forget that it might be easier to Plug In the answers on some of these problems.

i. $x + 6 = 9$ $x =$

ii. $33 = 11(4x - 4)$ $x =$

iii. $\dfrac{1}{2}x + \dfrac{1}{4}x + \dfrac{1}{8}x = 49$ $x =$

1. If $\dfrac{24}{x} = \dfrac{3}{4}$, then $x =$

(A)   16
(B)   18
(C)   30
(D)   32
(E)   36

2. If $(a + 3) + b = 0$, then $a + b =$

(A) -3

(B) $-\dfrac{3}{2}$

(C) 0

(D) $\dfrac{3}{2}$

(E) 3

3. If the sum of $q - 6$, $q - 3$, and q is 0, what is the value of q ?

(A)   5
(B)   4
(C)   3
(D)   2
(E)   0

3. If $\dfrac{400}{100(x + 3)} = 4$, then what does x equal?

(A) -4
(B) -3
(C) -2
(D) -1
(E) 0

4. If $5z = 10 + 2z$, what is the value of $9z$?

(A)   3
(B)   7
(C)   10
(D)   15
(E)   30

4. If $\dfrac{x + 4}{7} = \dfrac{4}{9}$, then x equals

(A) $-\dfrac{8}{9}$

(B) $-\dfrac{1}{4}$

(C) $\dfrac{1}{4}$

(D) $\dfrac{24}{9}$

(E) $\dfrac{36}{7}$

10. The smaller of two integers, r and $r + 3$, is multiplied by 3 and then subtracted from the other integer. Which of the following represents this operation?

(A) $(r + 3) - 3r$

(B) $\dfrac{r - 3}{r + 3}$

(C) $(3r + 9) + r$

(D) $r - (3r + 9)$

(E) $\dfrac{r(r - 3)}{3}$

14. If $\dfrac{8y}{3} - 4 = \dfrac{1}{6}$, then $\dfrac{1}{y}$ equals

(A)   16

(B) $\dfrac{25}{16}$

(C)   1

(D) $\dfrac{2}{3}$

(E) $\dfrac{16}{25}$

SIMULTANEOUS EQUATIONS

Remember: You can usually stack equations and find out what you need by combining the two equations—either add or subtract.

8. If $3x + 2y = 7$ and $2x + 2y = 9$, what is the value of x ?

(A) −2
(B)   2
(C)   7
(D)   9
(E) 16

11. If $-x - y = -2$ and $2x - y = -11$, what is the value of x ?

(A) −13
(B)   −9
(C)   −3
(D)   3
(E)   9

12. If $2x + 3y = 3x - 3y = 25$, what is the value of x ?

(A)   5
(B)   10
(C)   25
(D)   50
(E)   It cannot be determined from the information given.

13. Twice the sum of three positive numbers x, y, and z is 21. When the smallest of these numbers is subtracted from the product of the other two, the result is 32. If $z < y < x$, which of the following equations could correctly express the information above?

(A) $x + y + z = 42$
      $xy - z = 32$

(B) $2(x + y + z) = 21$
      $2xy - z = 32$

(C) $2(x + y + z) = 32$
      $xy - z = 21$

(D) $x + y + z = 21$
      $2(xy - z) = 21$

(E) $2(x + y + z) = 21$
      $xy - z = 32$

14. If $6j - 5k = 11$ and $5j - 6k = -22$, what is the value of $2j + 2k$?

(A) −33
(B) −11
(C)   −6
(D)   33
(E)   66

14. If $2a + b = 6$ and $3a + c = 13$, then $a - b + c =$

(A)   3
(B)   7
(C)   9
(D)   20
(E)   78

15. If $4r + 3s = 7$, $2r + s = 1$, and $2r + 2s = t - 4$, what is the value of t ?

(A)   6
(B)   8
(C)   10
(D)   12
(E)   It cannot be determined from the information given.

MATH

WRITING

READING

VOCABULARY

EXPONENTS AND ROOTS

When in doubt, expand it out. MADSPM.

2. If $q^2 = 81$, then which of the following could be the value of $(q + 1)(q - 1) =$

(A) 79
(B) 80
(C) 81
(D) 82
(E) 83

3. $10,000 + (3 \times 10^2) =$

(A) 4,000
(B) 10,003
(C) 10,030
(D) 10,300
(E) 13,000

3. $(3x^3y^4)^4 =$

(A) $12x^4y^8$
(B) $27x^9y^8$
(C) $81x^7y^8$
(D) $81x^{12}y^{16}$
(E) $81x^{81}y^{256}$

3. $(3^2)^2 =$

(A) 18
(B) 27
(C) 81
(D) 729
(E) 6,561

3. $\dfrac{5^9}{5^3} =$

(A) 5^{27}

(B) 5^{12}

(C) 5^6

(D) 5^3

(E) 5

4. $(\sqrt{24})(\sqrt{3}) =$

(A) $3\sqrt{6}$

(B) $2\sqrt{24}$

(C) 6

(D) $4\sqrt{3}$

(E) $6\sqrt{2}$

5. If $a = 25$ and $b = 16$, then for what value of c will $\sqrt{a} + \sqrt{b} + \sqrt{c} = 15$?

(A) 9
(B) 16
(C) 25
(D) 36
(E) 49

6. If $a = 5$ and $b = 2$, then $a^2b - ab^2 + (ab)^2 =$

(A) 20
(B) 50
(C) 100
(D) 130
(E) 170

6. If w is a positive integer, then $(2w)^3 =$

(A) $2w^3$
(B) $4w^2$
(C) $8w$
(D) $8w^3$
(E) $16w$

6. $\sqrt{\dfrac{1}{4}} + \sqrt{\dfrac{1}{16}} + \sqrt{\dfrac{9}{4}} =$

   (A) $\dfrac{1}{4}$

   (B) $\dfrac{11}{16}$

   (C) $\dfrac{9}{4}$

   (D) $\dfrac{41}{16}$

   (E) $\dfrac{83}{16}$

7. If $x^{\frac{2}{3}} + 6 = 10$, what is the value of x ?

   (A)   4
   (B)   6
   (C)   8
   (D) 27
   (E) 64

8. $(-3a^2 b^5)^3$

   (A) $-3a^5b^8$
   (B) $-3a^6b^{15}$
   (C) $-27a^5b^8$
   (D) $-27a^6b^{15}$
   (E) $27a^6b^{15}$

9. If $a = 2$ and $b = 3$, then what does

   $a^2 + b^2 - \sqrt{a^2 b^2}$ equal?

   (A)   5
   (B)   6
   (C)   7
   (D) 13
   (E) 19

10. $(-\dfrac{3}{4})^k$ will be greatest for which of the following

   values of k ?

   (A) 5
   (B) 4
   (C) 3
   (D) 2
   (E) 1

10. If z is a positive integer, which of the following is equal to $2\sqrt{16z^2}$?

   (A) $\sqrt{32z^2}$

   (B) $12z$

   (C) $8z^2$

   (D) $8z$

   (E) $4z$

14. If $x > 0$, which of the following is equal to $(x^{\frac{1}{2}})(x^2)$?

   (A) $x^{\frac{1}{4}}$

   (B) $x^{\frac{2}{5}}$

   (C) x

   (D) $x^{\frac{3}{2}}$

   (E) $x^{\frac{5}{2}}$

18. If $64^{12} = 4^x$, then $x =$

   (A)   4
   (B) 24
   (C) 36
   (D) 72
   (E) 192

18. Let m and n represent positive integers such that $5\sqrt{80} = m\sqrt{n}$ and $m > n$. What is the value of $m - n$?

MATH

WRITING

READING

VOCABULARY

SETS

4. If set *A* is the set of single-digit prime integers, how many elements are in set *A* ?

(A) 3
(B) 4
(C) 5
(D) 6
(E) 7

6. If set *C* = {2, 4, 6, 8, 10} and set *D* consists of all positive odd integers less than 10, then how many elements do *C* and *D* have in common?

(A)   0
(B)   1
(C)   5
(D)   8
(E)   10

12. If set *Q* = {1, 2, 5, 10} and set *R* is the positive factors of 15, then *Q* and *R* have how many elements in common?

14. There are five elements in set *S* and four elements in set *T*. Set *U* is the union of sets *S* and *T*. What is the minimum number of elements in set *U* ?

(A) 0
(B) 1
(C) 4
(D) 5
(E) 9

16. For sets *F* and *G*, if the union of sets *F* and *G* is the set of all positive factors of 36 and set *F* = {2, 3, 6, 9, 18}, then which of the following could be set *G* ?

(A) {36}
(B) {2, 4, 12, 36}
(C) {4, 12}
(D) {4, 12, 36}
(E) {1, 4, 12, 36}

MATH

WRITING

READING

VOCABULARY

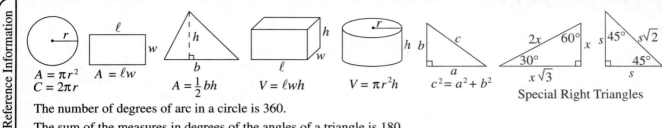

$A = \pi r^2$
$C = 2\pi r$

$A = \ell w$

$A = \frac{1}{2} bh$

$V = \ell wh$

$V = \pi r^2 h$

$c^2 = a^2 + b^2$

Special Right Triangles

The number of degrees of arc in a circle is 360.

The sum of the measures in degrees of the angles of a triangle is 180.

Reference Information

RIGHT TRIANGLES

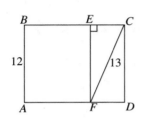

9. In the figure above, *ABCD* is a rectangle. What is the area of $\triangle ECF$?

(A)   5
(B)   30
(C)   65
(D)   78
(E)   156

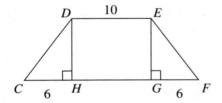

11. In the figure above, the area of rectangle *HDEG* is 80. What is the perimeter of quadrilateral *CDEF* ?

(A)   10
(B)   24
(C)   52
(D)   68
(E)   128

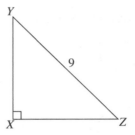

13. In $\triangle XYZ$ above, if $\angle Z = 45°$, what is the area of the triangle?

(A) $\dfrac{9\sqrt{2}}{2}$

(B) $\dfrac{81}{4}$

(C) $\dfrac{81}{2}$

(D) $\dfrac{81\sqrt{2}}{2}$

(E)   81

16. If the point (4, 3) lies on a circle with center at (0, 0), what is the area of the circle?

(A) 9π
(B) 10π
(C) 16π
(D) 25π
(E) 49π

TRIG? WHO NEEDS IT?

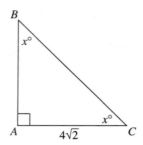

8. In △ABC, what is the length of $\overline{BC}$?

(A) 2

(B) 4

(C) $4\sqrt{2}$

(D) 8

(E) $8\sqrt{2}$

11. A straight ladder leaning against a wall creates a 30° angle with the wall. If the distance from the base of the ladder to the base of the wall is 7, what is the length of the ladder?

(A)   2
(B)   7
(C)   14
(D)   21
(E)   49

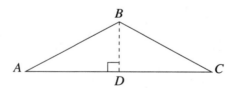

14. What is the perimeter of the isosceles triangle ABC shown above if the measure of ∠ABC is 120° and BD = 2 ?

(A) $4 + 4\sqrt{3}$

(B)   12

(C) $8 + 4\sqrt{3}$

(D) $8 + 8\sqrt{3}$

(E)   24

14. A rock climber stands on level ground, 100 feet from the base of a vertical cliff. The climber holds a taut rope that extends from the top of the cliff to the ground. If the rope makes an angle of 60° with the ground, how high is the cliff?

(A)   100 feet

(B) $100\sqrt{2}$ feet (approximately 141.42 feet)

(C) $100\sqrt{3}$ feet (approximately 173.20 feet)

(D)   200 feet

(E)   500 feet

14. In square WXYZ (not shown), YZ = 3. What is XZ ?

(A) $3\sqrt{2}$

(B) $3\sqrt{3}$

(C) 6

(D) $6\sqrt{2}$

(E) 9

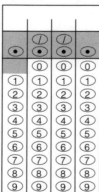

18. The triangle and the square shown above have equal areas. If AC = 5, what is EG ?

FOUR OR MORE SIDES?

5. If the sum of the measures of the interior angles of a certain polygon is 540°, how many sides does the polygon have?

    (A) 3
    (B) 4
    (C) 5
    (D) 6
    (E) 7

18. The sum of the degree measures of the interior angles of a 10-sided polygon is how much greater than the sum of the degree measures of those in a 9-sided polygon?

13. A certain equilateral polygon has 2 interior angles that add up to 240°. How many sides does the polygon have?

    (A) 6
    (B) 7
    (C) 8
    (D) 9
    (E) 10

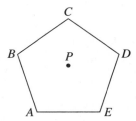

14. The pentagon above has equal sides and equal angles with point P in the center. What is the measure of angle APB ?

    (A) 54
    (B) 72
    (C) 96
    (D) 108
    (E) 124

16. If all the interior angles in hexagon JKLMNO are equal, what is the sum of the degree measures of any two of the interior angles?

    (A) 90
    (B) 120
    (C) 180
    (D) 240
    (E) 720

USING DATA

Package	Included	Price for first day	Price per day after first day
Snowboard only	1 snowboard	$15	$12
Snowboard package	1 snowboard, 1 pair of goggles	$20	$15
Skis only	1 pair of skis	$18	$15
Ski package	1 pair each of skis, boots, and poles	$22	$18

18. The chart above shows the rental prices for various combinations of equipment at a rental shop. A family rents equipment for 5 days. If the family rents 2 snowboards, 3 pairs of skis, and 3 pairs of boots, what is the least amount the family could pay to rent this equipment?

(A) $390
(B) $408
(C) $420
(D) $442
(E) $480

PERCENT OF LAND BY CATEGORY

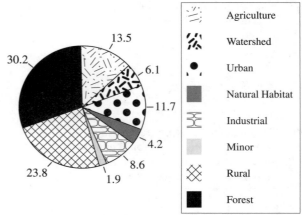

7. What is the approximate ratio of watershed land to rural land?

(A) 10:1
(B) 4:1
(C) 2:1
(D) 1:4
(E) 1:6

POPULATION IN COUNTRY *A* AND COUNTRY *B*

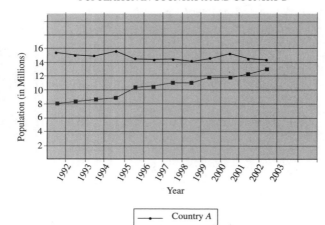

5. Of the following, which is the closest to the number of people living in country *B* in 1998 ?

(A) 20,000,000
(B) 14,000,000
(C) 11,000,000
(D) 1,200,000
(E) 110,000

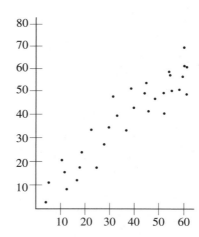

13. Which of the following best approximates the slope of the line that best fits the scatterplot above?

(A) –5
(B) –1
(C) 0
(D) 1
(E) 5

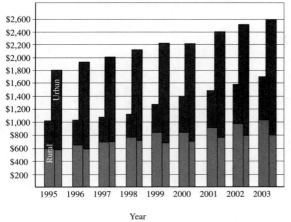

AVERAGE ANNUAL TOTAL CHARGES FOR PROGRAM FEES
AT AMERICAN OVERNIGHT CAMPS 1995–2003

■ Room & Board
■ Program Fee

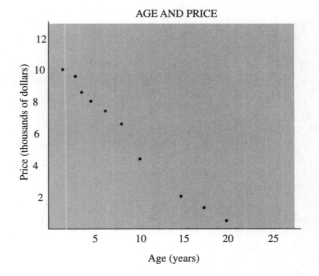

AGE AND PRICE

18. For the program year in which charges for room and board at rural camps was most nearly equal to $1,100, what was the approximate charge for the program fee at the urban camp?

(A) $2,650
(B) $1,800
(C) $1,025
(D) $980
(E) $895

12. The graph above shows the price and age for each of 10 cars of a certain model made by the Drive-o-Matic company. Which of the following is the best approximation for the price of a car that is 10 years old?

(A) $550
(B) $1,000
(C) $4,000
(D) $5,500
(E) $10,000

ENROLLMENT LAST YEAR AT GROVETON HIGH SCHOOL

Class	Total Number of Students in Class	Number of Students Who Passed Chemistry
Junior	80	42
Senior	70	30

18. All of the students who took chemistry last year at Groveton High School were juniors or seniors as shown in the chart above. If 80% of the students who took chemistry passed, what fraction of the students in the combined junior and senior classes took chemistry?

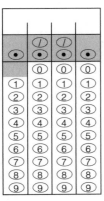

CONTENT REVIEW
EXPLANATIONS

WORKING WITH EQUATIONS

i. **3**   Isolate the variable by subtracting 6 from both sides. This gives you $x = 3$.

ii. $\dfrac{7}{4}$ Before we can isolate the variable, we need to distribute the 11 on the right side of the equation. This creates the equation $33 = 44x - 44$. Add 44 to both sides to get $77 = 44x$, and divide both sides by 44 to get $x = \dfrac{77}{44}$, which reduces to $x = \dfrac{7}{4}$.

iii. **56**   In order to add fractions, you must have a common denominator. Since the lowest common denominator for these fractions is 8, you can rewrite the equation as $\dfrac{4}{8}x + \dfrac{2}{8}x + \dfrac{1}{8}x = 49$. This simplifies to $\dfrac{7}{8}x = 49$. To isolate x, multiply each side by the reciprocal of $\dfrac{7}{8}$ to obtain $x = 49 \cdot \dfrac{8}{7}$, or $x = 56$.

1. **D**   Cross multiply! The problem becomes $3x = 24(4)$, or $3x = 96$. Divide each side by 3 to get $x = 32$, or (D).

2. **A**   Don't let those parentheses throw you off! Adding can be done in any order, so $(a + 3) + b = 0$ is the same thing as $a + 3 + b = 0$. Since the question wants the value of $a + b$, we can subtract 3 from each side to get $a + b = -3$, or (A). If you are at all wary, you can always plug in. Let's assume $a = 2$. Substituting that value into our original equation yields $(2 + 3) + b = 0$, or $5 + b = 0$. Subtracting 5 from each side tells us that $b = -5$. Therefore, $a + b = 2 + (-5) = -3$, or (A).

3. **C**   This is really a vocabulary question, so if you know that sum means add, you're okay! Our equation will read $(q - 6) + (q - 3) + q = 0$, which we can then simplify by combining like terms to $3q - 9 = 0$. Add 9 from each side to get $3q = 9$, and then divide each side by 3 for $q = 3$, or (C).

3. **C**   This problem becomes a lot simpler to solve when you realize that both sides can be written as fractions in order to cross multiply. Rewriting the equation in this way yields $\dfrac{400}{100(x+3)} = \dfrac{4}{1}$, which then turns into $400(1) = 100(x + 3)(4)$. Simplify this equation to read $400 = 400x + 1{,}200$ and subtract 1,200 from both sides for $-800 = 400x$. Finally, divide both sides by 400 to get $x = -2$, or (C). Don't forget that you can also Plug In The Answers! If $x = -2$, then the left side simplifies to 4, so that's the right answer.

4. **E**   You start solving this equation like any other: Combine like terms by subtracting $2z$ from both sides to get $3z = 10$. Now you could solve for z and then find the value of $9z$. However, like many SAT problems, this one can be done more simply. All you need to do is multiply both sides by 3 to get $9z = 30$, or (E).

4. **A**   Another lovely cross multiplication problem! Multiply diagonally across the equal sign to get $7(4) = (x + 4)(9)$, then simplify the expression to read $28 = 9x + 36$. Subtract 36 from both sides to get $-8 = 9x$, then divide both sides by 9 to find that $x = -\dfrac{8}{9}$, or (A).

10. **A**   Confused? If so, it's time to Plug In! Let's assume $r = 4$, in which case $r + 3 = 4 + 3 = 7$. The problem says that the smaller of the two integers is multiplied by 3 and then subtracted from the other integer. That means you should multiply $4 \times 3 = 12$, and then subtract it from 7 to get $7 - 12 = -5$. So, -5 is our target. With this target in mind, we can go straight to the answer choices, Plug In $r = 4$, and find the one that gives us the target. Only one answer choice gives us -5 when $r = 4$, so the correct answer must be (A).

14. **E**   Start solving this equation by adding 4 to both sides of the equation and converting to an improper fraction. This gives you $\dfrac{8y}{3} = \dfrac{25}{6}$, an equation you can solve by cross multiplication. Multiplying diagonally across the equal sign yields $8y(6) = 3(25)$, or $48y = 75$. Isolate the variable by dividing both sides by 48 to get $y = \dfrac{75}{48}$ which reduces to $\dfrac{25}{16}$. But if that's the value of y, why isn't (B) the correct answer? Because the value of y is not what the question asked you for! We need the value of $\dfrac{1}{y}$, which is equal to $\dfrac{16}{25}$, or (E).

© TPR Education IP Holdings, LLC

SIMULTANEOUS EQUATIONS

8. **A**   Stack the equations on top of each other and subtract the second equation from the first.

$$3x + 2y = 7$$
$$-(2x + 2y = 9)$$
$$\overline{x = -2}$$

Since the y variable cancels out, you're left with $x = -2$, or (A).

11. **C**   Stack the equations on top of each other and combine like terms by subtracting the first equation from the second.

$$2x - y = -11$$
$$-(-x - y = -2)$$
$$\overline{3x = -9}$$

Since the question wants the value of x, divide each side of the equation by 3 to get $x = -3$, or (C).

12. **B**   This equation looks odd because of the way it is written. However, you can separate it into two different equations, both equal to 25. At that point, you solve the system exactly the same way by stacking the equations on top of each other. Look for a way to combine the equations that results in the expression you want. In this case, adding does the trick.

$$2x + 3y = 25$$
$$+(3x - 3y = 25)$$
$$\overline{5x = 50}$$

Since the y variable cancels out, you're left with $5x = 50$, which simplifies to $x = 10$, or (B).

13. **E**   The first sentence says "twice the sum of the three numbers," so $2(x + y + z) = 21$. Eliminate (A), (C), and (D). The next one says that the smallest number, z, is subtracted from the product of the other two. So $xy - z = 32$, answer (E).

14. **E**   Stack the equations on top of each other and subtract the second equation from the first.

$$6j - 5k = 11$$
$$-(5j - 6k = -22)$$
$$\overline{j + k = 33}$$

In this problem, the question asks for the value of $2j + 2k$, so you need to multiply both sides by 2 to get $2j + 2k = 66$, or (E).

14. **B**   In this problem, there are three variables but only two equations. No worries! Just fill in the missing variable in each equation with a 0 coefficient. Then, stack the equations on top of each other and subtract the first equation from the second to get the expression you want.

$$
\begin{array}{r}
3a + 0b + c = 13 \\
- (2a + b + 0c = 6 \\
\hline
a - b + c = 7
\end{array}
$$

This gives you $a - b + c = 7$, or (B).

15. **C**   Even though the problem gives you three equations, start at the beginning and work on two at a time. Stack the first two equations on top of each other and subtract the second equation from the first.

$$
\begin{array}{r}
4r + 3s = 7 \\
-(2r + s = 1) \\
\hline
2r + 2s = 6
\end{array}
$$

At this point, turn your attention to the third equation provided in the problem, $2r + 2s = t - 4$. Since our first two equations simplified to tell us $2r + 2s = 6$, we can substitute this value into the third equation to get $6 = t - 4$. Add 4 to both sides, and you find $t = 10$, or (C).

EXPONENTS AND ROOTS

2. **B**   If $q^2 = 81$, then q could equal either 9 or –9. Substitute each of these values into the expression provided. Since $(9 - 1)(9 + 1) = (8)(10) = 80$, the answer is (B).

3. **D**   Order of operations tells us to take care of the multiplication before the addition, so let's first simplify 3×10^2. This is equal to 3×100, or 300. The final step is $10,000 + 300 = 10,300$, or (D).

3. **D**   To simplify the expression $(3x^3y^4)^4$, you need to raise each term inside the parentheses to the fourth power. So the expression becomes $3^4(x^3)^4(y^4)^4$. When raising a number or expression with an exponent to a power, you multiply the exponents. So the final expression should be written as $81x^{12}y^{16}$, or (D).

3. **C**   Start inside the parentheses to find that $3^3 = 9$. Now, square the 9 to get $9^2 = 81$, or (C).

3. **C**   When dividing two exponent expressions with the same base, you subtract the exponents. So $5^9 \; 5^3 = 5^{9-3} = 5^6$, or (C).

4. **E**   Plug this one into your calculator. Make sure you're careful with your parentheses.

MATH

WRITING

READING

VOCABULARY

5. **D** Plug In! Values for a and b are given, so we can substitute them into the equation provided to get $\sqrt{25} + \sqrt{16} + \sqrt{c} = 15$. Simplify the square roots to get $5 + 4 + \sqrt{c} = 15$, or $9 + \sqrt{c} = 15$. Subtract 9 from both sides for $\sqrt{c} = 6$, and square both sides to get rid of the radical. The final answer is $c = 36$, or (D).

6. **D** Plug In! Again, substitute the values provided for a and b into the expression, and you will get $(5)^2(2) - (5)(2)^2 + (5 \times 2)^2 = 25(2) - 5(4) + 10^2 = 50 - 20 + 100 = 130$, or (D).

6. **D** When raising a number with an exponent to a power, you multiply the exponents together. So this final expression can be rewritten as $2^3 w^3$, which equals $8w^3$, or (D). If you are at all uncertain, feel free to Plug In a value for w. Let's assume $w = 3$. The expression would then become $(2 \times 3)^3 = 6^3 = 216$. When you look for this target in the answer choices, the only option that will work is (D).

6. **C** Another job for the calculator. You should get $0.5 + 0.25 + 1.5 = 2.25$, answer (C).

7. **C** First, let's simplify. Subtract 6 from both sides, and we get $x^{\frac{2}{3}} = 4$. Now Plug In The Answers. (C) is the only answer that works.

8. **D** You can Plug In for both a and b. If you do it algebraically, make sure you distribute the exponent to each part of the problem. $(-3)^3 = -27$, so eliminate (A), (B), and (E). The next term would be $(a^2)^3$, which is a^6, so it must be (D).

9. **C** Plug In ... AGAIN! Substitute the values provided for a and b into the equation, and you will get $(2)^2 + (3)^2 - \sqrt{(2)^2(3)^2} = 4 + 9 - \sqrt{4 \times 9} = 13 - 6 = 7$, or (C).

10. **D** Since the question is asking for the value of k which will make the expression $\left(-\dfrac{3}{4}\right)^k$ the greatest, Plug In The Answers. A negative number raised to an odd exponent will always be negative, so we can eliminate (A), (C), and (E). Negative numbers raised to even exponents will always be positive, and positive numbers are always greater than negative numbers. Between $k = 4$ and $k = 2$, we can eliminate (B) because the higher the power to which a fraction is being raised, the smaller the fraction becomes. That leaves only one answer choice, (D).

10. **D**   To simplify the expression under the radical, put each term under its own radical. Doing so turns $2\sqrt{16z^2}$ into $2\sqrt{16}\sqrt{z^2}$, and makes it easier to see that the different terms reduce to $2(4)(z) = 8z$, or (D).

14. **E**   Variables in the answers means Plug In. Say $x = 4$. We get $2 \times 16 = 32$. Now Plug In $x = 4$ and see which answer gives you 32. Only (E) works.

18. **C**   There are two approaches to this problem. If you recognize that 64 can be rewritten as 4^3, you can substitute that into the equation to get $(4^3)^{12} = 4^x$. Since a number with an exponent is being raised to a power, you multiply the exponents to get $4^{36} = 4^x$, which tells you $x = 36$ or (C). Alternatively, you can plug the values from the answer choices in for x until you find the one that matches the value of 64^{12}. Just use your calculator! Either option will yield the same answer of (C).

18. **15**   Because $m > n$, we must simplify the $\left(\sqrt{80}\right)$ term, which becomes $\left(\sqrt{16} \times \sqrt{5}\right)$, or $4\sqrt{5}$.

Taking the initial coefficient of "5" into account, the term then becomes $5 \times 4\sqrt{5}$, or $20\sqrt{5}$.

Now, $m = 20$, and $n = 5$. Therefore, $m - n = 20 - 5$, or 15.

SETS

4. **B**   List all the single-digit prime integers: 2, 3, 5, and 7. Do not include 1 in this list because 1 is not prime. Therefore, set A is comprised of 4 elements, or (B).

6. **A**   Start by listing the elements of set D = {1, 3, 5, 7, 9}. Since no numbers appear in both set C and set D, the answer is 0, or (A).

12. **2**   We need to list all the positive factors of 15: set R = {1, 3, 5, 15}. Both set Q and set R include 1 and 5, so they have two elements in common.

14. **D**   Union refers to the result of combining all the elements of two different sets to make a new set. Since we know nothing at all about the sets, let's plug in values. Let's assume set S = {1, 2, 3, 4, 5} and set T = {6, 7, 8, 9}. The union of those sets would be {1, 2, 3, 4, 5, 6, 7, 8, 9}. But is that the MINIMUM number of elements possible? What if set T = {1, 2, 3, 4} instead? In that case, the union is {1, 2, 3, 4, 5}. It wouldn't be possible to make the union any smaller because all the elements of set S have to be included. So the answer must be 5, or (D).

16. **E** The union of sets F and G is $\{1, 2, 3, 4, 6, 9, 12, 18, 36\}$, the positive factors of 36. Since the union of two sets is a new set which includes all of the distinct elements from both sets, any element in the union that is not in set F must be in set G. The missing elements from set F are 1, 4, 12, and 36, or (E). Notice that you could have chosen (E) as soon as you realized that set G must contain 1.

RIGHT TRIANGLES

9. **B** Since $ABCD$ is a rectangle, we know that $\overline{EF}$ will have a length of 12. For triangle ECF, we know $EF = 12$ and the hypotenuse $CF = 13$, so by using the Pythagorean theorem we can determine that $EC = 5$. The question asks for the area of triangle ECF, and the formula for area of a triangle is $A = \dfrac{1}{2}\,bh$, so substitute in these values and solve: $A = \dfrac{1}{2}(12)(5) = 30$, or (B).

11. **C** According to the problem, the area of rectangle $HDEG$ is 80. Since the formula for area of a rectangle is $A = lw$, and the length is given as 10, we can calculate that $80 = 10w$, or $w = 8$. Therefore, for triangle EFG, the two sides are 8 and 6. Plug these values into the Pythagorean theorem to determine that the hypotenuse is equal to 10. Triangle EFG is identical to triangle DCH, so transfer the values onto the opposite side of the diagram. The final question asks for the perimeter of the quadrilateral $CDEF$. Add away! The perimeter equals $10 + 10 + 10 + 6 + 10 + 6 = 52$, or (C).

13. **B** Since we've got a 45°-45°-90° triangle, solve for the missing sides. $a\sqrt{2} = 9$, so each leg of the triangle must be $\dfrac{9}{\sqrt{2}}$. Now plug this into the formula for the area of triangle, and you'll get $\dfrac{81}{4}$, which is 20.25, answer (B).

MATH

WRITING

READING

VOCABULARY

16. **D**   If (4, 3) is a point on the circle, and the circle's center is at (0, 0), the line connecting these two points would be the radius of the circle. To determine the value of the radius, we need to find out the distance between the points. Graph the points and create a triangle in the coordinate plane.

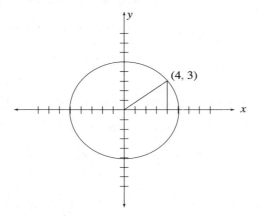

We know that the distance along the base of the triangle is 4 (since the *x* values go from 0 to 4) and the height is 3 (since the *y* values go up from 0 to 3). Using the Pythagorean theorem, we calculate that the hypotenuse is 5. However, the question asks for the area of the circle. If $r = 5$, and the formula for area of a circle is $A = \pi r^2$, then $A = \pi(5)^2 = 25\pi$, or (D).

TRIG? WHO NEEDS IT!

8. **D**   Since the diagram provided is a right triangle with two equal angles, we have a 45°-45°-90° right triangle. In these triangles, the hypotenuse is always the measure of the side times $\sqrt{2}$. Since the length of side $\overline{AC}$ is given as $4\sqrt{2}$, we can calculate that hypotenuse $BC = (4\sqrt{2})(\sqrt{2}) = 8$, or (D).

11. **C**   Draw it! If the ladder creates a 30° angle with the wall, that means it creates a 60° angle with the ground. What do you know—we have a 30°-60°-90° right triangle! Since the side opposite the 30° angle is 7 (the distance from the base of the ladder to the wall), the hypotenuse (ladder, in this case) is double that side. That means it has to be 14, or (C).

14. **C**   Since triangle ABC is isosceles and the measure of $\angle ABC = 120$, each of the angles BAC and BCA measure 30°. Line segment $\overline{BD}$ bisects angle ABC and creates two 30°-60°-90° right triangles. For triangle ABD, the long side, AB, is twice the short side, BD. So, $AB = 4$. To find the length of $\overline{AD}$, multiply the short side, BD, by $\sqrt{3}$ to get $AD = 2\sqrt{3}$. Since $DC = AD$ and $BC = AB$, the total perimeter is $8 + 4\sqrt{3}$, or (C).

MATH

WRITING

READING

VOCABULARY

14. **C** Draw it! If the rope creates a 60° angle with the ground, it creates a 30° angle with the cliff. That means we have a 30°-60°-90° right triangle. Since the side opposite the 30° angle has length 100 (the distance the climber stands from the base of the cliff), the height of the cliff is the other side of the triangle. As such, the height of the cliff is equal to the short side times $\sqrt{3}$, which works out to be $100\sqrt{3}$, or (C).

14. **A** Since the question asks about the diagonal of a square, we know that we have a 45°-45°-90° right triangle. In these triangles, the hypotenuse is always the measure of the side times $\sqrt{2}$. Since the length of $\overline{AC}$ is given as 3, we can calculate that hypotenuse $XZ = 3\sqrt{2}$, or (A).

18. **5** Start by writing down the formulas for the area of a square, $A = s^2$, and for the area of a triangle, $A = \frac{1}{2}bh$. To find the area of the square, find the length of a side of the square. Diagonal $\overline{AC}$ creates two 45°-45°-90° right triangles. To get from the hypotenuse to the side in such a triangle, divide by $\sqrt{2}$, giving you $\frac{5}{\sqrt{2}}$ as the side of the square. Using the formula $A = s^2$ we plug in $\frac{5}{\sqrt{2}}$ for s to find that $A = \left(\frac{5}{\sqrt{2}}\right)^2 = \frac{25}{2}$. This is also the area of triangle EFG, which is also a 45°-45°-90° right triangle because it has two angles marked x in addition to a 90° angle. Because a 45°-45°-90° right triangle has two sides equal in length, the formula for the area of the triangle can be written as $A = \frac{1}{2}s^2$. For triangle EFG, $\frac{25}{2} = \frac{1}{2}s^2$. So, s equals the square root of 25, or 5.

FOUR OR MORE SIDES

5. **C**   The angles inside a triangle add up to 180°, and every time you add another side to your figure, you have to add another 180° to the sum of the interior angles. So, the angles in a four-sided figure add to 360°, and those in five-sided figure add to 540°. Therefore, the polygon referred to in the question must be a pentagon, which has 5 sides, or (C).

8. **180**   Every time you add another side to your figure, you must add 180° to the sum of the interior angles. So since we're talking about a 9-sided figure and a 10-sided figure, whatever the sum of the interior angles in each, the 10-sided figure has one side, and therefore 180°, more than the 9-sided figure.

13. **B**   If the polygon has 2 interior angles that add up to 240°, then each interior angle must be 120°. Start adding up sides to see which polygon gives you 120° angles. A 6-sided figure would have 720° total, so each angle would be 120°.

14. **B**   Each angle in the pentagon is 540 ÷ 5 = 108°. Draw triangle APB. Angles A and B are each half of 108°, so together they are 108°. The remaining angle is 180° − 108° = 72°, answer (B).

16. **D**   The sum of the interior angles of a hexagon is 720°. Since the problem states that all the interior angles are equal, divide 720° by 6 to find that each angle measures 120°. The sum of two of these angles is 120° + 120° = 240°, or (D).

USING DATA

18. **B**   Unfortunately there is no faster way to approach this problem than to just try different combinations of packages from the chart. Ultimately you will hit upon the cheapest combination: two snowboard-only packages at $63 each ($15 for the first day and $12 for each of the 4 subsequent days) plus three ski packages at $94 each ($22 for the first day and $18 for each of the 4 subsequent days). This totals $408, or (B). And yes, you get the poles anyway.

5. **C**   The trick to this question is making sure you are reading the right line on the graph. Country B is represented on the graph by the line with squares on it. Find the line for 1998 on the graph to see where the line with squares intersects the line for 1998. The point of intersection is at 11,000,000, or (C).

7. **D**   To find the ratio of watershed land to rural land, find each category on the chart and set it up as a fraction. The chart tells us that 6.1 percent of the land is watershed, and 23.8 percent is rural, so the ratio would be $\dfrac{6.1}{23.8}$. This is about equal to $\dfrac{6}{24} = \dfrac{1}{4}$, or (D).

13. **D**   Ballpark to eliminate obviously wrong answer choices. The line of best fit has a positive slope, which eliminates (A), (B), and (C). A line with a slope of 5 would be very steep and close to the y-axis. As the scatterplot does not do this, we can eliminate (E). All that remains is (D).

18. **B**   The first challenge to this problem is locating which year room and board at rural camps was most nearly equal to $1,100. The only year in which the light grey bar goes up to $1,100 for rural camps was 2003, so that is the year we need to examine more closely. The question asks for the program fee at the urban camp, and most people want to circle (A) at this point. But the dark grey column does not start from $0 and go up to $2,600. Rather, it starts at $800. So the actual cost for the program fee would be the difference between these two values, $2,600 − $800 = $1,800, or (B).

18. $\dfrac{9}{15}$ According to the chart, 72 students passed chemistry. Those 72 students are 80 percent of all the students who took chemistry. So, the question becomes: "72 is 80 percent of what?" Now, translate this question into $72 = \dfrac{80}{100}x$. Therefore, $x = 90$. To find the fraction of all students in the combined classes who took chemistry, use the chart to find that there are 150 students in the combined classes. So, that's $\dfrac{90}{150}$, $\dfrac{9}{15}$, or $\dfrac{3}{5}$.

12. **C**   On the graph, the x-axis indicates the age of the car. So looking at $x = 10$, the closest dot on the graph is just above 4,000, or (C).

WRITING

SAT WRITING: GRAMMAR AND ESSAY

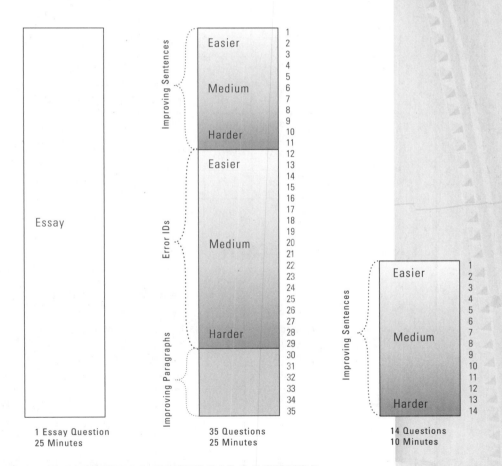

Essay		
1 Essay Question 25 Minutes	35 Questions 25 Minutes	14 Questions 10 Minutes

Improving Sentences — Easier, Medium, Harder (1–11)

Error IDs — Easier, Medium, Harder (12–29)

Improving Paragraphs (30–35)

Improving Sentences — Easier, Medium, Harder (1–14)

HOW IS THE WRITING SECTION SCORED?

The scaled Writing Section score (200–800) is derived from two components: the essay score and the multiple-choice grammar score. Two different people grade your essay, and each gives it a score on a scale of 1–6. The sum of these two scores is weighted to make the essay score worth approximately 30 percent of the total score; then the result is added to your grammar raw score to get your final Writing score.

Writing Scores

Grammar Score (Raw Points)	Essay Score						
	12	10	8	6	4	2	0
80 (49)	800	800	790	750	720	690	680
75 (47)	800	770	730	690	670	640	620
70 (45)	750	710	670	640	610	580	570
65 (42)	710	680	640	600	580	550	530
60 (38)	670	640	600	560	540	510	490
55 (33)	630	590	550	520	490	460	450
50 (28)	590	560	520	480	460	430	410
45 (22)	540	510	470	430	410	380	360
40 (16)	500	470	430	400	370	340	330
35 (10)	460	430	390	350	330	300	280
30 (5)	420	390	350	320	290	260	250
25 (2)	370	340	300	270	240	210	200
20 (−1)	320	290	250	210	200	200	200

Grammar Pacing Chart

To get: (scaled score)	You need: (raw points)	Answer this many questions		Total # of questions to attempt
		35-question section	14-question section	
35	10	10	5	15
40	16	13	7	20
45	22	18	8	26
50	28	22	9	31
55	33	26	10	36
60	38	27	11	38
65	42	31	all	45
70	45	all	all	49
75	47	all	all	49
80	49	all	all	49

 © TPR Education IP Holdings, LLC

SAT ESSAY:
HOW IT'S GRADED

UNDERSTANDING HOW GRADERS LOOK AT YOUR ESSAY

Learning to think like an ETS grader will help you improve your essay score. If you learn what graders look for and how they score essays, you can figure out how to improve your own essays. Start getting inside the graders' minds by reading the ETS Scoring Guidelines and sample scored essays. Next, find out how well you understand the scoring standards by grading some unscored essays.

MATH

WRITING

READING

VOCABULARY

ETS'S ESSAY SCORING GUIDELINES

Score of 6	Score of 5	Score of 4
An essay in this category is **outstanding**, demonstrating **clear and consistent mastery**, although it may have a few minor errors. A typical essay • effectively and insightfully develops a point of view on the issue and demonstrates outstanding critical thinking, using **clearly appropriate** examples, reasons, and other evidence to support its position • is **well organized and clearly focused**, demonstrating **clear coherence** and a smooth progression of ideas • exhibits **skillful use of language**, using a varied, accurate, and apt vocabulary • demonstrates **meaningful variety** in sentence structure • is free of most errors in grammar, usage, and mechanics	An essay in this category is **effective**, demonstrating **reasonably consistent mastery**, although it will have occasional errors or lapses in quality. A typical essay • effectively develops a point of view on the issue and demonstrates strong critical thinking, **generally using appropriate examples**, reasons, and other evidence to support its position • is **well organized and focused**, demonstrating **coherence** and progression of ideas • exhibits **facility in the use of language**, appropriate vocabulary • demonstrates **variety** in sentence structure • is generally free of most errors in grammar, usage, and mechanics	An essay in this category is **competent**, demonstrating **adequate mastery**, although it will have lapses in quality. A typical essay • develops a point of view on the issue and demonstrates competent critical thinking, using **adequate examples**, reasons, and other evidence to support its position • is **generally organized and focused**, demonstrating some coherence and progression of ideas • exhibits **adequate but inconsistent facility in the use of language**, using generally appropriate vocabulary • demonstrates **some variety** in sentence structure • has some errors in grammar, usage, and mechanics
Score of 3	**Score of 2**	**Score of 1**
An essay in this category is **inadequate**, but demonstrates **developing mastery**, and is marked by one or more of the following weaknesses: • develops a point of view on the issue, demonstrating some critical thinking, but may do so inconsistently or use **inadequate examples**, reasons, or other evidence to support its position • is **limited in its organization or focus**, but may demonstrate some lapses in coherence or progression of ideas • displays **developing facility in the use of language**, but sometimes uses weak vocabulary or inappropriate word choice • **lacks variety** or demonstrates problems in sentence structure • contains an accumulation of errors in grammar, usage, and mechanics	An essay in this category is **seriously limited**, demonstrating little mastery, and is flawed by one or more of the following weaknesses: • develops a point of view on the issue that is **vague or seriously limited**, demonstrating weak critical thinking, providing inappropriate or insufficient examples, reasons, or other evidence to support its position • is **poorly organized and/or focused**, or demonstrates serious problems with coherence or progression of ideas • displays **very little facility in the use of language**, using very limited vocabulary or incorrect word choice • demonstrates **frequent problems** in sentence structure • contains errors in grammar, usage, and mechanics so serious that meaning is somewhat obscured	An essay in this category is **fundamentally lacking**, demonstrating very little or no mastery, and is severely flawed by one or more of the following weaknesses: • develops **no viable point of view** on the issue, or provides little or **no evidence** to support its position • is **disorganized or unfocused**, resulting in a disjointed or incoherent essay • displays fundamental **errors in vocabulary** • demonstrates **severe flaws** in sentence structure • contains pervasive errors in grammar, usage, or mechanics that persistently interfere with meaning
Score of 0		
Essays not written on the essay assignment will receive a score of zero.		

SAMPLE ESSAYS

Read each of the following essays and try to explain why each received the score it did from SAT graders. Here are the instructions to test takers.

The essay gives you an opportunity to show how effectively you can develop and express ideas. You should, therefore, take care to develop your point of view, present your ideas logically and clearly, and use language precisely.

Your essay must be written on the lines provided on your answer sheet—you will receive no other paper on which to write. You will have enough space if you write on every line, avoid wide margins, and keep your handwriting to a reasonable size. Remember that people who are not familiar with your handwriting will read what you write. Try to write or print legibly for your readers.

You have twenty-five minutes to write an essay on the topic assigned below. DO NOT WRITE ON ANOTHER TOPIC. AN OFF-TOPIC ESSAY WILL RECEIVE A SCORE OF ZERO.

> The only way a government can function, and the only way a people's voice can be expressed, is through a process in which decisions are made by the majority. This is not a perfect way of controlling government, but the alternatives—decisions made by a minority, or by one person—are even worse.
>
> Adapted from Thomas Jefferson

Assignment: Is the opinion of the majority always right? Plan and write an essay in which you develop your point of view on this issue. Support your position with reasoning and examples taken from your reading, studies, experience, or observations.

YOU'RE THE GRADER!

On the next few pages you will find a series of essays. Give each a grade from 1 to 6, and be prepared to justify and discuss the grades you gave in class.

Essay A

Assignment: Is the opinion of the majority always right?

I believe that the opinion of the majority can be the wrong one. Just because many people believe something is right, does not make it right. The examples of the Nazis in World War II, The Scarlet Letter, and Lord of the Flies show this to be true.

One example in which the opinion of the majority was wrong is the Nazis in Germany during World War II. This group was following the orders of Adolf Hitler, who they thought was right. The Nazis did terrible things, such as kill innocent people, force people out of their homes and into concentration camps, and rape and pillage. If they had been individuals, certainly they would not have done these things. However, since they were following the majority, they committed deeds that were not right.

Another example of the majority being wrong is in the novel The Scarlet Letter. In this story, the young woman Hester Prynne is suspected of committing adultery. The townspeople decide that she should be punished, so she is made an outcast and must wear the letter "A" on her clothes so people will know she committed adultery. Actually,

Continue on the opposite side if necessary.

 © TPR Education IP Holdings, LLC

Hester did not commit adultery. The majority did not come up with the right conclusion and punished an innocent woman. This shows that the majority is not always right.

A final example that majority isn't always right is in the Lord of the Flies. In this novel, a group of boys becomes stranded on an island. As a group, they elect a leader to follow. Everyone has to follow this decision of the majority, but it eventually turns out to be a bad decision, causing a split in the group. Chaos follows. Had the boys not decided to go with the decision of the majority, they might have been happy and peaceful from the beginning. Clearly, the opinion of the majority was not the correct one in this situation.

The examples above show that the opinion of the majority can be wrong. If people would sometimes act as individuals and not part of a herd, they could make better decisions.

Grade: _____

Why: _____

_____

Essay B

Assignment: Is the opinion of the majority always right?

As citizens of the United States of America, we all possess basic freedoms and rights. All Americans have the ability to formulate beliefs based on their personal values and experiences. Some may formulate opinions that comply with the majority while other beliefs may deviate from that. Thus, the opinion of the majority can be considered a poor guide.

The presidential campaign of 2004 stirred quite a bit of controversy among supporters of both George Bush and John Kerry. Each presidential candidate had millions of proponents. In the end, George Bush won based on electoral college votes. However, just because Bush won, the entire nation did not sway their support to comply with our president. Many people continued to hold on to their beliefs which they had carefully formulated. For instance, one of my history teachers chose to deviate from the majority and stay true to his political values and beliefs. Clearly, not all citizens are forced to comply with the will of the many.

The opinion of the majority is shown in many situations outside the political realm. Hester Prynne, in Nathanial Hawthorne's _The Scarlet Letter_, exemplifies that the individual can remain apart from the community, but still do what is right. The majority looked down on Hester because she had committed adultery and wore the proof upon her bosom: a scarlet "A." Although she was frowned upon for her ignoble deeds, her daughter Pearl simply saw Hester as her mother; The views of society did not affect Pearl's love for her mother. When Hester removed her "A" in the forest, Pearl was greatly disturbed. Pearl knew Hester did not need to embrace the views of the town, because the majority simply did not understand the importance of acceptance.

Therefore, the opinion of the majority is a poor guide; we are all individuals.

Continue on the opposite side if necessary.

 © TPR Education IP Holdings, LLC

We are all free and able to formulate our own individual beliefs and exert them accordingly. People are sometimes condescended to, imprisoned, or killed for their beliefs, as in the cases of Columbus, Galileo, and Socrates, respectively. Were they wrong? No. The majority was wrong, and we should be glad they chose to ignore the majority.

Grade: _____

Why: _____

_____

Essay C

Assignment: Is the opinion of the majority always right?

I agree that the opinion of the majority is generally, 'a poor guide.' It is as true today as it was in 1492 — strong and intelligent leaders are needed to avoid mob rule. We are all slaves to our biases and prejudices and, in matters of importance, it takes clear, unbiased thinkers to overpower the majority. This theory can be proved by examining The Constitution of the United States and the Adventures of Huckelberry Finn by Mark Twain.

First, when America's Founding Fathers set forth to create The Constitution, they were very aware of the dangers of majority rule. Because of their studies, they new that a well run republic can't be a true democracy. Therefore, the created the "Electoral College" who would chose the President. Instead of being chosen directly by the people, the President is technically elected by a group of electors who are in turn chosen by their states. This was a ~~very~~ victory for the Anti-Federalists who wanted to guarantee each state had an equal voice and big states wouldn't dominate policies because of their numbers. This was challenged after the election of 2000 in which Al Gore won the popular vote and George W. Bush won the electoral vote. Whether you like Bush or not, you can agree that if the election was decided by majority, the

 © TPR Education IP Holdings, LLC

entire south and Midwest would be dominated by Northeast and West States. Thus, the Framers built a safeguard against majority rule into the Constitution because it is a poor guide.

Second, the Novel The Adventures of Huckelberry Finn by Mark Twain shows that the majority is not always right. Huck travels with an escaped slave named Jim. The majority of southerners (Huck's contemporaries) would have thought that Huck should report Jim. But, Huck was a strong individual and knew that slavery was wrong and Jim was a wise man who he could learn a lot from. Thus, Huck showed that the majority is often a poor guide.

In conclusion, through the examples of the electoral college and Huck Finn, I've shown that the majority is a poor guide. In the modern age, where pure democracy is easier to find, we all should remember the concers of our Founders and great authors and distrust the majority and make our own decisions.

Grade: _____

Why: _____

_____

Essay D

Assignment: Is the opinion of the majority always right?

The majority's opinion is not always a reliable, appropriate guide. In fact, in many instances, the viewpoint of the majority is incorrect and immoral. It is the opinion of the individual that matters most. This concept is evident in Nathaniel Hawthorne's The Scarlet Letter, the writings of Henry David Thoreau, and Mark Twain's The Adventures of Huckleberry Finn.

Consider the classic romantic novel The Scarlet Letter, whose protagonist, Hester Prynne, must endure isolation and humiliation from a Puritan society, because she committed adultery. However, through this ostracising, Hester is able to see the fallacies and inconsistencies of the larger Puritan community. She rises above their hypocritical beliefs and sees that their opinions are not ones that she shares. By developing her independence, Hester Prynne's experience demonstrates that the majority is not always right.

Similar to Hester's experiences are those of Henry David Thoreau, whose writings condemn immoral society and favor a life of solitude, independence, and reflection. Thoreau believed that a single voice was far greater than a majority's, and he encouraged individuals to escape from corrupt society, both physically and spiritually.

The life and works of Thoreau proves again that individual beliefs are better than the viewpoints of the majority.

A third example of the triumph of individuals over majority is in the great American novel Huck Finn. In this narrative, the young Huck chronicles his adventures along the Mississippi River. Throughout his experiences, he is constantly forced to question the morals that society has imposed on him. Huck eventually sees that society's - and thus the majority's - belief's are immoral and hypocritical, and he rejects them. Huck's moral education is an illustration of the power of individuality.

The examples of The Scarlet Letter, Henry David Thoreau, and Huck Finn prove that following the majority is not always the best path. If we can instead follow our own thoughts, we will find our true morals.

Grade: _____

Why: _____

_____

Essay E

Assignment: Is the opinion of the majority always right?

PICTURE THIS: IT'S THE MID-SEVENTEENTH CENTURY. THE SETTING IS A BUCOLIC VILLAGE SOMEWHERE IN MASSACHUSETTS. YOU ARE A YOUNG TEENAGE GIRL FROM A FAMILY RECENTLY ARRIVED IN TOWN. MAYBE YOU ARE QUITE STRIKING, AND THAT HAS AROUSED SOME MEN'S ATTENTION AND SOME WOMEN'S JEALOUSY. MAYBE BAD FORTUNE HAS COINCIDENTALLY OCCURED IN THE TOWN WITH YOUR ARRIVAL. WHATEVER THE VAGUE AND NEBULOUS REASONING, IMAGINE BEING WOKEN IN THE MIDDLE OF THE NIGHT BY AN ANGRY VILLAGE MOB. SOME VILLAGERS CARRY TORCHES, OTHERS PITCHFORKS, OR PLANKS OF WOOD. THEY DEMAND THAT YOU COME WITH THEM. THEY ACCUSE YOU OF WITCHCRAFT. THEIR EYES, WORDS TELL YOU THAT YOUR BLOOD IS TO BE SPILT. NOW I ASK YOU, DO YOU, CAN YOU, REASON WITH THEM?

THROUGHOUT HISTORY, INCIDENTS OF MOB RULE ABOUND. EVERYWHERE THAT RACISM OR PREJUDICE HAS EXISTED — AND WHERE HAS IT EVER NOT EXISTED? ONE CAN FIND INSTANCES WHERE PEOPLE HAVE FORSAKEN GOOD REASONING AND CALM LOGIC FOR BOILING HATRED, AND FEAR AND VIOLENCE. EVEN TODAY IN AN AGE OF POLITICAL CORRECTNESS AND TOLERANCE, ONE CAN FIND THAT SOCIAL OUTCASTS ARE OFTEN TREATED WITH CONTEMPT AND VIOLENCE BY THE MAJORITY. WHY IS THIS?

WHILE INDIVIDUALS LEFT TO THEIR OWN REASONING ARE QUITE CAPABLE OF SEPARATING FACTS FROM THEIR FEARS, LARGE GROUPS OF PEOPLE OFTEN FORSAKE FACTS AND FEED INTO EACH OTHER'S FEARS. IT IS AS IF THE FACT THAT SO MANY PEOPLE SHARE A FEAR THAT THIS FEAR IS STRENGTHENED AND MAGNIFIED. IT IS THEN NECESSARY FOR THESE PEOPLE TO FIND A CAUSE OF THE FEAR AND TO ELIMINATE IT. WHATEVER IS STRANGE TO THE MAJORITY IS A LIKELY TARGET.

 © TPR Education IP Holdings, LLC

MATH

WRITING

READING

VOCABULARY

It is no coincidence that the individuals singled out by the mob often have no power to stop the majority. Human nature has shown us that when individuals think and act as a group, the collective fears and desires win out over an individual's reasoning.

In the end, while an individual is capable of making an informed and rational decision, people as a whole are usually motivated by base fears and group desires. To protect the unfortunate individuals who may become the targets of a mob's fear, the power of the majority must be curbed.

Grade: _____

Why: _____

_____

MATH

WRITING

READING

VOCABULARY

Essay F

Assignment: Is the opinion of the majority always right?

History has shown that sometimes people can be misleaded. They do not have the point of view of what is right for the country. They see a good-looking figure and think that is what this country needs. The majority has been over-ruled for three reasons; the ability to make sacrifices, point of view, and lack of training.

The first reason that the majority is over-ruled is because of the ability to make sacrifices. Many events have occurred in history that the majority did not support. The First World War is an example. The people who made the decision knew their would be great loss of life, but they had to do it to protect the people.

The second reason that the majority is overruled is because of its point of view. Most people do not see the big picture. People with better judgement makes the choice for them. What people see is propoganda, designed to twist the truth.

The third reason that the majority is overruled is because of its lack of training. Government officials are trained to look past the propoganda and see the truth. People cannot do this and see only the misleading stories. Sometimes the past is not important, only the future.

Their are three reasons why the majority is overruled: the ability to make sacrifices, point of view, and lack of training. If the majority was heeded the germans might have won WWI. People are often led astray with misleading stories. The government can see through these stories with their extensive training.

Grade: _____

Why: _____

_____

Essays G through I are based on the following prompt.

The essay gives you an opportunity to show how effectively you can develop and express ideas. You should, therefore, take care to develop your point of view, present your ideas logically and clearly, and use language precisely.

Your essay must be written on the lines provided on your answer sheet—you will receive no other paper on which to write. You will have enough space if you write on every line, avoid wide margins, and keep your handwriting to a reasonable size. Remember that people who are not familiar with your handwriting will read what you write. Try to write or print legibly for your readers.

You have twenty-five minutes to write an essay on the topic assigned below. DO NOT WRITE ON ANOTHER TOPIC. AN OFF-TOPIC ESSAY WILL RECEIVE A SCORE OF ZERO.

When making a decision of minor importance, I have always found it advantageous to consider all the pros and cons. In vital matters, however, such as the choice of a mate or profession, the decision is by necessity limited, and rightly so: the decision should come from the unconscious, from somewhere within ourselves.

Adapted from Sigmund Freud

Assignment: Is having a large number of options preferable to having a small number of options? Plan and write an essay in which you develop your point of view on this issue. Support your position with reasoning and examples taken from your reading, studies, experience, or observations.

Essay G

Assignment: Is having a large number of options preferable to having a small number of options?

Having a large number of options does not make people happy because happiness depends on whether one gets what he or she needs. In order to illustrate this view, the examples of "Romeo and Juliet", the Soviet Union and the election of Adolf Hitler will be used.

The Example of "Romeo and Juliet" shows that though many options were available for both of them; they desired most what was "unavailable" for them. What actually made their happiness was not an option they did not have, at least in this lifetime. Indeed, the large number of options of eligible partners was not what made them happy; what was not available was.

During the 20th century, the Soviet Union exercised true nationalism, for a country once so great as Russia, it's citizens truly wanted Russia to be back to it's former glory, as they had gone through great poverty and famine. The Bolsheviks Revolution in 1917 brought about many options; the people of Russia

Continue on the opposite side if necessary.

 © TPR Education IP Holdings, LLC

MATH

WRITING

READING

VOCABULARY

followed communism, as their new religion. It soon became clear, however, that options were no longer available. Indeed, soon after Lenin died, Stalin took over and the dictatorship started and in fact did not end until 1989. By making one decision to follow the Communists, the people of Russia, who had the choice to decide who to follow, were not happy even though they had been given large options to begin with. Perhaps the large number of options, represents an even larger number of bad ones hence a greater risk to be unhappy.

The election of Adolf Hitler was very much similar. few people actually know that Hitler was never secretive about his intentions; his election campaign was based on the fact that Jews were to be blamed and in the democracy Germany was, the German electorate, as well as the German people, were truly unhappy with their decision amongst many others. This shows that no matter how many options were available; they could still pick the wrong one which causes unhappiness.

In the world of politics or in romance; the increasing number of options actually makes it more difficult for one to pick to right option. Hence in most cases; the essential will be forgotten as a consequence of the variety of choices, thus the decisions made will not be, one which causes happiness.

Grade: _____

Why: _____

_____

Essay H

Assignment: Is having a large number of options preferable to having a small number of options?

In life each person is given a large number of options. Yet, with increased choices comes increased confusion and pressure to choose the 'correct' one. I will show the confusion and pressure brought by many options using Catcher in the Rye, Death of a Salesman, and World War II.

In J.D. Salinger's Catcher in the Rye, the protagonist, Holden Caulfield, is expelled from boarding school for inadequate grades. He takes a trip to New York City to assert his independence. But, once in New York, he is faced with many difficult decisions and is unsure of the correct path to take. For instance, when faced with boredom, New York City provided a variety of activities that Holden had to choose from. Using poor judgement he hired a prostitute, when she arrived in his room he did nothing but cry like a child. This experience forced him to question further who he was, instead of helping him find his true identity. Holden was forced to choose from a myriad activities, but this choice only complicated his life.

In Arthur Miller's Death of a Salesman, the protagonist Willy Loman and his family strive for the "American dream." Lower middle-class Willy appears to have sight for nothing but this ideal that is

Continue on the opposite side if necessary.

© TPR Education IP Holdings, LLC

impossible to ever attain. Living in America, Willy, his wife Linda, and their two sons Happy, and Biff are given a myriad of opportunities. Yet, due to their single-mindedness, these choices complicate and confuse their lives. For example, Biff was a star football player in high school and recieved a football scholarship to college. His family and he saw this as the ultimate means to achieve the "American Dream." But when Biff was faced with to practice, socialize with friends or study, he never chose to study and his failing grades lost him his scholarship. Biff ruined his dream life because too many options caused him to choose incorrectly.

In World War II, the world had the benefit, or disadvantage, of technology never used before. In the past armies had used bows and arrows, then guns and cannons. But this was the first time the atomic bomb had been an option for a weapon. The United States were tempted by this seemingly fool-proof scare tactic that would end the war, despite the millions of possible casualties. When Franklin D. Roosevelt decided to wage nuclear warfare on Hiroshima, Japan in 1944, the death toll was enormous, and the loss of life from later radiation even more staggering. The United States were tempted by the new option of nuclear warfare, but in the usage set a dangerous and complicated precedent.

Catcher in the Rye, Death of a Salesman, and World War II all portrayed situations in which increased choices had negative consequences. More choices often do nothing but complicate situations unnecessarily.

Grade: _____

Why: _____

_____

Essay I

Assignment: Is having a large number of options preferable to having a small number of options?

It is definitely true that it is better to have a large # of options than to have a small # of options which I will show in this essay by using examples from history which are Randy Johnson's perfect game in 2008 and Anne Frank's life and the murder of famous rapper Tupac Shakur.

When Randy Johnson was pitcher for the Diamondbacks he threw a perfect game against the Braves who are from Atlanta. It is very difficult to throw

Continue on the opposite side if necessary.

a no hitter, particularly @ 40 years old, which is how old Randy Johnson was at the time. He had many options in that game, but he decided to throw a no-hitter and become the oldest pitcher to do so. If he had fewer options, he couldn't have done this.

One person who had fewer options was Anne Frank. Because she had fewer options b/c of the Nazis, she had to live in the attic with her family and write the book Diary Of Anne Frank by Anne Frank. She probably wanted the options available like to leave the country she lived in and go somewhere else.

My last example is Tupac Shakur who was a tal rtist+trapper. He was really starting to have his caree ust start to take off when tragically his life was stop + cut short by an unknown murderer (probaby Biggie). This removed the options he had. Tupac Shak should have had more options b/c he was very you + rich and talented but he had them taken sad away. In conclusion it is true what I said earlie

Grade: _____

Why: _____

_____

NICE TRY, KID.

Assignment: Is technology always beneficial?

Ralph Waldo Emerson believed that for every gain an individual or society makes towards more advanced technology something else is lost — stating, "The civilized man has built a coach, but has lost the use of his feet..." In many ways he is correct, with every advancement we grow more dependent on machines. When a society gives into such strides in technology they find themselves giving up the "old ways".

Let us use the example of automobiles — a wonderful invention — cars, trucks, vans, etc. have made transportation of goods and people easier and much more efficient. Think of how far behind we would be if it weren't for trucks to transport our goods across the country. This invention has created a more efficient and productive society. However, people rely too heavily on such inventions — for many, when in need of a trip down the street to the corner store they find themselves jumping into their car. What about the use of their feet? They've given into the technologicial advancement.

As I sit here I remember I've forgotten my calculator and I probably won't do too well. Why? Because I've grown quite dependent on such a tool — I use a calculator for even the simplest problems, I've given up my mind to let a machine think for me. Ladies and gentleman as opposed to before this is atrophy of the mind not the legs, but who is to say in the future we won't rely on machines for much simpler tasks?

To say the least, Emerson was right, with each advancement in technology we give something up, whether it be our mind, feet or something else. Though correct, Emerson, in my view, did not fully understand the good that came with such advancements. Society must take a step back and come to understand that

 © TPR Education IP Holdings, LLC

MATH

WRITING

READING

VOCABULARY

we are growing numb and take a stand on how to avoid such things. In time we will fall victim to our own creations, much like in the film Terminator. You guys ever see that movie?

Robots Eat Babies!

Grade: _____

Why: _____

_____

Selected Quotes from Past Princeton Review Essays

"If they had discovered electricity before Benjamin Franklin, the Greeks would not have been so easily conquered."

"The greatest invention of the 20th Century was the wheel."

"Good men and women who choose to abuse drugs can show depression, weakness or immorality."

"People are fickle. People will break your heart. But your Playstation is always there for you."

"In World War II, Germany lost a battle to the United Nations."

"Over-analization always causes stressful internal conflict."

"When you use your shoes to step on the street, you pick up all sorts of harmful microbes, dirt, and phlegm from old men."

"In the beginning, according to the Bible, the world was free of evil, pain, and suffering. Then a young woman named Pandora opened a mysterious box."

"In order to truly understand ourselves, we must never really understand anything at all."

"The Civil War began because Rosa Parks refused to sit at the back of the bus."

"The Great Depression was caused by the invention of credit cards. They said that everyone in America got a credit card at the same time without really knowing how they worked, and then they all got the bill at the same time and no one was able to pay it."

"Scientists made great genetic advances when they discovered the Gnome."

"Why would somebody skip graduation? That's like going to Denny's and not ordering cheese bread."

SAT ESSAY: CONSTRUCTION ZONE

3 Minutes	Brainstorm and write your examples.
17–20 Minutes	Write your essay.
2–5 Minutes	Write your conclusion.
DONE!!	

MATH

WRITING

READING

VOCABULARY

GETTING OFF ON THE RIGHT FOOT

ETS graders only spend a couple minutes grading your essay. Therefore, you need to make a good first impression. Here are some simple things to focus on that will put the grader on your side:

Length: While longer essays don't automatically receive higher scores, an essay that is too short is unlikely to provide a full treatment of the issue. We recommend that you write 1.5 to 2 pages.

Legibility: Graders won't give you the benefit of the doubt if they have to struggle to read your essay. Slow down and make sure you write legibly. If your cursive is hard to read, you should print.

Appearance: Make sure your essay looks organized: Indent clearly at the beginning of each paragraph, avoid excessive strikeouts or insertions, and don't write outside of the space provided.

THE BIG THREE

Writing a successful essay requires more than just good looks, however. Content matters, too. There are three things you must do to get a good score on your essay:

1. *Have a clear point of view.* Don't straddle the fence: Pick a side and stick to it.
2. *Support your position.* It's not enough to have an opinion: You need to back it up with appropriate and detailed examples.
3. *Have a logical structure.* A structure means more than just indenting for each new paragraph: You need a beginning, middle, and end.

BRAINSTORMING

STEP 1: ATTACK THE ASSIGNMENT

The assignment almost always asks a question that can be answered with either a "yes" or a "no." The quote usually provides one possible answer to the question. The quote may help you to determine your own position, but if you find it confusing, just ignore it! Your job is to answer the question in the assignment.

> Akira Kurosawa'a film masterpiece *Rashomon* portrays several people who have witnessed a death. As each observer recounts the event as he or she witnessed it, we come to realize that each person's story varies greatly from every other account. Watching the movie, we reflect that the truth of an experience—and perhaps all truth—is different for each person.
>
> Adapted from David Manning

Assignment: Is the truth different for each person? Plan and write an essay in which you develop your point of view on this issue. Support your position with reasoning and examples taken from your reading, studies, experience, or observations.

Start attacking the question by answering it with both a "yes" and a "no," in your own words.

Yes, _____

No, _____

Then, think about which side you want to take. Some points to consider include the following:

- Which side do *you* actually prefer?
- Why do you prefer it?
- Which side will you have an easier time supporting?

Now, pick a side and start thinking about examples to support your position.

MATH

WRITING

READING

VOCABULARY

STEP 2: CHOOSE YOUR EXAMPLES
Make your examples as concrete and detailed as possible. Avoid overly general or hypothetical situations. Which of the following examples do you think are most promising?

Good **Bad**   War is brutal

Good **Bad**   Brutality during the American Revolution

Good **Bad**   The brutality of Hessian Mercenaries during the Battle of Brooklyn

Good **Bad**   This one time I had to dig a hole in the backyard

Good **Bad**   The summer I spent digging wells in a Nicaraguan village

Good **Bad**   When people get rich, they do mean things to other people

Good **Bad**   *The Great Gatsby*

Good **Bad**   *Gossip Girl*

WHAT IF I CAN'T THINK OF ANY EXAMPLES?
Often, students get stuck trying to think of examples. Get around this by using a checklist and taking inventory of what you know. Start thinking today about a set of examples that you can adapt to almost any essay.

Literature: _____

History: _____

Current Events: _____

Pop Culture: _____

Personal Experience: _____

If you *still* can't think of any examples, go back to step 1 and reconsider your position. You might be better off taking the other side.

We recommend that you stick with two examples. Before you start writing, pick your examples and decide the order in which you want to present them.

TEMPLATES FOR YOUR ESSAY

INTRODUCTION

To write an effective introduction, use the following plan:

INTRO TEMPLATE

1) State your opinion.
2) Say why: Provide reasons that support your position.
3) Preview your examples.

Here are four examples that use the intro template. What would you give them, on a scale of 1-6?

I completely believe in the saying "the truth is different for each person." It is as true today as it has ever been. Two examples are the French Revolution and The Matrix.

Score _____

The quote "The truth is different for each person" is an interesting statement. Some people might agree with it, while some people might think its wrong. In some situations, truth is always the same. In other situations, people have different ideas about what is the truth. I will use one example to show that truth can be the same and another example to show that truth can be different.

Score _____

I agree with the statement "the truth is different for each person." People go through life differently, and their experiences and obstacles determine what they believe to be true. This can be demonstrated through the examples of the French Revolution and the movie The Matrix.

Score _____

In my opinion, truth is not an objective and universal concept. Rather, it is subjective, and determined by each individual according to his or her own values and morals. People grow up in different environments and develop their own unique beliefs, and these things influence what each individual perceives as true. By examining the events of the French Revolution and the classic movie The Matrix, we can see that the truth is not the same for everyone.

Score _____

MATH

WRITING

READING

VOCABULARY

BODY PARAGRAPH I

There are two keys to writing an effective body paragraph. First, make sure each example has a beginning, middle, and end. Second, provide an appropriate level of detail: Tell your readers everything they need to know—and nothing they don't—about the example. Here's a simple structure that will keep you on track.

BODY PARAGRAPH I TEMPLATE

1) Introduce the example.
2) Provide a brief summary.
3) Show how the example supports your point of view.
4) Restate your position.

Give each of the following body paragraphs a grade of 1-6.

Score _____

A good example is the French Revolution. This was a disturbing time. Some people did terrible things, like chopping other peoples heads off, believing that they were doing the right thing. But the people who were getting their heads chopped off believed that they were right too. Each of these people had their own version of the truth. This proves that truth is different for each person.

Score _____

My first example of how truth can vary is the French Revolution. The revolution happened because people were oppressed by the government. They lived in squalor and didn't have enough to eat. When Robespierre, who wanted to overthrow the government, accused the king of conspiring with Austria against the French people, the people immediately believed him. It didn't matter if the accusations were true or not: people believed what they wanted to believe. Their hatred of the king guaranteed that they would take Robespierre's side. This example shows that the truth depends on each person's unique point of view.

Score _____

History provides many illustrations of the subjective nature of truth. Take the French Revolution, for instance. In the Nineteenth Century, during the reign of Louis XVI, the French people demanded reform from government. Public discontent was at its height when Maximilian Robespierre, a well-known Frenchman, presented letters allegedly written by Louis XVI as evidence of a conspiracy between Louis and the King of Austria. The impoverished French masses immediately accepted these letters as true, while those loyal to Louis insisted with equal certainty that the letters had been fabricated. Whether the letters were authentic or false was beside the point: people based their judgments on their own beliefs, not on evidence. The events of the French Revolution demonstrate that truth is not founded on objective facts; rather, it is based on individual opinion.

BODY PARAGRAPH II

The big difference between the first and second body paragraphs is that the second body paragraph should start with a transition that connects the two examples. Transitions such as *"In addition to..."*, *"A similar situation to..."*, or *"Another good example of..."* would be good to use.

Here's the template for the second body paragraph.

BODY PARAGRAPH II TEMPLATE

1) Start with a transition that bridges the two examples.
2) Provide a brief summary.
3) Show how the example supports your point of view.
4) Restate your position.

What grade would you give the following body paragraphs?

Another good example that shows how the truth can be different for each person is the movie <u>The Matrix</u>. At the beginning of the movie, a man named Neo is living a normal life. But his comfortable life is disrupted by a character known as Morpheus, who presents Neo with evidence that the world as he knows it is an illusion. Morpheus offers Neo a choice: he can return to the reality he knows, or he can journey into the reality that Morpheus believes is true. Neo could have stayed in the world he was used to, but instead he chose to take a chance and find his own truth. This shows once again how truth is different for each person.

Score _____

Like the French Revolution, the classic movie <u>The Matrix</u> illustrates how truth is determined on an individual basis. Neo is a computer programmer dissatisfied with his humdrum life. Neo's ordinary existence is turned upside down when he encounters a group of rebels led by the legendary Morpheus. Morpheus tells Neo that the life Neo has been living is a mirage, created by a computer program known as The Matrix. He offers Neo a choice: If Neo takes a red pill, he can return to his comfortable existence inside the Matrix, but if he takes a blue pill, he will have to face a shocking and alien reality. Neo realizes that the truth is no longer something he can take for granted: he has to choose his own truth. Neo's journey through <u>The Matrix</u> reminds us that truth is something that all people must decide upon for themselves.

Score _____

MATH

WRITING

READING

VOCABULARY

CONCLUSION

The most important thing about a conclusion is to have one. Here's a basic template.

CONCLUSION TEMPLATE

1) Restate your position, and say why.

2) Recap your examples.

3) Give a concluding thought that comments on the topic.

Note: It's fine to vary the order of steps 1 and 2.

Give the following conclusions a grade:

Score _____

As the examples of the French Revolution and The Matrix have shown, the truth is different for each person. If everyone realized this, the world would be a better place.

Score _____

In conclusion, truth is determined by each person alone. As the examples of the French Revolution and the movie The Matrix demonstrate, we all have our own beliefs and ways of perceiving the world, and these things determine what we think truth is. My truth is not necessarily better than your truth — they are just different.

Score _____

In the final analysis, truth is not an objective set of facts that we all agree on. Instead, it something that is determined by each person individually. The events of the French Revolution and the provocative film The Matrix clearly demonstrate that truth is a product of each person's opinions, experiences, and ways of perceiving. In a world filled with intolerance and rigidity, we would all benefit from the realization that truth is relative, and that a truth that is not identical to yours and mine can still be valid.

 © TPR Education IP Holdings, LLC

GOING BEYOND THE TEMPLATES

Sticking with the templates can get you the highest possible score. However, if you find them too restrictive, just build more features into the templates. Here are some simple ways to add to your essay.

Introduction

Start with a rhetorical question

This is an easy way to jazz up your intro.

Is there an objectively right answer to every question? Can one look at everything in the world in black and white? Most of us would say no. There are many things in life that do not have a clear answer, and truth is one of them. Everyone uses his or her own life experiences to determine what is true, so everyone's truth is different. Reflecting on the French Revolution and the movie The Matrix, we can see that the truth is different for each person.

Attack the opposing point of view

Another option is to summarize the opposing point of view, and then refute it. Just be <u>absolutely</u> clear about which side you are on.

Some people believe that truth is the same for everyone. They see truth as something that is objective and unchanging. What these people fail to realize, however, is that human beings are not passive sponges who simply absorb the truth; we are active participants who create the truth out of our own life experiences, beliefs, and values. Therefore, we each have our own version of the truth. By considering the events of the French Revolution and the controversial film The Matrix, we come to the conclusion that the truth must be different for each of us.

Paint a picture with a suggestive example

While you shouldn't use a hypothetical situation in a body paragraph, it can be very effective to do so in your introduction. Just be sure you have real examples in your body paragraphs.

When a man or woman enters a courtroom to be judged, there are no fixed guidelines through which the jury determines what is honest and true. It is up to each jury member to use his or her mind and heart to understand what is true and what is not. The members of jury can hear the same testimony, observe the same evidence, and then violently disagree over what the truth is.

When considering the issue of truth, we realize that not only is truth subjective, but also that each individual's truth is determined by his or her environment and background. The truth of this can be clearly seen in the events of the French Revolution and the movie <u>The Matrix</u>.

CONCLUSION

Any of the techniques mentioned for the introduction will work in the conclusion as well. Here are a couple more options. If you have a hard time coming up with a "concluding thought," you might find these ideas helpful.

Give a shout out to the other side

Truth is not constant and unchanging. It is something that depends on a person's experiences and beliefs. Of course, there are certain things in life, like the law of gravity, which can objectively be proven true or false. But the law of gravity will not help us determine what is just or unjust: the cultural and moral truths that help us make sense of the human world have to be determined by each person alone. As the examples of the French Revolution and <u>The Matrix</u> show, the truth is different for each person.

Use an analogy

One's idea of truth is like one's fingerprints. While people's fingerprints more or less look alike at first glance, upon closer examination there are differences that completely set them apart. Truth works in much the same way: It is determined by each person individually and is shaped by each person's environment and experiences. As the confusion of the French Revolution and the shocking plot twists of the movie <u>The Matrix</u> show, truth can be different for every person in the world.

You can customize your templates however you want, but make sure you know <u>exactly</u> what you're going to do <u>before</u> you begin writing your essay.

 © TPR Education IP Holdings, LLC

Summary

What are the three things that will have the most impact on your score?

1) _____

2) _____

3) _____

What are the three parts of the intro template?

1) _____

2) _____

3) _____

What are the four parts of the body paragraph template?

1) _____

2) _____

3) _____

4) _____

What are the two parts of the conclusion template?

1) _____

2) _____

Name three ways that you can add to the basic template.

1) _____

2) _____

3) _____

I have accomplished _____ of my _____ stated goals in the Introduction chapter.

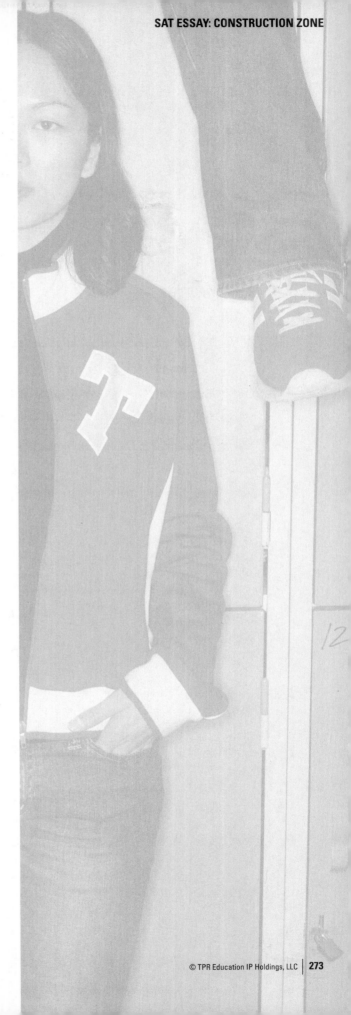

SAT ESSAY: YOUR TURN TO PLAY

MATH

WRITING

READING

VOCABULARY

EXAMPLES

So far we've talked about how to write your essay. Now let's talk about what to write. Keep the following rules in mind when selecting examples:

- **Name drop!** Use specific names and dates in your examples.
- Prepare some examples before the exam, but remember that not all essay topics lend themselves to using prepared examples.

In the following pages, you'll practice the valuable skill of defining examples. Here's what a well prepared example might look like.

Event:	American Revolution
Date:	1775–1783, began at Lexington
Description:	Declaration of Independence written in 1776, inspired by Enlightment philosophy. Americans fought for independence from Britain because they felt the British imposed intolerable conditions upon them. Americans won. French helped American colonists because France hated England.
Major Players:	George III (playing for Britain), George Washington (playing for America), Thomas Jefferson (wrote Declaration of Independence).
Big Ideas:	No taxation without representation, freedom is worth fighting for, majority isn't always right, sometimes breaking the rules is the right thing to do, power of ideas, the enemy of my enemy is my friend.

Samples

History: Fill in the appropriate information for two history examples below.

Event: _____

Date: _____

Description: _____
_____
_____
_____
_____
_____
_____

Major Players: _____
_____
_____

Big Ideas: _____
_____
_____

Event: _____

Date: _____

Description: _____
_____
_____
_____
_____
_____
_____

Major Players: _____
_____
_____

Big Ideas: _____
_____
_____

Current events: Recent events in the news.

Event: _____

Date: _____

Description: _____
_____
_____
_____
_____
_____
_____

Major Players: _____
_____
_____

Big Ideas: _____
_____
_____

Event: _____

Date: _____

Description: _____
_____
_____
_____
_____
_____
_____

Major Players: _____
_____
_____

Big Ideas: _____
_____
_____

MATH

WRITING

READING

VOCABULARY

MATH
WRITING
READING
VOCABULARY

Literature: Be it <u>Huckleberry Finn</u> or <u>Harry Potter</u>, be prepared to provide the specifics of the texts you choose.

Book: _____

Author: _____

Description: _____

_____

_____

_____

_____

_____

Major Players: _____

_____

_____

Big Ideas: _____

_____

_____

Book: _____

Author: _____

Description: _____

_____

_____

_____

_____

_____

Major Players: _____

_____

_____

Big Ideas: _____

_____

_____

Personal Experience: Choose experiences that have had a profound effect on you.

Event: _____

Date: _____

Description: _____

_____

_____

_____

_____

_____

Major Players: _____

_____

_____

Big Ideas: _____

_____

_____

Event: _____

Date: _____

Description: _____

_____

_____

_____

_____

_____

Major Players: _____

_____

_____

Big Ideas: _____

_____

_____

SAT GRAMMAR: GO BY SIGHT *NOT* SOUND

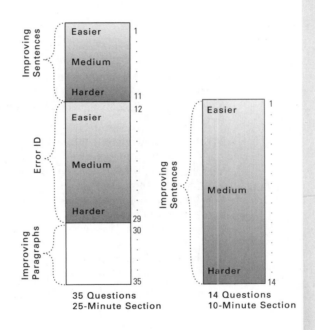

Improving Sentences

Easier — 1
Medium
Harder — 11

Error ID

12
Easier
Medium
Harder — 29

Improving Paragraphs

30
35

35 Questions
25-Minute Section

Improving Sentences

Easier — 1
Medium
Harder — 14

14 Questions
10-Minute Section

GRAMMAR ON THE SAT

Ah, grammar—your favorite subject, right? There are dozens and dozens of grammar rules that could be tested on the SAT, but the test writers are lazy, so they prefer to test the same handful of rules over and over again. Which rules does the SAT test? We'll look at the rules that are tested most often.

MATH

WRITING

READING

VOCABULARY

BUT IT *SOUNDS* GOOD!

The SAT tests simple grammar by disguising basic grammar concepts to make them look difficult. Joe Bloggs chooses answers based only on how they sound. *You* will find correct answers by comparing answer choices, applying a few basic grammar rules, and eliminating choices that are grammatically wrong.

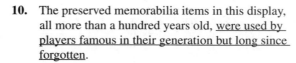

The Joe Bloggs Method
- Sounds good? No error.
- Sounds bad? Error.

The Princeton Review Method
- Eliminate four flawed answer choices.
- Know the basic grammar rules tested on the SAT.

Don't rely on your ear. Learn the rules that make sentences right or wrong.

10. The preserved memorabilia items in this display, all more than a hundred years old, <u>were used by players famous in their generation but long since forgotten</u>.

   (A) were used by players famous in their generation but long since forgotten

   (B) were used by famous players for the generation, which is now forgotten

   (C) had been used by a famous generation of players but then forgotten

   (D) were being used by a generation's famous players that we have now forgotten

   (E) having been used by players famous in their generation but long since forgotten

IMPROVING SENTENCES QUESTIONS

Here are a few key points about Improving Sentences questions.

- You never need to read choice (A) because it always repeats the underlined portion exactly as it is in the initial sentence.
- Approximately one-fifth of the sentences are correct as written, so don't be afraid to select answer choice (A).
- The NON-underlined portion of the sentence is always correct; however, you should always read that part to help find the answer.
- Don't try to revise the sentence in your head; your perfect revision may not be listed. Compare answer choices and use POE.
- The questions gradually get harder as the section progresses.

Basic Approach

The key to success on Improving Sentences questions is to identify errors and compare answer choices with each other. Use the following plan:

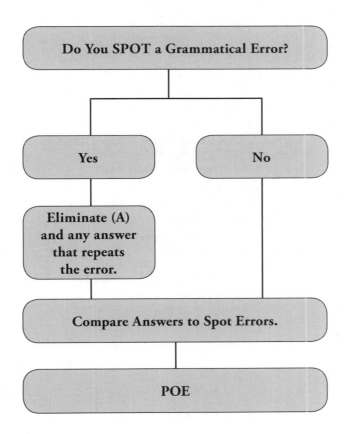

A "hard" grammar question is one that most students miss, not necessarily one that tests difficult grammar.

MATH

WRITING

READING

VOCABULARY

Three Rules to Live By

- Eliminate any answer choice that changes the intended meaning of the sentence.

- When you're down to two answer choices that contain no grammatical errors, choose the shorter and simpler one.

- If you have to choose between choice (A) and another answer choice, don't pick the other one unless you see a flaw in choice (A). Sometimes, it is correct as written.

Compare answers and make decisions.

3. The vivid descriptions and lively characterizations in the novel *Ahab's Wife* <u>give the reader a sense of participating in</u> Una's story.

   (A) *give the reader* a sense of participating in
   (B) *let the one* who is reading have a sense of participating in
   (C) *gives the one* who reads it a sense of participating in
   (D) *gives one* a sense of participation in the reading of
   (E) *give one* the sense, in the reading of it, of participating in

12. <u>Although the district attorney has begun to increase the security staff in the building</u>, she is still receiving calls from concerned employees.

   (A) Although the district attorney *has begun* to increase the security staff in the building
   (B) Although *beginning* to increase, as district attorney, the security staff in the building
   (C) The district attorney, *beginning* to increase the security staff in the building
   (D) The district attorney *has begun* to increase the security staff in the building,
   (E) The district attorney, *beginning* to increase the security staff in the building, however

SUBJECT-VERB AGREEMENT

Consider the following sentences:

The girl laughs.

The girls laugh.

Usually, when a subject ends in -s, the verb does not. When the subject does not end in -s, the verb does. The SAT plays with this rule constantly, with slightly longer sentences than the two listed above.

Consider the following sentences:

The lawyers representing the retired baseball star wants to correct the mistakes made by his previous advisors.

Barry's unfortunate weakness for plaid pants have led to his nomination as "Most Tragic Fashion Victim" in his class.

When a verb is underlined, find its subject and make sure the verb and subject agree. Watch for unnecessary filler, or "fat," separating the subject and verb.

3. The primary reasons given for the team's lackluster record <u>is that they have poor leadership and a relatively inexperienced coach</u>.

(A) is that they have poor leadership and a relatively inexperienced coach

(B) is poor leadership ability and they have a relatively inexperienced coach

(C) are that they have poor leadership and that they have a relatively inexperienced coach

(D) is having poor leadership and having a relatively inexperienced coach

(E) are poor leadership and a relatively inexperienced coach

MATH

WRITING

READING

VOCABULARY

5. The ideas for hats, little shoes, and bowties that fill the pages of *Dressing Up Your Pet Magazine* is crucial for those who want to make their pets look like little fuzzy people.

    (A) is crucial for those who want to make their pets look like little fuzzy people
    (B) are crucial for those whom are wanting to make their pets like little fuzzy people
    (C) is crucial to those who want to make their pets looking like little fuzzy people
    (D) for those wanting to make their pets look like little fuzzy people, is crucial
    (E) are crucial for those who want to make their pets look like little fuzzy people

6. The elements of good legal writing is clarity of expression and clearness of thought, not obscure legal terminology.

    (A) The elements of good legal writing is
    (B) The element of good legal writing are
    (C) Good legal writing are characterized by
    (D) In writing good legal documents is needed
    (E) The elements of good legal writing are

Often the key element of an answer choice can be found at the beginning or end of the choice. Compare the answers.

7. Because my friend Charles Jefferson, one of the team's best players, weigh 300 pounds, fans expect him to do well when the team plays Ridgemont High.

    (A) weigh 300 pounds, fans expect him
    (B) weighs 300 pounds, fans expecting him
    (C) weighs 300 pounds, and has fans that expect him
    (D) weighs 300 pounds, fans expect him
    (E) weigh 300 pounds, his fans expect

Collective Nouns

Consider the following sentences:

The chain of mountains that I can see from my back door are so beautiful that I often just stare at them.

The United States lead all other nations in many important economic categories.

5. The Philippines, although not famous for its <u>agriculture, they produce</u> some of the best tropical fruit in the world.

    (A) agriculture, they produce
    (B) agriculture, produces
    (C) agriculture, produce
    (D) agriculture, are producing
    (E) agriculture and it produces

8. The slow loris, a nocturnal and arboreal <u>creature, are unusual for a mammal in that their</u> bite is actually toxic.

    (A) creature, are unusual for a mammal in that their
    (B) creature, is unusual for a mammal in that its
    (C) creatures, are unusual for a mammal in that their
    (D) creatures, is unusual for mammals having a
    (E) creature, is unusual for mammals being that their

Put brackets around extra information that's surrounded by commas to trim the fat.

Consider the following sentences:

Takeru and my sister is well known as competitive hot dog eaters.

Neither my sister nor my brother are particularly interesting.

- Two singular nouns joined by "and" make a plural subject.
- If two or more nouns are joined by "or" or "nor," the verb agrees with the *last* element in the list.

9. Extracurricular activities, test scores, and grade point average, the relative importance of which <u>differs from school to school, is</u> the basis of the typical college application.

(A) differs from school to school, is
(B) differ from school to school, is
(C) differ from school to school, are
(D) differs from school to school, are
(E) differs between schools, is

10. Although they asked several times, <u>neither the time of the wedding nor its secret location have been revealed to the assembled media personnel</u>.

(A) neither the time of the wedding nor its secret location have been revealed to the assembled media personnel
(B) neither the time of the wedding nor the secret location of it had been revealed to the assembled media personnel
(C) both the time of the wedding or its secret location are not being revealed to the assembled media personnel
(D) neither the time of the wedding nor its secret location was revealed to the assembled media personnel
(E) it was not revealed to the assembled media personnel the time of the wedding but its secret location

Noun Agreement

Consider the following sentences:

People find it difficult to distinguish between alligators and the crocodile.

The cowboys stood out in the field, talking and chewing a toothpick.

6. Mr. Obama stood in the center of the auditorium and told the dozens of local residents who had come <u>to hear him speak that he wanted their vote</u>.

   (A) to hear him speak that he wanted their vote
   (B) to hear him speaking that he wanted their vote
   (C) to hear him speak that he wanted their votes
   (D) in order to hear him speaking and he wanted their vote
   (E) to hear him speak because he wanted their votes

11. The bartender recognized his regular customers, <u>so he poured and quickly served them their drink</u>.

    (A) so he poured and quickly served them their drink
    (B) so he poured and served quickly to them their drink
    (C) and so he poured and served quickly to them their drinks
    (D) so he poured and quickly served their drinks
    (E) he poured and served quickly their drink

MATH

WRITING

READING

VOCABULARY

Parallelism

Consider the following sentences:

The unusual sport known as haggis-hurling requires a haggis, a large open field, and you need a sense of humor.

Every morning I make sure I put on pants, socks, and I put on a shirt.

All items in a list must match in form.

6. The college students expressed their dissatisfaction to the dean, organized a picket line, <u>and were chanting slogans</u> in front of the administration building.

   (A) and were chanting slogans
   (B) and had chanted slogans
   (C) chanting slogans
   (D) and chanted slogans
   (E) and would chant slogans

Hint for #7:
Where does the list start?

7. In response to losing a significant part of its market share to a competitor, the soft drink company has cut costs by withholding executive bonuses, <u>changed their advertising agency, and have</u> redesigned the company logo.

   (A) changed their advertising agency, and have
   (B) changing their advertising agency, as well as
   (C) has changed its advertising agency, and
   (D) and changed its advertising agency, and has
   (E) changed its advertising agency, and

Comparisons

Consider the following sentences:

My cell phone plan, like many of my friends, includes unlimited text and picture messaging for a small fee per month.

My friend Matt and I both entered our poodles in the competition, but my poodle won first place, unlike Matt.

When you spot a comparison in a sentence, make sure the items are parallel: apples to apples and oranges to oranges.

11. The rules of written English are much more stringent than <u>spoken English</u>.

   (A) spoken English
   (B) English that is spoken
   (C) the rules dealing with English that is spoken
   (D) those of spoken English
   (E) English speech

14. <u>Unlike the East Coast</u>, California residents get to enjoy televised World Series night games at a reasonable hour.

   (A) Unlike the East Coast
   (B) Unlike the games viewed on the East Coast
   (C) Not similar to the residents on the East Coast
   (D) Like the residents who don't enjoy the games
   (E) Unlike East Coast residents

Watch for these comparison words: than, like, unlike, similar, different

MATH

WRITING

READING

VOCABULARY

If a pronoun ends with "body," "one," or "thing," it is singular.

Pronouns

Consider the following sentences:

Everyone should be careful to keep their hands and feet in the vehicle at all times; the bandicoots can be vicious if provoked.

France performed so well in the World Cup in 1998 that they won the championship.

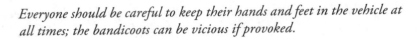

Every time a pronoun is underlined, check for two things:
agreement and **ambiguity**.

8. When you first taste *injera*, the customary bread of Ethiopia, <u>one may think one is</u> eating a sourdough crepe.

    (A) one may think one is
    (B) people may think they are
    (C) you may think you are
    (D) one may be thinking of
    (E) you might think you have been

9. Each of Jacob's students, some of whom had been working with him for years, <u>were accomplished pianists who could perform under even the most trying circumstances</u>.

    (A) were accomplished pianists who could perform under even the most trying circumstances
    (B) was an accomplished pianists who can perform under even the most trying circumstances
    (C) were accomplished pianists; who could have performed under even the most trying circumstances
    (D) was an accomplished pianist who could perform under even the most trying circumstances
    (E) was an accomplished pianist; and so they could have performed under even the most trying circumstances

Modifiers

Consider the following sentences:

While watching TV, the phone rang.

After rotting in the cellar for weeks, my brother brought up some oranges.

Staring down the ski slope, Bob's knees started to tremble.

Lauren made a cake for Emily with candles on top.

A modifier should be placed as closely as possible to the word it describes.

7. <u>Returning home for a visit, the backyard seemed much smaller to Richard</u> than he remembered.

   (A) Returning home for a visit, the backyard seemed much smaller to Richard
   (B) Returning home for a visit, it seemed a much smaller backyard to Richard
   (C) Returning to it for a visit, the backyard seemed much smaller to Richard
   (D) Richard returned home for a visit, the backyard seemed to him much smaller
   (E) When Richard returned home for a visit, the backyard seemed much smaller

12. Some families avoid cable television because they fear that seeing a movie <u>could be harmful to a young child which depicts excessive violence</u>.

   (A) could be harmful to a young child which depicts excessive violence
   (B) could be for young children harmful because they are excessively violent
   (C) that depicts excessive violence could be harmful to a young child
   (D) could be harmful for depicting excessive violence to a young child
   (E) could depict a young and harmfully violent child

Commas and Semicolons

Consider the following sentences:

My friend Merav is crazy, she has taken the SAT at least thirty times.

Mr. Jensen was known as a tough grader, all of his students had to study very hard.

Commas separate parts of a sentence that cannot stand alone. If a comma can be replaced with a period, the comma is incorrect.

3. The Wankel engine, developed in the 1950's, is based on the Otto <u>engine, Nikolaus Otto invented it</u> in 1876.

   (A) engine, Nikolaus Otto invented it
   (B) engine, then Nikolaus Otto inventing it
   (C) engine, Nikolaus Otto is the one who invented it
   (D) engine, invented by Nikolaus Otto
   (E) engine, it was an invention by Nikolaus Otto

9. <u>Most writers prefer</u> to work on computers, J.K. Rowling has resisted this trend, preferring to write her stories with pen and paper.

   (A) Most writers prefer
   (B) Most writers preferred
   (C) In that most writers prefer
   (D) Because most writers preferred
   (E) Although most writers prefer

Semicolons separate parts of sentences that can stand alone. If a semicolon can be replaced with a period, the semicolon is correct.

10. Many people believe that fortune cookies were invented in <u>China, and these cookies actually originated</u> in Japan and are almost unknown in China.

    (A) China, and these cookies actually originated
    (B) China, and it is true that these cookies actually originated
    (C) China, but these cookies actually originating
    (D) China; whereas these cookies were actually originating
    (E) China; however, these cookies actually originated

Conjunctions

Consider the following sentences:

Pop Rocks will rot your teeth but may cause your stomach to explode.

It is easy to learn the rules of chess, and it takes years to become a skilled player.

2. A review of the latest *Indiana Jones* movie called it thrilling because of its special <u>effects, and its uninspired acting makes it tedious</u>.

   (A) effects, and its uninspired acting makes it tedious
   (B) effects, and tedious with its uninspired acting
   (C) effects although tedious by having uninspired acting
   (D) effects since having uninspired acting that makes it tedious
   (E) effects but tedious because of its uninspired acting

7. After school, Jason buried his report card in the <u>woods; the reason is because he had failed</u> all his classes.

   (A) woods; the reason is because he had failed
   (B) woods; this was because he had failed
   (C) woods, in that he had failed
   (D) woods because he had failed
   (E) woods because of failing

Summary

Improving Sentences Basic Approach

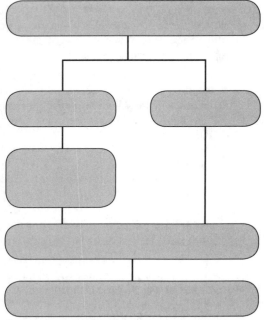

Three Golden Rules to Live By

- _____
- _____
- _____

Most Commonly Tested Errors

- _____
- _____
- _____
- _____
- _____
- _____

- I have accomplished _____ of my _____ stated goals in the Introduction chapter.

 © TPR Education IP Holdings, LLC

SAT GRAMMAR: MASTERING IMPROVING SENTENCES

Prepositions

Prepositions indicate location or direction. Prepositions occur frequently on the SAT and are key elements of questions. Below is the list of the prepositions you will see most often on the SAT.

about	by	outside	according to
above	down	over	because of
across	during	since	by way of
after	except	through	in addition to
against	for	throughout	in front of
around	from	to	in place of
at	in	toward	in regard to
before	inside	under	in spite of
behind	into	until	instead of
below	like	up	on account of
beneath	near	upon	out of
beside	of	with	
besides	off	without	
between	on		
beyond	out		

You must recognize these prepositions and, often, ignore the phrases that begin with them. Why? Well, prepositional phrases on the SAT are usually used to separate the subject of the sentence from the action in the sentence and thus confuse subject-verb agreement. You must Trim the Fat to find the subject-verb agreement.

6. For days, one ~~of the volleyball team's best players~~ ~~were performing so poorly that the coach worried~~ ~~that something was~~ wrong.

(A) were performing so poorly that the coach worried that something was

(B) was performing so poorly; the coach feared something to be

(C) were performing so poorly that the coach feared something has

(D) was performing very poorly; so the coach fearing something

(E) was performing so poorly that the coach feared something was

7. The impact ~~of the new student conduct board to~~ ~~which every student answers~~ shows that mutual respect, honesty, and their proper behavior are valued by all students.

(A) shows that mutual respect, honesty, and their proper behavior are valued by all students
(B) shows mutual respect, honesty, and proper behavior are valued by all students
(C) shows respect that is mutual, honesty, and proper behavior being valuable to all students
(D) show mutual respect, honesty, and proper behavior are valuable to all students
(E) show mutual respect, honest, and proper behavior are valued by all students

19. The number ~~of categories in this year's Academy~~
$\qquad\qquad\qquad\qquad$ A
~~Awards~~ illustrate the serious attempts being made by the
$\qquad$ B $\qquad$ C $\qquad$ D
producers to eliminate the excesses of previous

productions. No error
$\qquad\qquad$ E

21. Detractors assert that reforms ~~in baseball~~
$\qquad\qquad$ A
has not managed to reduce satisfactorily the
$\qquad$ B $\qquad\qquad$ C
proliferation of drug use in the sport. No error
$\qquad$ D $\qquad\qquad\qquad$ E

Unnecessary Prepositions

The SAT likes to test prepositions by including them where they don't belong.

They met ~~up with~~ the new principal in the auditorium.
The picture fell off ~~of~~ the wall.
He threw the clock out ~~of~~ the window.
The boy wouldn't let the dogs inside ~~of~~ the house.
Where did they go ~~to~~?
Where is the party ~~at~~?

PRONOUNS

The two types of pronouns that the SAT tests most often are subject pronouns and object pronouns. Use subject pronouns as the subjects of verbs. In other words, subject pronouns cause something to happen. Use object pronouns as the objects of verbs and as the objects of prepositions.

Subject pronouns do stuff; object pronouns have stuff done to them.

Subject Pronouns

I, He, She, We, They, Who, You

Here are some sentences that correctly use subject pronouns.

> *I* play chess.

> *He* bought the cake.

> *She* has been found guilty of sedition.

> *Who* does *he* think *he* is?

> *You* and *I* ate lunch together.

> The dogs are not as tired as *we* are.

As you can see in the last sentence above, subject pronouns aren't always at the beginning of a sentence.

Object Pronouns

Me, Him, Her, Us, Them, Whom, You

Object pronouns can be the objects of verbs, as in the following sentences:

> The coach picked *her*.

> Margaret took *him* to the park.

Jacques Brandenberger, inventor of cellophane, punched *him* in the neck.

The town has not been good to *us*.

With *whom* are you going to the rodeo?

They can also be the objects of prepositions, as in the following phrases:

"Between you and I" is always, always, always wrong.

between you and me

to you and me

between you and him

at you and her

except you and them

for Isaac and me

near her and me

above her and him

If there is ever any question about whether to use "I" or "me," draw a line through the extra person in the sentence.

Albert gave the book to ~~my brother and~~ I.

Albert gave the book to my brother and me.

MATH WRITING READING VOCABULARY

MATH

WRITING

READING

VOCABULARY

PRONOUN AGREEMENT DRILL

Circle the correct pronoun in each of the following sentences.

1. When one is successful, (*one/they*) should enjoy it.
2. Each of the students presented (*their/his*) own project.
3. Anyone who goes to college is in for the best years of (*their/her*) life.
4. The jury was sequestered until (*they/it*) reached a verdict.
5. One thing everyone knows about television news is that (*they're/it's*) biased.
6. Each of the women fought for (*their/her*) rights.
7. When one has to take a test, (*you/one*) ought to be prepared
8. Everyone who visits Argentina feels as if (*they are/he is*) visited by the ghosts of Eva and Juan Perron.
9. The guitar player is a more talented musician than (*he/him*) is.
10. It is well known that Alex is more soft-spoken than (*she/her*).
11. The professional baseball team gets paid more than (*them/they*).
12. No one else laughed at the joke, because it was just between David and (*I/me*)
13. Their class has fewer singers than (*us/we*).

IDENTIFY THE PRONOUN ERRORS

12. <u>Him and her</u> ran <u>hurriedly</u> to catch the ferry
    A   B

    <u>because</u> the boat was the last one <u>until</u> tomorrow.
    C   D

    <u>No error</u>
    E

13. Upon winning the volleyball championship, Charity

    leaped into the air <u>as if</u> she were <u>spiking</u> the
                         A   B

    ball, while the crowd cheered <u>uproariously</u> for
                                   C

    <u>she and the team.</u> <u>No error</u>
    D   E

19. It is difficult for my friends <u>and I</u>
                                     A

    <u>even to contemplate</u> <u>playing</u> chess against
    B   C

    someone accused <u>of cheating.</u> <u>No error</u>
                      D   E

22. It would be <u>better for</u> <u>you and I</u> to help each other
    A   B

    build one house <u>than</u> for <u>each of us</u> to work by
                      C   D

    ourselves. <u>No error</u>
                 E

24. My mother <u>was angry</u> because <u>although</u> she told
                A   B

    <u>Jenny and I</u> to go to the store, we <u>actually went</u> to
    C   D

    the movies. <u>No error</u>
                  E

25. Not one <u>of the doctors</u> treating my sister <u>know</u>
              A   B

    exactly <u>what is</u> wrong with <u>her.</u> <u>No error</u>
             C   D   E

26. After <u>engaging</u> in a spirited debate, everyone
           A

    except <u>Andrea and I</u> <u>decided</u> to watch the latest
            B   C

    action film, even though the rest of the group had

    <u>already seen</u> it. <u>No error</u>
    D   E

29. To those of us <u>who</u> had heard the rumors <u>about</u>
    A   B   C

    the staff cuts, the news of the editor's firing <u>was not</u>
                                                      D

    surprising. <u>No error</u>
                 E

SUBJECT-VERB AGREEMENT DRILL

Identify and correct any subject-verb agreement errors in the following sentences:

1. Although the directions that they sent out with the invitations show an easy way to get to their house, there **is** actually several different **ways** to get there faster by taking the back roads.
2. A high concentration of radioactive chemicals and other contaminants have been found in the drinking water at ETS headquarters, which may have caused brain damage in some of its test writers.
3. According to many children, neither a slice of apple pie nor a scoop of chocolate ice cream are more desirable than a huge batch of chocolate chip cookies.
4. His ridiculously unrealistic plots and his utterly unreadable style makes Joe Bloggs a completely unappealing writer, even to readers accustomed to buying books by Danielle Steele.
5. An understanding of irony and sarcasm are usually the last step in learning a language.
6. Sensationalism in television shows masquerading as "news" programs are making it difficult for serious journalism to compete for ratings.
7. Smoking cigarettes, although argued to be an attractive habit, are not known to help one befriend children, animals, or asthmatics.
8. When asked, the typical first-year student at Hackysack University will reply that either fingerpainting or snowshoeing are his intended major.
9. The typical first-year student changes his mind when he discovers that both the fingerpainting major and the snowshoeing major requires one hundred-page research projects.
10. Each of the contestants in the bodybuilding competition are required to participate in the talent competition; rippling of the muscles is not considered a display of talent.

IMPROVING SENTENCES DRILL 1

Remember to cross off wrong answers. We've done the first question for you.

1. Added to the raise and a company car, Bob demanded a four-day work week.

   (A) Added to the raise and a company car
   (B) In addition to the raise and a company car
   (C) In adding to the raise and a company car
   (D) Not only a raise and a company car
   (E) In addition to the raise and wanting a company car

2. For success in business, it is important not only to work hard but also to know the rules of the game.

   (A) to work hard but also to know
   (B) working hard but also to know
   (C) to work hard but also knowing
   (D) working hard but also knowing
   (E) that one work hard but also that you know

3. Vacationing in foreign countries provides one not only with relaxing experiences but also cultures different from theirs are better understood.

   (A) cultures different from theirs are better understood
   (B) a better understanding of cultures different from theirs
   (C) with a better understanding of different cultures
   (D) better understood are cultures different from theirs
   (E) cultures, although different, are better understood

4. Performing before an audience for the first time, fear suddenly overcame the child and she could not remember her lines.

   (A) fear suddenly overcame the child and she could not remember her lines
   (B) the lines could not be remembered by the child because she was overcome by fear
   (C) the child was suddenly overcome by fear and could not remember her lines
   (D) the child was suddenly overcome by fear, she could not remember her lines
   (E) suddenly the child was overcome by fear, and consequently not remembering her lines

5. The student of literature will learn many forms of criticism: psychoanalytic, Marxist, feminist, as well as the most popular, New Criticism.

   (A) as well as the most
   (B) as well as the moreover
   (C) as well. The most
   (D) as well, being that the much
   (E) and in addition, the most

5. Successful trials of a polio vaccine were completed in 1955, and whereby millions of American children were vaccinated that same year.

   (A) and whereby millions of American children were vaccinated
   (B) whereby millions of American children were vaccinated
   (C) and millions of American children were vaccinated
   (D) millions of American children were vaccinated
   (E) because millions of American children were vaccinated

6. After discussing plans for their seaside vacation, Victoria realized that she likes the ocean more than Doug; he has never been much of a swimmer.

   (A) she likes the ocean more than Doug
   (B) she likes the ocean more than Doug did
   (C) she does indeed like the ocean more than Doug
   (D) Doug does not like the ocean in the same way that she likes it
   (E) she likes the ocean more than Doug does

7. Richard III will not be remembered for his advocacy of the development of printing any more than they will remember Henry VIII for his compositions for lute and harpsichord.

   (A) any more than they will remember Henry VIII
   (B) as will Henry VIII not be remembered
   (C) any more than Henry VIII will be remembered
   (D) just as they will not remember Henry VIII
   (E) no more than Henry VIII will be remembered

7. The reason first-year college students often struggle academically is that you are not prepared to work independently to deadlines.

(A) is that you are not prepared
(B) is that they are not prepared
(C) is because one is not prepared
(D) is because of them not preparing
(E) is their preparing not

8. In towns throughout Texas, one can taste thousands of types of chili, each with a distinct flavor of its own.

(A) each with a distinct flavor of its own
(B) each having a distinct flavor of its own
(C) while they each have distinct flavors of their own
(D) which has a distinct flavor of its own
(E) they each have their own distinct flavor

8. Serving as a telephone, an internet connection, or a music library, the iPhone, it is increasingly a part of our lives.

(A) the iPhone, it is increasingly a part of our lives
(B) both the iPhone and its part in our lives has increased
(C) it has increasingly become a part of our lives
(D) the iPhone is increasingly a part of our lives
(E) iPhones are increasingly a part of our lives

8. Georg Büchner's writing is different from any other playwrights of his day because it exhibits many characteristics of modern drama.

(A) from any other playwrights
(B) from that of any other playwright
(C) from any other playwright
(D) than anyone
(E) than anyone else

9. Alex wanted to work as a lawyer, play in a band, and to travel around the world.

(A) work as a lawyer, play in a band, and to travel around the world
(B) work as a lawyer, play in a band, and travel around the world
(C) work as a lawyer, to play in a band, and travel around the world
(D) have worked as a lawyer, to play in a band, and to travel around the world
(E) work as a lawyer, to have played in a band, to have traveled around the world

9. Canada has a history of winning many Winter Olympic medals, perhaps because they live in one of the coldest climates on earth.

(A) perhaps because they live in one of the coldest climates on earth
(B) while living in one of the coldest climates on earth
(C) perhaps because of living in one of the coldest climates on earth
(D) although they are living in one of the coldest climates on earth
(E) perhaps because it is in one of the coldest climates on earth

10. Dogs generally make a better family pet than cats, because cats often damage furniture.

(A) a better family pet than cats, because cats
(B) better family pets than cats, though cats
(C) a better family pet than cats, though cats
(D) better family pets than cats, because cats
(E) a better family pet than the cat, which

10. Terry Fox, the courageous runner and cancer victim, could not continue his famous run across Canada until he can rely on the faith of his many supportive friends.

(A) can rely on the faith of his many supportive friends
(B) could rely on the faith of his many supportive friends
(C) would be able to rely on the faith of his many supportive friends
(D) can be reliant on the faith of his many supportive friends
(E) could be relying on the faith of his many supportive friends

10. The books I read as a child have made a greater impression on me than <u>any other time in my life</u>.

    (A) any other time in my life
    (B) that of any other time in my life
    (C) those from any other time in my life
    (D) any other time in my life has
    (E) has any other time in my life

11. The junior editor's experience at the publisher proved more challenging than he could have <u>expected, being put</u> in charge of a major book release when the senior editor fell ill.

    (A) expected, being put
    (B) expected; when he was put
    (C) expected; he was put
    (D) expected: one of which was putting him
    (E) expected and he had therefore been put

12. Students in the philosophy seminar hope to better understand the great thinkers of the past <u>and being enlightened by discussions</u> that will help them improve their critical thinking skills.

    (A) and being enlightened by discussions
    (B) as well as to participate in enlightening discussions
    (C) as well as enlightened discussions
    (D) and also by discussions being enlightened
    (E) in addition an expectation is enlightening discussions

13. <u>The uncertain origins of the ancient scrolls raising</u> many interesting questions for archeologists.

    (A) The uncertain origins of the ancient scrolls raising
    (B) The ancient scrolls with their uncertain origins having raised
    (C) Having uncertain origins, the ancient scrolls have
    (D) It is the uncertain origins of the ancient scrolls raising
    (E) The uncertain origins of the ancient scrolls raise

14. When Alice Randall wrote her book *The Wind Done Gone*, <u>the novel *Gone With the Wind* was used as inspiration, but it was never copied exactly by her</u>.

    (A) the novel *Gone With the Wind* was used as inspiration, but it was never copied exactly by her
    (B) the novel *Gone With the Wind* was used as inspiration, but she never copied it exactly
    (C) the novel *Gone With the Wind* was used as inspiration by her and not copied exactly
    (D) she used the novel *Gone With the Wind*, but it was not exactly copied
    (E) she used the novel *Gone With the Wind* as inspiration, but never copied it exactly

IMPROVING SENTENCES DRILL 2

1. The senator <u>told the angry protestors at the meeting that their concerns would be addressed as soon as possible</u>.

   (A) told the angry protestors at the meeting that their concerns would be addressed as soon as possible
   (B) told them of addressing their concerns as soon as possible, the protestors at the meeting were angry
   (C) told that their concerns would be addressed as soon as possible to the angry protestors at the meeting
   (D) telling the angry protestors at the meeting that their concerns would be addressed as soon as possible
   (E) tells the angriest protestors at the meeting, their concerns would be addressed as soon as possible

2. Many fans are surprised to learn that <u>Pink Floyd, one of the most influential rock bands of the 1960's receiving its name after two blues singers, Pink Anderson and Floyd Council</u>.

   (A) Pink Floyd, one of the most influential rock bands of the 1960's receiving its name after two blues singers, Pink Anderson and Floyd Council
   (B) Pink Floyd, one of the most influential rock bands of the 1960's, was named after two blues singers, Pink Anderson and Floyd Council
   (C) Pink Floyd's being one of the most influential rock bands of the 1960's received name after two blues singers, Pink Anderson and Floyd Council
   (D) they named Pink Floyd, one of the most influential rock bands after two blues singers, Pink Anderson and Floyd Council of the 1960's
   (E) the name of Pink Floyd having been one of the most influential rock bands of the 1960's after two blues singers, Pink Anderson and Floyd Council

3. <u>Becky feeling alert and awake, and</u> she fell asleep ten minutes after eating dinner.

   (A) Becky feeling alert and awake, and
   (B) Becky felt alert and awake,
   (C) Although Becky felt alert and awake,
   (D) Despite Becky felt alert and awake,
   (E) Nevertheless, Becky felt alert and awake,

4. Technology enthusiasts woke up before dawn to stand in line on a cold, windy <u>day, to be paying hundreds of dollars</u> to own the latest video game.

   (A) day, to be paying hundreds of dollars
   (B) and it is hundreds of dollars that they pay
   (C) day, they pay hundreds of dollars
   (D) day and pay hundreds of dollars
   (E) day, to have paid hundreds of dollars

5. The Sierra Club is an organization founded in the 1900's that <u>publishes maps and books for lovers of the outdoors and working to protect the environment</u>.

   (A) publishes maps and books for lovers of the outdoors and working to protect the environment
   (B) publishes maps, books, and the protecting of the environment for lovers of the outdoors
   (C) not only publishes maps and books for lovers of the outdoors but also works to protect the environment
   (D) has been publishing maps and books for lovers of the outdoors and were working to protect the environment
   (E) are publishing maps and books for lovers of the outdoors and having worked to protect the environment

6. Ultimate Frisbee and Frisbee Golf <u>are a type of non-traditional sports that</u> have grown in popularity.

   (A) are a type of non-traditional sports that
   (B) are types of non-traditional sports that
   (C) are types where non-traditional sports
   (D) typify a non-traditional sport that
   (E) typify non-traditional sports where they

7. Benjamin Franklin, a noted polymath, invented the lightning rod and <u>bifocals, also he established</u> the first public lending library, published *Poor Richard's Almanac*, and signed the Declaration of Independence.

   (A) bifocals, also he established
   (B) bifocals, and also he establishes
   (C) bifocals, he established
   (D) bifocals; he also established
   (E) bifocals by his establishing

8. Global warming, which is caused by gases that trap the sun's energy, is melting arctic ice, <u>and rising sea levels were caused by this by threatening communities</u> that are below sea level.

   (A) and rising sea levels are caused by this by threatening communities
   (B) rising sea levels are thereby caused and communities threatened
   (C) thereby causing sea levels to rise and threatening communities
   (D) thereby a cause of rising sea levels threaten communities
   (E) but this causes rising sea levels and communities are threatened

9. Consumer organizations praised the corporation for promising either to replace the defective products <u>nor repair</u> them free of charge.

   (A) nor repair
   (B) nor repairing
   (C) nor did they repair
   (D) or by repairing
   (E) or to repair

10. <u>Because bacterial growth causes the deterioration of gum tissue is the reason why</u> Dr. Lenkowitz urges all of his customers to buy a rotary toothbrush.

    (A) Because bacterial growth causes the deterioration of gum tissue is the reason why
    (B) Because bacterial growth causes the deterioration of gum tissue,
    (C) Bacterial growth causes the deterioration of gum tissue is the reason why
    (D) As a result of bacterial growth causing the deterioration of gum tissue;
    (E) The fact of bacterial growth is causing the deterioration of gum tissue is why

11. The foundation commissions new works by aspiring <u>artists and publicizes</u> those artists' earlier works.

    (A) artists and publicizes
    (B) artists, plus it will publicize
    (C) artists, in addition it will publicize
    (D) artists, and additionally, they also publicize
    (E) artists, it publicizes

12. The Rural Electric <u>Administration was created</u> to bring electricity to rural areas such as the Tennessee Valley, was criticized by some members of congress as a dangerous program that would bring the nation one step closer to socialism.

    (A) Administration was created
    (B) Administration is created
    (C) Administration, creating
    (D) Administration, which being created
    (E) Administration, created

13. During World War II, citizens of Great Britain had to make numerous sacrifices, <u>like when they rationed</u> most types of food, which were in short supply.

    (A) like when they rationed
    (B) and, for instance when they rationed
    (C) for instance, with rationing
    (D) as instantiated by when they rationed
    (E) such as rationing

14. Nicknamed "King James," LeBron James is a great basketball <u>player, one who can score at will and is</u> always willing to make the extra pass.

    (A) player, one who can score at will and is
    (B) player, he can score at will and is
    (C) player, and scoring at will in addition to being
    (D) player that scored at will and also is
    (E) player; thus, scoring at will and being also

© TPR Education IP Holdings, LLC

SAT GRAMMAR: NAME THAT (GRAMMAR) TUNE!

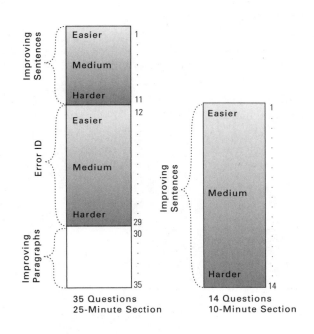

ERROR ID QUESTIONS

The Format

20. Singing about Americans whose plight was unbearable,
     ‾‾‾‾‾‾‾‾‾   ‾‾‾‾‾‾‾‾‾‾ ‾‾‾‾‾‾‾‾‾‾‾‾‾
          A   B   C
     Bob Dylan used the folk song to protest social
                                  ‾‾‾‾‾‾‾‾‾‾
                                      D
     conditions throughout his country. No error
                                        ‾‾‾‾‾‾‾‾
                                           E

The following are a few key points about Error IDs:

- Sentences never have more than one error each.
- Find what **MUST** be wrong instead of what COULD be wrong.
- The non-underlined portions of the sentence are always correct.
- Eliminate any underlined portion of the sentence that you know is error-free.
- Approximately one-fifth of the sentences have no error. Expect choice (E) to be correct for between two and six of the 18 Error ID questions.
- The questions in each Error ID set get progressively harder.

Basic Approach

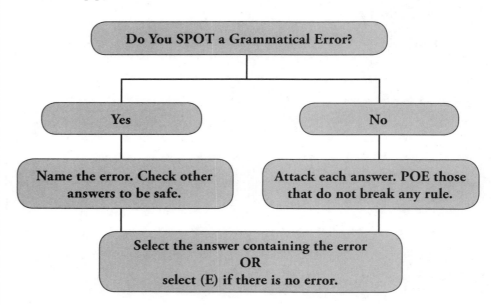

Drill

12. It is a more difficult task to learn to type than
    A   B   C
    mastering a simple word processing program.
    D
    No error
    E

13. The statistics released by the state department
                           A
    makes the economic situation look bleaker than it
    B   C
    already is. No error
             D   E

14. After deliberating for only one hour, the jury
    A   B
    found her actions pointless, cruel, and
    C
    they were unnecessary. No error
         D   E

15. Jeff and Sam, both of whom drive to work, is
                   A   B   C
    actually allergic to walking. No error
    D   E

16. The Halloween party was a great success: the
                        A
    children enjoyed bobbing for apples, playing
                     B   C
    party games, and to wear costumes. No error
                     D   E

19. Japan performed well in the 1980s because
                     A   B
    they were able to export the high quality
    C   D
    technology demanded by consumers. No error
                                     E

20. The American eagle was declared an endangered
                       A
    species in 1967, but in 1995 their status was
                                 B   C
    changed from endangered to merely threatened.
    D
    No error
    E

27. Like many writers , Arundhati Roy's stories about
    A   B
    the contradictions of post-colonial society balance
                                                C
    the author's personal views with those of an entire
                                   D
    culture. No error
             E

28. The marathoner paused briefly during the race to
                         A   B
    drink a few sips of water after he had ran the first
                                           C
    half at a record-setting pace. No error
    D   E

29. Although the peach grows naturally in many
    A   B
    places, bananas must be carefully tended in order
            C
    to flourish. No error
    D   E

MATH

WRITING

READING

VOCABULARY

PRONOUN AMBIGUITY

As we have seen, the first thing you should check about underlined pronouns is agreement. But there are a few other pronoun errors that ETS will occasionally throw at you.

There should be no confusion about what word a pronoun replaces.

Watch out for *it*, *they*, and *this*.

13. Even though Jane and Donna reminded each other
  A
to arrive early at the airport on Friday for their trip to
  B
Boston, she still arrived late, causing them both to
  C   D
miss the flight. No error
  E

15. One of the most influential women in history , Harriet
  A
Tubman was responsible for the escape of thousands of
  B   C
slaves via the Underground Railroad; to Southern society,

however, this was wrong. No error
  D   E

16. The team's research into an experimental treatment for
  A
diabetes made it one of the most promising in the
  B   C   D
field of medicine. No error
  E

18. When the comedian confronted the obnoxious heckler
  A   B
in the front row, he looked embarrassed. No error
  C   D   E

IDIOMS

Consider the following sentences:

The company is just as happy to sell plasma TVs than it is to sell fruit smoothies.

No sooner had one clown left but another one arrived.

It's hard to distinguish Mary-Kate Olsen and Ashley Olsen; they look so much alike.

I gave you the responsibility of deciding which MP3 player to buy, so don't complain.

You just gotta know the idioms. Go to the Practice section after this chapter.

12. Roger was prohibited, by his conscience as well as
             A   B   C
    the team dress code, to wear steel shin guards to the
                       D
    football scrimmage. No error
                  E

13. Olympic skater Tonya Harding wanted not only to win
    a gold medal, which is the goal of every competitive
                 A   B
    skater, plus to break the leg of her rival. No error
             C   D   E

15. The reason why many people vote for a specific
             A
    candidate in a general election is often based less on
                   B   C
    issues than we would like to believe. No error
                  D   E

16. Neither the cellist or the violinist was enamored with
                 A   B
    the music chosen for the evening's recital, but they both
                                C
    played it nonetheless. No error
            D   E

17. The choice the budget committee now has to make is
                                                   A   B
between building the proposed children's playground or
                                                      C
upgrading the park's antiquated facilities. No error
                         D   E

19. The blurb on the novel's jacket cover claimed that the
        A   B
writer's science fiction story was at once imaginative
                                C
and plausible. No error
 D   E

22. The child claimed that the reason he could not find his

shoes was because he had not been wearing them
      A   B   C
when he last came back into the house. No error
        D   E

23. The initial decision for most new car buyers is if they
                        A   B C
want to purchase a new car or a used one. No error
                                     D   E

WHO, WHEN, WHERE, AND IN WHICH

Consider the following sentences:

The doctor is the person which wrote the prescription.

The Triassic period was where the earliest turtles evolved.

Phrenology, what was a theory discredited before the beginning of the twentieth century, was influential despite the fact that it is completely crazy.

Who is used for people, *when* is used for time, and *where* is used for places. Use *in which* for everything else: concepts, ideas, or to indicate that something happens within a situation, condition, or time period.

12. An acrophobic is <u>when you have</u> an <u>unusually</u> strong
                             A   B
      <u>fear of</u> <u>extreme</u> heights. <u>No error</u>
        C   D   E

16. Blind Willie Johnson, a blind guitarist and singer <u>which</u>
                                             A
      is well known for his bottleneck guitar playing, <u>died of</u>
                                            B
      pneumonia <u>shortly after</u> the house he <u>was living in</u>
                  C   D
      burned down, leaving him homeless. <u>No error</u>
                                 E

17. Caisson sickness, <u>which</u> is a condition resulting from
                    A
      rapid decompression, <u>was named</u> by Dr. Andrew Smith,
                                B
      <u>who</u> worked as chief physician <u>during</u> the construction
       C   D
      of the Brooklyn Bridge. <u>No error</u>
                         E

© TPR Education IP Holdings, LLC

MATH · WRITING · READING · VOCABULARY

MATH

WRITING

READING

VOCABULARY

REDUNDANCY
Consider the following sentences:

There is nothing more better than eating butter you have churned yourself.

Steve believes that the complete collapse of human society is imminent and going to happen soon in the future.

The car's speakers hardly never worked.

16. The performer simultaneously juggled bowling pins and

    sang Ave Maria at the same time before transitioning
    ‾‾‾‾ A   ‾‾‾‾‾‾‾‾‾‾‾‾ B
    into his final trick, to the delight of the crowd.
         ‾‾‾ C   ‾‾‾‾‾‾‾‾ D
    No error
    ‾‾‾‾‾‾‾ E

27. The moon has some of the most immense

    and the largest craters in the solar system, including
    ‾‾‾‾‾‾‾‾‾‾‾‾‾ A   ‾‾‾‾‾‾‾‾ B
    the South Pole-Aitken basin, which is larger than the
                                 ‾‾‾‾‾ C ‾‾ D
    size of Mexico. No error
                    ‾‾‾‾‾‾‾ E

29. Mount St. Helens, a volcano that is undergoing
                                      ‾‾ A
    a period of nearly continuous eruption, annually grows
    ‾‾‾‾‾‾‾‾‾ B ‾‾‾‾‾‾ C
    at a rate of approximately 100 feet per year. No error
                                       ‾‾‾‾‾‾‾ D ‾‾‾‾‾‾‾ E

GRAMMAR ET CETERA

12. Photosynthesis <u>is</u> a process <u>when</u> carbohydrates
    $\quad$ A $\quad\quad$ B
    <u>are</u> synthesized from carbon dioxide and water
    C
    using light <u>as</u> an energy source. <u>No error</u>
    $\quad\quad$ D $\quad\quad\quad\quad\quad\quad$ E

13. The best action to take if you come across a snake

    <u>is</u> to <u>slow and quiet</u> move away, <u>leaving</u> a passage
    A $\quad\quad$ B $\quad\quad\quad\quad\quad\quad\quad$ C
    by which <u>it</u> can escape. <u>No error</u>
    $\quad\quad$ D $\quad\quad\quad\quad$ E

14. Jim <u>has</u> <u>less</u> reasons <u>to move</u> to the country <u>than</u>
    $\quad\quad$ A $\quad$ B $\quad\quad$ C $\quad\quad\quad\quad\quad\quad$ D
    he has to stay in the city. <u>No error</u>
    $\quad\quad\quad\quad\quad\quad\quad\quad$ E

15. Of the two competing theories, Dr. Andrew's

    hypothesis <u>is</u> the <u>most</u> credible because his
    $\quad\quad\quad$ A $\quad\quad$ B
    <u>analysis of</u> the relevant research <u>is</u> so thorough.
    $\quad$ C $\quad\quad\quad\quad\quad\quad\quad\quad\quad$ D
    <u>No error</u>
    $\quad$ E

16. Libertarianism <u>is</u> a political belief system <u>where</u>
    $\quad\quad\quad\quad$ A $\quad\quad\quad\quad\quad\quad\quad\quad$ B
    individual rights <u>are</u> maximized and the <u>role of</u>
    $\quad\quad\quad\quad\quad$ C $\quad\quad\quad\quad\quad\quad$ D
    the state is minimized. <u>No error</u>
    $\quad\quad\quad\quad\quad\quad\quad$ E

17. In demand <u>as</u> yearbook editor and co-captain
    $\quad\quad\quad$ A
    of the basketball team, Jerome <u>has never been</u>
    $\quad\quad\quad\quad\quad\quad\quad\quad\quad\quad$ B
    more <u>busier</u> than <u>he is</u> this semester. <u>No error</u>
    C $\quad\quad\quad$ D $\quad\quad\quad\quad\quad\quad$ E

18. Students <u>which</u> take extra classes and participate
    $\quad\quad\quad$ A
    <u>in</u> too many outside activities <u>can</u> sometimes exert
    B $\quad\quad\quad\quad\quad\quad\quad\quad\quad$ C
    <u>themselves</u> to the point of exhaustion. <u>No error</u>
    $\quad$ D $\quad\quad\quad\quad\quad\quad\quad\quad\quad\quad$ E

19. <u>Between</u> the field of competitors, there <u>were</u> fierce
    $\quad$ A $\quad\quad\quad\quad\quad\quad\quad\quad\quad\quad$ B
    rivalries <u>stemming from</u> many years <u>of</u> conflict
    $\quad\quad\quad$ C $\quad\quad\quad\quad\quad\quad$ D
    and misunderstandings. <u>No error</u>
    $\quad\quad\quad\quad\quad\quad\quad$ E

20. <u>Because</u> we have not had a moment to spare, <u>we</u>
    $\quad$ A $\quad\quad\quad\quad\quad\quad\quad\quad\quad\quad$ B
    <u>have not barely</u> started thinking <u>about</u> our trip.
    $\quad$ C $\quad\quad\quad\quad\quad\quad\quad$ D
    <u>No error</u>
    $\quad$ E

MATH

WRITING

READING

VOCABULARY

21. The prisoner, <u>along with</u> his accomplice, <u>was</u>
    $\overset{\text{A}}{}$ $\overset{\text{B}}{}$
    <u>visual to the guard</u> <u>observing</u> the road. <u>No error</u>
    $\overset{\text{C}}{}$ $\overset{\text{D}}{}$ $\overset{\text{E}}{}$

22. <u>Even though</u> common sense might
    $\overset{\text{A}}{}$
    <u>suggest otherwise</u> , the invention of the parachute
    $\overset{\text{B}}{}$
    <u>actually occurred</u> prior to the <u>airplane</u>. <u>No error</u>
    $\overset{\text{C}}{}$ $\overset{\text{D}}{}$ $\overset{\text{E}}{}$

23. Only after Martin <u>drives</u> <u>aimlessly</u> for several
    $\overset{\text{A}}{}$ $\overset{\text{B}}{}$
    miles was <u>he willing</u> to stop <u>in order to</u> ask for
    $\overset{\text{C}}{}$ $\overset{\text{D}}{}$
    directions. <u>No error</u>
    $\overset{\text{E}}{}$

24. Between you and <u>I</u> , it is unclear <u>whether</u> <u>our</u> gym
    $\overset{\text{A}}{}$ $\overset{\text{B}}{}$ $\overset{\text{C}}{}$
    teacher can tie his own shoes <u>much less</u> lead us in
    $\overset{\text{D}}{}$
    calisthenics drills. <u>No error</u>
    $\overset{\text{E}}{}$

25. In her senior thesis, Grace <u>studied</u> the relationship
    $\overset{\text{A}}{}$
    between the engineering prowess <u>of</u> the ancient
    $\overset{\text{B}}{}$
    Romans <u>with</u> the subsequent success <u>of their</u>
    $\overset{\text{C}}{}$ $\overset{\text{D}}{}$
    empire building. <u>No error</u>
    $\overset{\text{E}}{}$

26. Not <u>surprisingly</u> , Katie and Michelle, <u>members of</u>
    $\overset{\text{A}}{}$ $\overset{\text{B}}{}$
    the Reilly High soccer team, <u>scored</u> several goals
    $\overset{\text{C}}{}$
    <u>each</u> in the state championship. <u>No error</u>
    $\overset{\text{D}}{}$ $\overset{\text{E}}{}$

27. If both parties <u>would know</u> <u>how long</u> and difficult
    $\overset{\text{A}}{}$ $\overset{\text{B}}{}$
    the conflict was <u>likely to be</u> , the earlier settlement
    $\overset{\text{C}}{}$
    talks might have been more <u>fruitful</u>. <u>No error</u>
    $\overset{\text{D}}{}$ $\overset{\text{E}}{}$

28. My trainer told me <u>that if</u> my arm <u>hurts after</u>
    $\overset{\text{A}}{}$ $\overset{\text{B}}{}$
    lifting a weight during exercise, <u>I should</u> apply ice
    $\overset{\text{C}}{}$
    to <u>it</u> rather than heat. <u>No error</u>
    $\overset{\text{D}}{}$ $\overset{\text{E}}{}$

29. The labor dispute <u>was</u> <u>caused</u> by both long hours
    $\overset{\text{A}}{}$ $\overset{\text{B}}{}$
    <u>as well as</u> <u>unsafe</u> working conditions. <u>No error</u>
    $\overset{\text{C}}{}$ $\overset{\text{D}}{}$ $\overset{\text{E}}{}$

MISCELLANEOUS GRAMMAR

Active Voice

Consider the following sentences:

Ichiro hit the ball. He hit the ball.

The ball was hit by Ichiro. The ball was hit by him.

4. After Nixon spent months trying to counter bad press and pressure from his own party, <u>resignation was chosen by him instead of facing the impeachment process</u>.

   (A) resignation was chosen by him instead of facing the impeachment process
   (B) resignation was chosen instead of impeachment
   (C) resignation was the choice made by him rather than facing the impeachment process
   (D) he chose to resign rather than face impeachment
   (E) he chose resignation rather than being impeached

6. <u>When difficult classes are taken by Kate, she finds</u> it difficult to complete all the homework that is assigned.

   (A) When difficult classes are taken by Kate, she finds
   (B) When difficult classes are taken by Kate finding
   (C) Kate takes difficult classes she finds
   (D) When Kate takes difficult classes, she finds
   (E) When the taking of difficult classes is by Kate, she finds

ETS wants you to use the active voice whenever possible. So while the passive voice isn't grammatically incorrect, avoid it if possible.

MATH

WRITING

READING

VOCABULARY

Excess Nounification

Consider the following sentences:

Sally has a shellfish allergy, which prevents her from the consumption of clam chowder.

The university had given us the preparation to succeed in the world.

On the SAT, when you have a choice, use a verb.

6. <u>Political activists, often by means of aggressive propagandizing, have tried to increase its</u> lead among undecided voters.

   (A) Political activists, often by means of aggressive propagandizing, have tried to increase its
   (B) The aggressiveness of the propagandizing of political activists in trying to increase their
   (C) By means of often aggressive propagandizing, political activists, in trying to increase its
   (D) Political activists have often used aggressive propaganda to increase their
   (E) Often by means of aggressive propagandizing, political activists have tried to increase their

Awkward -*ing* Constructions

Consider the following sentences:

Einstein was the first scientist having conceived that there was no privileged frame of reference in the universe.

People are afraid to take risks because of knowing the danger that risk-taking involves.

Andrew was often found at the library, being that he loved to read books.

My desiring to help the police solve the crime led me to call the anonymous tip line.

Watch for verbs with -*ing* endings (being, having, etc.) They frequently make a sentence awkward and unnecessarily wordy.

5. After the snow stopped falling, my friends and I, <u>being excited over school having been canceled and excited over freeing us from homework, decided</u> to go sledding.

(A) being excited over school having been canceled and excited over freeing us from homework, decided

(B) excited that school was cancelled and that we were free from homework, decided

(C) excited over school being canceled, also over the freedom from homework, made a decision

(D) in that we were excited about the cancellation of school and also about the freedom from homework, made a decision

(E) because of our excitement concerning the cancellation of school, also concerning our freedom from homework, decided

MATH

WRITING

READING

VOCABULARY

Verb Tense

Tenses should be consistent unless the meaning of the sentence requires a change.

The majority of sentences you will encounter on the SAT will stick to simple past, simple present or simple future tense.

The basic tenses are the following:

Past: *I **played** basketball yesterday.*

Present: *I **play** basketball every day.*

Future: *I **will play** basketball next week.*

Present Perfect

The present perfect is constructed with the helping verb *has* or *have* (depending on whether the subject is singular or plural). It describes events that were completed in the past at an unspecified time. Perfect tenses are not tested often on the SAT.

*I **have been** to Costa Rica.*

*He **has read** <u>The Three Musketeers</u>.*

*They **have told** you before not to run with scissors.*

The present perfect is also used for events that started in the past and continue into the present.

*I **have lived** in Minneapolis for six years.*

*He **has been** president of the university since July.*

*Jeff **has played** billiards every day this week.*

Past Perfect

The following sentences correctly use the past perfect tense.

> I **had planned** to watch the "Love Boat" TV marathon until I **came** to my senses.

> My brother **had played** foosball every day before he **broke** his wrist.

> Delilah **had thought** nothing could be worse than Ewoks, but then she **saw** Jar Jar Binks.

Subjunctive

The following sentences correctly use the subjunctive.

> **If** politicians **told** the truth, then voters would not be so cynical.

> I wish I **were** back in Norwalk.

- Do NOT use "would" in an "if" clause. Use either the past tense or "were" in the "if" part of the sentence.
- After verbs that express a wish (insist, recommend, demand, desire, urge, require, mandate, ask), use the basic form of the verb, which is the infinitive form without the "to" (run, be, go, dance, sing).

Subjunctive is rarely tested, so don't sweat if you're not an expert.

MATH

WRITING

READING

VOCABULARY

REVIEW
Try the following questions on your own.

8. I <u>just stepped</u> out into the street when a car came speeding past me, missing me by inches.

   (A) just stepped
   (B) just stepping
   (C) had just stepped
   (D) would have just stepped
   (E) was to have just stepped

9. The Roman general could not invade his enemy's territory until he <u>can gather an army at least twice the size of his opponent's</u>.

   (A) can gather an army at least twice the size of his opponent's
   (B) could gather an army at least twice the size of his opponent's
   (C) would be able to gather an army at least twice the size of his opponent's
   (D) can gather an army at least twice the size of his opponent
   (E) could gather an army at least twice the size of his opponent

10. Delia <u>has been planning to attend</u> Boston College; however, after visiting the campus, she changed her mind.

    (A) has been planning to attend
    (B) has been planning on attending
    (C) had planned to attend
    (D) would have planned to attend
    (E) was to have planned to attend

11. Perhaps Karen <u>would be more popular if she would stop</u> correcting people's grammar all the time.

    (A) would be more popular if she would stop
    (B) would be more popular if she was to stop
    (C) were more popular if she would stop
    (D) will be more popular if she would stop
    (E) would be more popular if she stopped

Summary

Every SAT Grammar category you see in this table could be tested. What isn't here won't be tested; so, master this Rules Table!

If the underlined portion is a...	...check for...
verb	agreement parallelism tense
pronoun	agreement case ambiguity/vagueness redundancy
noun	agreement parallelism redundancy
preposition	improper idiom
phrase or clause	misplaced modifiers conjunction errors redundancy improper idiom parallelism

adjective or adverb	adjective/adverb
	   confusion
	diction error
	double negative
	counting error
	comparative/
	   superlative
	   confusion
	parallelism
	modification error

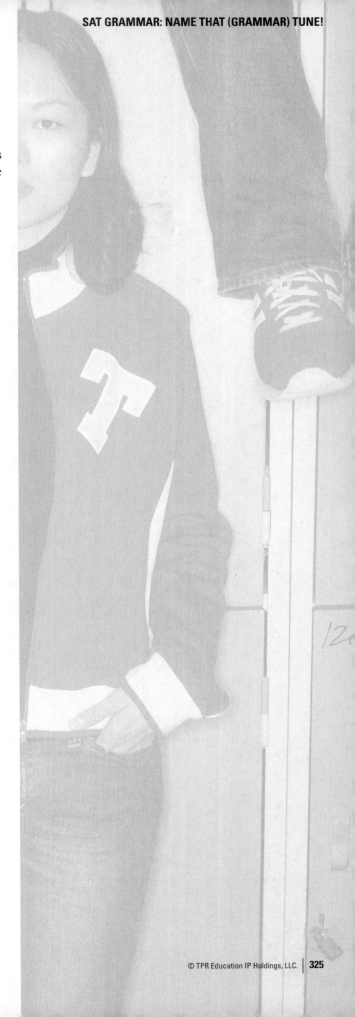

SAT GRAMMAR:
MASTERING ERROR ID

IDIOM LIST

Here's a list of the idioms tested most frequently on the SAT. Learn them!

About

Worry…about

If you **worry** too much **about** the SAT you'll develop an ulcer.

As

Define…as

Some people **define** insanity **as** repeating the same action but expecting a different outcome.

Regard…as

Art historians **regard** the *Mona Lisa* **as** one of the greatest works of art.

Not so…as

He is **not so** much smart **as** cunning.

So…as to be

She is **so** beautiful **as to be** exquisite.

Think of…as

Think of it more **as** a promise than a threat.

See…as

Many people **see** euthanasia **as** an escape from pain.

The same…as

Mom and Dad gave **the same** punishment to me **as** to you.

As…as

Memorizing idioms is not **as** fun **as** playing bingo.

At

Target…at

The commercials were obviously **targeted at** teenage boys.

For

Responsible for

You are **responsible for** the child.

From

Prohibit…from

He was **prohibited from** entering the public library after he accidentally set the dictionary on fire with a magnifying glass.

Different…from

Democrats are not so **different from** Republicans in the United States.

Over

Dispute over

The men had a **dispute over** money.

That

So…that

He was **so** late **that** he missed the main course.

Hypothesis…that

The **hypothesis that** aspartame causes brain tumors has not been proven yet.

To be

Believe…to be

His friends do not **believe** the ring he bought at the auction **to be** Jackie O's; they all think he was tricked.

Estimate…to be

The time he has spent impersonating Elvis is **estimated to be** longer than the time Elvis himself spent performing.

To

Forbid…to

I **forbid** you **to** call me before noon.

Ability…to

If you take the test enough times, you might develop the **ability to** choose the credited responses without reading the questions.

Attribute…to

Many amusing quips are **attributed to** Dorothy Parker.

Require…to

Before you enter the house you are **required to** take off your hat.

MATH

WRITING

READING

VOCABULARY

MATH

WRITING

READING

VOCABULARY

Responsibility...to

You have a **responsibility to** take care of the child.

Permit...to

I don't **permit** my children **to** play with knives in the living room.

Superior...to

My pasta sauce is far **superior to** my mother-in-law's.

Try...to

Try to stay awake during the essay section of the test.

With

Credit...with

Many people **credit** Christopher Columbus **with** the discovery of America, but Native Americans were here first.

Associate...with

Most politicians prefer not to be **associated with** the Mafia.

Contrast...with

My father likes to **contrast** my grades **with** my brother's.

No preposition

Consider...(nothing)

Art historians **consider** the *Mona Lisa* one of the greatest works of art.

More than one preposition

Distinguish...from

I can't **distinguish** day **from** night.

Distinguish between...and

I can **distinguish between** black **and** white.

Native (noun)... of

Russell Crowe is a **native of** Australia.

Native (adjective)...to

The kangaroo is **native to** Australia.

Comparisons and Links

Not only…but also

She is **not only** beautiful, **but also** smart.

Not…but

The review was **not** mean-spirited **but** merely flippant.

Either…or

I must have **either** chocolate ice cream **or** carrot cake to complete a great meal.

Neither…nor

Because Jenny was grounded, she could **neither** leave the house **nor** use the telephone.

Both…and

When given the choice, I choose **both** ice cream **and** cake.

More…than; Less…than

The chimpanzee is much **more** intelligent **than** the orangutan.

As vs. like

As is used to compare actions.

Like is used to compare nouns.

He did not vote for the Libertarian Party, **as** I did.

Her coat is just **like** mine.

Like vs. such as

Like means *similar to.*

Such as means *for example.*

The mule, **like** the donkey, is a close relative of the horse.

Many of my favorite ice cream flavors, **such as** chocolate chip and strawberry, are also available as frozen yogurt.

The more…the -er

The more you ignore me, the **closer** I get.

From…to

Scores on the SAT range **from** 200 **to** 800.

Just as…so too

Just as I crossed over to the dark side, **so too** will you, my son.

© TPR Education IP Holdings, LLC

MATH

WRITING

READING

VOCABULARY

MATH

WRITING

READING

VOCABULARY

Miscellaneous

<u>Each vs. all or both</u>

Use *each* when you want to emphasize the separateness of the items.

Use *both* (for two things) or *all* (for more than two things) when you want to emphasize the togetherness of the items.

Each of the doctors had his own specialty.

Both of the women went to Bryn Mawr for their undergraduate degrees.

All of the letters received before January 15 went into the drawing for the $10 million prize.

<u>Whether vs. if</u>

Use *whether* when there are *two possibilities*.

Use *if* in *conditional statements*.

Eduardo wasn't sure **whether** he could make it to the party.

If Eduardo comes to the party, he will bring a bag of chips.

Yes, These Are Real Words

Sometimes the SAT likes to use big words to frighten you. If you see these in an Improving Sentences or Improving Paragraphs question, see if ETS has given you an option to use a simpler, more direct word.

Furthermore	Nonetheless
Heretofore	Notwithstanding
Hereinafter	Ought
Inasmuch	Ongoing
Insofar	Therefore
Likewise	Thereby
Moreover	Whereas
Nevertheless	Whereby

 © TPR Education IP Holdings, LLC

Idiom Drill 1

Fill in the blanks below, if necessary. If you need some review first, make idiom flashcards!

1. I am indebted _____ you.

2. I am resentful _____ you.

3. I am jealous _____ you.

4. I am different _____ you.

5. The women had a dispute _____ you.

6. Lindsay's books fell off _____ the wall.

7. In our secret clubhouse, a majority is defined _____ two-thirds or more.

8. You have a responsibility _____ take care of your pet.

9. You are responsible _____ your pet.

10. He was horrified to read his sister's diary and find himself depicted _____ a jerk.

11. Jessie was named _____ president of her senior class.

12. I am planning _____ get my driver's license soon.

13. Lindsay will try _____ attend Morgan's party.

14. Ana intends _____ major in mathematics.

15. It is **not so much** a question of knowing rules _____ it is memorizing the idioms that show up frequently.

16. This memorization can easily be **achieved** _____ using flash cards.

17. **Just as** this will improve your essay, _____ will it increase your score on the multiple-choice section.

MATH

WRITING

READING

VOCABULARY

Idiom Drill 2

Some idioms do not even involve prepositions. Give these a try.

1. ETS loves to test **not only** idioms _____ parallelism on some of these questions.

2. The writers are just **as** happy to test one _____ they are to test the other.

3. That disc jockey is **at once** interesting _____ offensive.

4. **Both** Carin _____ Graham worked very hard to finish their work over the weekend.

5. **Between** you _____ me, I am not sure that they did.

6. **Either** one _____ the other had extra math homework to do.

7. **Neither** John _____ Alex has any free time anymore.

8. It is hard to **determine** _____ Christine ever sleeps.

9. The last four months have been **so** intense _____ I sometimes forget what day it is.

10. **No sooner** had I finished one project _____ another one arrived.

11. Sometimes I **prefer** green tea _____ coffee when I need to stay awake at night, even though there is firm evidence _____ support the claim _____ coffee contains four times **more** antioxidants _____ green tea does.

12. Tea is certainly **no more** flavorful _____ coffee.

13. Furthermore, coffee contains **from** two _____ five times _____ much caffeine _____ tea does.

14. Still, I am just **as** fond of tea _____ my friend Roger is.

Pronoun Practice

Take a look at these sentences. If necessary, correct the use of pronouns.

1. Between you and me, Harry is not a very good dancer.

   _____

2. Who did that work? It was him.

   _____

3. I'm going to get myself some new shoes.

   _____

4. I've completed more assignments than they.

   _____

5. Kelly can yodel better than him.

   _____

6. To whom shall I give it?

   _____

7. You can count on Al and me to do a good job.

   _____

8. It's me!

   _____

9. There's nobody here except for us chickens.

   _____

Pronoun Patrol

In the following sentences, decide which of the choices is the better one to use in the blank.

1. You and _____ will rule the world.
   I/me

2. Just between you and _____, I think the bus
   I/me

   driver is hot.

3. If anyone deserves recognition for their contribution,

   it is _____.
   they/them

4. _____ cheerleaders are planning to burn our
   We/Us

   pompoms.

5. It is _____ right to have a bad hair day.
   my/myself

6. You can't have that tofu; it belongs to _____!
   she/her

7. _____ is planning an overthrow of the school
   He/Himself

   government.

8. If it were _____ decision, I wouldn't give
   my/mine

   _____ the time of day.
   he/him

9. That pair of platform shoes is _____.
   herself/hers

10. If Ellen did it _____, she could save at least
    herself/hers

    10 cents.

11. _____ dog is better looking than _____
    We/Our   we/our

    cat is.

12. Let's just keep this secret between you and

    _____ .
    my/me

13. At _____ did you throw that paper airplane?
    who/whom

14. To _____, you sound terrible
    we/us

15. Perhaps they should keep their opinions to

    _____ .
    theirself/themselves

SOME OF ETS'S FAVORITE DICTION ERRORS

The SAT does not test spelling, but you may see one of these commonly confused words. These diction errors are not frequently tested on the SAT.

_____ allusion vs. illusion _____

_____ implicate vs. imply _____

_____perspective vs. prospective _____

_____ describe vs. ascribe_____

_____ deduce vs. induce_____

_____consciousness vs. conscience_____

_____ compliment vs. complement _____

_____ elude vs. allude _____

_____ desirous vs. desirable _____

_____ principal vs. principle _____

_____ accept vs. except _____

_____indict vs. induct_____

_____ declined vs. descended _____

_____ precede vs. proceed_____

_____ affect vs. effect_____

ERROR ID DRILL 1

The following sentences contain problems with grammar, usage, diction (word choice), and idioms. No sentence contains more than one error. Select (E) if there is no error. If you find an error, circle it. Then, name the grammatical error in the blank next to the question number.

Verb Tense **12.** Despite the existence of scientific proof
A
to the contrary, the Flat Earth Society continues
B
(to have argued) that we do not live on a globe.
C   D
No error
E

13. Robert felt that the novelist was trying

not only to incite her readers to arms,
A   B
but also educating them. No error
C   D   E

14. Revered as one of the world's most versatile
A
geniuses, Leonardo da Vinci excelled in
B
every endeavor and serving as a prototype of
C   D
the Renaissance man. No error
E

15. Jill, Marie, and Dana was seriously affected
A
by the high temperatures and the humidity

when they were traveling through the
B   C   D
South Pacific. No error
E

16. Her final suggestions were to increase the
A
size of the staff, install a refrigerator and
B
coffeemaker and, most important,
C
the firing of the personnel director. No error
D   E

17. Educators and parents agree that a daily
A
reading time will not only enhance a child's
B
education but also helping the child to read
C   D
independently. No error
E

18. Michael later discovered that Melissa and
A
he were the only people in the class to score
B C   D
higher than eighty on the test. No error
E

19. Pilot carelessness, rather than equipment
A
malfunctions, were responsible for the
B   C
near disaster at Kennedy Airport. No error
D   E

20. The continual improvements in athletic
A
training methods has made performances
B
that would have been considered impossible
C
a generation ago everyday occurrences.
D
No error
E

_____21. Most of the contestants feel that the rules
                A   B
that pertains to the race are far too strict.
        C   D
No error
   E

_____22. If you invite Joanna to the party, then
               A
you have no choice but to invite her
   B   C
boyfriend Rico as well . No error
                  D   E

_____23. Doug is so fond of chocolate that he eats
                A   B   C
at least three candy bars a day or more .
                               D
No error
   E

_____24. Yesterday, much to the dismay of his wife,
                          A
the new anchorperson has worn a red
                       B
necktie that did not match his green suit.
              C   D
No error
   E

_____25. Just last month, 92-year-old Fyodor, two

weeks after the announcement of elections
      A   B
in Georgia, has cast his first vote in 70
             C   D
years. No error
         E

_____26. Many young adults find it extremely difficult
                              A
to return home from college and abide with
   B   C
the rules set down by their parents. No error
                      D   E

_____27. The Eastern Arrente people of Australia's
                                    A
Northern Territory preserve traditions in age-
                    B
old carvings that serve as records of ancient
                C   D
cultural practices. No error
                      E

_____28. An ongoing argument rages between

Akil and I as we have such wildly different
   A   B
ideas about which we cannot agree. No error
      C   D   E

_____29. Rick said that he would hire more people to
                          A   B
work in the office if Adam would prove it
   C   D
was absolutely necessary. No error
                            E

ERROR ID DRILL 2

The following sentences contain problems with grammar, usage, diction (word choice), and idioms. No sentence contains more than one error. Select (E) if there is no error. If you find an error, circle it. Then, name the grammatical error in the blank next to the question number.

_____ 12. The children enjoyed playing pin-the-tail-
                                     A   B
on-the-donkey, going on a scavenger hunt,
                        C
and to bob for apples. No error
       D   E

_____ 13. The new course schedule worked out
                                              A
splendid for all students
   B   C
who had been worried . No error
        D   E

_____ 14. The secretary must attend all meetings, call
                              A   B
the roll, and collect the minutes from past
                C   D
board conferences. No error
                        E

_____ 15. Instead of concentrating on doing their
                  A   B
homework as they should, many teenagers
           C
watch television, talk on the phone, and

they listen to the radio. No error
       D   E

_____ 16. She hunted frantic through the grass,
                           A
trying to find the diamond ring that had just
       B   C
slipped off her finger. No error
       D   E

_____ 17. When I reached the back of the clubhouse,
                  A   B
I saw Brian flirting with Jess and Mary at the

pool side, something she seemed to enjoy
                        C
immensely . No error
   D   E

_____ 18. The members of the board listened patiently
                           A   B
to the excuses the director gave , but in the
                             C
end they decided to fire him . No error
                          D   E

_____ 19. I bet that between you and I , we could
                        A   B   C   D
split a six-foot submarine sandwich.

No error
   E

_____ 20. For we city dwellers, it is difficult to
                  A   B
imagine life without taxicabs that cost so
                                    C
little and subways that run all night.
                         D
No error
   E

MATH

WRITING

READING

VOCABULARY

_____**21.** For hours on end, he <u>repeated</u> the same
　　　　　　　　　　　　A
tired old phrases <u>until</u> someone finally
　　　　　　　　　B
demanded that he <u>sit down and be quiet</u> .
　　C　　　　　　　　　D
<u>No error</u>
　E

_____**22.** <u>Although</u> the professor had <u>heretofore</u>
　　　　　　A　　　　　　　　　　　B
been quite entertaining, today's lecture <u>put</u>
　　　　　　　　　　　　　　　　　　　　C
<u>half</u> of the class to sleep. <u>No error</u>
　D　　　　　　　　　　　E

_____**23.** John is a musician who <u>has</u> perfect pitch
　　　　　　　　　　　　　　A
<u>and</u> <u>a person who can</u> play by ear <u>nearly</u>
　B　　C　　　　　　　　　　D
every song he hears. <u>No error</u>
　　　　　　　　　　E

_____**24.** She <u>ought to have</u> defended <u>her</u> principles
　　　　　　　A　　　　　　　　　B
rather <u>than giving</u> in to the majority.
　　C　　D
<u>No error</u>
　E

_____**25.** <u>Although</u> the weatherman <u>has forecast</u>
　　　　　　A　　　　　　　　　B
rain, the students <u>are</u> planning <u>on attending</u>
　　　　　　　　C　　　　　　D
Saturday's picnic in the park. <u>No error</u>
　　　　　　　　　　　　　E

_____**26.** Doug and Joey both <u>need</u> <u>a moth</u> for <u>their</u>
　　　　　　　　　　A　　B　　　C
insect collections <u>to be</u> complete. <u>No error</u>
　　　　　　　D　　　　　　　E

_____**27.** The winds kicked up so much dust <u>during</u>
　　　　　　　　　　　　　　　　A
the storm <u>that</u> the air-traffic controllers
　　　　B
<u>could not</u> scarcely see the planes they
　C
<u>were guiding</u> . <u>No error</u>
　D　　　　　E

_____**28.** The <u>question of</u> <u>whether to stay</u> at home or
　　　　　A　　　B
to visit other countries <u>are</u> difficult for both
　　　　　　　　　　　C
him and me to answer. <u>No error</u>
　D　　　　　　　　E

_____**29.** Mrs. Olivera rarely <u>complemented</u> students;
　　　　　　　　　　　A
<u>they</u> <u>would have to</u> <u>accomplish</u> a near
　B　　C　　　　　D
miracle in order to receive any recognition.

<u>No error</u>
　E

ERROR ID DRILL 3

The following sentences contain problems with grammar, usage, diction (word choice), and idioms. No sentence contains more than one error. Select (E) if there is no error. If you find an error, circle it. Then, name the grammatical error in the blank next to the question number.

_____ **12.** During the American Civil War, skilled
              A
     horsemen <u>were</u> used to fill the ranks
             B
     of <u>the cavalry</u> as well as <u>scouting</u> enemy
           C   D
     locations. <u>No error</u>
              E

_____ **13.** The model car <u>was taking</u> an extremely
                 A
     long time to <u>put together</u> , because Tommy's
             B
     father <u>having lost</u> the instructions <u>for</u> the
           C   D
     assembly of the vehicle. <u>No error</u>
                    E

_____ **14.** The director told the star of the production

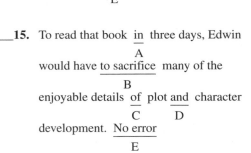

     that <u>he</u> <u>was making</u> far too much money
         A   B
     to <u>tolerate</u> such nasty treatment <u>from</u> the
         C   D
     producer. <u>No error</u>
             E

_____ **15.** To read that book <u>in</u> three days, Edwin
                  A
     would have to <u>sacrifice</u> many of the
             B
     enjoyable details <u>of</u> plot <u>and</u> character
                C   D
     development. <u>No error</u>
               E

_____ **16.** My art history professor prefers
     Michelangelo's paintings <u>to viewing</u> his
                      A
     sculptures, <u>even though</u> Michelangelo
              B
     himself <u>was</u> prouder <u>of</u> the latter.
           C   D
     <u>No error</u>
       E

_____ **17.** Rome is an <u>exceedingly</u> beautiful city
                 A
     <u>largely</u> because <u>they have</u> <u>successfully</u>
       B   C   D
     blended the modern with the ancient.

     <u>No error</u>
       E

_____ **18.** Dieting and exercise <u>is</u> not the answers <u>to</u>
                         A   B
     all weight problems, but they <u>should</u> be
                      C
     effective for <u>most</u> waistlines. <u>No error</u>
            D   E

_____ **19.** Most critics <u>agreed that of</u> the two movies
               A
     <u>shown</u> on the opening day of the film
      B
     festival, the first <u>was the</u> <u>better</u> . <u>No error</u>
                C   D   E

_____20. A dilemma is <u>when</u> a person <u>is faced</u> with
             A   B
two or more choices, <u>each</u> of <u>which</u> leads
                    C   D
to undesirable consequences. <u>No error</u>
                          E

_____21. Maps <u>of</u> the city are <u>available at</u> the front
          A   B
desk <u>but</u> they <u>can be picked up</u> any time
      C   D
during the day. <u>No error</u>
              E

_____22. The two poets <u>are</u> famous throughout
           A
their <u>respective</u> countries, <u>and</u> they are
        B   C
completely unknown <u>in this</u> country.
                 D
<u>No error</u>
  E

_____23. <u>After</u> a thorough physical examination, the
      A
doctor <u>reviewed</u> the test result data <u>with</u>
       B   C
Melissa, and <u>she</u> was very pleased.
         D
<u>No error</u>
  E

_____24. Jonathan found it <u>quite</u> challenging to
              A
<u>illicit</u> responses from the students in <u>his</u>
  B   C
7:30 A.M. class; <u>they</u> were all half asleep
           D
from studying too much. <u>No error</u>
                E

_____25. The <u>finish</u> of the 100-meter race was so
       A
close that each of the first five finishers
    B
thought <u>that</u> <u>they</u> had won. <u>No error</u>
      C   D   E

_____26. The doctor warned all of his patients <u>to be</u>
                             A
especially careful <u>because</u> the upcoming
      B   C
season's flu promised to be highly
<u>communicative</u> . <u>No error</u>
     D   E

_____27. The principle is <u>clear, all</u> contestants should
                A
<u>be given</u> an equal opportunity to <u>fully</u>
  B   C
<u>prepare for the science fair</u> . <u>No error</u>
         D   E

_____28. Although <u>their</u> conceptual foundations are
           A
quite different, <u>both</u> biology and chemistry
      B   C
are considered <u>as</u> natural sciences.
             D
<u>No error</u>
  E

_____29. Although Beyoncé has a better voice than
          A
<u>him</u> , Billy <u>insists on</u> leading his class
  B   C
<u>during</u> the national anthem. <u>No error</u>
  D   E

ERROR ID DRILL 4

The following sentences contain problems with grammar, usage, diction (word choice), and idioms. No sentence contains more than one error. Select (E) if there is no error. If you find an error, circle it. Then, name the grammatical error in the blank next to the question number.

_____12. The exacting editor looked close
                                           A
at the young author's final manuscript, but
    B
could find no typographical, grammatical,
                 C
or other errors . No error
        D   E

_____13. The entry requirements state that all
                              A
skateboarders must have been wearing
                          B
protective gear while performing in the
                          C
competition, regardless of their age.
                  D
No error
   E

_____14. The enforcement of Hammurabi's complex
                        A
legal code did not extend to territories
              B
on the border of Mesopotamia, where
      C
there was barely no loyalty to the great
                D
Babylonian leader. No error
                       E

_____15. The concept of black holes

was first proposed a century ago, but
       A   B
not until more advanced technology
            C
became available did the detection of such

occurrences become a reality. No error
    D   E

_____16. Discount coupons are accepted at the
                                   A
designer's downtown location, and they
                                 B   C
are not accepted at the designer's suburban
              D
locations. No error
              E

_____17. Because the elderly dog's physical condition
                   A
rapidly descended , the veterinarian decided
   B   C
at long last to undertake the risky operation.
        D
No error
   E

_____18. Mark Twain wrote novels where he
                             A   B
described the joys and trials of life on the
                                 C
Mississippi in the nineteenth century .
                      D
No error
   E

_____19. The chief obligations of the vice president
                              A
of the United States are to preside over the
                        B
Senate and assuming the presidency
               C
should the current president be
    D
incapacitated. No error
                   E

20. Although <u>Katrina and I</u> realize that the risk
A
of injury <u>while</u> bungee jumping is
B
<u>small from</u> an objective standpoint, the
C
prospect of making a leap still sounds fairly

frightening to both her and <u>me</u>. <u>No error</u>
D   E

21. The visiting team <u>scores</u> a winning
A
touchdown with seconds <u>to go</u> , <u>just when</u>
B   C
the hometown fans expected certain victory

for <u>their</u> team. <u>No error</u>
D   E

22. The impact <u>of</u> air pollution, <u>far from</u> being
A   B
evenly distributed throughout the state,

seems to be concentrated <u>in</u> its metropolitan
C   D
areas. <u>No error</u>
E

23. For all their <u>size</u> , elephants,
A
<u>plant-eating animals</u> <u>indigenous to</u> Asia
B   C
<u>but also</u> Africa, are remarkably passive.
D
<u>No error</u>
E

24. The district attorney <u>was not able to</u>
A
<u>precede</u> with her investigation <u>until</u> she
B   C
convinced a judge to grant her <u>extensive</u>
D
search warrants. <u>No error</u>
E

25. <u>Despite</u> Sam's shaky beginning <u>at</u> the start
A   B
of the term, the average of his scores on the

midterm quizzes <u>were</u> high and by the end
C
of the term he had achieved an <u>outstanding</u>
D
final grade. <u>No error</u>
E

26. If someone will be late for the party, <u>they</u>
A
<u>should</u> call in advance <u>to let</u> the hosts know
B   C
<u>as soon as possible</u>. <u>No error</u>
D   E

27. In some regions of the state <u>,</u> May's average
A   B
rainfall <u>is greater</u> than <u>April</u> . <u>No error</u>
C   D   E

28. The accomplished author has found that he

<u>can express</u> his ideas more <u>clearly</u> through
A   B
his use <u>of metaphor</u> and <u>in</u> his use of
C   D
simile. <u>No error</u>
E

29. The <u>senator's proposed</u> incentive program
A
<u>included</u> a provision <u>where</u> each recipient
B   C
of the tax rebate was to receive his or her

<u>payment on</u> a quarterly basis. <u>No error</u>
D   E

ERROR ID DRILL 5

The following sentences contain problems with grammar, usage, diction (word choice), and idioms. No sentence contains more than one error. Select (E) if there is no error. If you find an error, circle it. Then, name the grammatical error in the blank next to the question number.

_____ 12. The purpose of George Bernard Shaw's
                      A
plays is more to instruct than providing
      B   C   D
entertainment. No error
                E

_____ 13. Lance Armstrong, winner of the Tour de
                                        A
France, recommended that every serious
                        B
cyclist invest in the best bicycle that
        C
he or she can afford. No error
    D   E

_____ 14. The enthusiastic participants

in the state fair's pie-eating contest, which
          A   B
ranged in age from seven to seventy, all said
                   C   D
that they had eaten nothing that morning.

No error
  E

_____ 15. It is a surprising plus true fact that more
          A   B
ice cream is consumed in the month of
          C
January than in the month of July. No error
        D   E

_____ 16. The cheering by the home team's fans in

the stadium was so deafening as the buzzer
           A
went off that the spectators could not hardly
      B   C
hear the announcement that the final play

had been disallowed . No error
        D   E

_____ 17. The latest version of the software has less
                                A   B
flaws in it than does the previous version.
      C   D
No error
  E

_____ 18. The population of New York City is larger
                  A   B
than that of any other city in the United
    C   D
States. No error
         E

_____ 19. In some European capitals—such as
                        A   B
Madrid—they eat dinner late in the
           C   D
evening. No error
           E

_____ 20. The team of surgeons worked slowly and
                                A
steady during the most delicate phase of the
      B   C
operation on the newborn infant's heart.
      D
No error
  E

_____ 21. It was difficult to decide from among
                      A   B
the girls in the junior class, who wore the

more outrageous costume to the school
  C   D
Halloween Dance. No error
                   E

_____22. The collection of short stories by
                        A   B
Hemingway contains not only comic
                              C
elements but also contains tragic elements.
                     D
No error
   E

_____23. The third game of the series was delayed
                          A
when the two referees disagreed among
  B   C
each other about a critical play. No error
              D   E

_____24. Fire officials attributed the large amount
                          A
of property damage to the fact that not
   B
one of the hotel's more than two thousand
                      C
rooms were equipped with the latest
        D
sprinklers. No error
              E

_____25. Nobody ever achieved true success—
                  A
whether in sports, business,
   B
or any other field —all by themselves .
        C   D
No error
   E

_____26. While visiting the Statue of Liberty, Mr.
                  A
Johnson's hat was blown into the harbor
                 B
waters and quickly sank beneath the
            C   D
turbulent waves. No error
                   E

_____27. Sophomores outnumbered juniors and
                       A
seniors at the school dance, so the principal
                                        B
decided that she should open an additional

room for them . No error
      C   D   E

_____28. The amount of people who go to the library
             A
these days is far smaller now that so much
    B   C
research is accessible on the Internet.
   D
No error
   E

_____29. Tim and Jack want to get an A in their
                              A   B
ethics class, and each student is prepared to
                                  C
do whatever it takes to achieve his goal.
                                   D
No error
   E

© TPR Education IP Holdings, LLC

MATH

WRITING

READING

VOCABULARY

ERROR ID DRILL 6

The following sentences contain problems with grammar, usage, diction (word choice), and idioms. No sentence contains more than one error. Select (E) if there is no error. If you find an error, circle it. Then, name the grammatical error in the blank next to the question number.

_____**12.** No matter how <u>careful</u> you drive during
    A
the day or night, <u>you</u> should always wear a
    B
seatbelt because <u>there</u> is always the chance
    C
of an accident . <u>No error</u>
    D   E

_____**13.** The supportive words of the teacher

offering <u>little</u> <u>consolation</u> to the despondent
    A   B
athlete, <u>who had</u> been <u>disqualified</u> on a
    C   D
technicality. <u>No error</u>
            E

_____**14.** A picture of the All-Star Team, <u>composed of</u>
                    A
players <u>from</u> different leagues, <u>were</u>
    B   C
<u>given to</u> each member. <u>No error</u>
    D   E

_____**15.** A talented athlete <u>just like</u> his older
                    A
brother, Harold <u>enjoys</u> biking, skiing, and
    B   C
<u>to play</u> golf. <u>No error</u>
    D   E

_____**16.** After months of campaigning the

<u>council member finally</u> <u>had</u> enough support
        A   B
for her <u>proposal</u> , so she <u>calls</u> for an
        C   D
immediate vote. <u>No error</u>
                E

_____**17.** The coach <u>often</u> worked with her
                A
<u>athletes individually</u> , carefully selecting
        B
<u>challenging drills</u> <u>and would adapt</u> her
        (no letter)   C
approach to each girl's particular needs.
            D
<u>No error</u>
    E

_____**18.** While crossing the North Pole

<u>with his dog team</u> , Admiral Byrd was
        A
<u>so close</u> to dying from starvation that the
    B
very thought of food made him <u>queasy</u> .
    C   D
<u>No error</u>
    E

_____**19.** The <u>sheer</u> number of Thomas Edison's
            A
<u>inventions is</u> <u>indicative of</u> a uniquely
        B   C
<u>imaginary</u> mind. <u>No error</u>
    D   E

_____**20.** The academic <u>habits</u> and <u>expectations</u> of
                    A   B
teenage girls <u>are very</u> different
            C
from teenage boys . <u>No error</u>
    D   E

MATH

WRITING

READING

VOCABULARY

21. *Titus Andronicus*, one of Shakespeare's

lesser-known works and the inspiration for
           A

the popular movie *Gladiator*, is a play where
                      B   C

the noble protagonist suffers a tragic fate.
                     D

No error
  E

22. Tim promised his doubtful mother that
          A   B

by the time she returned home from her trip,
    C

he will complete his history term paper.
    D

No error
  E

23. A paradox is a situation when an
        A   B

apparently reasonable statement leads to a
                     C

contradictory or inexplicable conclusion.
         D

No error
  E

24. A confirmed perfectionist, Kara was less
                  A   B

satisfied with her painting than
   C

her art teacher. No error
      D   E

25. The consequences of the senator's alleged
             A

offense is serious, so unless he addresses the
      B

charge soon he will face disciplinary action
                        C

and possible expulsion from the senate
           D

itself. No error
    E

26. Madeline is a better badminton player
           A

than me even though she learned the game
   B   C

only a few months ago. No error
  D   E

27. The causes of the American Civil War

were not just social, but also
 A   B   C

economical and technological . No error
         D   E

28. All of the former classmates are planning
          A

on attending the formal reunion ceremony,
      B

and most have said that they will also
    C   D

attend the reception party afterwards.

No error
  E

29. Were it not for the downturn of the local
     A   B

economy last year, the then-popular mayor
                C

would surely have been reelected . No error
      D   E

GRAMMAR IN REAL LIFE

Pop lyrics are a great source of bad grammar. See if you can find the error in each of the following.

Pronouns

Katy Perry: *In another life, I would make you stay, so I don't have to say you were the one that got away.*

Taylor Swift: *Somebody tells you they love you, you got to believe 'em.*

Whitney Houston: *It's the second time around for you and I...*

Lady Gaga: *You and me could write a bad romance.*

Verb Tense

Justin Timberlake: *When you cheated girl, my heart bleeded girl.*

Dave Matthews Band: *And the world's done/Ours just begun/It's done/Ours just begun.*

Ke$ha: *And yes of course we does/We running this town just like a club.*

Timbaland: *Can you handle me the way I are?*

Modifier

Lee Greenwood: *I'm proud to be an American, where at least I know I'm free.*

Redundancy

Britney Spears: *My loneliness ain't killing me no more/I don't need no body.*

Rolling Stones: *I can't get no satisfaction.*

Gwen Stefani: *I'm restless/Can't you see I try my bestest.*

Backstreet Boys: *As time goes by, you will get to know me a little more better.*

One Direction: *Everyone else in the room can see it/Everyone else but you.*

SAT GRAMMAR: IMPROVING PARAGRAPHS

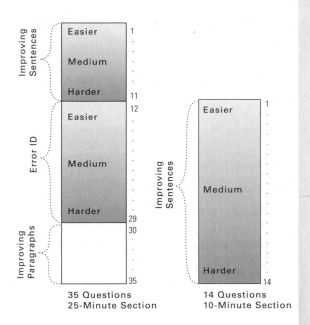

Improving Sentences

Easier
Medium
Harder
1
.
.
.
11

Error ID

12
Easier

Medium

Harder
29
30

Improving Paragraphs
35

35 Questions
25-Minute Section

Improving Sentences

Easier
1
.
.
.
Medium

Harder
14

14 Questions
10-Minute Section

In the previous Writing lessons you learned how to tackle the two most important question types: Improving Sentences and Error IDs. Now we're going to look at the third question type: Improving Paragraphs. This is the least common question type, accounting for only 6 of your 49 grammar questions.

MATH

WRITING

READING

VOCABULARY

THE FORMAT

Improving Paragraphs questions are based on a short "first draft" essay of two to four paragraphs. Most questions will ask you to improve the essay in some way.

Here are a few key points about Improving Paragraphs questions.

- These questions should be in everyone's POOD. They may take a bit longer to do, but are nearly always of easy or medium difficulty.
- The "20% are correct as written" rule doesn't apply here.
- There are many more flaws within the passage than you will be asked about. Therefore, do not edit as you read.
- Most questions will be of medium difficulty, so do your best to reach these. You may even choose to skip a few of the hardest Error ID questions in order to do so.

Improving Paragraphs Basic Approach

1. Skim the passage and quickly identify the following things:
   - The main idea of the entire passage
   - The point of each paragraph
2. Read the question and go back to the passage for context when necessary.
3. POE what you can, reading vertically when need be.
4. Repeat Steps 2 and 3 until you are down to one answer.

More than Grammar

Improving Paragraphs questions involve more than the grammar rules you've already seen. You'll also need to think about how the parts of the passage fit together.

Questions

You'll see three basic types of questions: revision, combination, and weird.

Revision

Treat these like Improving Sentences questions. If you spot the error, eliminate answers that contain that error, then read vertically and use POE. If more than one seems grammatically correct, go back to the passage to find the one that fits the context.

Combination

These questions are really a type of revision question, but you're working with two sentences instead of one.

Weird

These relate to the content and flow of the passage. Handling a weird question depends on what you're specifically asked to do. Here are a few guidelines.

- When swapping sentences, focus on the **order of ideas**. Where do ideas flow in an illogical order?
- **Stick as closely to the passage as you can**. Something preceding the passage should tie directly into the first sentence.
- In general, maintain focus on the main idea of the passage.

MATH
WRITING
READING
VOCABULARY

(1) Conservation and ecology are becoming important topics at our school. (2) Some of us wondered how we could make a difference. (3) Students used to just throw everything out in one big garbage pail. (4) Sure, it was easy. (5) It wasn't good for the environment.

(6) I volunteered to head up the conservation team. (7) My friends and I decided to map out our strategies. (8) Implementing a recycling program seemed like the most important thing. (9) First, we talked to the town officials, they agreed to supply the recycling bins. (10) We also checked that the sanitation department would be able to collect our recycled materials. (11) Making sure that people would use the recycling bins correctly was a thing to do. (12) Paper needed to go in one bin, plastic and glass in another.

(13) We decided to run a poster contest. (14) Its purpose was to increase awareness. (15) Aspiring artists found many ways to illustrate our new motto: "Reuse, recycle, renew." (16) The winners are hanging in our halls, reminding everyone to do his part. (17) When I saw that most of the posters had been drawn on the back side of old posters, I knew that our conservation program was well on its way.

Revision Questions

Revision questions are like Improving Sentences, but answer (A) isn't necessarily the same as the original sentence.

30. In context, which of the following is the best version of sentence 11 (reproduced below) ?

    Making sure that people would use the recycling bins correctly was a thing to do.

    (A) A thing to do was to make sure that people would use the recycling bins correctly.
    (B) Making sure that people would use them correctly was one thing to do.
    (C) To make sure that people would use the recycling bins correctly, it had to be done.
    (D) Next, we had to make sure that people would use the recycling bins correctly.
    (E) Another thing to do correctly was making sure that people would use the recycling bins.

31. What is the best way to deal with sentence 16 ?

    (A) Change "his" to "their."
    (B) Change "reminding" to "as reminders of."
    (C) Change "winners" to "winning posters."
    (D) Omit the word "hanging."
    (E) Add the words "and they are" after the comma.

Combination Questions

32. Which of the following is the most effective combination of sentences 4 and 5 ?

   (A) It sure was easy, and it wasn't good for the environment.

   (B) It was easy, but it wasn't good for the environment.

   (C) It was easily not good for the environment.

   (D) I was sure that it was easy, not good for the environment.

   (E) It was easy; therefore, it wasn't good for the environment.

Combination questions are often about which conjunction to use.

33. Which of the following is the best revision of the underlined portion of sentences 13 and 14 (reproduced below) ?

We decided to run a poster <u>contest. Its purpose was</u> to increase awareness.

   (A) (as it is now)

   (B) contest. We hoped

   (C) contest, its purpose being

   (D) contest with the intention

   (E) contest in order

Weird Questions

34. Which of the following sentences, if inserted at the end of the first paragraph, would best serve to link the first two paragraphs?

   (A) Separating your trash is not as difficult as it may seem.

   (B) We knew that we needed to change our habits.

   (C) People can be very unmotivated sometimes.

   (D) Over half of our school's garbage comes from the cafeteria.

   (E) Also, students driving cars to school cause unnecessary pollution.

Look at the main idea for each paragraph.

MATH
WRITING
READING
VOCABULARY

(1) Censorship in the media was an extreme important issue throughout the twentieth century. (2) In the 1950s television programs and movies had to comply with codes that enforced strict standards of propriety. (3) Couples were shown sleeping in separate beds, and the concept of nudity or verbal profanity was unheard of. (4) In reaction to them, in the 1960s and 70s the media abandoned the codes in favor of more realistic representations of relationships and everyday life. (5) Filmmakers and songwriters were able to express themselves more honestly and freely. (6) The idea that in the early 60s the Rolling Stones had to change their lyrics from "let's spend the night together" to "let's spend some time together" seemed almost unlikely by the end of the decade.

(7) Yet in the mid-1980s a period of conservative reaction occurred, turning the cycle around. (8) Explicit song lyrics began to be censored. (9) Warning labels were added to the covers of albums. (10) The labels indicated that some of the language might be "offensive" to the consumer. (11) It is unfortunate that people feel the need to blame the media for societal problems instead of realizing that the media only brings to light the problems that already exist.

(12) Hopefully, our reactions will ultimately break free of all previous patterns. (13) Yet until this happens we must remain content to know that the good parts of the past, as well as the bad, repeat themselves.

30. In context, what is the best version of the underlined portion of sentence 1 (reproduced below)?

Censorship in the media was an extreme important issue throughout the twentieth century.

(A) (as it is now)
(B) was an extremely
(C) having been an extremely
(D) has been extreme as an
(E) will be an extremely

31. Which of the following would be the best subject for a paragraph immediately preceding this essay?

(A) The types of movies most popular in the 1950s
(B) The changing role of the media over the last ten years
(C) The ways in which the economy affects society's political views
(D) The role of the media in European countries
(E) The roots of media censorship

32. The author wishes to divide the first paragraph into two shorter paragraphs. The most appropriate place to begin a new paragraph would be

(A) between sentences 1 and 2.
(B) between sentences 2 and 3.
(C) between sentences 3 and 4.
(D) between sentences 4 and 5.
(E) between sentences 5 and 6.

33. What is the best way to deal with sentence 4?

(A) Replace "them" with "the programs of the 1950s."
(B) Change "abandoned" to "had abandoned."
(C) Change "in favor of" to "in favor for."
(D) Eliminate the phrase "and everyday life."
(E) Eliminate sentence 4 altogether.

34. What is the best way to revise sentence 7?

(A) Change "turning" to "had turned."
(B) Replace "Yet" with "Although."
(C) Change it from the passive to the active voice.
(D) Change it from the active to the passive voice.
(E) Eliminate "period of."

35. Which would be the best way to revise and combine the underlined portions of sentences 9 and 10 (reproduced below)?

Warning labels were added to the covers of albums. The labels indicated that some of the language might be "offensive" to the consumer.

(A) albums, indicating
(B) albums, which indicated
(C) albums, and they indicated
(D) albums, the indication being
(E) albums, being indicative

Summary

The Format

- Most questions will be of medium difficulty, so do your best to attempt these before time is up.

The Approach

- _____

- _____

- _____

The Questions

- Revision questions: Eliminate answer choices with the error. If more than one choice is grammatically correct, pick what fits the context.

- Combination questions: Treat them as if you were working a revision question, and think about how the sentences are related.

- Weird questions: Stick closely to the passage, and make sure ideas flow logically.

- I have accomplished _____ of my _____ stated goals in the Introduction chapter.

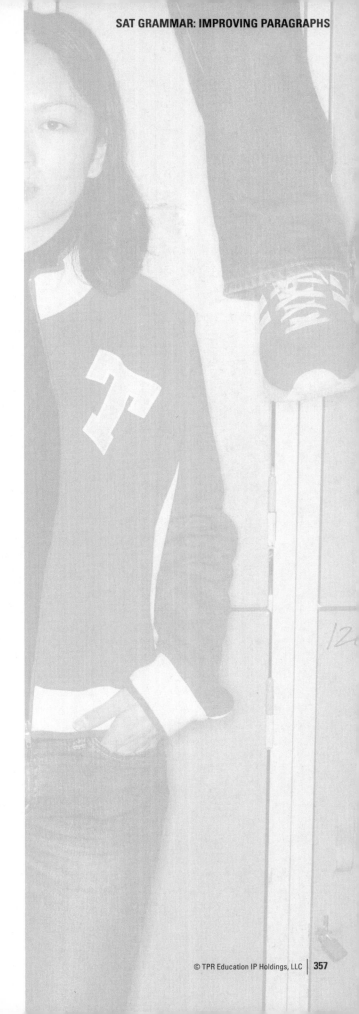

IMPROVING PARAGRAPHS PRACTICE

MATH

WRITING

READING

VOCABULARY

DOWN TO TWO DRILL

If you were down to the following pairs of answer choices on an Improving Paragraphs question, which would you eliminate?

(A) The school insisted on a rigorous curriculum, which made them

(B)

(C) An insistence on a rigorous curriculum in the school made them

(D)

(E)

(A)

(B) having the ability to live in the town of their birth is more important

(C)

(D)

(E) living in the town of their birth is more important

(A)

(B)

(C)

(D) and they could formulate theories easily

(E) and to formulate theories was easy for them

(A) a discovery that was remarkable

(B) an idea that was remarkable in its discovery

(C) you should speak slowly

(D) your speech should be slow

(E)

(A) the convoluted language of the book was hard for him to follow

(B)

(C)

(D)

(E) he found the convoluted language of the book hard to follow

MATH

WRITING

READING

VOCABULARY

IMPROVING PARAGRAPHS DRILL

Questions 30-35 are based on the following passage.

(1) I guess that bread baking is not a very common hobby for a guy, but that has never bothered me. (2) I have been making bread ever since I was five years old, and my grandmother let me climb up on the kitchen stool to help her punch down the dough, knead it, and formed it into loaves. (3) By the time I was twelve, I was combing through cookbooks in the public library, looking for new recipes.

(4) A lot of it has to do with timing: how long to let the yeast foam, how much rising time to give the dough, when to take the loaves out of the oven, and how long to wait before slicing the fresh loaves. (5) It takes quite a while to get the hang of baking bread.

(6) Once one gains an understanding of basic bread-baking technique, you can get creative, making up variations on recipes. (7) Whole-wheat flour can be substituted for white flour in a French bread recipe, and dried apricots are used in place of raisins in cinnamon rolls. (8) I will admit that I have had my share of failures: somehow, tomato-rye bread did not end up tasting as good as I hoped it would, and my recipe for chocolate-chip buns is not one that I will ever try again.

(9) Some recipes are just not as good as others. (10) Still, my family has been very supportive through the ups and downs of my baking. (11) They have bravely eaten the bad along with the good. (12) My friends might laugh at my baking now, but some day, when I open my own bakery, they'll all wish that they knew their way around a kitchen as well as I do!

30. Which of the following is the best version of the underlined portion of sentence 2 (reproduced below)?

I have been making bread ever since I was five years old, and my grandmother let me climb up on the kitchen stool to help her punch down the dough, knead it, and formed it into loaves.

(A) (as it is now)
(B) and I help her punch down the dough, knead it, and form
(C) to be a help to her punching down the dough, kneading it and forming
(D) to help her punch down the dough, knead it, and form
(E) to have helped her in punch down the dough, knead it, and formed

31. In context, which of the following could best replace the word "you" in sentence 6?

(A) they
(B) people
(C) I
(D) one
(E) bakers

32. Which of the following sentences could best be omitted from the passage?

(A) Sentence 2
(B) Sentence 4
(C) Sentence 6
(D) Sentence 9
(E) Sentence 10

33. Which two sentences, if their order were reversed, would most improve the organization of the essay?

(A) Sentence 2 and sentence 3
(B) Sentence 4 and sentence 5
(C) Sentence 7 and sentence 8
(D) Sentence 9 and sentence 10
(E) Sentence 10 and sentence 11

34. In context, which of the following versions of the underlined portion of sentence 7 (reproduced below) is the best?

Whole-wheat flour can be substituted for white flour in a French bread recipe, and dried apricots are used in place of raisins in cinnamon rolls.

(A) (as it is now)
(B) or dried apricots used in place of
(C) however much dried apricots are used for
(D) while substituting dried apricots instead of
(E) dried apricots are as good as

35. How could the author best revise and combine the underlined portions of sentences 10 and 11 (reproduced below)?

Still, my family has been very supportive through the ups and downs of my baking. They have bravely eaten the bad along with the good.

(A) baking, eating with bravery
(B) baking; having bravely eaten
(C) baking, bravely eating
(D) baking: they have been brave and eaten
(E) baking and eating bravely

Questions 30-35 are based on the following passage.

(1) Many animals have a group mindset. (2) This manner of thinking ensures the survival of the species. (3) Some examples of such animals include ants, fish, and birds.

(4) Ants work together to live through the winter and have enough food. (5) Together, they can lift large food like apples or pieces of animal carcasses and bring them into their underground storage. (6) Other insects like bees behave similarly and can direct other bees to a delicious field of flowers by dancing.

(7) Fish stay together for protection against predators in a group called a school. (8) When fish are in schools, their sheer number can save them from being picked out by an enemy. (9) Together, they swim through the seas and move as one unit.

(10) Migration and group protection are why birds unite. (11) They also seem to have a method of communicating or a group idea of where they are going. (12) When birds like geese migrate, each bird takes a turn as the lead bird, so they all know where south, or north, is.

(13) All these animals seem to have a group mind that directs them to find food or protection or a predetermined location. (14) Do other animals have a similar mindset? (15) In fact, this mentality reaches all the way up the food chain. (16) Even humans, the most advanced animal, has a similar mindset at times.

30. In context, which word best replaces the underlined phrase in sentence 2 (reproduced below)?

   This _manner of thinking_ ensures the survival of the species.

   (A) omnipotence
   (B) mentality
   (C) wisdom
   (D) excellence
   (E) thoughtfulness

31. The removal of which of the following would best improve the second paragraph?

   (A) Sentence 4
   (B) Sentence 5
   (C) Sentences 4 and 5
   (D) Sentence 6
   (E) Sentences 5 and 6

32. In context, which version of sentence 7 (reproduced below) is the best?

   Fish stay together for protection against predators in a group called a school.

   (A) Fish stay together in schools for protection against predators.
   (B) Fish stay together in groups and schools for protection against predators.
   (C) For protection against predators, fish stay together in a protective group called a school.
   (D) Together for protection, fish stand against predators in a group called a school.
   (E) For protection against predators, fish in schools stay together protectively in a group.

33. Which of the following sentences would provide the best transition into the fourth paragraph?

   (A) Migration and group protection unite birds as well as fish.
   (B) Fish and bees use their group mentality to help their species survive.
   (C) All animals are social creatures that can perpetuate only in a community.
   (D) Fish and other animals protect themselves by staying together.
   (E) Like fish, birds also travel together.

34. In context, which version of the underlined part of sentence 12 (reproduced below) is the best?

   When birds like geese migrate, each bird takes a turn as the lead bird, so they all know where south, or north, is.

   (A) each bird takes a turn leading
   (B) each bird is the lead bird
   (C) each bird alternates as the lead bird
   (D) each bird takes a turn as the leading bird
   (E) the birds each take a turn as the lead bird

35. If added to the last paragraph, which of the following would most enhance it?

   (A) An example of how humans show their group mindset
   (B) A list of additional reasons animals act as one
   (C) Examples of at least three other types of animals that have a group mentality
   (D) A judgment as to which animal is the least individualized
   (E) More questions about other animal communities

Questions 30-35 are based on the following passage.

(1) Embargos are often done with good intentions but can wind up having negative consequences. (2) For example, the embargos on Cuban sugar and cheese made from unpasteurized milk wind up hurting Americans in the long run.

(3) Cuba is the number one exporter of sugar in the world and exports 3 million tons a year. (4) Americans only get their sugar from Hawaii and California which only produce 1 million ton of sugar though. (5) The result is that processed food like soda and candy is made with corn syrup instead of the much more pricey sugar. (6) Sugar is more expensive in the U.S. than other countries because of this embargo.

(7) Right now, cheese made from unpasteurized milk is illegal in the U.S., but the FDA has not enforced the law but now the American cheese industry is encouraging the FDA to take a strong stand and view this cheese as a huge health risk. (8) These companies argue that this cheese carries bacteria like *E. coli* and *listeria*. (9) But Europeans eat cheese made from unpasteurized milk every day and they're fine. (10) American cheese companies pasteurize cheese because it takes a long time to get from production to the table whereas in Europe they eat the cheese shortly after it's made.

(11) If the FDA decides to enforce this embargo, some of the best cheeses in the supermarket like parmigiano reggiano and other expensive block cheeses will disappear and vanish from the shelves. (12) Our country needs to decide if the loss is worth it.

30. In context, which revision of sentence 3 (reproduced below) is the best?

    Cuba is the number one exporter of sugar in the world and exports 3 million tons a year.

    (A) Cuba, the number one exporter of sugar in the world, exports 3 million tons a year.
    (B) Cuba is the primary world exporter of sugar and exports 3 million tons a year.
    (C) Although Cuba is the first exporter of sugar in the world, it exports 3 million tons a year.
    (D) As the leading exporter of sugar in the world, Cuba exports 3 million tons a year.
    (E) Cuba exports 3 million tons a year and is the number one exporter of sugar in the world.

31. Inclusion of which of the following would most enhance this essay?

    (A) Definitions of embargo and pasteurization
    (B) Reasons for the American embargo on all Cuban exports
    (C) An explanation of the controversy surrounding *E. coli* and *listeria*
    (D) The history of the FDA's positions on various dairy products
    (E) An analysis of American relations with Cuba

32. Where would sentence 6 be better placed in the essay?

    (A) After sentence 1
    (B) Before sentence 3
    (C) After sentence 5
    (D) After sentence 8
    (E) Before sentence 11

33. The main rhetorical purpose of the essay is to

    (A) analyze American embargos.
    (B) demonstrate the problems with American food consumption.
    (C) show how the FDA controls the sugar and cheese industries.
    (D) prove that the embargo on cheese is more detrimental than the one on sugar.
    (E) explain that embargos can have negative effects.

34. In context, which version of the underlined part of sentence 11 (reproduced below) is the best?

    If the FDA decides to enforce this embargo, some of the best cheeses in the supermarket like parmigiano reggiano and other expensive block cheeses will disappear and vanish from the shelves.

    (A) will disappear and will vanish
    (B) disappear and vanish
    (C) will disappear from the shelves
    (D) will, from the shelves, disappear and vanish
    (E) vanished from the shelves

35. Which of the following suggestions would most improve the last paragraph?

    (A) Mention more cheeses that consumers will no longer be able to purchase.
    (B) Discuss the unfavorable effects of embargos other than sugar and cheese.
    (C) Include inexpensive sugar as another American loss.
    (D) Describe the average American's response to the embargos.
    (E) Theorize the effect that the removal of the sugar embargo would have on the corn syrup industry.

SAT READING: INTRODUCTION

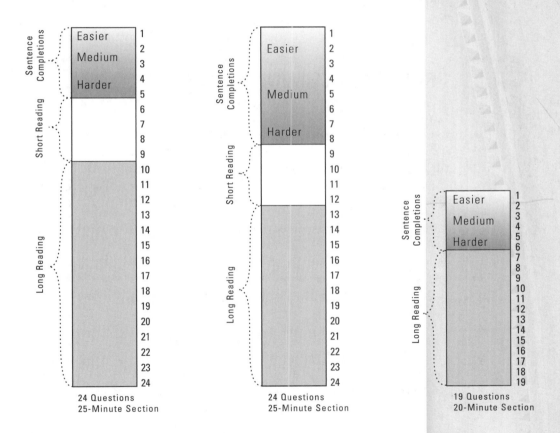

24 Questions
25-Minute Section

24 Questions
25-Minute Section

19 Questions
20-Minute Section

*The SAT will have 67 Critical Reading questions total. The exact # of questions per section may vary by 1 question.

MATH

WRITING

READING

VOCABULARY

CHOOSING THE BEST ANSWER

Critical Reading is not about selecting the *right* answer, but the *best* answer. An answer choice that looks bad can actually be the one that gets you the point, as long as all the other choices are even worse. An answer choice that looks good can be wrong if another choice is even better.

The best ETS answers

- are supported by the text of the sentence (for sentence completions)
- are supported by the text of the passage (for short and long reading)
- agree with the main idea of the passage
- answer the question that is being asked

Critical Reading questions, even ones that require you to "read between the lines," are <u>not</u> a matter of opinion. ETS **must have one single justifiable answer** for each question; otherwise, they'd face a flood of lawsuits and challenged scores.

Wrong answers are easier to find, because there are more of them!

PROCESS OF ELIMINATION (POE)

To avoid choosing trap answers, don't just skim the choices looking for one to pick. Go through all five choices, one at a time, decide how likely it is to be the best answer, and *make a mark* to indicate what you think. Put a ✓ if you like it, a **W** if it's weak, or a **?** if you're not sure. Cross off wrong answers. Once you've gone through all five choices, decide which one you'll finally pick. Use the answer choices below to practice doing this for different scenarios that might arise on test day.

(A)	(A)	(A)	(A)
(B)	(B)	(B)	(B)
(C)	(C)	(C)	(C)
(D)	(D)	(D)	(D)
(E)	(E)	(E)	(E)

Use Process of Elimination to get rid of the answers that you know are wrong, and guess aggressively.

 © TPR Education IP Holdings, LLC

PACING

To get: (scaled score)	You need to earn: (raw points)	Attempt approximately this many questions			
		24 question section	24 question section	19 question section	Total # of questions to attempt
300	5	6	6	3	15
350	9	8	8	4	20
400	16	11	11	8	30
450	23	14	14	10	38
500	31	16	16	11	43
550	40	19	19	13	51
600	46	22	22	16	60
650	53	23	23	17	63
700	59	23	23	18	64
750	63	all	all	all	67
800	67	all	all	all	67

PERSONAL ORDER OF DIFFICULTY (POOD)

While the pacing chart gives you an idea of how many questions to do, it doesn't dictate to you *which* questions to do. If the chart tells you to do 20 questions in a particular section, that doesn't necessarily mean you should do the *first* 20. The arrangement of Sentence Completion questions follows an order of difficulty.

Rely on your POOD to decide if you want to do a reading or sentence completion question.

Work with your teacher to figure out where you should focus your time.

MATH

WRITING

READING

VOCABULARY

SAT READING: SENTENCE COMPLETIONS

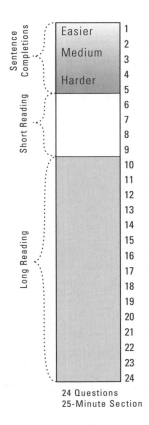

Sentence Completions
Easier
Medium
Harder
Short Reading
Long Reading

1
2
3
4
5
6
7
8
9
10
11
12
13
14
15
16
17
18
19
20
21
22
23
24

24 Questions
25-Minute Section

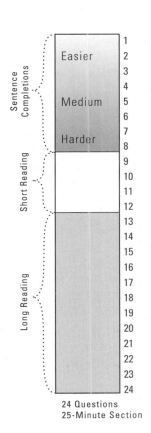

Sentence Completions
Easier
Medium
Harder
Short Reading
Long Reading

1
2
3
4
5
6
7
8
9
10
11
12
13
14
15
16
17
18
19
20
21
22
23
24

24 Questions
25-Minute Section

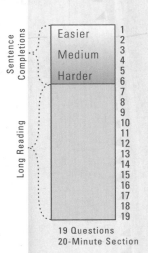

Sentence Completions
Easier
Medium
Harder
Long Reading

1
2
3
4
5
6
7
8
9
10
11
12
13
14
15
16
17
18
19

19 Questions
20-Minute Section

THE JOE BLOGGS METHOD

Joe heads straight for the answer choices. He sticks each word in the blank and decides whether it "sounds right."

> **2.** Early scientists knew relatively little about the behavior of ------- animals… *blah blah blah blah blah blah blah.*
>
> (A) tropical (B) aggressive (C) migratory
> (D) carnivorous (E) nocturnal

WHAT JOE DOESN'T KNOW

The correct answer to a Sentence Completion has nothing to do with how the word *sounds* in the sentence. ETS deliberately designs the answer choices to sound good in the sentence so that you'll be less likely to pick out the right answer.

The correct answers to Sentence Completions are based on what the words *mean*, not on how they *sound*.

WORK SMARTER, NOT HARDER

1. **Cover the answers.**
   Cover the answer choices and read through the sentence carefully to get an idea of what it's about.

2. **Speak for yourself.**
   Choose a word or phrase for the blank that makes sense based on what you've read. *Write your word or phrase down.* You don't need to come up with a fancy vocabulary word. As long as you've got the *meaning* right, you're in great shape.

3. Use **POE and guess aggressively.**
   Uncover the answer choices and compare them to your word. Eliminate answers that aren't close in meaning to your word.

1. When the Hubble telescope was first launched into space, its mirrors were ------- and therefore provided blurred images.

   Your word: _____

   (A) efficient (B) homogenous (C) augmented
       (D) imperfect (E) enormous

1. Filmmaking is a ------- effort, since the director, cinematographer, writer, editor, and many others must work together to produce a movie.

   Your word: _____

   (A) creative (B) lucrative (C) glamorous
       (D) collaborative (E) concentrated

2. Jazz singer Sarah Vaughan is known chiefly for her ------- and inventiveness in scat singing, an improvisational vocal technique.

   Your word: _____

   (A) apprehension (B) originality (C) perfection
       (D) terseness (E) conviction

If you don't know a word in an answer choice, don't eliminate it. Put a ? next to it and move on.

Recycle a word or phrase from the sentence whenever possible.

MATH

WRITING

READING

VOCABULARY

GET A CLUE

2. Museums that house many paintings and sculptures are good places for students of -------.

   (A) art (B) music (C) religion
       (D) democracy (E) paleontology

The clue is a word or phrase that makes one answer choice better than the others. Every sentence has one.

Want to see a neat trick? Even if the *topic* of the sentence remains the same, change the *clue* and watch the answer change too...

4. Museums that house many rare fossils are good places for students of -------.

   (A) art (B) music (C) religion
       (D) democracy (E) paleontology

  © TPR Education IP Holdings, LLC

CLUELESS?

If you are having trouble finding the clue, ask yourself the following:

- Who or what is the blank talking about?
- What *information* does the sentence give you about that person or thing?

Find the clue in each of the following sentences and <u>underline</u> it. Then, choose your own word. Try to recycle clue words when you can.

1. Tamson was so gifted a singer that her colleagues were often dazzled by her ------- and failed to appreciate her other talents.

2. Before it could be worn, the cheap suit required such ------- alterations that in the end it was no bargain.

3. The appeal of Cirque de Soleil is ------- because it has been enjoyed by audiences of all ages and backgrounds.

4. Playing to sell out audiences around the country, the concert pianist was extolled by critics as a gifted, even -------, performer.

5. According to legend, Romulus and Remus, the founders of Rome, were ------- children, raised in the wild by a wolf.

6. Art critics have characterized Jackson's latest work as a ------- of different ideas, all thrown together with little thought to any unifying theme.

7. Normally -------, many solar features become visible only during a lunar eclipse.

8. Some researchers have described light as ------- even though it travels at nearly two hundred thousand miles per second.

Write down your word or phrase. Yes, on the page. Write it down!

MATH

WRITING

READING

VOCABULARY

TRIGGERS

Trigger words indicate whether the word that fills the blank agrees or disagrees with the clue.

Answer the following questions in your own words:

1. I really like you, and _____ .

2. I really like you, but _____ .

The words "and" and "but" indicate what sorts of words will fit in the blanks.

Not every sentence has a trigger.

Trigger Words	
Same Direction	*Change Direction*
Because	Although/though
And	However
Since	Yet
In fact	But
Colon (:)	Rather
Semicolon (;)	In contrast to
Thus	Despite
So	Even though
Also	Unlike
As well as	Instead

Time Triggers

Some sentences talk about two different time periods, and this itself is a trigger, as in the following sentence:

Once a sad and lonely soul, Chip is now _____ and _____ .

The reference to the past ("once") and the present ("now") contrasts two periods and lets you know that the sentence is changing direction or degree.

 © TPR Education IP Holdings, LLC

<u>Underline</u> the clues. (Circle) the triggers.

1. Initially, the factory workers ------- the recommendations of the efficiency expert, but they soon embraced the changes as beneficial.

   (A) resisted (B) accepted (C) applauded
     (D) created (E) predicted

4. The governor's reputation, though ------- by the false allegations of conspiracy, emerged from the crisis intact.

   (A) tarnished (B) misconstrued (C) destroyed
     (D) satiated (E) emboldened

6. Although the Harlem Globetrotters are ------- basketball players, it is their humorous antics rather than their skills that have brought them worldwide popularity.

   (A) stolid (B) trivial (C) adept
     (D) cavalier (E) novel

7. Most of Alice's comments were -------; they directed the conversation away from the topic being discussed.

   (A) focused (B) obtuse (C) intermittent
     (D) equivocal (E) tangential

8. The tour guide was known for both his ------- and his -------: frequently dishonest, he was nonetheless uniquely charming.

   (A) evasiveness . . irascibility
   (B) ambivalence . . charisma
   (C) bravado . . extravagance
   (D) mendacity . . corruption
   (E) duplicity . . panache

MATH

WRITING

READING

VOCABULARY

TWO BLANKS = TWICE AS EASY

So far we've worked with one-blank sentences, but many sentences have two blanks. Are two-blank questions harder? Not if you use POE.

Step 1: Cover the answers.

Step 2: Decide which blank is easier to figure out.

Step 3: Using clues and triggers, fill in a word for that blank.

Step 4: Eliminate the entire answer choice when one word doesn't match.

Step 5: Now do the same for the other blank.

1. After living in a cramped and ------- studio apartment for several years, Roberta moved to a house that was commodious and ------- .

    (A) expensive . . cluttered
    (B) inhospitable . . comfortable
    (C) congested . . remote
    (D) expansive . . roomy
    (E) undecorated . . historical

3. Tragically, the independent stores of America's downtowns are so ------- by the loss of customers to huge suburban shopping centers that they may ------- in a few short years.

    (A) threatened . . revive
    (B) imperiled . . vanish
    (C) troubled . . consume
    (D) encouraged . . disappear
    (E) isolated . . expire

4. Although popular images of the 1950s often portray the era as a time of ------- in America, this decade was actually a time of great -------, marked by the nation's growing fear of Communism and nuclear proliferation as well as mounting racial tensions.

    (A) uncertainty . . equality
    (B) turbulence . . benevolence
    (C) serenity . . apprehension
    (D) equanimity . . tranquility
    (E) emotion . . philanthropy

MATH

WRITING

READING

VOCABULARY

5. Considering the strength of her earlier ------- the legislation, the senator's decision to vote for the bill was -------, even shocking.

(A) support for . . surprising
(B) indifference to . . predictable
(C) resistance to . . belligerent
(D) promotion of . . astonishing
(E) opposition to . . unexpected

6. Although in dry seasons mosses may appear to be dead, they can ------- during periods of extended drought and will quickly ------- with the first rain.

(A) perish . . regress
(B) thrive . . flourish
(C) decline . . dissipate
(D) survive . . revive
(E) germinate . . wilt

7. The reviewer neither ------- nor ------- the director's latest work; she discussed the film's strengths and weaknesses with all due fairness.

(A) aggrandized . . favored
(B) maligned . . criticized
(C) lauded . . derided
(D) celebrated . . adapted
(E) disregarded . . plagiarized

On some two-blank questions, you won't have enough information to fill in either blank: The clue itself will have been blanked out! Fortunately, this situation is rare. When it happens, look for a relationship between the blanks. Are they kind of similar or kind of opposite?

6. Norton is a seemingly ------- critic; he writes a ------- review of every play he sees.

(A) indifferent . . lukewarm
(B) unintelligent . . masterful
(C) exuberant . . negative
(D) condescending . . warm
(E) merciful . . combative

Clueless questions are uncommon. There is a clue 95% of the time.

VOCAB IN CONTEXT

Now here is a quick preview of a Critical Reading question type that we will approach the same way as Sentence Completions. For these, merely cross off the identified word (or phrase) and create your own blank. Then follow the steps you already know.

> The Greek theater, that is, theater altogether, began
> when Thespis arrived in Athens from Icaria with his
> startling invention: the use of one performer to keep up
> *Line* a dialogue with the chorus, instead of the chorus merely
> 5 reciting the poetry as was the practice until then…

7. The word "practice" in line 5 most nearly means

(A) exercise
(B) recitation
(C) custom
(D) rehearsal
(E) repetition

It is very rare that the correct answer is the primary definition. The secondary or tertiary definition is usually the answer.

> White-collar criminals are rarely subjected to the
> various indignities the common criminal suffers. The
> accused is usually informed of the authorities' intent to
> *Line* arrest, given a time and place to meet (with counsel), and
> 5 offered the various courtesies afforded an invited guest.
> Dissimilarly, the common criminal is often arrested in
> his home or at his place of work, in full public view, and
> held in temporary custody until he can get an attorney and
> provide bail. He is usually treated roughly and unfairly,
> 10 and is often abused…

10. The word "afforded" in line 5 most nearly means

(A) budgeted
(B) permitted
(C) purchased
(D) denied
(E) requited

Neil Armstrong used to summer in Avalon, taking
long walks with his wife and two children along the
soda-sticky boardwalk and the reeling lighted rides. I was
Line seven, and through Life magazine, I had been offered a
5 hero, a nobleman, a man of honest greatness. Through
the glamour and glitz, this luminary strolled, taking the
occasional perfunctory toss of a softball at a stand of milk
cans, or pausing awkwardly, even shyly, at the requests
for photographs. Mostly, he stayed to the beach, sipping
10 vanilla Cokes and watching the brilliant octopus lights
rotate over and over and over…

9. In line 6, the word "luminary" means

    (A) gloomy soul
    (B) tyrant
    (C) brilliant light
    (D) person of distinction
    (E) ambassador

VOCABULARY DRILL

Remember these words? Really? Let's see.

adept: _____

stolid: _____

terse: _____

augmented: _____

duplicity: _____

cavalier: _____

irascible: _____

ambivalent: _____

laud: _____

mendacity: _____

obtuse: _____

tangential: _____

germinate: _____

Add any unknown words
to your blank flashcards!

MATH
WRITING
READING
VOCABULARY

Summary

- Steps for answering Sentence Completion questions include:

  - _____

  - _____

  - _____

- Sentence Completions have a clear order of difficulty.

  True / False

- Choose answers based on _____, not on sound.

- Usually, the correct answer to a very hard question will be _____ challenging vocabulary.

- For two blanks, follow the steps for one blank at a time. Eliminate answers using two passes.

  True / False

- In the Reading section, you should approach _____ questions the same way as you approach Sentence Completions.

- I have accomplished _____ of my _____ stated goals in the Introduction chapter.

SENTENCE
COMPLETIONS PRACTICE

WARM UP!

On each of the following questions

- underline the clue and circle the triggers
- write your own word or phrase for each blank

1. The leading lady's rehearsals were so ------- that she was fired, and her part given to the understudy.

1. Shockingly ------- conditions prevail in some remote, isolated American villages, where many homes lack electricity and indoor plumbing.

1. Nearsightedness is to some degree -------; if your parents wear glasses, you probably will, too.

2. When one considers how ------- the commercial appeared, it is remarkable how many people remember having seen it.

3. After the dramatic gains achieved during the 1960s, some civil rights leaders now fear that the pace of social progress has -------.

3. Once considered a rare experimental procedure, organ transplants are increasingly -------.

3. Vitamins should be consumed with caution: at high doses, they can be -------.

4. The letters that were incorrectly -------, and therefore did not arrive at their intended destination, have been ------- the sender.

4. Cézanne was a -------; if every detail in a painting was not exactly correct, he would unhesitatingly destroy his creation.

5. Like Mohandas Gandhi, who ------- nonviolent protest, Martin Luther King Jr. championed change without bloodshed.

5. Paul resented that he had to shovel the driveway rather than go sledding; he therefore completed the task -------, complaining to his father as they worked.

6. Shaken by two decades of virtual anarchy, the majority of people was ready to buy ------- at any price.

6. Although the heavy rain fell -------, the darkening clouds and distant thunder had warned that a storm was -------.

7. Even the author admits that the favorable reviews of her latest book were ------; the critics may have been unduly influenced by her previous best-sellers.

7. Many criminals achieve infamy only -------; had they received the same attention while alive, they might not have become felons.

7. Unfortunately, some of the most advanced civilizations have been capable of the most ------- acts.

8. In a pluralistic society such as ours, in which so many different groups coexist, a political ------- on any single issue may be impossible.

8. Her shrewd campaign managers used political slogans that were actually forgotten clichés revived and ------- with new meaning.

ONE BLANK AT A TIME

In each of the following examples, decide which blank is easier to do first. Use the clue and triggers to come up with your own word for the blank. Eliminate any answer choice that doesn't match your word for that blank. Then, repeat the process for the other blank.

1. Because the textbook includes chapters that ------- the traditions and customs of ancient civilizations, it is often used by students majoring in -------.

   (A) detail . . anthropology
   (B) criticize . . psychology
   (C) overlook . . politics
   (D) emphasize . . biology
   (E) misunderstand . . literature

2. The artifacts that were improperly -------, and thus misplaced within the museum's storage room for years, have been found and are now being ------- by archeologists.

   (A) showcased . . explained
   (B) preserved . . disregarded
   (C) catalogued . . studied
   (D) interpreted . . examined
   (E) discovered . . purchased

3. As ------- a scientist as he was an artist, Leonardo da Vinci was perhaps the most diversely ------- genius the world has ever known.

   (A) accomplished . . affected
   (B) exceptional . . talented
   (C) historical . . read
   (D) energetic . . knowledgeable
   (E) practical . . published

4. Many scientists believe that the existence of extraterrestrial intelligence is -------, while others maintain that we will someday find ------- that proves we are not alone in the universe.

   (A) assured . . data
   (B) improbable . . evidence
   (C) controversial . . corroboration
   (D) inevitable . . criteria
   (E) doubtful . . authorization

5. The school's new policy, which ------- students who repeatedly arrive late to class, will not affect those who are consistently -------.

   (A) targets . . inattentive
   (B) penalizes . . punctual
   (C) recognizes . . conscientious
   (D) punishes . . tardy
   (E) identifies . . absent

6. Modern writers, ------- to drape reality with pretty phrases, show us everything, putrid and pure, with a grim -------.

   (A) aspiring . . reality
   (B) hesitating . . innocuousness
   (C) disdaining . . candor
   (D) purporting . . determination
   (E) endeavoring . . fascination

On the SAT about half of the Sentence Completions are the 2 blank variety.

SENTENCE COMPLETION DRILL 1

We've done the first one for you.

1. The onset of the earthquake was gradual; the tremors occurred ------- at first, then with greater frequency. *infrequently*
   - ~~(A) continuously~~
   - ~~(B) intensely~~
   - ✓ (C) sporadically
   - ~~(D) unexpectedly~~
   - ~~(E) chronically~~

2. When speaking before an audience, Marcus always expresses himself clearly, projecting his voice and ------- his words.
   - (A) mincing (B) enunciating (C) interpreting
   - (D) alternating (E) regretting

3. Desktop publishing eventually received ------- as the improved quality of laser printers helped to create documents as ------- as those of typesetters.
   - (A) acceptance . . readable
   - (B) disapproval . . defined
   - (C) resistance . . creative
   - (D) accuracy . . questionable
   - (E) criticism . . detached

4. Warnings concerning drunk driving, no matter how ------- they may be, cannot alone ------- people from endangering the lives of all of us.
   - (A) gruesome . . resist
   - (B) deficient . . prohibit
   - (C) inevitable . . arrest
   - (D) prolific . . transport
   - (E) persuasive . . deter

5. Although she lived at a time during which American poetry was valued and -------, as a black woman Phillis Wheatley was ------- pursuing her artistry.
   - (A) enjoyed . . discouraged from
   - (B) appraised . . frightened of
   - (C) insulted . . encouraged in
   - (D) recognized . . supported in
   - (E) abandoned . . praised by

6. Since toxic chemicals have been dumped in the Colorado River, the ------- of freshwater trout has been severely -------.
   - (A) environment . . protected
   - (B) growth . . miscounted
   - (C) habitat . . threatened
   - (D) diversion . . regulated
   - (E) population . . examined

7. The final proposal represented a ------- of the committee's ideas: the opinions of the diverse members were each taken into account.
   - (A) revision (B) misinterpretation (C) synthesis
   - (D) repetition (E) proliferation

8. The roller coaster ride lasts for only two short minutes; the thrill, therefore, is -------, and ends when the ride comes to a stop.
   - (A) arduous (B) transient (C) obtuse
   - (D) tenacious (E) perfunctory

The OOD in 5 question Sentence Completion sections increases more rapidly than the OOD in 8 question Sentence Completion sections.

SENTENCE COMPLETION DRILL 2

1. Although on the surface the final draft appeared to ------- the first draft, upon close inspection it was ------- that major changes had been made.

   (A) mimic . . distant
   (B) contradict . . clear
   (C) reproduce . . apparent
   (D) resemble . . deceptive
   (E) critique . . suggested

2. Mrs. Dundon is a colorful and ------- commentator, equally knowledgeable in matters of art, music, theology, and politics.

   (A) pleasant (B) versatile (C) prosaic
       (D) panoramic (E) heretical

3. Although this strain of bacteria has ------- effects on certain animals, scientists have found no evidence that it is harmful to humans.

   (A) constrained (B) deleterious (C) questionable
       (D) salutary (E) regenerative

4. Parker could not allow her criticism to remain -------; she openly ------- the members of the committee for their indolence and lackadaisical attitude.

   (A) judgmental . . scolded
   (B) unspoken . . censured
   (C) constant . . excoriated
   (D) tacit . . lauded
   (E) unheeded . . cited

5. After reading a negative review in a consumer magazine, many potential buyers became ------- the manufacturer's claims regarding the high quality of this model.

   (A) assuaged by (B) intrigued by
       (C) commensurate with (D) censured by
           (E) dubious of

When there are only 5 questions in a Sentence Completion section, you may find difficult questions as early as #2.

SENTENCE COMPLETION DRILL 3

1. The grateful owner was ------- by the rescuer's gracious ------- not to accept the reward she had offered for the return of her prized Dalmatian.

   (A) intrigued . . efforts
   (B) confused . . service
   (C) impressed . . insistence
   (D) enlightened . . assistance
   (E) prejudiced . . attempt

2. A chess master is ------- at ------- the tiniest advantage, transforming a slight edge into a winning position.

   (A) slow . . sacrificing
   (B) skilled . . overturning
   (C) fierce . . playing
   (D) competitive . . judging
   (E) adept . . exploiting

3. The introduction of a powerful fertilizer was able to ------- nutrients missing in the soil, so crops finally ------- in the formerly drought-stricken area.

   (A) yield . . increased
   (B) gather . . enlarged
   (C) harvest . . eroded
   (D) supplement . . flourished
   (E) multiply . . developed

4. If we are to ------- certain failure, immediate corrective action is -------; nothing else matters if we falter at this critical juncture.

   (A) forestall . . heedless
   (B) allow . . necessary
   (C) record . . steadfast
   (D) avert . . paramount
   (E) prevent . . detrimental

5. The objectivity of the biologist's findings was so compromised by a conflict of interest that even those who had once ------- his work, now criticized it.

   (A) repudiated (B) censored (C) championed
       (D) ignored (E) suppressed

6. Because the ocean vessel's cargo sank in an inaccessible region, ------- efforts were abandoned as -------.

   (A) ineffectual . . technical
   (B) fervent . . cumbersome
   (C) relief . . irretrievable
   (D) salvage . . impracticable
   (E) rescue . . feasible

7. The historian reminded her students that seemingly ------- periods belie the turmoil that is an inescapable aspect of human society.

   (A) tiresome (B) oblivious (C) serene
       (D) liberal (E) radical

8. Given the gravity of his offenses, the convicted executive displayed astonishingly little ------- when he addressed the court before sentencing.

   (A) ambivalence (B) compunction (C) resolution
       (D) petulance (E) vindication

 © TPR Education IP Holdings, LLC

SENTENCE COMPLETION DRILL 4

1. The actor was shorter in person than he appeared on stage: apparently his stature had been ------- by the play's scenery.

   (A) diminished (B) viewed (C) magnified
   (D) created (E) blocked

2. The attorney cautiously refused to ------- for the media on whether the jury would exonerate his client.

   (A) testify (B) search (C) practice
   (D) speculate (E) litigate

3. Rather than using explicit signals that others might -------, the teammates relied on ------- communication of each other's intentions.

   (A) misconstrue . . an instinctive
   (B) intercept . . a tacit
   (C) observe . . a humorous
   (D) exemplify . . an overt
   (E) receive . . a solicitous

4. His classmates began to refer to their seminar as a soliloquy because of the domineering way that Roland ------- every discussion.

   (A) monopolized (B) invigorated (C) censured
   (D) amplified (E) embraced

5. Although the amateur inventor's claims were outlandish, they had not yet been definitively -------.

   (A) publicized (B) jeopardized (C) agitated
   (D) disproved (E) neutralized

6. The narrative was ------- rather than chronological because one scene leaped to another randomly and did not follow a timeline.

   (A) regressive (B) incalculable (C) episodic
   (D) intricate (E) structural

7. Hoping to ------- the public's skepticism surrounding electricity, Edison held numerous demonstrations to show that this phenomenon had no ------- effects.

   (A) elucidate . . vacillating
   (B) galvanize . . deleterious
   (C) quell . . adverse
   (D) counter . . salutary
   (E) address . . mitigating

8. Like all human beings, scientists are not ------- observers of the world, but rather struggle to recognize and overcome their own biases and -------.

   (A) meticulous . . notions
   (B) impartial . . antipathies
   (C) calculating . . perceptions
   (D) disinterested . . preconceptions
   (E) philosophical . . experiences

© TPR Education IP Holdings, LLC

SENTENCE COMPLETION DRILL 5

1. For someone with a well-earned reputation for ------- , he was surprisingly restrained at his own birthday party.

   (A) repression (B) exuberance (C) tranquility
      (D) pessimism (E) dispassion

2. The land development threatened the territorial habits of indigenous species, so animal rights advocates proposed creating a nearby ------- .

   (A) subterfuge (B) paragon (C) seclusion
      (D) archive (E) sanctuary

3. The undergraduate was happy to learn that the professor who seemed so ------- and grave while lecturing was quite approachable after class.

   (A) distant (B) academic (C) frivolous
      (D) abstruse (E) insufferable

4. Having all but ------- their vacation funds in the first week, the group resolved to conserve their ------- remaining savings to last them the rest of their trip.

   (A) captivated . . modest
   (B) depleted . . scant
   (C) ascertained . . interminable
   (D) bypassed . . terse
   (E) safeguarded . . insatiable

5. His manner in front of adults was so ------- that it seemed affected; no teenager behaves that ------- all the time without consciously trying to impress his or her elders.

   (A) banal . . gratuitously
   (B) compliant . . flippantly
   (C) hackneyed . . obediently
   (D) polished . . impeccably
   (E) genteel . . tediously

6. Her knowledge of ornithology was truly ------- : she knew more about birds than anyone else in the world.

   (A) impressionable (B) encyclopedic (C) circumspect
      (D) incredulous (E) vociferous

7. Because the singer had won a Grammy Award, he was clearly in ------- mood and so in accepting indulged in ------- acknowledgement of his fellow nominees.

   (A) an obstreperous . . a haughty
   (B) a dynamic . . an overweening
   (C) a morbid . . a disingenuous
   (D) a magnanimous . . a generous
   (E) an enigmatic . . a fastidious

8. A renowned ------- , Pablo Picasso broke from conventional painting styles and forged his own avant-garde idiom.

   (A) iconoclast (B) patriarch (C) advocate
      (D) aesthete (E) ideologue

SENTENCE COMPLETION DRILL 6

1. Proponents of yoga say they enjoy it because it has been proven to ------- the effects of stress.

   (A) emphasize (B) alleviate (C) allocate
       (D) expand (E) aggravate

2. Doctors are reluctant to prescribe antibiotics without good reason because many kinds of bacteria in the human body are harmless, or even ------, to our well-being.

   (A) beneficial (B) serious (C) virulent
       (D) chronic (E) debilitating

3. It was difficult to ignore so ------- a landmark building, standing out as it did among ------- surrounding structures.

   (A) distinguished . . magnificent
   (B) prominent . . commonplace
   (C) residential . . dilapidated
   (D) historic . . important
   (E) central . . massive

4. The success of diminutive Muggsy Bogues in professional basketball is -------: only someone so short could reveal how the height of other players could be a disadvantage.

   (A) a hypocrisy (B) a paradox (C) a memory
       (D) an epitome (E) a eulogy

5. The critic apologized for the ------- review but said it was impossible to be concise about such ------- and complex work.

   (A) harsh . . a visionary
   (B) laudatory . . a plagiarized
   (C) rambling . . a literary
   (D) caustic . . an arcane
   (E) lengthy . . a multifaceted

6. That cactus plants survive, let alone -------, in such an arid and ------- environment never ceased to amaze the botanist.

   (A) thrive . . inhospitable
   (B) vitiate . . desolate
   (C) aerate . . fertile
   (D) grow . . nurturing
   (E) negate . . malevolent

7. The commissioner pointed out to the applicant that until final approval had been granted, the permit should be viewed as ------- and revocable.

   (A) tangible (B) tentative (C) obvious
       (D) onerous (E) permanent

8. For all the professor's scorn for commercial enterprises, his outrageous salary demands showed that he too had ------- side.

   (A) an idealistic (B) a philanthropic (C) a quixotic
       (D) a venal (E) a frugal

MATH

WRITING

READING

VOCABULARY

SENTENCE COMPLETION DRILL 7

1. Like every -------, he always rationalized why he put off until tomorrow what could easily have been done today.

   (A) opportunist (B) utilitarian (C) scholar
       (D) procrastinator (E) detractor

2. The discovery of a new element occasioned little surprise from chemists and physicists because the substance's properties were entirely ------- previous hypotheses.

   (A) consistent with (B) negligible to (C) relevant to
       (D) antagonistic to (E) incongruous with

3. Despite his dislike of ------- and popular acclaim, the reclusive poet attended the gala ceremony ------- the achievements of his late mentor.

   (A) delegation . . celebrating
   (B) pretension . . fabricating
   (C) autonomy . . belittling
   (D) fanfare . . commemorating
   (E) exultation . . undermining

4. Government regulations require drug companies to submit potential new drugs to ------- and comprehensive battery of tests to ------- safety.

   (A) a rigorous . . ensure
   (B) a typical . . guarantee
   (C) a dangerous . . secure
   (D) a cautious . . examine
   (E) an experimental . . legislate

5. Today's consumer is so overwhelmed by the sheer ------- of choices that purchasing even the simplest item becomes an exhausting decision.

   (A) protection (B) anarchy (C) frequency
       (D) dearth (E) multiplicity

6. Even though the philosophers lived in different eras and were not -------, they shared a kind of intellectual ------- through similar ideas and values.

   (A) adversaries . . indictment
   (B) zealots . . component
   (C) alternatives . . institution
   (D) dilettantes . . attribute
   (E) contemporaries . . fraternity

7. The book's chief revelation was so ------- that popular opinion was polarized; readers might agree or disagree with the author, but nobody was likely to remain -------.

   (A) nonchalant . . indifferent
   (B) quizzical . . misinformed
   (C) divisive . . neutral
   (D) controversial . . biased
   (E) promulgated . . personal

8. The legends depicted in ancient literature have been largely ignored by scholars as ------- tales, but advances in archaeology and anthropology continue to unearth corroborative findings.

   (A) redoubtable (B) ubiquitous (C) perfidious
       (D) egregious (E) apocryphal

SENTENCE COMPLETION DRILL 8

1. The mood at the school dance Saturday night was decidedly ------- after the football team had lost the homecoming game in the final seconds.

   (A) trivial (B) frightening (C) unadorned
       (D) gloomy (E) contrived

2. Even the greatest fashion designers must find it difficult to reinvent their styles continually to keep up with the public's need for -------.

   (A) appeal (B) cajolery (C) novelty
       (D) certainty (E) connotation

3. Jazz as an art form is a textbook example of how ------- and potentially discordant elements can be combined into a coherent and ------- whole.

   (A) placid . . euphonious
   (B) unique . . majestic
   (C) subordinate . . obscure
   (D) disparate . . harmonious
   (E) hierarchical . . melodious

4. The coach was exasperated by her player's ------- remarks to reporters, and urged her to practice more ------- and discretion during interviews.

   (A) candid . . brevity
   (B) rambunctious . . melodrama
   (C) spontaneous . . tact
   (D) impromptu . . interpretation
   (E) indecent . . repetition

5. Simon's theory says resources can never become ------- because, as creations of human ingenuity, they are as ------- as our imaginations.

   (A) scarce . . inexhaustible
   (B) benign . . intelligible
   (C) pervasive . . pernicious
   (D) economical . . common
   (E) desirable . . exorbitant

6. Although the artist's career had a less than ------- start, she soon reached the ------- of her profession and saw her work internationally recognized.

   (A) auspicious . . crossroads
   (B) latent . . zenith
   (C) exceptional . . destruction
   (D) promising . . pinnacle
   (E) litigious . . manifestation

7. Carrie's friends invariably described her as ------- because of her apathetic attitude towards just about everything.

   (A) contentious (B) magnanimous (C) facetious
       (D) pragmatic (E) nonchalant

8. The debater's playful demeanor suggested that his real attitude was -------, notwithstanding the seriousness of his talk.

   (A) funereal (B) sinister (C) insouciant
       (D) scrupulous (E) egalitarian

MATH

WRITING

READING

VOCABULARY

SENTENCE COMPLETION DRILL 9

1. A classic is an ------- literary work that is read and analyzed by generation after generation.

   (A) enduring (B) authoritarian (C) unknown
   (D) exclusively (E) immaterial

2. Benjamin Franklin was the ultimate -------: he was less concerned with speculating than with testing his ideas experimentally.

   (A) idealist (B) essayist (C) orator
   (D) theoretician (E) empiricist

3. The introduction of improved helmets on the game's safety was -------: because helmets encouraged reckless play, the number of head injuries actually increased.

   (A) exhilarating (B) presupposed (C) aggressive
   (D) counterproductive (E) fortifying

4. Far from being ------- by a succession of setbacks in his life, Billy Mills was inspired by his adversity and went on to win an Olympic gold medal.

   (A) daunted (B) validated (C) accessed
   (D) corrected (E) foreshadowed

5. The committee's recommendation represented not simply ------- change for appearances, but a true departure from previous policy.

   (A) unexpected (B) redundant (C) inexpedient
   (D) cosmetic (E) political

6. The virtues of meals prepared by the best chefs are not ------- and require the discriminating palate of a connoisseur to fully -------.

   (A) gullible . . encompass
   (B) consuming . . savor
   (C) sagacious . . distinguish
   (D) flagrant . . appease
   (E) conspicuous . . appreciate

7. The heroic rescuer was remarkably ------- about her feat: as soon as the news personnel arrived to interview her, she quietly ------- the scene.

   (A) conciliatory . . persevered with
   (B) meritorious . . extrapolated from
   (C) humble . . retired from
   (D) eloquent . . advanced toward
   (E) prolix . . mulled over

8. After months of an unrelentingly ------- schedule on the campaign trail, the investigative journalist was left completely -------.

   (A) dilatory . . listless
   (B) soporific . . burgeoning
   (C) frenetic . . enervated
   (D) torpid . . moribund
   (E) noisome . . obdurate

SENTENCE COMPLETION DRILL 10

1. It was hard not to laugh at the kitten's ------- gestures intended to frighten us away from its food bowl.

   (A) menacing (B) precise (C) disconnected
      (D) feline (E) domesticated

2. After years of feeling that their concerns were merely ------- to mainstream interests, a faction of marginalized citizens have rejected ------- and become more vocal.

   (A) arbitrary . . action
   (B) secondary . . lobbying
   (C) clamorous . . narcissism
   (D) squandered . . reclamation
   (E) peripheral . . passivity

3. Sadly, most academic writing is perplexing if not downright -------, and certainly not a model of writing to be emulated by students.

   (A) archetypal (B) impenetrable (C) special
      (D) creative (E) ostensible

4. The effects of Brian Regan's brilliant comedy routine are ------- and -------; they sneak up on the audience, slowly gathering an irresistible comic force.

   (A) surprising . . cumulative
   (B) negligent . . hilarious
   (C) deadly . . vivid
   (D) obvious . . striking
   (E) acquisitive . . morose

5. By dismissing his opponent's views as -------, the speaker hoped that the audience would fail to notice that his own position was anything but
   -------.

   (A) tenable . . debatable
   (B) irrefutable . . preposterous
   (C) spurious . . plausible
   (D) partisan . . dubious
   (E) moderate . . inscrutable

6. Only the aging actor's biggest fans could overlook that his heart was no longer in his
   ------- performances and that he relied on -------
   when nuanced portrayals were required.

   (A) mercenary . . paradigms
   (B) perfunctory . . histrionics
   (C) laborious . . parodies
   (D) callow . . machinations
   (E) trenchant . . kudos

SENTENCE COMPLETION DRILL 11

1. The club's budget had been drastically cut, so their year-end celebration was less ------- than usual.

   (A) refined (B) popular (C) defined
       (D) lavish (E) sedate

2. Honesty is important, but Melissa carries frankness with others to the point of being -------.

   (A) introverted (B) equivocal (C) diplomatic
       (D) brusque (E) wary

3. The dance performance was so ------- that even the most reserved critic gave it a rave review.

   (A) mendacious (B) vacuous (C) spellbinding
       (D) superfluous (E) strenuous

4. The mathematician was not sure of his conclusion, but his colleagues agreed that it was a promising -------.

   (A) exposition (B) conjecture (C) abstraction
       (D) fundamental (E) requisite

5. The customer's anger was so ------- that the store manager gave up trying to ------- her.

   (A) equable . . forsake
   (B) vitriolic . . mollify
   (C) cloying . . confound
   (D) bilious . . reprimand
   (E) vapid . . proscribe

 © TPR Education IP Holdings, LLC

SENTENCE COMPLETION DRILL 12

1. Skilled animal trainers condition their animals to associate a specific ------- with a given behavior, so that each stimulus will ------- an expected response.

   (A) discipline . . vanquish
   (B) pattern . . subvert
   (C) habitat . . elicit
   (D) temperament . . illustrate
   (E) cue . . trigger

2. The political candidate's ------- owed as much to her positive appeal with voters as to the negative views they held of her rival.

   (A) apprehension (B) transference (C) success
   (D) elitism (E) erudition

3. Every new scientific theory that challenges the reigning orthodoxy is viewed as ------- until it is supported by mounting evidence and eventually adopted as truth.

   (A) dichotomous (B) heretical (C) critical
   (D) relative (E) inconsequential

4. When a public figure's every expression and gesture is scrutinized, successful politicians become skilled at ------- and masking their true feelings.

   (A) relegating (B) coercing (C) vilifying
   (D) dissembling (E) perpetrating

5. Aspiring actors sometimes forget that fame is not guaranteed but rather -------; and even if achieved, not ------- but rather ephemeral.

   (A) intransigent . . transient
   (B) elusive . . immutable
   (C) hopeful . . permanent
   (D) mercurial . . impersonal
   (E) inevitable . . futile

SENTENCE COMPLETION DRILL 13

1. The company's president is an autocrat: he expects employees to follow his orders without question and tolerates no ------- .

   (A) dissent (B) diffusion (C) congeniality
       (D) communication (E) optimism

2. Although the candidate's speech was eloquent, he alienated his audience with ------- comments about his rivals.

   (A) disparaging (B) sympathetic (C) whimsical
       (D) affable (E) scholarly

3. Elizabeth played six musical instruments equally well; her ------- musical skills made her a valuable member or the orchestra.

   (A) grandiose (B) residual (C) pristine
       (D) fluent (E) versatile

4. Anyone unable to discern the characteristic traits of charlatans is ------- their -------.

   (A) coddled by . . depravity
   (B) impressed by . . idiosyncrasies
   (C) vulnerable to . . chicanery
   (D) patronized . . misgivings
   (E) surpassed by . . veracity

5. The monotone with which the announcer spoke about the details of the discovery ------- her true excitement.

   (A) vitrified (B) embodied (C) catalyzed
       (D) striated (E) belied

SAT READING: THE APPROACH

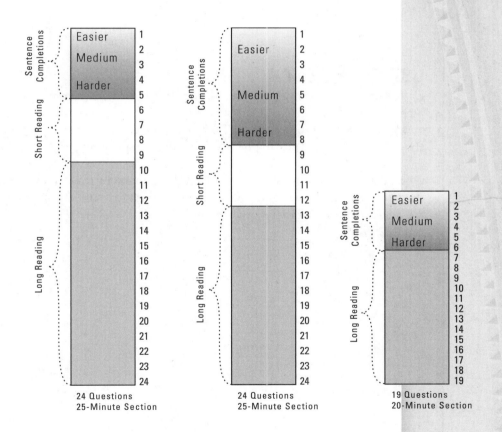

24 Questions
25-Minute Section

24 Questions
25-Minute Section

19 Questions
20-Minute Section

Question 1:   Why does the SAT Reading section always seem so hard?

Question 2:   How is it possible to answer every reading question correctly on the SAT without knowing one correct answer?

MATH

WRITING

READING

VOCABULARY

PASSAGE-BASED READING PHILOSOPHY

Yes, you know how to read, but you get too many Reading questions wrong on the SAT. The reason? This isn't English class. You don't have to know anything but what you are given in the passage. *There is no deep interpretation.* Everything is supported on the surface in the passage, and you can actually point to the evidence. However, just as with the Math and Writing sections, the test makers design questions that make simple ideas seem hard. For this reason, the one major technique that you must execute throughout the Reading section is, as always, POE.

Your job: seek bad answers. Eliminate four of them.

USE YOUR PENCIL

First of all, a reminder: For all your SAT practice with TPR, you should be using a pencil, not a pen. This includes your practice in this manual, your homework, and your diagnostic tests. You will not be using a pen on the real thing, so you should not be using a pen to practice. Yes, this actually matters.

One of the biggest mistakes that SAT students make in this section is doing all the work in their heads. You **must** underline and circle important things in the passage—and even jot down quick notes.

BASIC APPROACH FOR PASSAGE-BASED READING

1. **Read the Blurb.** Do not skip the little italicized summary of what the passage is about.
2. **Work the Passage.** Don't let all of the details make you lose sight of the main idea.
3. **Select and Understand a Question.** Skip any confusing or time-consuming questions and do the questions that you understand first.
4. **Mark the Reference Window.** Most answers will be located within a small portion of the passage. Find that window. Read.
5. **Predict the Answer.** Use your own words first before working the given answer choices.
6. **POE.** Find your answer by eliminating four bad answers.
   - Information that is **not mentioned** in the passage.
   - **Extreme language** that is too strong than the tone of the reference window.
   - **Half-right but half-wrong.** For an answer to be right, every word in it must be true.

Purposefully skim the passage but never skim the questions or the answer choices.

Common question: What about skipping the passage? That works for some people, but not all. Try it. Either way, you're going back to the passage for every question.

MATH

WRITING

READING

VOCABULARY

© TPR Education IP Holdings, LLC

DIGGING DEEPER...

To attack SAT Reading passages, search for the following items as these will help you make long and usually boring passages a little more manageable.

Line References: If the lines are numbered for us, let's use them! Many questions will contain line references for you know from where you should base your answer.

Find the Window: For those questions that have line references, now read 5 lines up and 5 lines down from the line reference to establish your reference window. The answer WILL come from within this window! However, if there is no line reference in the question...

Chronology: ETS will generally order the questions in the order in which answers can be found in the passage. Therefore, if a question doesn't have a line reference for you to mark your reference window, check out the question before or after to get some indication as to where you should find your window.

POOD: Save the time-consuming questions for last!

Mark your reference windows so that you won't fall for answers that may be true but don't answer the question.

Got it? Now let's practice finding reference windows utilizing line references, chronology, and POOD in the following passage:

Questions 7-12 are based on the following passage.

The following passage discusses the annexation of Hawaii by the United States.

On January 28, 1893, Americans read in their evening newspapers a bulletin from Honolulu, Hawaii. Two weeks earlier, said the news report, a group of
Line American residents had overthrown a young native
5 queen and formed a provisional government. Marines from the U.S.S. *Boston* had landed at the request of the American minister in order to protect lives and property. Violence had ended quickly. The rebels were in full control and were said to have enthusiastic support
10 from the populace. Most noteworthy of all, they had announced the intention of asking the United States to annex the islands.

The proposal was not as startling as it might have seemed. Most of the large landowners in the islands
15 were Americans or the children of Americans. So too were the men who grew, refined, and shipped the sugar that was Hawaii's principal export. In addition, many of the kingdom's Protestant clergymen, lawyers, bankers, factory owners, and other leading personages
20 were also American citizens. Though numbering only two thousand of the island's total population of around ninety thousand, these Americans had already given Hawaii the appearance of a colony. This influence could be seen as far back as 1854 when they nearly persuaded
25 a native monarch to request annexation by the United States. Subsequently, the American element helped secure tariff reciprocity from the United States while the island ceded a naval station to the United States. Such measures sparked enough concern by the United States
30 to lead presidents from Tyler on down to periodically warn European powers against meddling in Hawaiian affairs. Thus, by 1893, the new proposal might have been characterized as simply a plan to annex a state already Americanized and virtually a protectorate.
35 Nonetheless, the proposition came unexpectedly, and neither politicians nor journalists knew quite what to make of it. Editorials and comments from Capitol Hill were at first noncommittal. The molders of public opinion seemed intent on learning what mold the public
40 wanted.

San Francisco's leading Republican and Democratic dailies, the *Chronicle* and *Examiner*, declared that Hawaii should certainly be accepted as a state. On January 29, the *Chronicle* reported a poll of local
45 businessmen demonstrating overwhelming support for this view. Some businessmen focused on potential profits. Claus Spreckels, for example, who owned Hawaii's largest sugar plantation, hoped to obtain the two-cent-a-pound bounty paid by the United States
50 government to domestic sugar producers. In addition, he anticipated increased freight for his Oceanic Steamship line as well as more plentiful and cheaper raw sugar for his California sugar refinery company.

Businessmen elsewhere on the Pacific coast followed
55 their lead. San Diego, for example, was virtually the property of the Spreckels family. Moreover, in Los Angeles, Fresno, and San Jose, the Spreckels were allied, to some extent, in the battle against the railroad with merchants, bankers, warehouse owners, real
60 estate dealers, and contractors; and the Chambers of Commerce of Portland and Seattle had long cooperated with that of San Francisco in pressing for national policies advantageous to the West. It was not long before businessmen all along the coast were reported as
65 favoring annexation.

7. What event occurred "two weeks earlier" (line 3) than January 28, 1893 ?

8. According to the second paragraph, Americans on the Hawaiian Islands

9. The tone of the author's statement in lines 36-40 ("Editorials...public wanted") is best described as

10. In describing the response of the "molders" (lines 38-39) the author suggests that they

11. All of the following served as reasons that Claus Spreckels supported annexation EXCEPT

12. In line 62, "pressing" most nearly means

MATH

WRITING

READING

VOCABULARY

FIND THE WINDOW DRILL

The following passage is adapted from a 2010 short story about a woman who comes back to the United States after living for four years in Europe.

By the time I was 22, my girlhood home seemed like the *real* foreign country, not the language or even the people, but that combination of familiarity and fear. In
Line that combination, I sensed my own closed-mindedness
5 and open-heartedness all at once. I had my way of life, and I'd have to learn a new one to come here.

It's said that you can never really be at home in a foreign country, that your national origins are attached to you like fingerprints. And, of course, when people
10 are conversing easily and fluidly in a language you may never perfect, you're on the outside, and they're on the inside.

I definitely know what it means to be on the outside. I was born and raised in a place that could not be more
15 American, but for those four college years, every time I stepped out of my front door, I could feel myself cycling through thousands of different identities. I belonged here as much as anyone else. Like a local, I could assimilate the collection of odd sights on my walk to
20 school: the homeless man with a different dog every day, the park with shards of classical sculpture, and the former government buildings that now sold American electronics at a huge markup.

I embraced the strangeness, walking down the
25 street with my eyes and ears as open as vast doorways. I embraced the way that leaving my apartment, in pursuit of newspapers in soothing, familiar English or breads so light and fluffy they might've been made from clouds, never felt like entering one foreign country, but like
30 entering *many* of them, with all the world's cultures and races represented in a panoply of storefronts, restaurants, languages, clothing, and people.

Imagine a rainbow with three times as many colors as it normally has.

35 But my days on the rainbow were short-lived. It was four years altogether, my four years of college, first in London then in Paris, until my school's commencement, which felt like an ironic name when all I could feel was the end. I came back to Virginia that July, and after
40 months of kicking and screaming that I did not belong here anymore, I couldn't help feeling that I had never left. I both loved and hated this feeling. I felt like a stranger in a very familiar land, as if I had been hired to play a difficult role that only I could play.

45 My jetsetter persona from college would be appalled if she knew that this is what waited for her after her travels. I wanted to make the United States, especially my little corner of Virginia, a fond memory, an object of nostalgia rather than a real home, as I spent the rest
50 of my days in Europe. Instead, here I was in the car with my parents, riding in the passenger seat as I had when I was a teenager, and there they all were, behind every familiar door, every address plaque, every twist and turn of the driveways: all the people that I knew from my
55 youth were here and looked oddly the same, but I looked like them, too.

"How does it feel to come back?" asked my father, and after a moment of consideration (a long moment, for my father is never in a hurry), I knew that "come back"
60 had different meanings for the two of us. For him, it was "back home," the place that he and I would always return to, but for me it was "back in time," as I had always imagined my future to be on the other side of the Atlantic Ocean.

65 My hometown—for that much it surely is—lies just to the west of the Shenandoah Valley. The town is tiny, maybe 500 people altogether, but I learned on our drive back from the airport in Washington, D.C., that my "hometown" has much more capacious borders
70 than I had ever realized. The majestic Shenandoahs tower above the scenery, and you can take them in from many miles away. Once you leave the D.C. suburbs in Virginia, you can feel the warmth of communities that historically had only their own resources on which to
75 rely. Every trip here *was* a trip "back" as only a few technological updates made secret changes within a visually unchanged landscape. I was coming back not only to my own home but also to the homes of many others before me.

80 I wanted to be like all my favorite American expatriates from the 1920s, and maybe I could have been. But my circumstances brought me back here. I should consider it a great privilege rather than an insufferable burden that I had nothing to escape from,
85 so why pretend otherwise? I could've made it in Paris, I think, but now, I finally realize that I can just as well make it here, too. I didn't have to be a foreigner to feel like myself. This community doesn't have to swallow everything that makes me an individual. It can take me
90 in, and in fact, it can give me the freedom to be myself in a way that the hustle and bustle, the true unfamiliarity, of Paris and London never could. At home, I can be a local or a stranger as I please.

14. The central contrast in the passage is between

15. In the passage, the narrator is concerned primarily with

16. As it is used in line 9, the word "fingerprints" is a simile for

17. Lines 20-23 ("the homeless...markup") are similar to lines 52-54 ("every door...driveways") in the way they

18. Lines 24-32 are characterized by the use of

19. The use of italics in line 30 serves to emphasize a distinction between

20. In context, the phrase "my days on the rainbow" (line 35) refers mainly to a time that the narrator was

21. Lines 42-44 ("I both ... play") are notable for their description of

22. In line 52, the word "they" refers to

23. In line 76, "secret" most nearly means

24. The narrator's description of the "warmth" (line 73) chiefly reveals her

25. In lines 82-85 ("I should ... otherwise"), the narrator poses a question that primarily

MATH

WRITING

READING

VOCABULARY

Reading Hit Parade

Here are the vocabulary words that have the biggest impact throughout the Reading section. Of course, you will have decisive moments involving other vocabulary. However, if you aren't good at studying hundreds of words, this short list will have the biggest impact on your Reading score.

These are some of the most commonly occurring vocabulary words on the SAT, especially in the Reading Comprehension sections. Know them!

aesthetic	dismissive	plausible
allusion	disparage	pragmatic
ambivalent	disparity	prove
anecdote	dispassionate	provoke
assert	dubious	qualified
assess	elicit	reconcile
belied	endorse	refute
challenge	equivocate	relevant
characterize	exemplify	repudiate
compare	fallacy	resigned
concur	hypothesis	reverent
contempt	hypothetical	rhetoric
contrast	illustrate	satire
conventional	indifferent	scornful
convey	interpret	scrutinize
debunk	ironic	speculate
diffident	justify	subjective
discern	nostalgia	substantiate
discredit	objective	undermine
disengaged	partisan	underscore
disinterested	phenomenon	yield

Summary

- What are the 6 steps of the Basic Approach to Passage-Based Reading?

  1. _____

  2. _____

  3. _____

  4. _____

  5. _____

  6. _____

- The answers to questions will always be within _____.

- Do _____ questions first and save the _____ questions for last.

- Passage-based questions are generally in _____ order.

- I have accomplished _____ of my _____ stated goals in the Introduction chapter.

SAT READING: P & P

READING BASIC APPROACH

1. Read the Blurb

2. Work the Passage

3. Select and Understand a Question

4. Mark the Reference Window

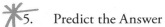5. Predict the Answer

6. POE

Using Reference Windows to Predict the Answer

Here are two examples that show the importance of going above and below the exact line reference you are given.

Line   …Our understanding of the composition of matter
15   has changed radically in the past one hundred years.
Before Ernest Rutherford posited the existence of
protons, neutrons, and electrons in 1911, even the most
accomplished scientist conceived of the atom as the
smallest possible unit of matter. There was nothing
20   smaller. Now, we know that there are myriad subatomic
particles, ranging from protons and electrons to quarks
and neutrinos….

8. The author states that "protons, neutrons, and electrons" (line 17) are

   …It has been documented that the best chess players
do not view the playing pieces in isolation, noting their
locations individually. Rather, they visualize sections
10   of the chessboard in a process known as chunking; they
may not remember exactly where each piece is on the
board, but they know the position of each piece relative
to the others. Researchers in artificial intelligence have
tried to duplicate this sort of vision in their chess-
15   playing computer programs, with varying degrees of
success. In an attempt to beat the human players at
their own game, the programmers have turned away
from the computer's traditional strength—the ability to
perform an astonishing number of calculations quickly
20   and flawlessly—and begun to model their programs
after the cognitive structures of the most successful
humans….

13. The author refers to "chunking" (line 10) as

PROCESS OF ELIMINATION (POE) REVIEW

Remember the Reading Comprehension POE symbols? Labeling the answer choices with these symbols will be very important for Reading Comprehension score improvement. Let's run through several more examples as a reminder.

(A)   (A)   (A)

(B)   (B)   (B)

(C)   (C)   (C)

(D)   (D)   (D)

(E)   (E)   (E)

Now use the **POE symbols** to label each answer choice when comparing all of them to your predicted answer.

Line
15   ...Our understanding of the composition of matter has changed radically in the past one hundred years. Before Ernest Rutherford posited the existence of protons, neutrons, and electrons in 1911, even the most accomplished scientist conceived of the atom as the smallest possible unit of matter. There was nothing
20 smaller. Now, we know that there are myriad subatomic particles, ranging from protons and electrons to quarks and neutrinos....

8. The author states that "protons, neutrons, and electrons" (line 17) are

(A) particles created by Ernest Rutherford
(B) only a few of many subatomic particles
(C) atomic components developed in 1911
(D) molecules formed by atoms
(E) units of matter currently unimaginable

    ...It has been documented that the best chess players do not view the playing pieces in isolation, noting their locations individually. Rather, they visualize sections
10 of the chessboard in a process known as chunking; they may not remember exactly where each piece is on the board, but they know the position of each piece relative to the others. Researchers in artificial intelligence have tried to duplicate this sort of vision in their chess-
15 playing computer programs, with varying degrees of success. In an attempt to beat the human players at their own game, the programmers have turned away from the computer's traditional strength—the ability to perform an astonishing number of calculations quickly
20 and flawlessly—and begun to model their programs after the cognitive structures of the most successful humans....

13. The author refers to "chunking" (line 10) as

(A) the most successful cognitive process applied by the brain
(B) a process some programmers have tried to replicate
(C) the traditional strategy of computers when playing chess
(D) the visualization technique used by all chess players
(E) the ability to perform calculations flawlessly

PREDICT THE ANSWER AND POE: DRILL 1

In the passage below, work the passage and mark the reference window for each question, where appropriate. Then, write in your predicted answer for each question.

The following passage is excerpted from an autobiographical novel by Maya Angelou and describes an incident from her youth.

One summer afternoon, sweet-milk fresh in my memory, Mrs. Flowers stopped at the Store to buy provisions. Another Negro woman of her health and age
Line would have been expected to carry the paper sacks home
5 in one hand, but Momma said, "Sister Flowers, I'll send Bailey up to your house with these things."

She smiled that slow dragging smile. "Thank you, Mrs. Henderson. I'd prefer Marguerite, though." They gave each other age-group looks.
10 Momma said, "Well, that's all right then. Sister, go and change your dress. You going to Sister Flowers's."

There was a little path beside the rocky road, and Mrs. Flowers walked in front swinging her arms and picking her way over the stones.
15 She said, without turning her head, to me, "I hear you're doing very good school work, Marguerite, but that it's all written. The teachers report that they have trouble getting you to talk in class." We passed the triangular farm on our left and the path widened to allow us to
20 walk together. I hung back in the separate unasked and unanswerable questions.

"Come and walk along with me, Marguerite." I couldn't have refused even if I wanted to. She pronounced my name so nicely. Or more correctly, she
25 spoke each word with such clarity that I was certain a foreigner who didn't understand English could have understood her.

"Now no one is going to make you talk—possibly no one can. But bear in mind, language is man's way of
30 communicating with his fellow man and it is language alone which separates him from the lower animals." That was a totally new idea to me, and I would need time to think about it.

"Your grandmother says you read a lot. Every chance
35 you get. That's good, but not good enough. Words mean more than what is set down on paper. It takes the human voice to infuse them with the shades of deeper meaning."

She said she was going to give me some books and that I not only must read them, I must read them aloud.
40 "I'll accept no excuse if you return a book to me that has been badly handled." My imagination boggled at the punishment I would deserve if in fact I did abuse a book of Mrs. Flowers's. Death would be too kind and brief.

The odors in the house surprised me. Somehow I had
45 never connected Mrs. Flowers with food or eating or any other common experience of common people. There must have been an outhouse, too, but my mind never recorded it.

The sweet scent of vanilla had met us as she opened
50 the door.

"I made tea cookies this morning. You see, I had planned to invite you for cookies and lemonade so we could have this little chat."

They were flat round wafers, slightly browned on
55 the edges and butter-yellow in the center. With the cold lemonade they were sufficient for childhood's lifelong diet. Remembering my manners, I took nice little lady-like bites off the edges. She said she had made them expressly for me. So I jammed one whole cake in my
60 mouth and the rough crumbs scratched the insides of my jaws, and if I hadn't had to swallow, it would have been a dream come true.

As I ate she began the first of what we later called "my lessons in living." She said that I must always be
65 intolerant of ignorance but understanding of illiteracy. That some people, unable to go to school, were more educated and even more intelligent than college professors. She encouraged me to listen carefully to what country people called mother wit.
70 When I finished the cookies she brushed off the table and brought a thick, small book from the bookcase. I had read *A Tale of Two Cities* and found it up to my standards as a romantic novel. She opened the first page and I heard poetry for the first time in my life.
75 "It was the best of times and the worst of times . . ."

Her voice slid in and curved down through and over the words. She was nearly singing. I wanted to look at the pages. Were they the same that I had read? Or were there notes, music, lined on the pages, as in a hymn book?
80 "How do you like that?"

It occurred to me that she expected a response. The sweet vanilla flavor was still on my tongue and her reading was a wonder in my ears. I had to speak.

I said, "Yes ma'am." It was the least I could do, but it
85 was the most also.

On that first day, I ran down the hill and into the road (few cars ever came along it). I was liked, and what a difference it made. I was respected not as Mrs. Henderson's grandchild or Bailey's sister but for just
90 being Marguerite Johnson.

16. The narrative point of view of the passage is that of

17. Lines 22-27 ("I couldn't...her") primarily serve to

18. In line 37, "shades" most nearly means

19. Marguerite's statement in lines 41-43 ("My imagination...Mrs. Flowers's") suggests that

20. In lines 63-69 ("As I...wit"), Mrs. Flowers indicates that

21. Marguerite's statement in lines 71-73 ("I had... novel") suggests that she initially viewed *A Tale of Two Cities* as

22. The question posed in lines 78-79 ("Were they... book") primarily serves to

23. Marguerite's attitude toward Mrs. Flowers in lines 81-85 ("It occurred...also") is best described as one of

24. Mrs. Flowers's main objective in inviting Marguerite to her house was to

Now use the POE symbols to label each answer choice when comparing all of them to your predicted answer.

16. The narrative point of view of the passage is that of

(A) a woman explaining the importance of reading

(B) a child presenting her opinions on a particular novel

(C) an adult recounting a memorable childhood event

(D) a writer describing why she chose to write

(E) an objective narrator explaining the perspectives of several characters

17. Lines 22-27 ("I couldn't...her") primarily serve to

(A) present an example

(B) recount an anecdote

(C) note an impression

(D) describe a theory

(E) resolve a conflict

18. In line 37, "shades" most nearly means

(A) shadows

(B) levels

(C) insights

(D) reflections

(E) signals

19. Marguerite's statement in lines 41-43 ("My imagination...Mrs. Flowers's") suggests that

(A) Mrs. Flowers is known for her strict and unforgiving nature

(B) Mrs. Flowers is overly concerned with the importance of books

(C) Marguerite is having difficulty understanding Mrs. Flowers

(D) Marguerite would fear for her life if she harmed one of Mrs. Flowers's books

(E) Marguerite is unlikely to mistreat one of Mrs. Flowers's books

20. In lines 63-69 ("As I...wit"), Mrs. Flowers indicates that

(A) intellectuals are not as clever as many people suppose

(B) Marguerite does not truly understand how to live

(C) intelligence is not dependent upon formal education

(D) well-educated people lack common sense

(E) impoverished people are deserving of compassion

21. Marguerite's statement in lines 71-73 ("I had... novel") suggests that she initially viewed *A Tale of Two Cities* as

(A) satisfactory

(B) sentimental

(C) incomprehensible

(D) stunning

(E) original

22. The question posed in lines 78-79 ("Were they... book") primarily serves to

(A) imply that Marguerite was bewildered by Mrs. Flowers's unusual speech patterns

(B) convey Marguerite's admiration for the eloquence of Mrs. Flowers's reading

(C) indicate that Mrs. Flowers had set the words of the book to music

(D) show the religious fervor that Mrs. Flowers brought to her reading

(E) suggest that Marguerite was not familiar with modern poetry

23. Marguerite's attitude toward Mrs. Flowers in lines 81-85 ("It occurred...also") is best described as one of

(A) grudging acceptance

(B) respectful awe

(C) guarded fear

(D) well-disguised dislike

(E) relaxed affection

24. Mrs. Flowers's main objective in inviting Marguerite to her house was to

(A) help Marguerite to appreciate the importance of the spoken word

(B) urge Marguerite to spend less time reading and more time living

(C) inspire Marguerite to put more effort into her schoolwork

(D) convince Marguerite to overcome her shyness and become more outgoing

(E) expose Marguerite to a wide variety of literary influences

DRILL 1 REVIEW

1. I was able to predict the answer for _____ questions.

2. Compared to the given answer choices, my predicted answers matched _____ times.

3. I used POE symbols for all answer choices on all questions.
    TRUE / FALSE

4. Some new vocabulary words that I need to learn from this passage are as follows:

    _____

    _____ .

PREDICT THE ANSWER AND POE: DRILL 2

In the passage below, work the passage and mark the reference window for each question, where appropriate. Then, write in your predicted answer for each question.

The following passage is adapted from a 2010 short story about a woman who comes back to the United States after living for four years in Europe.

By the time I was 22, my girlhood home seemed like the *real* foreign country, not the language or even the people, but that combination of familiarity and fear. In
Line that combination, I sensed my own closed-mindedness
5 and open-heartedness all at once. I had my way of life, and I'd have to learn a new one to come here.

It's said that you can never really be at home in a foreign country, that your national origins are attached to you like fingerprints. And, of course, when people
10 are conversing easily and fluidly in a language you may never perfect, you're on the outside, and they're on the inside.

I definitely know what it means to be on the outside. I was born and raised in a place that could not be more
15 American, but for those four college years, every time I stepped out of my front door, I could feel myself cycling through thousands of different identities. I belonged here as much as anyone else. Like a local, I could assimilate the collection of odd sights on my walk to
20 school: the homeless man with a different dog every day, the park with shards of classical sculpture, and the former government buildings that now sold American electronics at a huge markup.

I embraced the strangeness, walking down the street
25 with my eyes and ears as open as vast doorways. I embraced the way that leaving my apartment, in pursuit of newspapers in soothing, familiar English or breads so light and fluffy they might've been made from clouds, never felt like entering one foreign country, but like
30 entering *many* of them, with all the world's cultures and races represented in a panoply of storefronts, restaurants, languages, clothing, and people.

Imagine a rainbow with three times as many colors as it normally has.
35 But my days on the rainbow were short-lived. It was four years altogether, my four years of college, first in London then in Paris, until my school's commencement, which felt like an ironic name when all I could feel was the end. I came back to Virginia that July, and after
40 months of kicking and screaming that I did not belong here anymore, I couldn't help feeling that I had never left. I both loved and hated this feeling. I felt like a stranger in a very familiar land, as if I had been hired to play a difficult role that only I could play.

45 My jetsetter persona from college would be appalled if she knew that this is what waited for her after her travels. I wanted to make the United States, especially my little corner of Virginia, a fond memory, an object of nostalgia rather than a real home, as I spent the rest of
50 my days in Europe. Instead, here I was in the car with my parents, riding in the passenger seat as I had when I was a teenager, and there they all were, behind every familiar door, every address plaque, every twist and turn of the driveways: all the people that I knew from my
55 youth were here and looked oddly the same, but I looked like them, too.

"How does it feel to come back?" asked my father, and after a moment of consideration (a long moment, for my father is never in a hurry), I knew that "come back"
60 had different meanings for the two of us. For him, it was "back home," the place that he and I would always return to, but for me it was "back in time," as I had always imagined my future to be on the other side of the Atlantic Ocean.
65 My hometown—for that much it surely is—lies just to the west of the Shenandoah Valley. The town is tiny, maybe 500 people altogether, but I learned on our drive back from the airport in Washington, D.C., that my "hometown" has much more capacious borders than I had
70 ever realized. The majestic Shenandoahs tower above the scenery, and you can take them in from many miles away. Once you leave the D.C. suburbs in Virginia, you can feel the warmth of communities that historically had only their own resources on which to rely. Every trip here was
75 a trip "back" as only a few technological updates made secret changes within a visually unchanged landscape. I was coming back not only to my own home but also to the homes of many others before me.

I wanted to be like all my favorite American
80 expatriates from the 1920s, and maybe I could have been. But my circumstances brought me back here. I should consider it a great privilege rather than an insufferable burden that I had nothing to escape from, so why pretend otherwise? I could've made it in Paris, I think, but now,
85 I finally realize that I can just as well make it here, too. I didn't have to be a foreigner to feel like myself. This community doesn't have to swallow everything that makes me an individual. It can take me in, and in fact, it can give me the freedom to be myself in a way that
90 the hustle and bustle, the true unfamiliarity, of Paris and London never could. At home, I can be a local or a stranger as I please.

14. The central contrast in the passage is between

15. In the passage, the narrator is concerned primarily with

16. As it is used in line 9, the word "fingerprints" is a simile for

17. Lines 20-23 ("the homeless…markup") are similar to lines 52-54 ("every door…driveways") in the way they

18. Lines 24-32 are characterized by the use of

19. The use of italics in line 30 serves to emphasize a distinction between

20. In context, the phrase "my days on the rainbow" (line 35) refers mainly to a time that the narrator was

21. Lines 42-44 ("I both … play") are notable for their description of

22. In line 52, the word "they" refers to

23. In line 76, "secret" most nearly means

24. The narrator's description of the "warmth" (line 73) chiefly reveals her

25. In lines 81-84 ("I should … otherwise"), the narrator poses a question that primarily

Now use the POE symbols to label each answer choice when comparing all of them to your predicted answer.

14. The central contrast in the passage is between

(A) anger and redemption
(B) foreignness and sophistication
(C) maturity and childishness
(D) familiarity and unfamiliarity
(E) artistry and drabness

15. In the passage, the narrator is concerned primarily with

(A) extending a heated disagreement with her parents
(B) settling reluctantly into an shocking new reality
(C) reminiscing about the most difficult period of her life
(D) characterizing her acceptance of a change in life
(E) remembering the ways her life was better before

16. As it is used in line 9, the word "fingerprints" is a simile for

(A) manual labor
(B) criminal proceedings
(C) inescapable marks
(D) celebratory gestures
(E) foreign accents

17. Lines 20-23 ("the homeless…markup") are similar to lines 52-54("every door…driveways") in the way they

(A) correct a misrecognition
(B) create a fantastic setting
(C) describe a scene
(D) evoke a paradox
(E) imbue the passage with nationalism

18. Lines 24-32 are characterized by the use of

(A) subtlety and nuance
(B) irony and cynicism
(C) simile and metaphor
(D) citation and allusion
(E) overstatement and hyperbole

19. The use of italics in line 30 serves to emphasize a distinction between

(A) enjoyment and displeasure
(B) singularity and multiplicity
(C) race and national origin
(D) foreignness and familiarity
(E) immaturity and adulthood

20. In context, the phrase "my days on the rainbow" (line 35) refers mainly to a time that the narrator was

(A) living a pleasantly varied and diverse lifestyle
(B) flying back and forth between continents often
(C) denying the natural beauty of her home state
(D) ignoring her studies for extracurricular activities
(E) feeling nostalgia for her home in the United States

21. Lines 42-44 ("I both … play") are notable for their description of

(A) unscrupulous actions
(B) theatrical performances
(C) deep-seated antipathies
(D) nostalgic longings
(E) conflicted feelings

22. In line 52, the word "they" refers to

(A) "travels" (line 47)
(B) "days" (line 50)
(C) "parents" (line 51)
(D) "driveways" (line 54)
(E) "people" (line 54)

23. In line 76, "secret" most nearly means

(A) unspoken
(B) invisible
(C) embarrassing
(D) shameful
(E) private

24. The narrator's description of the "warmth" (line 73) chiefly reveals her

(A) anger
(B) comfort
(C) foreignness
(D) age
(E) short-sightedness

25. In lines 81-84 ("I should … otherwise"), the narrator poses a question that primarily

(A) shows her defensive stance
(B) argues for an older way of life
(C) demonstrates her calm acceptance
(D) evokes her international experience
(E) states an obvious moral truth

DRILL 2 REVIEW

1. I was able to predict the answer for _____ questions.

2. Compared to the given answer choices, my predicted answers matched _____ times.

3. I used POE symbols for all answer choices on all questions.
   TRUE / FALSE

4. Some new vocabulary words that I need to learn from this passage are as follows:

   _____

   _____ .

PREDICT THE ANSWER AND POE: DRILL 3

In the passage below, work the passage and mark the reference window for each question, where appropriate. Then, write in your predicted answer for each question.

The following passage is adapted from a novel set in the early twentieth century. Lily Bart, a New York socialite, is speaking with her friend Lawrence Selden about some of the differences between the lives led by women and men.

Lily sank with a sigh into one of the shabby leather chairs.

"How delicious to have a place like this all to one's
Line self! What a miserable thing it is to be a woman." She
5 leaned back in a luxury of discontent.

Selden was rummaging in a cupboard for the cake.

"Even women," he said, "have been known to enjoy the privileges of a flat."

"Oh, governesses—or widows. But not girls—not
10 poor, miserable, marriageable girls!"

"I even know a girl who lives in a flat."

She sat up in surprise. "You do?"

"I do," he assured her, emerging from the cupboard with the sought-for cake.

15 "Oh, I know—you mean Gerty Farish." She smiled a little unkindly. "But I said marriageable—and besides, she has a horrid little place, and no maid, and such odd things to eat. Her cook does the washing and the food tastes of soap. I should hate that, you know."

20 She began to saunter about the room, examining the bookshelves. Suddenly her expression changed from desultory enjoyment to active conjecture, and she turned to Selden with a question. "You collect, don't you—you know about first editions and things?"

25 He had seated himself on an arm of the chair near which she was standing, and she continued to question him, asking which were the rarest volumes, whether the Jefferson Gryce collection was really considered the finest in the world, and what was the largest price ever
30 fetched by a single volume.

It was so pleasant to sit there looking up at her, as she lifted now one book and then another from the shelves, fluttering the pages between her fingers, while her drooping profile was outlined against the
35 warm background of old bindings, that he talked on without pausing to wonder at her sudden interest in so unsuggestive a subject. But he could never be long with her without trying to find a reason for what she was doing, and as she replaced his first edition of *La Bruyère*
40 and turned away from the bookcases, he began to ask himself what she had been driving at. Her next question was not of a nature to enlighten him. She paused before him with a smile which seemed at once designed to admit him to her familiarity, and to remind him of the
45 restrictions it imposed.

"Don't you ever mind," she asked suddenly, "not being rich enough to buy all the books you want?"

He followed her glance about the room, with its worn furniture and shabby walls.

50 "Don't I just? Do you take me for a saint on a pillar?"

"And having to work—do you mind that?"

"Oh, the work itself is not so bad—I'm rather fond of the law."

"No; but the being tied down: the routine—don't you
55 ever want to get away, to see new places and people?"

"Horribly—especially when I see all my friends rushing to the steamer."

She drew a sympathetic breath. "But do you mind enough—to marry to get out of it?"

60 Selden broke into a laugh. "God forbid!" he declared.

She rose with a sigh.

"Ah, there's the difference—a girl must, a man may if he chooses." She surveyed him critically. "Your coat's a little shabby—but who cares? It doesn't keep people
65 from asking you to dine. If I were shabby no one would have me: a woman is asked out as much for her clothes as for herself. The clothes are the background, the frame, if you like: they don't make success, but they are a part of it. Who wants a dingy woman? We are expected to
70 be pretty and well-dressed till we drop—and if we can't keep it up alone, we have to go into partnership."

Selden glanced at her with amusement: it was impossible, even with her lovely eyes imploring him, to take a sentimental view of her case.

75 "Ah, well, there must be plenty of capital on the lookout for such an investment. Perhaps you'll meet your fate tonight at the Trenors'."

10. Lily's tone in lines 3-10 ("How delicious...girls") is one of

11. In line 9 ("Oh, governesses—or widows"), Lily's comment serves to

12. Lily's remarks in lines 15-19 ("Oh,...you know") help to convey her

13. In lines 37-42 ("But he...him"), Selden is best described as

14. In line 43, "designed" most nearly means

15. Selden's response to Lily in line 50 ("Don't I... pillar") most directly suggests that he

16. Lily's observation in lines 63-64 ("Your coat's... cares") serves primarily to

17. Lily's remarks about marriage primarily indicate that she views marriage as a

18. In line 74, "sentimental" most nearly means

19. In line 76, Selden's use of the word "fate" refers to the

Now use the POE symbols to label each answer choice when comparing all of them to your predicted answer.

10. Lily's tone in lines 3-10 ("How delicious...girls") is one of

  (A) surprise
  (B) indignation
  (C) delight
  (D) sarcasm
  (E) self-pity

11. In line 9 ("Oh, governesses—or widows"), Lily's comment serves to

  (A) express anger about a change in social status
  (B) bemoan the lack of help in Selden's apartment
  (C) call attention to a person's arrogant behavior
  (D) indicate exceptions to a perceived rule
  (E) demonstrate remorse for an unkind remark

12. Lily's remarks in lines 15-19 ("Oh,...you know") help to convey her

  (A) dislike of a former friend
  (B) distaste for a certain lifestyle
  (C) fear of an uncertain future
  (D) concern for a close friend
  (E) contempt for the lower class

13. In lines 37-42 ("But he...him"), Selden is best described as

  (A) irritated by Lily's childish questions about literature
  (B) puzzled by Lily's fascination with financial matters
  (C) disturbed by Lily's casual treatment of his book collection
  (D) uncertain about the motivation for Lily's actions
  (E) concerned about the reasons behind Lily's sudden mood swings

14. In line 43, "designed" most nearly means

  (A) renovated
  (B) charted
  (C) intended
  (D) allowed
  (E) visualized

15. Selden's response to Lily in line 50 ("Don't I... pillar") most directly suggests that he

  (A) resents not having the time to read more
  (B) regrets his decision to become a lawyer
  (C) wishes to be seen as deeply religious
  (D) hopes to move to a wealthier neighborhood
  (E) agrees that wealth has certain advantages

16. Lily's observation in lines 63-64 ("Your coat's... cares") serves primarily to

  (A) ridicule a character
  (B) dismiss a belief
  (C) highlight a discrepancy
  (D) voice a concern
  (E) issue a warning

17. Lily's remarks about marriage primarily indicate that she views marriage as a

  (A) natural result of a prolonged courtship
  (B) happy coincidence that cannot be counted on
  (C) distant dream for the average person
  (D) practical necessity for a young woman
  (E) romantic delusion that may be hazardous

18. In line 74, "sentimental" most nearly means

  (A) melodramatic
  (B) nostalgic
  (C) sympathetic
  (D) subjective
  (E) amused

19. In line 76, Selden's use of the word "fate" refers to the

  (A) possibility that Lily will meet a potential suitor
  (B) likelihood that Lily will be forced to remain single
  (C) conviction that people's lives are largely predetermined
  (D) probability that a business venture will be profitable
  (E) belief that Lily faces an unpleasant situation

DRILL 3 REVIEW

1. I was able to predict the answer for _____ questions.

2. Compared to the given answer choices, my predicted answers matched _____ times.

3. I used POE symbols for all answer choices on all questions. TRUE / FALSE

4. Some new vocabulary words that I need to learn from this passage are as follows:

_____

_____ .

MATH

WRITING

READING

VOCABULARY

PREDICT THE ANSWER AND POE: DRILL 4

In the passage below, work the passage and mark the reference window for each question, where appropriate. Then, write in your predicted answer for each question.

The following is an adaptation of an essay published by a journalist in a collection of essays on the cultural history of newspapers.

There was a time when journalists were rogue heroes who showed society's hidden workings and did so fearlessly. While the rogue journalist may still
Line exist, our own news-media landscape has altered, and
5 we are necessarily much worse-informed because of it. Particularly on television news, the copywriters have all become editors. That is to say, those who were previously tasked with dredging up the cold, hard facts are now much more likely to provide viewers with
10 predetermined opinions and personal perspectives.

One possible cause for this shift is the increasingly vicious fight for viewers and readers. Not only are there hundreds of channels on the television, there are now literally millions of attention-grabbing options on
15 computers, tablets, and smartphones. After a long, hard day at the office, the average viewer wants an easy time at home, not a mental challenge (life provides enough of those) but a comfortable retelling of the day's events. That retelling can be made most comfortable when it is
20 delivered in an entertaining package by people whose view of the world will basically square with the viewer's own.

A crucial historical example offers the comforting reminder that things were not always this way. Joseph
25 Pulitzer was born in Mako, Hungary, in 1847. In his younger years, Pulitzer wanted to be a soldier. He was turned away from the Austrian Army, but in Germany, he was eventually recruited to fight as a mercenary in the U.S. Union Army. After the Civil War ended,
30 Pulitzer made his way to St. Louis, where he began to study English and law. A chance meeting with two German newspaper owners led to Pulitzer's first job as a copywriter.

Pulitzer was a tireless and innovative journalist. He
35 worked doggedly to write high-quality stories and to increase the circulation of his papers. At the shockingly young age of 31, Pulitzer was the owner of the English-language *St. Louis Post-Dispatch*, where he oversaw all aspects of the newspaper's publication. In this era,
40 Pulitzer became particularly interested in championing the causes of the common man. His paper commonly featured exposes of the corruption of the rich and

powerful. Circulation of the *Post-Dispatch* rose to such heights, in fact, that Pulitzer was able to purchase the
45 much larger *New York World* in 1883. Pulitzer's same commitment to exposing corruption and educating his underrepresented public created what has been called a "one-man revolution" in the *World's* editorial policies and in newspaper publishing more generally.

50 One of the most vicious circulation battles of Pulitzer's career came from 1896 to 1898, the period of the Spanish-American War. This war famously stretched the limits of journalistic objectivity, and Pulitzer's main competitor, William Randolph Hearst, famously said to
55 one of his photographers, "You supply the pictures, and I'll supply the war." In the context of Pulitzer's larger career, it is especially unfortunate that Pulitzer was equally guilty of these kinds of fabrications, though the battled soured him on this kind of sensationalist
60 journalism for the remainder of his career.

With Hearst at the forefront of this new "yellow journalism," newspapers became the mouthpieces for the ideologies of their editors, not for the hard realities of common men. Pulitzer withdrew from this method of
65 journalism, and in time, the *New York World* became a more nuanced newspaper. With the paper's help and at its prodding, the U.S. government protected American business by passing new antitrust legislation and by regulating an increasingly out-of-control insurance
70 industry.

Pulitzer's name is best-known today because of its association with the Pulitzer Prize, awarded every year to works ranging from journalism to drama. The prize, especially the prize awarded for journalism, serves as a
75 constant reminder that journalism is most valuable when it at its most honest. Pulitzer explained his journalistic credo this way: "An able, disinterested, public-spirited press, with trained intelligence to know the right and courage to do it, can preserve that public virtue without
80 which popular government is a sham and a mockery." He would surely be disappointed in the direction that journalism has taken today, and we should be, too. We can only hold out the hope that someone with Pulitzer's courage and perseverance can come along to restore
85 journalism to its rightful place as teller of things as they really are. Only then can we begin to change those things to how they really should be.

17. The primary purpose of the passage is to

18. The author's attitude toward the situation described in lines 7-10 ("That is … perspectives") is best characterized as

19. The information in lines 24-33 ("Joseph Pulitzer … copywriter") serves primarily to

20. The information in lines 36-39 ("At the … publication") reveals Pulitzer's

21. The misfortune referred to in lines 56-60 ("In the … career") is that

22. The author's comment in lines 81-82 ("He would … too") is best described as

23. The "hope" referred to in line 83 is that

24. Which of the following, if true, is the author most likely to see as an unfortunate consequence of modern journalistic practices?

© TPR Education IP Holdings, LLC

MATH

WRITING

READING

VOCABULARY

Now use the POE symbols to label each answer choice when comparing all of them to your predicted answer.

17. The primary purpose of the passage is to
   (A) detail the contributions of immigrants to contemporary journalism
   (B) garner support for the return of print in place of electronic media
   (C) blame the reading public for its lack of interest in current events
   (D) draw the reader's attention to an issue in contemporary news reporting
   (E) champion a particular newspaper in today's media landscape

18. The author's attitude toward the situation described in lines 7-10 ("That is … perspectives") is best characterized as
   (A) confused
   (B) obstinate
   (C) open-minded
   (D) jealous
   (E) disapproving

19. The information in lines 24-33 ("Joseph Pulitzer … copywriter") serves primarily to
   (A) explain the reasons behind Pulitzer's change in career
   (B) sketch the early career of a historical figure
   (C) preview the conflicts outlined in the following paragraph
   (D) decry the state of contemporary journalism and media
   (E) suggest that the army provides excellent preparation for a career in journalism

20. The information in lines 36-39 ("At the … publication") reveals Pulitzer's
   (A) apathy
   (B) immaturity
   (C) humbleness
   (D) kindness
   (E) precociousness

21. The misfortune referred to in lines 56-60 ("In the … career") is that
   (A) Pulitzer stopped competing with Hearst for readers and lost the circulation battle
   (B) Pulitzer built the remainder of his career on a series of dubious journalistic practices
   (C) a career built on journalistic integrity should be compromised by this particular lapse
   (D) many journalists used sensationalist tactics to gain an edge in circulation
   (E) Hearst and Pulitzer mischaracterized the reality of the Spanish-American War

22. The author's comment in lines 81-82 ("He would … too") is best described as
   (A) an overstatement
   (B) a critique
   (C) a hypothesis
   (D) a concession
   (E) a metaphor

23. The "hope" referred to in line 83 is that
   (A) journalists will stop listening to the corporate interests of their editors
   (B) a brave individual will come along and change the face of journalism forever
   (C) news reporting will free itself from sensationalism and return to an era of purer objectivity
   (D) journalistic integrity will be recognized as the true way to produce social change
   (E) a young journalist from a major news outlet will aspire to win a Pulitzer Prize

24. Which of the following, if true, is the author most likely to see as an unfortunate consequence of modern journalistic practices?
   (A) A rural journalist accepts a higher salary to transfer to a popular newspaper published in an urban area.
   (B) A newspaper editor is reluctant to state his political views because he fears doing so may decrease the popularity of his paper.
   (C) A newspaper receives public scrutiny for uncovering the details of corruption within a state government.
   (D) A television news station that claims to be fair to all political ideologies represents the viewpoints of only one political perspective.
   (E) A reader writes a letter to the editor of a newspaper asking him to explain the contents of a particular article.

 © TPR Education IP Holdings, LLC

DRILL 4 REVIEW

1. I was able to predict the answer for _____ questions.

2. Compared to the given answer choices, my predicted answers matched _____ times.

3. I used POE symbols for all answer choices on all questions. TRUE / FALSE

4. Some new vocabulary words that I need to learn from this passage are as follows:

   _____

   _____ .

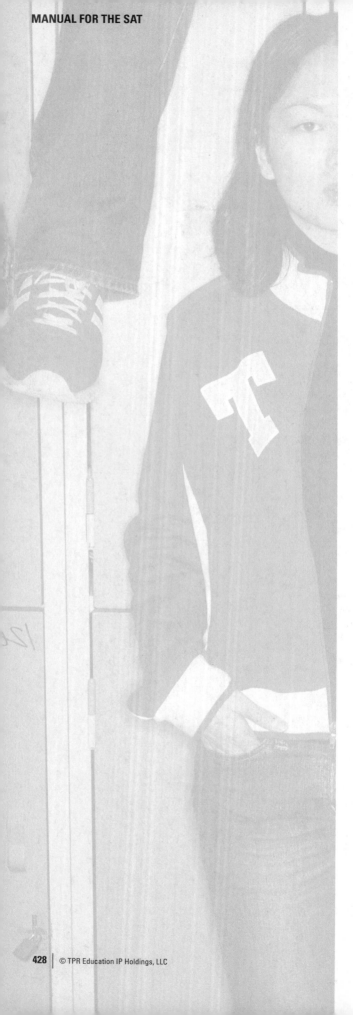

Summary

- After marking the reference window and reading the lines in it, I should _____.

- The POE symbols used to label answer choices in Passage-Based Reading are as follows:

  1. _____

  2. _____

  3. _____

  4. _____

- Reasons for eliminating answer choices could be the following:

  1. _____

  2. _____

  3. _____

- I have accomplished _____ of my _____ stated goals in the Introduction chapter.

SAT READING: IDENTIFYING QUESTION TYPES

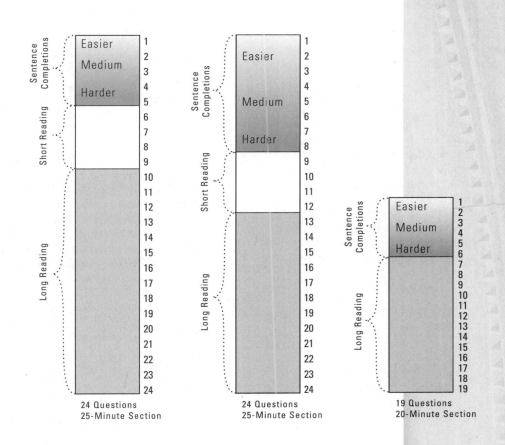

Sentence Completions
Short Reading
Long Reading

Easier
Medium
Harder

1
2
3
4
5
6
7
8
9
10
11
12
13
14
15
16
17
18
19
20
21
22
23
24

24 Questions
25-Minute Section

Sentence Completions
Short Reading
Long Reading

Easier
Medium
Harder

1
2
3
4
5
6
7
8
9
10
11
12
13
14
15
16
17
18
19
20
21
22
23
24

24 Questions
25-Minute Section

Sentence Completions
Long Reading

Easier
Medium
Harder

1
2
3
4
5
6
7
8
9
10
11
12
13
14
15
16
17
18
19

19 Questions
20-Minute Section

QUESTION TYPE: DETAIL

Questions that ask for details from the passage are among the more straightforward and direct questions. Most of these questions (about 80%) have line references. Remember to predict the answer after marking your reference window!

...I grew up believing that I hated tomatoes. I used to describe the raw fruit as tasting like curdled water and preferred tomato sauce from a can. But it was not by accident that the tomato rapidly insinuated itself into
45 the world's cuisines after 1492: it grows like a weed, and wherever this weed took root, locals fell in love with it. To grow a bad tomato takes careful planning. Unfortunately, careful planning is exactly what the North American food industry has provided. It has
50 carefully crafted tomatoes that can be hauled long distances and still look great, and the only casualty is taste. And it has done so for so long now that most of us have forgotten, or have never learned, what tomatoes are supposed to taste like.
55 I am certainly not arguing that we should go back to the days when all produce was local and no American ever tasted a cherimoya....

16. The problem with the "careful planning" (line 47) mentioned in the passage is that

(A) tomato fields are still plagued by weeds
(B) despite its best efforts, the American food industry has not been able to breed a tomato that tastes good
(C) local tomatoes are still more expensive at supermarkets than at farmers' markets
(D) it has been directed toward enhancing qualities in produce other than taste
(E) it has not been enough to keep foreign produce out of the marketplace

The haiku's relative simplicity explains its popular use worldwide as a means to introduce young children
Line to poetry. The brief Japanese poem consists of three
5 lines with a set number of syllables for each line. But the form is not as simple as it seems. The poem must also describe a single event taking place in the present, as well as make reference to the four seasons. Although a haiku can seem timeless, its reference to the changes
10 in nature serves to indirectly highlight the ephemeral quality of life.

6. Which one of the following best describes a contrast made in the passage?

(A) Although seemingly simple, the haiku is used to introduce young children to poetry.
(B) Haikus look relatively simple but are difficult to understand.
(C) The haiku enjoys worldwide popularity although most haiku poets are Japanese.
(D) While expressing eternal themes, a haiku can also convey a sense of the brief and passing nature of life.
(E) Despite the haiku's lengthy history in Japan, its popularity worldwide has only been a recent phenomenon.

7. The author most likely views the haiku as

(A) a poetic style focusing on solely natural themes
(B) the preferred form of poetry in Japanese society
(C) the best introduction to poetry
(D) a deceptively simple verse form
(E) a poem that emphasized rhythm

QUESTION TYPE: IMPLY/INFER/SUGGEST/CONCLUDE

You'll see this question type frequently. The SAT presents many questions that suggest you'll have to solve something or look very deeply into the passage. This is not the case. In the real world, these words involve subtlety, deep meaning, and a secondary level of understanding. But this isn't the real world. On the SAT, every correct answer is solidly supported by the passage. Don't get creative or try to "read between the lines" because all you'll need is direct information from the passage.

What **MUST** be true based on what was stated in the passage?

People often base their perceptions of similarity between fraternal twins on factors other than actual physical resemblance. Mannerisms such as similar gestures and *Line* facial expressions can substantially amplify even a minor
5 resemblance. Fraternal twins, who are no closer genetically than ordinary siblings, are very likely to share many of these behavioral quirks, since they often spend more time together than do siblings with a separation in age. Consequently, because they constantly provide each other with nonverbal feedback,
10 they tend to converge in many of their unconscious habits, leading to a closer perceived resemblance to one another.

7. The passage implies that "behavioral quirks" (line 7) are

   (A) mannerisms that are determined by genetic factors
   (B) behaviors that are shared only by fraternal twins
   (C) characteristics that are influenced by social interaction
   (D) traits that help parents distinguish between identical twins
   (E) peculiarities that often cause children to feel uncomfortable

...The nuns of Mankato raise interesting questions about how the brain functions as we age. These women, many of whom are older than ninety, believe that they must avoid an idle mind, *Line* and so they challenge themselves doggedly. Common leisure
35 activities among the nuns include vocabulary quizzes, puzzles, and debates. They hold seminars on current events, keep journals, and teach, many well into their eighties and nineties. They also suffer far fewer cases of dementia, Alzheimer's, and other brain diseases than does the general public...

10. The author of the passage suggests that the nuns of Mankato are very

   (A) intelligent
   (B) pious
   (C) decrepit
   (D) industrious
   (E) strict

MATH

WRITING

READING

VOCABULARY

A recent theory, which is still contested, claims
that disease can travel from one continent to another in
dust clouds. According to the theory, the Sahara Desert,
Line which has grown over the past thirty years due to the
5 near constant drought conditions in northern Africa, is
polluted with pesticides and laced with diseases from
human and animal waste. The dust from the desert,
when picked up by wind, can travel thousands of miles,
carrying the disease-laden particles around the world.

9. The passage suggests that the "recent theory"
(line 1) is

(A) unlikely to be an explanation of disease
dispersal
(B) based on faulty evidence and unsound logic
(C) currently a subject disputed by some
individuals
(D) too focused on contemporary conditions to be
useful
(E) appealing but marred by simplistic reasoning

Art is life. Life is art. Sophie Calle blends the two
so completely that it is hard to tell the two apart. The
documentation of her own life and the lives of others
Line are presented as photographs accompanied by text in
5 museums and in books. Her work has recorded people as
they sleep through the night and compiled blind people's
ideas of beauty. She has reported her experiences of
following people and having a private investigator follow
her. One revealing piece, *The Hotel*, displays people's
10 lives as seen from Calle's position as a hotel maid. Each
of her projects could be a sociology experiment as well
as a work of art.

9. In lines 10-12 ("Each...art"), the author suggests
that sociology experiments

(A) can involve chronicling people's daily
experiences
(B) were used as the basis for much of Calle's
art
(C) frequently investigate aspects of humanity
other people ignore
(D) are typically similar to works of art
(E) enhance the artistic qualities of Calle's
projects

Line
50 ...enterprise. Achievement was demanded of them. They
recognized the greatness of the prize, studied the strong
and weak points of their rivals, and with a cautious
forecast and a daring energy set themselves to the task of
defeating them.
55 If the English colonies were comparatively strong
in numbers, their numbers could not be brought into
action; while if the French forces were small, they were
vigorously commanded, and always ready at a word. It
was union confronting division, energy confronting
60 apathy, military centralization opposed to industrial
democracy; and, for a time, the advantage was all on one
side.
The demands of the French were sufficiently
comprehensive. They repented of their enforced
65 concessions at the Treaty of Utrecht, and in spite of that
compact, maintained that, with a few local and trivial
exceptions, the whole North American continent, except
Mexico, was theirs of right; while their opponents
seemed neither to understand the situation nor to see the
70 greatness of the stakes at issue.
The French did not forget the West; and towards
the middle of the century they had occupied points
controlling...

13. The statement in lines 61-62 ("for a...side")
implies the advantage was held by

(A) the Mexicans
(B) the French
(C) the English
(D) the native tribes
(E) the colonists

14. The author implies that the "Treaty of Utrecht"
(line 65)

(A) placed some North American land under non-
French rule
(B) did not include territory south of the present-
day United States
(C) was an agreement solely between the French
and the English
(D) contained confusing statements and vague
language
(E) stopped the French from invading English
colonies

QUESTION TYPE: PURPOSE

Now it's time to introduce one of the most important concepts you will encounter on the SAT: *purpose.* Reading Comprehension passages are filled with questions of purpose; they deal with *why* the passage tells us certain information, or *how* the passage works. For these questions, knowing *what* happened (details) is not enough.

The author's use of _____ primarily serves to…

The author mentions _____ in order to…

The purpose of the fourth paragraph is to…

Look for the following phrases:

- purpose
- mentions in order to
- serves to
- to indicate

These questions ask

- "What does the author want you to think?"
- "How does this information fit in with the rest of the passage?"
- "Why did the author bother to talk about this?"
- "Why does the author put this information here?"

These questions *do not* merely ask

- "What is the topic?"
- "What detail is stated?"
- "What did the author say?"

Line
50   … As the European Union both matures and grows,
adding more member states and attempting to integrate
their diverse laws, there has been an increasing call
for the creation of a constitution. Interestingly, many
among both those who want to limit the power of the
55   central European government and those who want to
see its power expand favor such a document. The former
believe it will create strict boundaries, whereas the latter
feel that the laws delineated in such a document will be
a further step toward the "ever closer union" promised in
60   the 1957 Treaty of Rome. …

18. The "Treaty of Rome" (line 60) is most likely
mentioned in order to

(A) defend a historical precedent
(B) challenge a faulty assumption
(C) undermine an argument
(D) show an earlier incarnation of an idea
(E) compare a similar theory

…of a tomato for a salad and found myself faced with
the usual unsavory tableau.
Most of the tomatoes I found had been shipped
Line   in from Canada, where they had been grown
5   hydroponically in greenhouses. These were salad-sized
"beefsteak" tomatoes, each one more perfectly round
than the last, and basically indistinguishable in taste
and appearance from a large, deep pink racquetball.
This would be bad enough in January, but at the time of
10   my visit it was the height of tomato season in the state
of Washington, where I live. Later that day I went to
a farmer's market in Seattle's university district, and
sampled over a dozen different varieties of Washington-
grown tomatoes—sweet yellow Taxi, complex and
15   bulging Brandywine, tart Roma. Prices ranged from
sixty cents to a dollar a pound. At the supermarket, the
only concession to the season had been a sad pile of
"local tomatoes," variety unknown, picked green and
smelling faintly of wax, marked at $1.99 a pound.
20   Ripe fruit wants to be eaten. Plants will use every
means at their disposal to attract animals to come eat
their fruit and spread…

16. The author mentions his visit to a farmers'
market (lines 12-16) primarily in order to point
out that

(A) Washington tomatoes are superior to those of
any other region
(B) most consumers are chiefly concerned with
the price of produce
(C) Taxi, Brandywine, and Roma tomatoes are the
best tomato varieties
(D) the affordability of supermarket tomatoes is
part of their appeal
(E) supermarkets do not always sell the best
available produce

Line   …in love with it. To grow a bad tomato takes careful
45   planning. Unfortunately, careful planning is exactly
what the North American food industry has provided. It
has carefully crafted tomatoes that can be hauled long
distances and still look great, and the only casualty is
taste. And it has done so for so long now that most of us
50   have forgotten, or have never learned, what tomatoes are
supposed to taste like.
I am certainly not arguing that we should go back to
the days when all produce was local and no American
ever tasted a cherimoya. But something is deeply
55   wrong when quality local tomatoes are available, but
supermarkets, where most Americans do all their food
shopping, carry only inedible tomatoes trucked in from
the other side of a national border. The next time I travel
to Italy, I intend to bring one of these supermarket
60   tomatoes along to show people as a practical joke. I have
no doubt it will survive in my carry-on luggage. …

17. What role does the mention of a cherimoya
(line 54) play in the author's argument?

(A) It concedes that long-distance shipping of
produce has some advantages.
(B) It specifies that the tomato is not the only
produce adversely affected by industrial
farming techniques.
(C) It suggests that tomatoes were not the only
fruit hated by the author as a child.
(D) It explains the object of the author's proposed
trip to Italy.
(E) It draws the reader's attention to another
item available at Seattle-area farmers'
markets.

Sometimes the SAT will ask for the primary purpose of a short reading passage.

On Primary Purpose questions, ask yourself "Why is the author telling me this? Why? Why? Why?"

In 1752, Benjamin Franklin demonstrated through a series of kite experiments that lightning is a form of electricity. More than 250 years later, scientists
Line still know relatively little about the causes of this
5 phenomenon. Yet lightning plays such a significant role in weather and climate that it could eventually become a powerful tool in storm prediction. Current technology can detect the direction of a storm's wind flow but cannot tell if these winds will pick up or die
10 down. Lightning commonly occurs during tornadoes, and flashes increase significantly right before a twister touches ground. If understood, lightning, once considered a mysterious and frightening occurrence, could do much to save lives.

6. The primary purpose of the passage is to

(A) assert that a theory will resolve a dilemma
(B) demonstrate that lightning helps predict wind direction
(C) suggest that a subject is in need of further study
(D) claim that lightning is a relatively harmless phenomenon
(E) imply that progress in a scientific field has stopped

People often base their perceptions of similarity between fraternal twins on factors other than actual physical resemblance. Mannerisms such as similar
Line gestures and facial expressions can substantially amplify
5 even a minor resemblance. Fraternal twins, who are no closer genetically than ordinary siblings, are very likely to share many of these behavioral quirks, since they often spend more time together than do siblings with a separation in age. Consequently, because they constantly
10 provide each other with nonverbal feedback, they tend to converge in many of their unconscious habits, leading to a closer perceived resemblance to one another.

6. The primary purpose of the passage is to

(A) evaluate the opinions of experts in a related field
(B) provide a plausible explanation for an observed phenomenon
(C) disprove an alternative explanation with new data
(D) question a commonly held superstition
(E) describe a scientific experiment that explains an event

Why do we know so little about the life of William Shakespeare when we know comparatively so much about the lives of his less accomplished peers? Our
Line lack of knowledge about Shakespeare has inspired
5 countless conspiracy theories. The actual writing of Shakespeare's works has been attributed to others from contemporary playwrights Christopher Marlowe and Ben Johnson to the brilliant Renaissance scientist and philosopher Francis Bacon. Shakespeare was an
10 immensely successful dramatist as well as a prosperous property owner. Circumspect, and only too aware of the government-inspired branding of Johnson, its torture of Thomas Kyd, and its murder of Marlowe, Shakespeare kept himself nearly anonymous. Wary to the end,
15 Shakespeare led a life virtually without memorable incident, as far as we can tell.

9. The phrase "as far as we can tell" (line 16) primarily serves to

(A) suggest another interpretation
(B) refute an erroneous theory
(C) question a belief
(D) advocate a novel position
(E) offer additional evidence

10. The primary purpose of the passage is to

(A) argue that Shakespeare is not as important as many people think he is
(B) compare Shakespeare's works to those of his less successful contemporaries
(C) take issue with theorists who suggest that Shakespeare did not write his plays
(D) show how a brutal and repressive government affected Shakespeare's career
(E) suggest that Shakespeare himself influenced our knowledge of his life

MATH

WRITING

READING

VOCABULARY

Primarily/Mainly/Chiefly

The SAT uses the words *primarily*, *most nearly*, or *most likely* on almost half of the reading questions. Why? Because they want to stay as close to the passage as possible. They're not looking for far-out interpretations; they want to know the BIG, PRIMARY, MOST LIKELY reason something happened. Remember that when an author uses quotations, parentheses, or italics, it's for the same reasons we all do—for emphasis and clarity. Keep in mind that authors have a purpose behind what they write.

10   ...The human body is not an ideal model of biological
efficiency; it is more like a garbage dump. Buried
deep within the genetic code of all humans is the
unfortunate record, the genetic "trash," of our less
successful evolutionary cousins and ancestors. Consider
15   hemoglobin. Modern human hemoglobin consists of
four different protein chains known as globins. Many
of the genes that could produce globins are redundant,
and several others are inactive, damaged in such a way
as to make protein production impossible. What is
20   the significance of these dysfunctional genes? Quite
simply, these damaged genes are the legacy of our
less successful ancestors, the biological remnants of
evolutionary mutations that didn't work out well enough.

9. In line 14, the sentence "Consider hemoglobin" serves primarily to

(A)   summarize a new argument
(B)   extend a metaphor
(C)   introduce an example
(D)   provide a summary
(E)   determine a pattern

While many rivers have long been utilized and
harnessed by the people who congregate near them, the
Mekong River, though it snakes through five countries
in Southeast Asia, has eluded human control until recent
Line   times. The low water level in dry seasons impedes travel
5   down the river, as does the Mekong's habit of splitting
into wide networks of smaller channels. Annual flooding
during the monsoon season thwarts attempts at long-
term agriculture. But in recent years, modern technology
and burgeoning human populations have begun to
10   encroach upon the Mekong's independence. Soon, the
Mekong may be as readily manipulated as many of its
peers around the world.

9. The reference to annual flooding (lines 7-9) primarily serves to

(A)   provide a specific illustration of a prior statement
(B)   resolve the conflict between two points of view
(C)   confirm the necessity of technological innovations
(D)   analyze the veracity of the author's argument
(E)   provide support for an argument against the river's development

MATH

WRITING

READING

VOCABULARY

QUESTION TYPE: VOCABULARY IN CONTEXT

You will likely see about five of them on your SAT.

1. Find the word in context in the passage.

2. Draw a line through it and treat it like a blank.

3. Fill in your own word for the blank. (Do not use the answers.)

4   POE (usually a secondary definition will be correct).

Approach these questions just as you would a
SENTENCE COMPLETION.

Line
30   …mirror copy much like a colored photograph:
nature with its infinite mass of details crowded into the
picture, unsifted, unassimilated, and unarranged. Even
if it were possible to put in everything seen, it would
not be art any more than copying a poem is creating
35   poetry. The painter uses nature not as a copybook but
as a source of inspiration, picks such details as suits his
or her purpose, and arranges them in a picture with a
discriminating regard for pictorial effect.

… Most of the tomatoes I found had been shipped
in from Canada, where they had been grown
hydroponically in greenhouses. These were salad-sized
Line   "beefsteak" tomatoes, each one more perfectly round
10   than the last, and basically indistinguishable in taste
and appearance from a large, deep pink racquetball.
This would be bad enough in January, but at the time of
my visit it was the height of tomato season in the state
of Washington, where I live. Later that day I went to
15   a farmer's market in Seattle's university district, and
sampled over a dozen different varieties of Washington-
grown tomatoes—sweet yellow Taxi, complex and
bulging Brandywine, tart Roma. Prices…

Line
10   …but as I stepped through and into the clearing, the
worst of my suspicions was confirmed. The source
of the noise that had drawn me far from my planned
route turned out to be the smaller bear cub, scared and
wailing, its foot fast in a trap. I did not see the mother,
15   yet I knew I must act quickly. With my pulse rising, I
stepped closer with measured steps in order to…

Line
35   …but not if she continued to lead such a reckless
life. It was becoming her habit to daily court potential
disaster by barely sleeping or eating. She had long ago
started ignoring the warnings of her family and friends.
Her doctor too, suggested that the greatest risk to her
health at that point, was not her diagnosed disease, but
40   the careless lifestyle that was consistently…

13. In line 38, the word "discriminating" is used to
mean

(A) prejudiced
(B) hostile
(C) selective
(D) artistic
(E) reflective

12. In line 13, the word "height" is used to mean

(A) elevation
(B) altitude
(C) summer
(D) excellent taste
(E) best part

14. In line 14, "fast" most nearly means

(A) slipping slightly
(B) shaking rapidly
(C) caught firmly
(D) dragging noticeably
(E) moving quickly

16. In line 35, "court" most nearly means

(A) legislate
(B) sue
(C) prefer
(D) provoke
(E) judge

MATH   WRITING   READING   VOCABULARY

QUESTION TYPE: TONE

Though less common than other question types, tone questions are likely to show up on your test. There are a few basic things to remember when dealing with anything that asks about the author's tone or opinion in an SAT question.

First ask yourself: did the author kind of like it, kind of dislike it, or was he or she in the middle?

First, authors almost never go to extremes. If you ever want to say an author is "scornful," for example, there has to be proof in the passage. Authors **often** have the following (less extreme) attitudes or tones:

+	neutral	–
agreement	ambivalent	disagreement
acceptance	unbiased	criticism
support	impartial	rejection
advocate	informing	question
praise	disinterested	doubt

Authors **rarely** have the following extreme attitudes:

ecstatic	overwhelming joy	exuberance
indulgent	hostile	exasperated
hatred	anger	disgust

In addition, authors care what they write about, and they know what they are saying. Authors are **rarely**

confused	bewildered
puzzled	befuddled
uninterested	indifferent

If they were that confused, would they have written the boring passages you have to read? ETS tries this when there is a rhetorical question somewhere in the passage and the exam asks you why the question was asked. Well, it's not because the author needs more information.

Tone questions often test hard vocab words. Keep studying the Hit Parade!

10 …If there is one imaginative work of the Romantic era that scientists should pay attention to, it is Mary Shelley's *Frankenstein*. Shelley was familiar with some of the most exciting scientific developments of her day, especially Galvani's experiments with electricity as a
15 life-force. Very much rooted in the science of its day, *Frankenstein* embodies a profound awareness of the larger human context of scientific endeavor. Despite the cheap thrills offered by all the horror movies…

20 …Economist Benjamin Grant believes differently. His group, Citizens Against Debt, works to educate people regarding the danger of easy access to loans. As he recently pointed out, "credit cards have become the new life preserver. How will I pay for that new massage
25 chair? A credit card. How will I pay off my credit card? Another credit card. How will I pay the fine to get released from debtors' prison? Does the court take credit cards?"

23. The author's attitude toward "Mary Shelley's *Frankenstein*" (lines 11-12) is best characterized as one of

(A) curiosity
(B) indignation
(C) nostalgia
(D) suspicion
(E) admiration

15. The tone of Benjamin Grant's comment in lines 23-25 is best described as

(A) laudatory
(B) decisive
(C) guarded
(D) wry
(E) despondent

Characters, in the passage however, can occasionally go to extremes. Look for words or phrases that describe what that person was thinking or feeling. Stick close to the passage.

The doctor packed his instruments and left Keswick manor, stepping into the cool grey fog of a London morning. As he passed Whitehouse Street, his lip curled
Line and his pace quickened. Here were the shabby offices
5 of his nominal peers, untrained nurses and midwives, mostly, although the doctor thought of the gulf between him and them as large as that between the captain of an ocean liner and the oarsman of one of the small rowboats that scurry across the Thames…

12. The doctor's attitude towards the "nurses and midwives" in line 5 is best described as

(A) ambivalent
(B) contemptuous
(C) suspicious
(D) furious
(E) combative

MATH

WRITING

READING

VOCABULARY

If the question asks what someone would think about something,
ask yourself what you *know* about that person from the passage.

...I grew up believing that I hated tomatoes. I used
to describe the raw fruit as tasting like curdled water
and preferred tomato sauce from a can. But it was not
by accident that the tomato rapidly insinuated itself into
45 the world's cuisines after 1492: it grows like a weed,
and wherever this weed took root, locals fell in love
with it. To grow a bad tomato takes careful planning.
Unfortunately, careful planning is exactly what the
North American food industry has provided. It has
50 carefully crafted tomatoes that can be hauled long
distances and still look great, and the only casualty is
taste. And it has done so for so long now that most of us
have forgotten, or have never learned, what tomatoes are
supposed to taste like.
55   I am certainly not arguing that we should go back to
the days when all produce was local and no American
ever tasted a cherimoya....

22. The author of the passage would most likely
agree with which of the following statements?

(A) We should spend more time finding better
produce.

(B) Tomatoes are not worth eating any more
unless they are from a can.

(C) People did not appreciate the taste of the
tomato until 1492.

(D) The quality of current produce could be
improved.

(E) We do not know what good tomatoes taste
like.

23. The North American food industry would be
most likely to agree with which of the following
statements?

(A) The main consideration when growing a
tomato is its taste.

(B) No one cares whether tomatoes taste good
anymore.

(C) It takes careful planning to grow a bad
tomato.

(D) The appearance of a tomato is an important
characteristic.

(E) Canned tomatoes taste better than those
grown on a vine.

...Archibald Suttle, quivering, set his teacup on the
35 table and stood up, so he could have free reign to make
his next point.
    "Well then, there must be thoughts of propriety.
Propriety, madam! A woman in this day and age cannot
just marry the first stagecoach driver that comes along.
40 A marriage requires, as in all things, a firm footing. Not
to say love should not enter into the thing, far from it.
I am quite fond of my Mrs. Suttle. It was, however, a
fondness born of our compatibility in financial matters:
we both came from the same place, as it were. Horse
45 before the cart, Elizabeth, not the other way around!"...

11. Archibald Suttle's comments in lines 37-45
indicate that he would agree with a marriage that

(A) develops naturally to fulfill both partners'
emotional needs

(B) has been sanctioned by the local government
officials

(C) is between two people of the same economic
standing

(D) was arranged and approved of by family
members

(E) involves a formal and elaborate ceremony

Passage 1

Scores of movies released in the past ten years—
The Matrix comes to mind—are so overloaded with
computer images that the experience is mind-numbing.
Special effects appear to have become more of an arms
race and less about supporting a story. Most blockbuster
special effects movies leave audiences with a feeling of
numbness rather than wonder.

It is a misguided pretense that too many studio check-
writers adopt: to get your money's worth; audiences need
to notice the effects, not forget about them. The best
special effects movie of the past ten years was *Master
and Commander: The Far Side of the World*—in which
every computer-assisted cannonball, amputation, and
gale force wind looked as if it actually happened in the
1800s on the open sea. In the end, many people did not
even know it was a special effects film. Which is just the
way it should be.

Passage 2

When director John Guillermin remade *King Kong* in
1976, he and producer Dino De Laurentis went to great
lengths to convince moviegoers that they were seeing an
actual giant ape on the screen in front of them. With a
film like 1999's *The Matrix*, however, co-directors Andy
and Larry Wachowski used computer-generated imagery
not intending to produce lifelike results, but to put a
highly stylized accent on the visuals. In one now-famous
fight scene, the female character Trinity is about to boot
a bad guy when she is frozen in mid-air; the camera then
sweeps around her, providing a panoramic view of the
kick to come. The Wachowski brothers were not trying
to convince viewers that a person could suspend herself
as Trinity does. Instead, they were trying to come up
with a shot that would make jaws drop.

9. The tone of lines 25-29 ("In one...come") is best
characterized as

(A) wistful
(B) ambivalent
(C) cynical
(D) apologetic
(E) enthusiastic

10. Which best describes the relationship between
Passage 1 and Passage 2?

(A) Passage 1 presents an opinion that Passage 2
calls into question.
(B) Passage 1 highlights an important
development whereas Passage 2 questions
its use.
(C) Passage 1 discusses a concern whereas
Passage 2 resolves that concern.
(D) Passage 1 argues against a changing
dynamic whereas Passage 2 argues for that
change.
(E) Passage 1 note problems for which Passage 2
offers solutions.

11. The author of Passage 2 would most likely
respond to lines 1-5 ("Scores . . . story") by

(A) arguing that the author is biased against a
certain type of movie
(B) suggesting that audiences can tolerate a
surprising number of computer images
(C) observing that special effects may legitimately
serve more than one purpose
(D) questioning the objectivity of reviews by well
known movie critics
(E) noting that the movie in question has become
a modern classic

12. The two passages differ in their discussion of
special effects primarily in that Passage 1

(A) presents special effects as useful but overused,
whereas Passage 2 explores their necessary
realism
(B) suggests that special effects are constantly
evolving, whereas Passage 2 argues that
they have stagnated
(C) describes typical uses of special effects,
whereas Passage 2 argues those uses
overwhelm a film's more subtle aspects
(D) notes that special effects can be distracting,
whereas Passage 2 suggests they exist for
the purpose of entertaining
(E) praises nontraditional use of special effects,
whereas Passage 2 contends they should be
used only in limited instances

 © TPR Education IP Holdings, LLC

MAIN IDEA

Though you will need to know the main idea of each passage in order to attack the questions, you will not see many questions that ask for the main idea directly. You're more likely to see questions on primary purpose, which we've already seen.

The key word here is *main*. Bad answers to these questions will often have choices with information that is either too specific or too general.

It is commonly assumed that the government's insuring bank deposits makes them safer. If the bank somehow fails by investing customer deposits in risky
Line loans that are not repaid, the government will make
5 good the lost funds. Thus reassured, the public will not find itself in the grips of financial panic and create "runs" on the bank to demand back their money, as occurred during the Great Depression in the 1930s.

Ironically, the perception of this "safeguard"
10 induces banks to extend far riskier loans than they would otherwise, thereby increasing the likelihood of catastrophic bank failures. In the final analysis, bank deposit insurance may undermine rather than bolster public confidence in our financial institutions.

6. Which of the following is the main idea of this passage?

(A) The government's insuring of bank deposits may have unintended consequences.

(B) Financial panics and bank runs are not likely to occur in the future because bank deposits are insured.

(C) If the government had taken the proper steps, the Great Depression could have been prevented.

(D) The government should take greater steps to insure customer deposits.

(E) Banks should not put customer deposits at risk by making loans that might not be repaid.

ANALOGY

Analogy questions are odd and, thankfully, rare. The exact topic of each answer choice is not important. The key is that the answer choice has to be parallel to the analogy in the question stem. Look at the example below.

Line

5   …of a tomato for a salad and found myself faced with the usual unsavory tableau.

Most of the tomatoes I found had been shipped in from Canada, where they had been grown hydroponically in greenhouses. These were salad-sized "beefsteak" tomatoes,
10   each one more perfectly round than the last, and basically indistinguishable in taste and appearance from a large, deep pink racquetball. This would be bad enough in January, but at the time of my visit it was the height of tomato season in the state of Washington, where I live.
15   Later that day I went to a farmer's market in Seattle's university district, and sampled over a dozen…

8. The author's comparison of a supermarket tomato to a racquetball in lines 9-12 is most analogous to

   (A) a horticulturalist explaining that peaches and nectarines are identical except for a single gene
   (B) a child jeering that his baby brother looks exactly like a monkey
   (C) a baker warning that bread left out too long will become inedibly hard
   (D) an art critic remarking that the painting in front of her is the worst she has ever seen
   (E) a native of a forested island declaring that a certain type of berry found there is poisonous

MATH

WRITING

READING

VOCABULARY

WEAKEN/STRENGTHEN

Like Analogy questions, these are rare. The key is to determine what the author believes, then be sure to read the question carefully. You could be asked either to strengthen or weaken the author's argument. Try the example below.

> In 1752, Benjamin Franklin demonstrated through a series of kite experiments that lightning is a form of electricity. More than 250 years later, scientists still know
> *Line* relatively little about the causes of this phenomenon. Yet
> 5 lightning plays such a significant role in weather and climate that it could eventually become a powerful tool in storm prediction. Current technology can detect the direction of a storm's wind flow but cannot tell if these winds will pick up or die down. Lightning commonly
> 10 occurs during tornadoes, and flashes increase significantly right before a twister touches ground. If understood, lightning, once considered a mysterious and frightening occurrence, could do much to save lives.

7. Which of the following would most weaken the author's argument as stated in the last two sentences?

(A) Scientists have much to learn about the phenomenon of lightning.

(B) Death by electric shock has decreased significantly.

(C) Lightning flashes steadily and predictably decreases after a tornado touches down.

(D) The technology to detect lightning flashes is not yet available.

(E) Lightning flashes fluctuate erratically during a tornado-producing storm.

MATH

WRITING

READING

VOCABULARY

The SAT doesn't really care about the difference between similes, metaphors, and analogies. As far as the SAT is concerned, they're all comparisons.

LITERARY DEVICES 101

Literary terms are only occasionally used on the SAT Reading section. The few that you will need to know are listed below.

Analogy: A comparison between things which have similar features.
Example: *The programmer drew an analogy between the human brain and the computer.*

Simile: A direct comparison of two things using the words "like" or "as."
Example: *My love is like a red, red rose.*

Metaphor: A literally false statement meant to be taken as a comparison between two things.
Example: *Juliet is the sun.*

Personification: A figure of speech in which human qualities are attributed to an animal, object, or idea.
Example: *The yellow fog rubs its back on the windowpanes.*

Hyperbole: Deliberate exaggeration.
Example: *There are a million questions about literary terms on the SAT.*

Verbal irony: The use of words to express the opposite of their literal meaning.
Example: *So you locked your keys in your car, then set off the alarm pulling on the door handle? Brilliant!*

Dramatic irony: When events turn out the opposite of the way those involved expect.
Example: *A man sells his watch to buy a comb for his wife, only to find that she has sold her hair to a wigmaker in order to buy him a watch chain.*

Allusion: Casual reference; an incidental mention of something.
Example: *The president made no allusion to the war in his speech.*

Rhetoric: The skilled use of language effectively, persuasively or excessively.
Example: *The preacher's rhetoric convinced my grandmother to donate all her savings to his church.*

Characterize: To describe something by stating its main qualities.
Example: *In his essay, he characterized the 1960s as a period of radical change.*

Dramatize: To express or represent vividly, emotionally, or strikingly, as in a drama.
Example: *Oh, my friend always dramatizes everything that happens to her as if it were the worst thing ever.*

Line
5   ...But I had lost something, too. I had lost something which could never be restored to me while I lived. All the grace, the beauty, the poetry had gone out of the majestic river! I still keep in mind a certain wonderful sunset which I witnessed when steamboating was new

10   to me. A broad expanse of the river was turned to blood; in the middle distance the red hue brightened into gold, through which a solitary log came floating, black and conspicuous...

14. The phrase "A broad expanse of the river was turned to blood" (line 10) is an example of

(A) irony
(B) anecdote
(C) metaphor
(D) personification
(E) hyperbole

45   ...Extracting the venom from the rattlesnake could be euphemistically described as "hard." If a rattlesnake gave up its venom easily, it could cause problems for the animal itself (leading to the old joke about the snake biting its tongue). The venom collector's job, therefore, is

50   to give the rattlesnake a simulated prey for it to bite and release venom into. This is when "milking a snake," as it is known, is more of an art than a science...

14. The sentence in which "hard" appears suggests that the author believes the word to be

(A) a contradiction
(B) an exaggeration
(C) an allusion
(D) an understatement
(E) a preconception

MATH

WRITING

READING

VOCABULARY

MATH

WRITING

READING

VOCABULARY

EXCEPT/NOT/LEAST QUESTIONS

These questions should be done later in the section. Even though the test writers put the key word in capital letters, students often miss it or forget about it. These questions take extra time, but they can be fairly straightforward. It's POE as usual. Remove the four answers that are true according to the passage. The one you have left is the correct answer.

... But the ordinary person's idea of imitation is the setting down with the utmost precision every visible fact in a subject—"making it look like the real thing." Imitation
Line in a painting is, for example, flowers that one can botanize,
5 or fruit that "looks good enough to eat" and has a fly on it one feels the urge to brush off. Such deceptive resemblance gives people the pleasure of surprise rather than aesthetic pleasure. Carefully realistic pictures may please, but the pictures people enjoy living with leave
10 something to the imagination. "The secret of being a bore," said Voltaire, "is to tell everything."

Actually, a few painters try to carry imitation to the point of deceptive resemblance. It cannot be done at all unless the object painted is small enough to be reproduced
15 full size. A true artist never tries to make us believe that his or her medium is anything except a medium. It is paint with which great painters express themselves.

What the ordinary person generally means by imitation of a large subject—say a landscape—is a...

Cross off any answers that DO work, so that what's left DOESN'T work. That's your answer.

12. It can be inferred from the passage that a painter who wished "to carry imitation to the point of deceptive resemblance" (lines 12-13) might have difficulty depicting all of the following EXCEPT

(A) a vase of flowers
(B) a seascape
(C) a field with distant trees
(D) a street scene
(E) the interior of a small cottage

GENERAL QUESTIONS

Do general questions after you've done enough specific ones to understand the big ideas in the passage.

People often base their perceptions of similarity between fraternal twins on factors other than actual physical resemblance. Mannerisms such as similar
Line gestures and facial expressions can substantially amplify
5 even a minor resemblance. Fraternal twins, who are no closer genetically than ordinary siblings, are very likely to share many of these behavioral quirks, since they often spend more time together than do siblings with a separation in age. Consequently, because they constantly
10 provide each other with nonverbal feedback, they tend to converge in many of their unconscious habits, leading to a closer perceived resemblance to one another.

6. In the passage above, the goal of the author is to

(A) evaluate the opinions of experts in a related field
(B) provide a plausible explanation for an observed phenomenon
(C) disprove an alternative explanation with new data
(D) question a commonly held superstition
(E) describe a scientific experiment that explains an event

Art is life. Life is art. Sophie Calle blends the two so completely that it is hard to tell the two apart. The documentation of her own life and the lives of others
Line are presented as photographs accompanied by text in
5 museums and in books. Her work has recorded people as they sleep through the night and compiled blind people's ideas of beauty. She has reported her experiences of following people and having a private investigator follow her. One revealing piece, *The Hotel*, displays people's lives
10 as seen from Calle's position as a hotel maid. Each of her projects could be a sociology experiment as well as a work of art.

8. The primary purpose of the passage is to

(A) favor a certain method of collecting data
(B) highlight an artist's approach
(C) reveal previously unknown information
(D) declare an artistic philosophy
(E) question a hotel's methodology

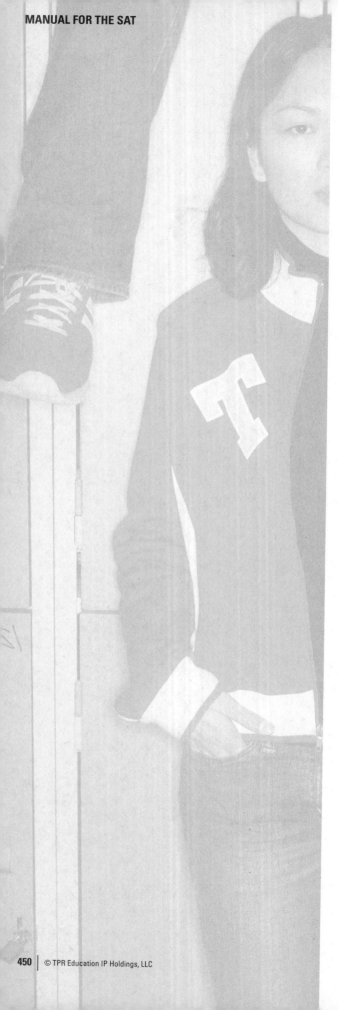

Summary

- **Detail Questions:** These are straightforward questions that usually have line references, so these are questions that we definitely want to do first.

- **Inference Questions:** *Imply, infer/inference, suggest, conclude, or interpret* on an SAT question STILL means that you will be able to find direct evidence to support your predicted answer and, ultimately, the correct answer choice.

- **Purpose Questions:** This question type asks for the *why* and the *how* of a part of the passage and not just the *what*.

- **Primarily/Mainly/Chiefly Questions:** Be careful not to fall for answers that may be "true" but don't encompass the overall idea of what the question asks.

- **Vocabulary In Context Questions:** Treat these types of questions just as you would Sentence Completions.

- **Tone Questions:** These usually test harder vocabulary, so learn more words!

Less Frequent Question Types

- *Main Idea Questions:* Bad answers to these questions will often be too specific or too general.

- *Analogy Questions:* Identify the key parts of the story, relate them in your own words, and then select the answer choice that matches the story that you've created.

- *Weaken/Strengthen Questions:* Know which side of the fence the author is on and select the appropriate answer choice.

- *Literary Device Questions:* Know the tools that ETS will sometimes use in its passages.

- *Except/Not/Least Questions:* Circle these words any time they appear in questions as they are easy to forget when predicting an answer.

- I have accomplished _____ of my _____ stated goals in the Introduction chapter.

SAT READING:
DUAL PASSAGES

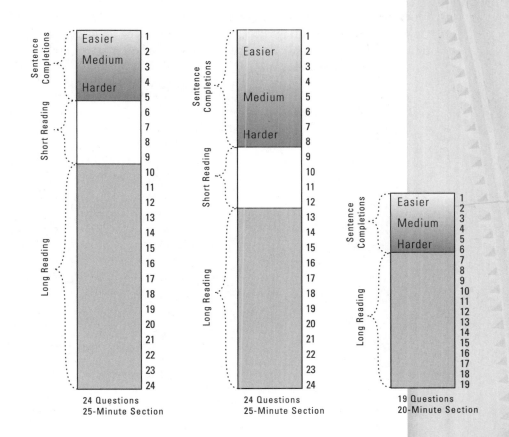

DUAL PASSAGES

Every SAT has two sets of dual passages: one set of long passages and one set of short passages. When working on dual passage questions, it's very important to have a strategy. POOD is important here, because, as in all reading questions, an incredibly tough question could show up anywhere.

Dual Short Reading

For dual short reading passages, go ahead and read both passages. Then ask yourself the following three questions:

> What are both passages about?
> What does the author of Passage 1 think about that subject?
> What does the author of Passage 2 think about that subject?

Questions often ask you things like "The author of Passage 1 would most likely view (something) in Passage 2 as..." Remember, on the SAT, we don't have to infer or read the author's mind. The answer will be based on what the author of Passage 1 *has already said* about that subject.

Questions 6-9 are based on the following passages.

Passage 1

Tibetans refer to the colossal Himalayan peak known in the West as Everest as *Chomolungma*, or "mother goddess of the world." The Nepalese residing to
Line the south have given the mountain a title that similarly
5 reflects their reverence for it: *Sagarmatha*, "forehead of the sky." The Sherpas who live in the region viewed the peak for centuries as the residence of the earth goddess Miyo Lungsangma, and considered it blasphemous to think of achieving the summit. Like the mountain
10 itself, which is often cloaked by clouds, these local perspectives are unfortunately obscured by the more familiar and less reverential name of a nineteenth-century British surveyor: Sir George Everest.

Passage 2

In 1953, a British expedition supported by the Royal
15 Geographical Society attempted an unprecedented feat: climbing to the summit of Mount Everest and returning safely home. On May 29, two of the expedition's members, New Zealand's Edmund Hillary and Sherpa guide Tenzing Norgay, crested the peak. Though neither
20 man had been born in Britain, the British viewed the Everest triumph as a watershed moment in their nation's history. News of the expedition's success reached London on the eve of Queen Elizabeth II's coronation, a coincidence which enabled commentators and
25 editorial writers to present the Everest achievement as a culminating moment of an empire which had begun in North America in the reign of the first Elizabeth.

6. The "Sherpas" referred to in line 6, Passage 1, would most likely view the "triumph" mentioned in line 21, Passage 2, with

   (A) reverence
   (B) indifference
   (C) disdain
   (D) wonder
   (E) amusement

7. The two passages differ in that Passage 1 suggests that Mount Everest

   (A) is truly revered only by native Tibetans, while Passage 2 claims that other cultures attach symbolic importance to the peak
   (B) has taken on a lesser role in Sherpa religious culture, while Passage 2 implies that Westerners have no appreciation for the peak
   (C) is less respected by modern Himalayan peoples than by their ancestors, while Passage 2 notes that the peak has never been so popular a spiritual symbol as it is today
   (D) is an integral part of Tibetan religious culture, while Passage 2 contends that the peak's symbolic importance is not exclusive to Tibet
   (E) is not revered by non-Tibetans, while Passage 2 asserts that the mountain is more important to Britain than it is to any other nation

8. Unlike the author of Passage 2, the author of Passage 1 makes use of

   (A) personal experience
   (B) historical analysis
   (C) hypothetical assumptions
   (D) literary sources
   (E) direct translation

9. Both authors acknowledge which of the following points?

   (A) The summit of Mount Everest was first reached in 1953.
   (B) British citizens are often insensitive to local customs.
   (C) Britain has figured prominently in the history of Mount Everest.
   (D) Mount Everest is actually known by several different names.
   (E) The British version of history is considered controversial.

Questions 9-12 are based on the following passages.

Passage 1

While some contemporary scientists dispute the
popular belief that dreams are more than a random
series of visions, many inventors and scientists since
Line DaVinci's time have documented receiving useful
5 ideas from dreams. Sleep researchers speculate that if
a person actively seeks a solution during the day, the
mind continues to work on it in sleep, with access to the
dreamer's entire storehouse of knowledge and memories.
Because of the brain's very different biochemical and
10 psychological states during the stages of dreaming, the
mind combines all available information in ways that
never would have occurred to the dreamer when awake.

Passage 2

During the course of a night, a person cycles
between two distinct phases of sleep. During REM
15 sleep, frantic brain waves show activity levels akin to
those of the waking state. In slow-wave sleep, neurons
fire across the brain in synchronized waves. Some
scientists postulate that REM sleep is just the brain
firing up the neurons to test the work completed
20 during slow-wave sleep. Although many feel there is a
psychological component involved in dreaming, dreams
may actually be nothing more than a by-product of the
maintenance processes of the brain.

9. The author of Passage 1 mentions DaVinci
   (line 4) in order to emphasize the

   (A) importance of artistic inspiration
   (B) brilliance of a historical figure
   (C) longevity of certain beliefs
   (D) origins of a common misconception
   (E) gullibility of the average person

10. The "researchers" mentioned in line 5 of Passage
    1 would probably respond to the last sentence of
    Passage 2 with

    (A) appreciation
    (B) skepticism
    (C) outrage
    (D) boredom
    (E) confusion

11. The passages differ in their discussion of dreams
    primarily in that

    (A) Passage 1 emphasizes the impact of dreams
        on visual perception, whereas Passage
        2 stresses that dreams affect abstract
        reasoning
    (B) Passage 1 discusses the potential importance
        of dreaming, whereas Passage 2 suggests
        that dreams play a secondary role
    (C) Passage 1 presents a historically based theory
        of dreams, whereas Passage 2 underscores
        the psychological aspect of dreams
    (D) Passage 1 describes a popular view of dreams,
        whereas Passage 2 rejects that view as
        unscientific
    (E) Passage 1 asserts that dreams are the result
        of chemical processes, whereas Passage 2
        claims that dreams result from neurological
        processes

12. The author of Passage 2 would most likely
    respond to the "contemporary scientists" (line 1)
    mentioned in Passage 1 by

    (A) concurring that dreams have no discernibly
        useful function
    (B) rejecting the narrow-minded opinions of
        modern scientists
    (C) arguing that dreams are only one way the
        body replenishes itself
    (D) admitting that dreams may be more than a
        random series of visions
    (E) agreeing that there is some doubt as to the
        psychological benefits of dreams

DUAL LONG READING

Since dual long passages are basically two whole passages, it can be tough to get through both of them in a timely fashion. It's also easy to confuse what happened in Passage 1 with what happened in Passage 2. So focus on one passage at a time.

Dual Long Reading Tips

1. Do the questions that deal with **Passage 1** only <u>first</u>.

2. Do the questions that deal with **Passage 2** only <u>next</u>.

3. Do the questions that deal with **both passages** <u>last</u>.

Dual Long Reading

Q's 13-25 are based on the following passages.

The following passages discuss the impact of suburbanization on American culture.

Passage 1

Pull up to a traffic light in Anytown, U.S.A. and look around. On one side sits an army of national chain stores and "family friendly" restaurants, with names designed to evoke memories of small town Americana. On the
5 other side are endless waves of identical cookie-cutter tract homes with perfectly trimmed lawns, separated by wide streets named for bucolic features of the landscape long since obliterated. In front and behind lie streams of red brake lights and bright white headlights, stretching
10 as far as the eye can see.

Welcome to Suburbia. Although suburbs have been around since the 1800's, the explosive growth of American suburbs began in the 1940's as a way to effectively utilize the large swaths of land needed
15 to house a booming population. By adopting mass-production techniques to home construction, suburban developers were able to make home ownership more accessible to the average American family than ever before. But this achievement came with a price.
20 Suburban culture and its principles of residential planning, while bringing certain material benefits, have in fact diminished our standing as an inquisitive, expressive people.

Identical-looking, prefabricated houses have deprived
25 neighborhoods of hundreds of years of original and beautiful home design: mechanized, impersonal construction has trumped all. Suburban sprawl has engulfed the natural landscape, devouring millions of acres of prime forest, carving up family farms into
30 nondescript little subdivisions, and turning the fragile habitats of threatened animal species into golf courses and swimming pools. Family-owned businesses that existed for generations have been swept away by gargantuan super-stores, fast-food restaurants, and
35 national retailing chains; these newcomers, which spring up seemingly overnight and often disappear just as quickly, have no stake in their communities and no higher purpose other than the accumulation of profits. A culture founded on the almighty automobile has filled the air
40 with smog, choked our freeways with suffocating traffic, and condemned suburbanites to endless hours behind the wheel. Operating on the assumption that "everybody drives," suburban planners have created communities that are relentlessly hostile to pedestrians. As a result,
45 people rarely get to know one another and may live their entire lives without learning their neighbor's names. The ultimate results of suburban growth are communities with no center, no soul, few social bonds, and no reason to exist other than to consume.

50 It is perhaps too much of a stretch to claim that the growth of suburbs is responsible for all of contemporary society's problems; crime, global warming, and other modern maladies constitute more immediate and pervasive threats. Nevertheless, suburban culture, with
55 its emphasis on uniformity and materialism, illustrates the gaping contradictions of a culture hungry for individual expression in the way it thinks, shops, lives, and dreams.

Passage 2

Suburbia has long had its detractors: urban
60 intellectuals, professors at elite East Coast universities, Hollywood screenwriters, and earnest city planners. But it has had its proponents as well, although these tend to be far less vocal, for the simple reason that they are busy working routine office jobs, driving the kids to
65 soccer practice, or attending PTA meetings. What these defenders lack in scholarly credentials, they make up for in authenticity as bona fide suburbanites.

The most common charges leveled against suburbs since the 1940's—that they are bland, boring places
70 that breed conformity, encourage rampant consumerism, and discourage the formation of communal bonds—can easily be answered: "Of course. That's why people move there in the first place!"

Obvious as it may seem, suburbs are not cities. To
75 criticize them for their lack of urbanity is to make no criticism at all. People don't move to the suburbs because they're looking for vibrant neighborhoods, unique and tasteful architecture, or convenient mass-transit options; they move to the suburbs because they
80 want safe streets, plenty of shopping options, and a little bit of space in which to breathe and be left alone. The last thing most of these people want is to be reminded of the urban landscapes they left behind. Recent attempts by devotees of the New Urbanism movement
85 to create "urban" suburbs prove the point: in seeking to import urban values into suburban communities, these well-meaning planners succeed only in combining the worst of both worlds. Small wonder that a prominent New York newspaper described Celebration, a New
90 Urbanist community in Florida, as being like "living in a Disneyland theme park."

For years, government bureaucrats and public policy experts have attempted to entice people out of the suburbs and back into cities. They have imposed zoning
95 restrictions and anti-growth ordinances on suburban development, while simultaneously encouraging urban development with tax-free zones and lavish mass-transit subsidies. And yet, population growth in the suburbs continues to dramatically outpace population growth
100 in traditional urban centers. The fact is that people choose to live where they do because their environment provides them with what they most value. Americans have cast their votes for suburbia, and there can't be any harm in letting them have what they want, no matter
105 what the experts say.

13. Both authors would most likely agree that suburbs

    (A) inhibit social interaction
    (B) are garishly amusing
    (C) make home ownership affordable
    (D) threaten sensitive ecosystems
    (E) would benefit from increased regulation

14. The primary purpose of Passage 1 is to

    (A) describe a typical American suburb
    (B) defend a widely held point of view
    (C) compare urban and suburban lifestyles
    (D) present a strongly held opinion
    (E) clarify a common misconception

15. The author of Passage 2 would most probably regard lines 2-8, Passage 1 ("On one . . . obliterated") as a description of

    (A) landscapes that cause people to feel a sense of alienation
    (B) features that make suburbs less expensive than cities
    (C) structures that make inefficient use of available land
    (D) characteristics that suburbanites may find appealing
    (E) peculiarities that are not typical of most suburbs

16. In line 8, the word "lie" most nearly means

    (A) recline
    (B) extend
    (C) deceive
    (D) pause
    (E) reside

17. In line 19, "price" refers to the

    (A) benefits that come from investing in suburban property
    (B) problems caused by unscrupulous developers
    (C) costs of a typical suburban home
    (D) penalties paid by construction firms for environmental damage
    (E) consequences that have resulted from the growth of suburbs

18. The author of Passage 1 criticizes the "newcomers" (line 35) because the author believes that they

    (A) have an unfair advantage over local businesses
    (B) charge exorbitant prices for their merchandise
    (C) lack integral connections to their surrounding neighborhoods
    (D) are unwilling to hire local residents
    (E) primarily benefit residents of urban neighborhoods

19. In response to the claim made in lines 42-46 of Passage 1 ("Operating . . . names"), the author of Passage 2 would most likely assert that

    (A) suburbs were not designed with pedestrians in mind
    (B) people move to the suburbs in search of solitude
    (C) suburbanites tend to be passionate about their likes as well as their dislikes
    (D) many suburbs now provide easy access to mass transit
    (E) suburban residents are surprisingly friendly and outgoing

20. The author of Passage 1 would most likely view the "charges" mentioned in line 68, Passage 2 with

    (A) veiled suspicion
    (B) cynical detachment
    (C) marked agreement
    (D) cheery optimism
    (E) considerable surprise

21. The author of Passage 2 argues that suburbia functions as a

    (A) destination for young families
    (B) laboratory for social experimentation
    (C) haven for automobile owners
    (D) model for future development
    (E) refuge from city life

22. It can be inferred that the author of Passage 2 regards the "recent attempts" (lines 83-84) as

    (A) ill-conceived failures
    (B) misunderstood creations
    (C) unsophisticated designs
    (D) shoddy efforts
    (E) unpopular imitations

23. In the last paragraph of Passage 2, the author argues that the efforts of public policy experts

    (A) place unfair burdens on suburban homeowners

    (B) have had little effect on where people choose to live

    (C) make poor use of taxpayers' money

    (D) exploit the fears of suburban residents

    (E) reduce overcrowding in suburban neighborhoods

24. The argument from Passage 1 that best refutes the statement in lines 102-105 of Passage 2 ("Americans . . . say") is that suburban development

    (A) hastens the deterioration of urban neighborhoods

    (B) discourages communities from investing in mass transit

    (C) fails to appreciate the beneficial qualities of cities

    (D) has adverse consequences for the environment

    (E) pressures people into buying homes that they are unable to afford

25. Unlike the author of Passage 1, the author of Passage 2 develops his or her argument by

    (A) tracing the development of American suburbs since the 1940's

    (B) noting that suburbs tend to encourage uniformity, rather than individual expression

    (C) citing the qualifications of those who share his or her opinion

    (D) pointing out the problems caused by excessive automobile traffic

    (E) dismissing those who fail to understand the complexities of modern life

MATH

WRITING

READING

VOCABULARY

Summary

- When faced with dual passages, approach the passage as you normally would (questions first, passage first, skim, etc.), but go through the passages and problems in a more specific order.

    - _____

    - _____

    - _____

- Remember to keep your POOD in mind and look out for time-sucker questions.

- I have accomplished _____ of my _____ stated goals in the Introduction chapter.

SAT READING:
MASTER THE POE!

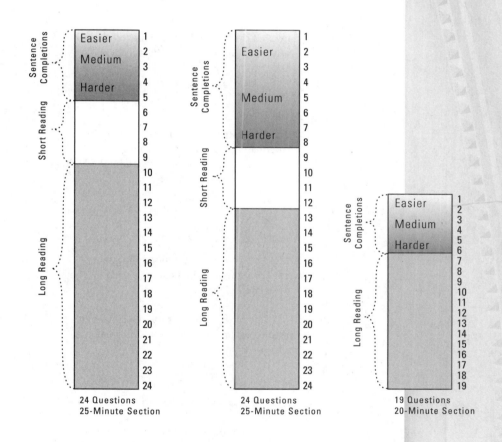

Sentence Completions

Short Reading

Long Reading

Easier	1
Medium	2
	3
Harder	4
	5
	6
	7
	8
	9
	10
	11
	12
	13
	14
	15
	16
	17
	18
	19
	20
	21
	22
	23
	24

24 Questions
25-Minute Section

Sentence Completions

Short Reading

Long Reading

Easier	1
	2
	3
Medium	4
	5
	6
	7
Harder	8
	9
	10
	11
	12
	13
	14
	15
	16
	17
	18
	19
	20
	21
	22
	23
	24

24 Questions
25-Minute Section

Sentence Completions

Long Reading

Easier	1
	2
Medium	3
	4
Harder	5
	6
	7
	8
	9
	10
	11
	12
	13
	14
	15
	16
	17
	18
	19

19 Questions
20-Minute Section

DOWN TO TWO

Let's turn to our friend Joe Bloggs for guidance on what NOT to do. Joe *always* gets it down to two answers, and he gets frustrated because he *always* seems to pick the wrong one. Joe's problem is that he is trying to pick the right answer. What does he do wrong?

POE is more important than ever when you're down to two answers!

Let's look at some answers, no questions or passages involved. Which of the following is more likely to be an ETS "best" answer?

(A) seek a greater understanding of the choices his
     father made in his life

(B)

(C) show that everything he had believed about his
     father was false

(D)

(E)

(A)

(B) attempts to establish a third major party in
     American politics are destined for failure

(C) dominance of the two-party system in the United
     States is likely to continue

(D)

(E)

(A)

(B) by the late nineteenth century, immigrants
     from the mainland had gained a great deal of
     influence in Hawaii

(C)

(D) by the late nineteenth century, the Hawaiian
     people had proven themselves incapable of
     self-governing

(E)

(A) refuses to acknowledge the variable of gravity in
     a theory

(B) accounts for a seemingly paradoxical element
     within a hypothesis

(C)

(D)

(E)

Half Right = All Wrong

… the poet you have so long desired to know personally is a moody and abstracted middle-aged gentleman, who fails to catch your name on introduction,
Line whose phrases are awkward and ironically commonplace.
55   The witty and ferocious critic—whose frequently negative reviews give the impression he has a vicious appetite for new literature—destroys this demonic portrait when he appears by appearing before you as a shy and uncomfortable soul. His is of slender limb and
60 deprecating glance. He stammers and makes a painful spectacle of himself when you ask his opinion of the latest best seller or hit play...

Passage 1

In the Greek type of democracy, all the citizens could listen to a series of orators and vote directly on questions of legislation. Hence their philosophers held that a
Line small city was the largest possible democratic state. The
5 English invention of representative government made a democratic nation possible, and the possibility was first realized in the United States. Since the development of broadcasting in the twentieth century, it has once more become possible for every citizen to listen to the
10 political views of representative orators, and the future may perhaps see the return of the national state to the Greek form of democracy.

Passage 2

The term "democracy" by all accounts must be one
Line of the all-time most overused vocabulary items in the
15 modern political and philosophical lexicon. It seems almost impossible to go more than a few days without hearing of wars fought to defend it, of institutions that proudly symbolize it, of deeds done in its name, and of efforts to spread it as far as can be conceived by human
20 minds. Countless hours are devoted to cultivating it both in theory and in fact. But for all this effort and expense, democracy still eludes more people than it serves. Even many of those who reportedly have it can be dissatisfied with it for one reason or another, and some go so far as
25 to doubt that what they have is actually democracy at all.

12. The passage suggests the critic's work is best described as

(A)
(B)
(C)
(D) routine denigration
(E) awkward observations

9. Which best describes the relationship between Passage 1 and Passage 2 ?

(A)
(B) Passage 1 compares Greek and American democracies whereas Passage 2 catalogues problems caused by the rise of modern democracies.
(C) Passage 1 discusses different styles of democracy whereas Passage 2 illustrates some difficulties surrounding the use of the word "democracy."
(D)
(E)

10. Both authors imply that

(A)
(B) democracy is an important and misunderstood concept
(C)
(D)
(E) democratic participation can become still more widespread

11. The author of Passage 2 would most likely believe that the views of the "philosophers" (line 3) are

(A)
(B)
(C) limited
(D)
(E) evasive

12. Unlike Passage 1, Passage 2 makes reference to

(A) a specific historical example of a form of government
(B)
(C) a discrepancy between a label and its limited implementation in reality
(D)
(E)

Recycled Words

Beware of answers that repeat *exact phrases* from the passage but do not maintain the meaning.

To get ready for my trip, for weeks I had studied maps, large-scale and small. But maps are not reality at all—they can be tyrants. I know people who are so immersed in

Line road maps that they never see the countryside they pass

5 through, and others who, having traced a route, are held to it as though held by flanged* wheels to rails.

* A protruding rim on the train's wheels, used to hold each wheel in place on the tracks.

10. The author would most likely agree with which of the following statements?

(A) Large scale maps do not represent the reality of countryside roads.

(B) Strict adherence to a planned route can affect one's enjoyment while traveling.

(C)

(D)

(E)

…In 1876, Roberts Brothers launched a line of books they called the 'No Name Series.' At the time, Roberts Brothers was a well-known publisher of such literary

Line luminaries as Robert Louis Stevenson, Walt Whitman, and

35 Louisa May Alcott. Fervent public interest greeted the line's debut work, *Mercy Philbrick's Choice*, because the author's name was kept secret. The marketing gimmick of the new series was that these books would be published anonymously. At the top of the title page of each volume

40 appeared the following quotation: "Is the gentleman anonymous? Is he a great unknown?" In reality the majority of the series' works were written by women…

8. Which of the following can be inferred about the No Name Series from the passage?

(A) Louisa May Alcott was a literary luminary who contributed to the No Name Series.

(B)

(C) The title pages of many novels in the No Name Series misrepresented gender.

(D)

(E)

MATH

WRITING

READING

VOCABULARY

Too Literal

Also, beware of Purpose questions with overly literal answers.

What exactly did the Wright Brothers invent? It rankles my sensibilities to hear such an indefensible and irresponsible opinion. Every once in a while a silly
Line controversy gets started because somebody realizes
5 that almost everything about the airplane was really quite well understood long before the Wrights, and he foolishly announces, "They didn't invent the airplane after all!"

9. The primary purpose of the passage is to

(A)

(B)

(C) question the Wright Brothers' accomplishments

(D)

(E) dismiss superfluous criticism

Goes Too Far

Eliminate any answers that draw conclusions that can't be reached from the information given in the passage.

Line …In 1876, Roberts Brothers launched a line of
25 books they called the 'No Name Series.' At the time, Roberts Brothers was a well-known publisher of such literary luminaries as Robert Louis Stevenson, Walt Whitman, and Louisa May Alcott. Fervent public interest greeted the line's debut work, *Mercy Philbrick's*
30 *Choice*, because the author's name was kept secret. The marketing gimmick of the new series was that these books would be published anonymously. At the top of the title page of each volume appeared the following quotation: "Is the gentleman anonymous? Is he a great
35 unknown?" In reality the majority of the series' works were written by women.

8. The passage implies which of the following about *Mercy Philbrick's Choice*?

(A) Its anonymous authorship inspired public curiosity.

(B)

(C) It sold out and required a second printing.

(D)

(E)

Though it has become a bit of a clichéd image in our world of telescopes and internet images, supernovae seen up-close can still be an awe-inspiring sight. But
Line we sometimes overlook how rarely supernovas actually
5 occur. In fact, the last supernova in our galaxy visible from Earth was observed only five years before the telescope was first used for celestial observation in 1609.

9. The passage supports which of the following statements about supernovas?

(A)

(B) Supernovae occur less frequently in our galaxy than in neighboring galaxies.

(C)

(D) It is possible to see supernovas from earth with an unaided eye.

(E)

To get ready for my trip, for weeks I had studied maps, large-scale and small. But maps are not reality at all—they can be tyrants. I know people who are
Line so immersed in road maps that they never see the
5 countryside they pass through, and others who, having traced a route, are held to it as though held by flanged* wheels to rails.

* A protruding rim on a train's wheels, used to hold each wheel in place on the tracks.

9. It can be inferred from the passage that maps

(A) can influence people's decisions when traveling

(B)

(C)

(D)

(E) often indicate the best routes for travel

Extreme Answers

Check to see if any answers contain extreme language. They don't immediately indicate a wrong answer, but be aware of the following words:

always	none	no	worst	will
never	only	once	impossible	must
every	all	best	should	

...Language is always changing. When two groups
Line of people speaking the same language are separated and
15 remain in comparative isolation, change continues in the language of both groups, but naturally it does not continue in the same direction and at the same rate with both of them. The languages thus tend to become different...

14. The author uses the word "comparative isolation" (line 15) in order to

(A) indicate a condition that facilitates the evolution of a language
(B) describe a situation that inevitably results in the creation of a new language
(C)
(D)
(E)

The opposition is indispensable. A good statesman, like any other sensible human being, always learns more from his opponents than from his fervent supporters.
Line For the supporters will push him to disaster unless his
5 opponents show him where the dangers are. So if he is wise he will often pray to be delivered from his friends, because they will ruin him. But, though it hurts, he ought also to pray never to be left without opponents; for they keep him on the path of reason and good sense.

11. The author uses "for the supporters... dangers are" in order to

(A)
(B) show an opponent's only purpose is to point out hazards
(C) emphasize the value of listening to opponents
(D)
(E)

One last note on extreme answers

(A) All answers containing extreme language are always wrong and never right.
(B) Most answers containing extreme language are incorrect, but there are exceptions.

 © TPR Education IP Holdings, LLC

DOWN TO 2 DRILL

Questions 9-12 are based on the following passages.

Passage 1

Life in medieval castles has often been romanticized in novels and popular films, but hardships were plenty even for the wealthiest individuals. Despite

Line our impressions of their grandiose castles, one aspect

5 of medieval life hard for people today to comprehend is the lack of individualism. There was literally little room for privacy. The cramped living quarters, even for some nobles, did much to foster togetherness. So did the lack of central heating. Most medieval homes—and castles

10 were no exception—were so cold, damp, and dark that during the dead of winter, it was not uncommon for the members of an entire household to huddle and sleep together in a single huge bed to keep warm.

Passage 2

Line An essential component of modern comfort—the

15 adequate heating of houses—was barely possible during the Middle Ages, even for the great ones of the earth. Peasants were more fortunate in this respect than were nobles. Living in small houses, they were better able to keep warm. But the nobleman, the prince, the

20 king, and the cardinal inhabited palaces of a grandeur corresponding with their social positions. They received guests in vast halls like athletic stadiums; they marched in solemn processions along galleries as long and as drafty as Alpine tunnels. A great man in those days

25 had to spend a large portion of time performing solemn symbolical charades and pompous ballets that required a great deal of room to accommodate numerous actors and spectators. How splendid, how magnificent! But oh, how bleak!

9. Both authors acknowledge that in the Middle Ages

   (A) it was difficult for many people to live in solitude
   (B) ~~~~
   (C) ~~~~
   (D) the benefits of nobility did not include warmth
   (E) ~~~~

10. Unlike Passage 1, Passage 2 makes use of

    (A) expert and amateur analysis
    (B) ~~~~
    (C) historical and contemporary comparison
    (D) ~~~~
    (E) ~~~~

11. According to Passage 1, the relative lack of privacy in the Middle Ages was most directly attributable to the

    (A) ~~~~
    (B) ~~~~
    (C) ~~~~
    (D) size of extended families
    (E) dimensions of large households

12. Which of the following best characterizes the relationship between the two passages?

    (A) Passage 1 considers the problem of staying warm, whereas Passage 2 contends that warmth was less a problem than that of overlong social ceremonies.
    (B) ~~~~
    (C) ~~~~
    (D) ~~~~
    (E) Passage 1 discusses difficulties faced by many people, whereas Passage 2 focuses on the troubles endured by the upper class.

...Irrespective of the fact that some philosophers or linguists claim there are no rules for deciding whether one translation is better than another, everyday activity
Line in a publishing house tells us that it is easy to establish
55 that a translation is wrong and deserves severe editing; maybe it is only a question of common sense, but common sense must be respected.

Let us suppose that in a novel a character says, "You're just pulling my leg." To render such an idiom
60 in Italian by *stai solo tirandomi la gamba* or *tu stai menandomi per la gamba* would be literally correct, but misleading. In Italian, one should say *mi stai prendendo per il naso*, thus substituting an English leg with an Italian nose. If literally translated, the
65 English expression, absolutely unusual in Italian, would make the reader suppose that the character (as well as the author) was inventing a provocative rhetorical figure; which is completely misleading, as in English the expression is simply an idiom. By choosing "nose"
70 instead of "leg," a translator puts the Italian reader in the same situation as the original English one. Thus, only by being literally unfaithful can a translator succeed in being truly faithful to the source text. Which is like echoing Saint Jerome, patron saint of translators, that
75 in translating one should not translate *verbum e verbo sed sensum exprimere de sensu* (word for word instead of sense for sense), even though the notion of the right sense of a text can imply some ambiguities.

In the course of my experiences as a translated
80 author, I have always been torn between the need to have a translation that respected my intentions and the exciting discovery that my text could elicit unexpected interpretations and be in some way improved when it was re-embodied in another language...

16. In lines 59-62 ("To render such . . . misleading."), the author states that it would be misleading to so translate the English statement because

(A)
(B) the word-for-word translation would not have the same sense
(C)
(D) in Italian there is no equivalent idiom
(E)

17. In line 68, "figure" most nearly means

(A)
(B)
(C)
(D) character
(E) expression

18. In lines 71-73 ("Thus, only by . . . text."), the author

(A)
(B)
(C) poses a paradox
(D) proves a theory
(E)

19. The author's attitude towards translation is best described as

(A)
(B) ponderous familiarity
(C)
(D)
(E) veiled disgust

20. In referring to the "ambiguities" (line 78), the author

(A) admits that translators might differ regarding their determination of the sense of a text
(B) points out that words have more than one meaning
(C)
(D)
(E)

TONE REVIEW

Let's gain more insight into Tone questions, which are a common place for ETS to test your vocabulary knowledge. Mark where on the "positive-neutral-negative" scale the word is, if possible. If you don't know the word, admit it and look up the definition. Make sure to put any you don't know on flashcards and memorize them!

ambivalent: + Neutral −

_____

analytical: + Neutral −

_____

apathetic: + Neutral −

_____

baffled: + Neutral −

_____

condescending: + Neutral −

_____

contemptuous: + Neutral −

_____

cynical: + Neutral −

_____

defiant: + Neutral −

_____

detached: + Neutral −

_____

didactic: + Neutral −

_____

disdainful: + Neutral −

_____

dismayed: + Neutral −

_____

dismissive: + Neutral −

_____

earnest: + Neutral −

_____

Often, merely knowing if a word is positive or negative is enough to help answer the question.

MATH

WRITING

READING

VOCABULARY

MATH

WRITING

READING

VOCABULARY

ecstatic: + Neutral −

_____

equivocal: + Neutral −

_____

exasperated: + Neutral −

_____

incredulous: + Neutral −

_____

indignant: + Neutral −

_____

indulgent: + Neutral −

_____

intrigued: + Neutral −

_____

ironic: + Neutral −

_____

mocking: + Neutral −

_____

nonchalant: + Neutral −

_____

nostalgic: + Neutral −

_____

objective: + Neutral −

_____

optimism: + Neutral −

_____

pessimistic: + Neutral −

_____

puzzled: + Neutral −

_____

qualified: + Neutral −

_____

resigned: _____ + Neutral –

reverential: _____ + Neutral –

revulsion: _____ + Neutral –

sarcastic: _____ + Neutral –

sentimental: _____ + Neutral –

skeptical: _____ + Neutral –

solemn: _____ + Neutral –

unabashed: _____ + Neutral –

whimsical: _____ + Neutral –

wistful: _____ + Neutral –

disengaged: _____ + Neutral –

scornful: _____ + Neutral –

naive: _____ + Neutral –

facetious: _____ + Neutral –

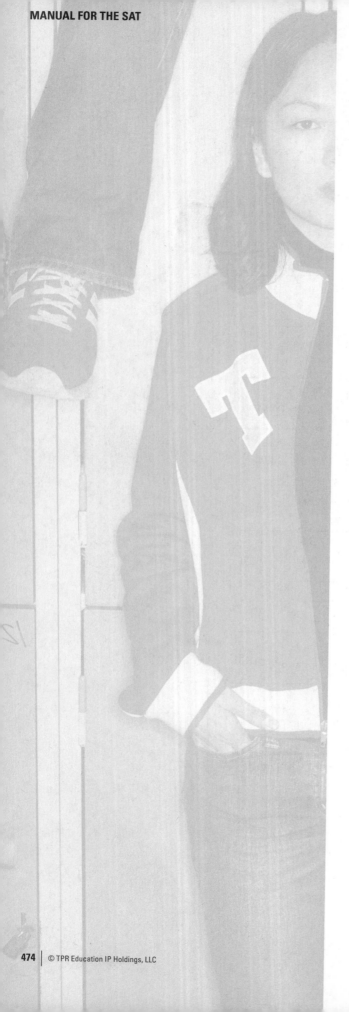

Summary

- When down to two answers, remember to search for the _____, not the _____. It's easier to pick out the word or phrase within an answer choice that makes it wrong than it is to pick out the word or phrase that makes it right.

- Feeling stuck? Use your POE techniques:

    - _____
    - _____
    - _____
    - _____

- When you're down to two answers, _____!

- I have accomplished _____ of my _____ stated goals in the Introduction chapter.

SAT READING:
TIMED DRILLS

"I'm a man of few words."

MATH

WRITING

READING

VOCABULARY

DRILL 1 (8 minutes)

Questions 18-24 are based on the following passage.

The following passage is adapted from a memoir. The author had worked for several years as a steamboat pilot on the Mississippi River before becoming a writer.

Now when I had mastered the language of this water and had come to know every trifling feature that bordered the great river as familiarly as I knew the
Line letters of the alphabet, I had made a valuable acquisition.
5 But I had lost something, too. I had lost something which could never be restored to me while I lived. All the grace, the beauty, the poetry had gone out of the majestic river! I still keep in mind a certain wonderful sunset which I witnessed when steamboating was new
10 to me. A broad expanse of the river was turned to blood; in the middle distance the red hue brightened into gold, through which a solitary log came floating, black and conspicuous; in one place a long, slanting mark lay sparkling upon the water; in another the surface was
15 broken by boiling, tumbling rings, that were as many-tinted as an opal; where the ruddy flush was faintest, was a smooth spot that was covered with graceful circles and radiating lines, ever so delicately traced; the shore on our left was densely wooded, and the somber shadow
20 that fell from this forest was broken in one place by a long, ruffled trail that shone like silver; and high above the forest wall a clean-stemmed dead tree waved a single leafy bough that glowed like a flame in the unobstructed splendor that was flowing from the sun. There were
25 graceful curves, reflected images, woody heights, soft distances; and over the whole scene, far and near, the dissolving lights drifted steadily, enriching it, every passing moment, with new marvels of coloring.
I stood like one bewitched. I drank it in, in a
30 speechless rapture. The world was new to me, and I had never seen anything like this at home. But as I have said, a day came when I began to cease from noting the glories and the charms which the moon and the sun and the twilight wrought upon the river's face;
35 another day came when I ceased altogether to note them. Then, if that sunset scene had been repeated, I should have looked upon it without rapture, and should have commented upon it, inwardly, in this fashion: This sun means that we are going to have wind tomorrow; that
40 floating log means that the river is rising, small thanks to it; that slanting mark on the water refers to a bluff reef which is going to kill somebody's steamboat one of these nights, if it keeps on stretching out like that; those tumbling "boils" show a dissolving bar and a changing
45 channel there; the lines and circles in the slick water over yonder are a warning that that troublesome place is shoaling up dangerously; that silver streak in the shadow

of the forest is the "break" from a new snag, and he has located himself in the very best place he could have
50 found to fish for steamboats; that tall dead tree, with a single living branch, is not going to last long, and then how is a body ever going to get through this blind place at night without the friendly old landmark?
No, the romance and the beauty were all gone from
55 the river. All the value any feature of it had for me now was the amount of usefulness it could furnish toward compassing the safe piloting of a steamboat. Since those days, I have pitied doctors from my heart. What does the lovely flush in a beauty's cheek mean to a doctor but
60 a "break" that ripples above some deadly disease? Are not all her visible charms sown thick with what are to him the signs and symbols of hidden decay? Does he ever see her beauty at all, or doesn't he simply view her professionally, and comment upon her unwholesome
65 condition all to himself? And doesn't he sometimes wonder whether he has gained most or lost most by learning his trade?

18. The primary purpose of the passage is to show that
  (A) sunsets are not as beautiful as many people assume
  (B) a steamboat pilot must be wary of various dangerous river conditions
  (C) technical knowledge can detract from aesthetic appreciation
  (D) being a steamboat pilot is not a worthy profession for most people
  (E) danger and disease can be hidden behind pleasing appearances

19. The author mentions he had "lost something" (line 5) to express his belief that
  (A) the sunsets were less colorful than they had been in the past
  (B) he was too concerned with studying the river to appreciate its beauty
  (C) he had decided to make a career writing fiction instead of poetry
  (D) the river had capsized a steamboat that he used to pilot
  (E) he had not been paid enough in his profession as he deserved

20. In line 20, "broken" most nearly means

    (A) smashed
    (B) disabled
    (C) unused
    (D) interrupted
    (E) defeated

21. The primary purpose of the second paragraph (lines 29-53) is to

    (A) illustrate the author's lack of experience as a steamboat pilot
    (B) emphasize the pleasure the author received in seeing two nearly identical sunsets
    (C) describe the numerous perils in piloting a steamboat
    (D) contrast two different ways of perceiving a particular event
    (E) compare the conceptions different people often have to similar events

22. The author's attitude towards the "sunset scene" (line 36) after working on the river for several years is best described as

    (A) pleased
    (B) nostalgic
    (C) skeptical
    (D) irate
    (E) pragmatic

23. The author suggests that a steamboat pilot must keep track of all of the following EXCEPT the

    (A) time of the sunset
    (B) weather conditions
    (C) location of reefs
    (D) landmarks on the riverbank
    (E) depth of the river

24. The author probably mentions that he "pitied doctors" (line 58) because he feels that they

    (A) view people in a purely analytical fashion
    (B) do not treat their patients with respect
    (C) are able to notice indicators of disease
    (D) would make poor steamboat pilots
    (E) tend to be judged on outward appearances

DRILL 2 (10 minutes)

Questions 16-24 are based on the following passage.

Defining a uniquely American educational system was one of the challenges faced by the Revolutionary generation. The following passage discusses the views on education of two of America's most important eighteenth-century political figures.

Benjamin Franklin and Thomas Jefferson shared basic ideas about the importance of education and its social implications in the early American Republic because both
Line
5 were greatly influenced by the liberal Enlightenment thinkers, but they differed on more specific points of organization, funding, and subject matter.

Benjamin Franklin's outlook on education was tempered by his humble background and his rise to fame through self-motivation and hard work. He did not feel
10 that publicly funded education was necessary because personal ability and initiative to educate oneself would be (as it had been in his case) enough to drive the most worthy candidates to the top. Education beyond the elementary level, he claimed, was simply not necessary or
15 desirable to all people. Franklin was critical of a strictly classical education, for he felt it served no purpose in the new era and perpetuated the elitist trend in higher education, a trend which ran counter to the democratic ideals of the age. His model for a new private academy,
20 as put forth in his "Proposals Relating to the Education of Youth in Pennsylvania" of 1743, answered growing middle class needs while still including traditional elements of the classical model. The curriculum of the private academy would reflect the current trends of the day—empiricism,
25 sense realism, and science—as well as Franklin's personal utilitarian and commercial interests. True to his deistic inclinations, scientific study was included in the curriculum, as were basic moral principles, but sectarian religious views were not.
30 In contrast to Franklin, whose ideas against publicly funded education found a wide audience, Thomas Jefferson felt that universal education was imperative for democratic participation in community development; therefore, he strongly advocated state control of secular
35 education. Like Franklin, Jefferson acknowledged that there were those who had a greater predilection for scholarship, but while Franklin seemed content to let the more able students scramble to the top on their own with no state assistance, Jefferson wanted the state to
40 fund secondary schooling for more academically capable youth, as well as universal elementary education for all children. Jefferson also strongly advocated the retention of the classical curriculum in higher education. In 1779 he tried unsuccessfully to reform the college of William
45 and Mary, which at that time offered only religious instruction for future church leaders and a liberal curriculum for the aristocracy. Jefferson felt that a classical education was still the most appropriate for the training of leaders who must understand basics of
50 democracy and human political interaction; in short, he wanted education for civic leadership to be part of university curriculum. Jefferson, like the French philosophers Condorcet and Rousseau before him, was a little ahead of his time on this issue; eventually
55 his models for both state-supported, secular education and university curricula for civic leadership were more widely accepted in the nineteenth century than they were in his own time.

Overall, the disparities between the educational
60 views of Jefferson and Franklin are attributable in large part to the fact that the two men concerned themselves with different elements of education, even though they were influenced by the same philosophical beliefs. Franklin's efforts targeted secondary schooling, while
65 Jefferson concerned himself with improving higher level curriculum. Franklin's reforms benefited the commercial classes, with whom he had many contacts and a personal interest in assisting, while the efforts of Jefferson, who mistrusted capitalism and the mercantile
70 mentality, were intended to improve the lot of the democratic political elite.

However, there is still much the two men had in common; both Franklin and Jefferson envisioned the building of a democratic society in the new Republic.
75 They were both against strong central government, religious authoritarianism, and elitism in public institutions. They both felt that the educational structure should serve the greater needs of society and produce citizens, not just religious leaders and aristocrats.
80 Both were also hostile to organized religion because European history had already shown the kind of violence and cultural stagnation that resulted from the dogmatic, intolerant strains of religious sectarianism. A democratic state by definition required a citizenry that
85 identified itself as members of a larger community—of humanity—as opposed to a specific religious group. This was one of the primary goals of Enlightenment education in America—to educate all people in order to enable them to fulfill their civic responsibilities.

16. The passage is primarily concerned with

   (A) describing the historical roots of the modern American educational system
   (B) evaluating the relative merits of Franklin and Jefferson's proposals
   (C) comparing and contrasting two points of view on education
   (D) contrasting Franklin's upstart nature with Jefferson's elitism
   (E) showing how two views have more in common than was previously believed

17. In lines 7-9 the phrase "tempered by...work" most directly suggests that Benjamin Franklin

(A) believed that others would educate themselves in the same way he had
(B) disregarded the importance of maintaining a well-informed populace
(C) was conflicted over the impact of a university education
(D) questioned the usefulness of labor and industriousness
(E) was unlikely to change his opinions based on the views of others

18. The author observes that "Franklin was critical" (line 15) primarily to emphasize Franklin's belief that classical education was

(A) restricted exclusively to people from wealthy backgrounds
(B) essential to the development of the new middle class
(C) useless for students accustomed to more modern educational methods
(D) incompatible with contemporary political aspirations
(E) concerned primarily with moral and religious studies

19. Which of the following would best fit the author's description of Franklin's "new private academy" (line 19)?

(A) A liberal arts college with a largely classical curriculum
(B) A private religious institution
(C) A state-funded public school
(D) A school that specializes in science and business
(E) A home-schooling program

20. Lines 37-39 ("but while...assistance") are intended to

(A) stress that Franklin's educational system was bound to fail the average citizen
(B) convey the inherent similarities between the two important political figures
(C) contrast Franklin's belief in self reliance with Jefferson's emphasis on governmental participation
(D) criticize Franklin's lack of compassion for people of limited intelligence
(E) address the difficulty of providing quality instruction in publicly funded schools

21. Jefferson's endorsement of a classical curriculum is based on the assumption that

(A) classical authors had previously designed a democratic system similar to ours
(B) a degree from a university is required for a position of civil leadership
(C) people who learn democratic principles will become effective leaders
(D) only the aristocracy is able to comprehend a classical curriculum
(E) Condorcet and Rousseau also advocated a classical education

22. It can be inferred from the passage that, for Jefferson, training in "civic leadership" does NOT consist of

(A) study of political behavior
(B) a university education
(C) a foundation in religious doctrine
(D) state-controlled secular education
(E) study of democratic principles

23. Franklin and Jefferson would BOTH most likely agree with which one of the following statements?

(A) Religion has no place in the education of children.
(B) One goal of education should be to teach civic responsibility.
(C) Capitalism and the mercantile mentality are not to be trusted.
(D) Democracy requires citizens who align themselves with specific religious groups.
(E) The modern American educational system most resembles Jefferson's model.

24. The primary purpose of the fourth paragraph (lines 59-71) is to

(A) suggest that a previously stated view should be called into question
(B) explain the contemporary relevance of a disagreement
(C) dramatize the contrast between two points of view
(D) offer an explanation for a difference of opinion
(E) call into question the social significance of a belief

DRILL 3 (6 minutes)

Questions 10-14 are based on the following passage.

The following passage presents the reader with a view of art, specifically painting, as something more than just imitation.

"I always paint what I see," said Turner; yet no painter ever departed further from close imitation or took more liberties with subjects. He elongated steeples,
Line reconstructed buildings, changed the course of rivers,
5 even the course of the sun. Yet one critic says Turner was sincere in thinking that he painted what he saw; that he seemed to be swept along as by a dream, and the changes he made "came into his head involuntarily."
    But the ordinary person's idea of imitation is the
10 setting down with the utmost precision every visible fact in a subject—"making it look like the real thing." Imitation in a painting is, for example, flowers that one can botanize, or fruit that "looks good enough to eat" and has a fly on it one feels the urge to brush off.
15 Such deceptive resemblance gives people the pleasure of surprise rather than aesthetic pleasure. Carefully realistic pictures may please, but the pictures people enjoy living with leave something to the imagination. "The secret of being a bore," said Voltaire, "is to tell
20 everything."
    Actually, a few painters try to carry imitation to the point of deceptive resemblance. It cannot be done at all unless the object painted is small enough to be reproduced full size. A true artist never tries to make us believe that
25 his or her medium is anything except a medium. It is paint with which great painters express themselves.
    What the ordinary person generally means by imitation of a large subject—say a landscape—is a mirror copy much like a colored photograph: nature
30 with its infinite mass of details crowded into the picture, unsifted, unassimilated, and unarranged. Even if it were possible to put in everything seen, it would not be art any more than copying a poem is creating poetry. The painter uses nature not as a copybook but as a
35 source of inspiration, selects such details as suits his or her purpose, and arranges them in a picture with a discriminating regard for pictorial effect.
    If a painting is an unsifted mass of objects, it fails at the very point where art begins, the point that marks the
40 difference between art and imitation. One of the pathetic fallacies of art is that realism of fact creates realism of effect, that increasing the facts of nature in a picture or sculpture increases the "feeling of Nature" in it. On the contrary, such techniques decrease the sensation because
45 fullness of fact leaves too little to the imagination. That is the trouble with wax figures and with pictures

in which every detail is perfectly defined. What could better give us the facts of nature than a stuffed bird with glass eyes? Yet an artist, employing only one percent of
50 the facts of nature, can give us a rough sketch of a bird that is infinitely better.

10. The primary purpose of the passage is to

    (A) praise an artist
    (B) contrast two viewpoints
    (C) conduct an experiment
    (D) test two theories
    (E) examine a career

11. The author's statement in lines 3-5 ("He elongated...sun") serves chiefly to

    (A) provide support for an assertion made in the previous sentence
    (B) demonstrate how Turner achieved mastery over nature
    (C) suggest how Turner's paintings might be interpreted by modern audiences
    (D) put two different interpretations of Turner into historical perspective
    (E) begin a digression away from the thesis of the passage

12. In line 11, "fact" most nearly means

    (A) scripture
    (B) certainty
    (C) feature
    (D) word
    (E) statistic

13. The author would most likely characterize the "deceptive resemblances" (line 15) as

    (A) unnerving
    (B) inspiring
    (C) thought-provoking
    (D) appetizing
    (E) unsatisfying

14. In the fourth paragraph (lines 27-37), the author indicates that part of a painter's job is to

    (A) inspire people to develop a love of art
    (B) present nature in all of its infinite variety
    (C) reproduce images with photographic precision
    (D) choose elements from a range of possibilities
    (E) create works that express a diverse range of emotions

DRILL 4 (5 minutes)

Questions 9-12 are based on the following passages.

Passage 1

Any decent meteorologist can predict, with a reasonably high degree of certainty, the weather of the following day and even the week ahead. While *Line* sudden storms and shifting weather fronts do require
5 meteorologists to constantly update and amend their forecasts, these scientists have the great benefit of working with a more limited set of variables than do their counterparts, the long-term climatologists. Scientists attempting to predict weather patterns over the next
10 decade or century must understand both the immense history of such climate change and, perhaps more importantly, the still undetermined effect that human activities have on the environment.

Passage 2

Much has been said and written about the probable
15 effects of human activities on the Earth's climate. Without question, the concentrations of carbon dioxide and the other greenhouse gases that act to keep the planet warm—and therefore habitable—are increasing very rapidly. While a wealth of information has been gathered
20 on different aspects of the problem, consensus on the meaning of these findings has yet to be reached. While some climatologists argue that climate change to date falls well within an acceptable and predictable range, others fear that the recent rise in world temperatures
25 indicates a dangerous trend for decades to come.

9. Both passages support which of the following statements about the impact of human activity on the Earth's change?

(A) It has been underestimated by meteorologists in predicting the weather.
(B) It presents a challenge to those attempting to predict long-term climate change.
(C) It has only been accounted for in long-term predictions during the last decade.
(D) It will prove valuable to both meteorologists and long-term climatologists.
(E) It has worsened recently due to the emissions of greenhouse gases.

10. The author of Passage 1 uses the phrase "with a reasonably high degree of certainty (lines 1-2)," in order to

(A) allow for the minor inaccuracies involved in short-term weather predictions
(B) account for the poor reputation of meteorologists and their work
(C) indicate that no science can be truly exact
(D) highlight the similarity between meteorology and long-term climatology
(E) praise the improvements made in short-term weather predictions

11. Both authors would agree that the "effects" (line 15, Passage 2) are

(A) of limited importance
(B) potentially hazardous
(C) easy to overlook
(D) intentionally ignored
(E) difficult to quantify

12. It can be inferred that the "greenhouse gases" (line 17, Passage 2)

(A) cause irreparable damage
(B) modify the planet's temperature
(C) threaten Earth's environment
(D) remain essentially mysterious
(E) will eventually disperse

MATH
WRITING
READING
VOCABULARY

DRILL 5 (13 minutes)

Questions 13-24 are based on the following passage.

The following excerpt is from a book of literary criticism written by John Gardner.

The language of art critics, and of artists of the kind who pay attention to critics, has become exceedingly odd: not talk about feelings or intellectual
Line affirmations— not talk about moving and surprising
5 twists of plot or wonderful characters and ideas—but sentences full of large words like hermeneutic, heuristic, structuralism, formalism, or opaque language, and full of fine distinctions—for instance those between modernist and post-modernist—that would make
10 even an intelligent cow suspicious. Though more difficult than ever before to read, criticism has become inconsequential.

The trivial has its place, its entertainment value. I can think of no good reason that some people should
15 not specialize in the behavior of the left-side hairs of an elephant's trunk. Even at its best, its most deadly serious, criticism, like art, is partly a game, as all good critics know. My objection is not to the game but to the fact that contemporary critics have for the most part lost track
20 of the point of their game, just as artists, by and large, have lost track of the point of theirs. Fiddling with the hairs on an elephant's nose is indecent when the elephant happens to be standing on the baby.

At least in America, art is not thought capable, these
25 days, of tromping on babies. Yet it does so all the time, and what is worse, it does so with a bland smile. I've watched writers, composers, and painters knocking off their "works" with their left hands. Nice people, most of them. Artists are generally pleasant people, childlike
30 both in love and hate, intending no harm when they turn out bad paintings, compositions or books. Indeed, their ambition guarantees that they will do the best they know how to or think they ought to do. The error is less in their objects than in their objectives. "Art is play, or
35 partly play," they'll tell you with an engaging smile, serving up their non-nutritious fare with the murderous indifference of a fat cook serving up hamburgers. What they say is true enough, as far as it goes, and nothing is more tiresome than the man who keeps hollering, "Hey,
40 let's be serious!" but that is what we must holler.

In a world where nearly everything that passes for art is tinny and commercial and often, in addition, hollow and academic, I argue—by reason and by banging on the table—for an old-fashioned view of what art is
45 and does and what the fundamental business of critics therefore ought to be. Not that I want joy taken out of the arts; but even frothy entertainment is not harmed by a touch of moral responsibility, at least an evasion of too fashionable simplifications. My basic message is

50 as old as the hills, drawn from Homer, Plato, Aristotle, Dante, and the rest, and standard in Western civilization down through the eighteenth century: one would think all critics and artists should be thoroughly familiar with it, and perhaps many are. But my experience is that in
55 university lecture halls, or in kitchens at midnight, after parties, the traditional view of art strikes most people as strange news.

The traditional view is that true art is moral: it seeks to improve life, not debase it. It seeks to hold off, at least
60 for a while, the twilight of the gods and us. I do not deny that art, like criticism, may legitimately celebrate the trifling. It may joke, or mock, or while away the time. But trivial art has no meaning or value except in the shadows of more serious art, the kind of art that, if you
65 will, makes the world safe for triviality. The art which tends toward destruction, the art of cynics and nihilists, is not properly art at all. Art is essentially serious and beneficial—a game played against chaos and death, against entropy. It is a tragic game, for those who have
70 the wit to take it seriously, because our side must lose: a comic game because only a clown with sawdust brains would take our side and eagerly join in.

Like legitimate art, legitimate criticism is a tragiccomic holding action against entropy. Art builds
75 temporary walls against life's leveling force, against the ruin of what is splendidly unnatural in us: consciousness. Art rediscovers, generation by generation, what is necessary to humanness. Criticism restates and clarifies, reinforces the wall.

13. The author would most likely characterize the approach of the "critics" referred to in line 1 as

   (A) strongly expressive
   (B) invigorating
   (C) carefully reasoned
   (D) unsophisticated
   (E) unnecessarily intricate

14. As used in line 8, the word "fine" most nearly means

   (A) subtle
   (B) excellent
   (C) attractive
   (D) aesthetic
   (E) impressive

MATH

WRITING

READING

VOCABULARY

15. The main point of the first paragraph (lines 1-12) is that

(A)   art critics should use simpler, more understandable language

(B)   artists should not concern themselves with the opinion of critics

(C)   art critics have lost touch with their public

(D)   art criticism has been rendered trivial by its use of overly complex language

(E)   artists have become suspicious of art critics

16. The author's statement in lines 21-23 ("Fiddling…baby") serves to

(A)   resolve a contradiction

(B)   exaggerate a danger

(C)   defend a theory

(D)   dramatize an argument

(E)   offer a prognosis

17. In line 27, "knocking off" most nearly means

(A)   observing

(B)   simulating

(C)   pilfering

(D)   damaging

(E)   producing

18. The author most likely views the "works" (line 28) of artists with

(A)   curiosity

(B)   detachment

(C)   reverence

(D)   dismissiveness

(E)   indifference

19. In line 39, "the man" represents

(A)   the public's opinion

(B)   the author's point of view

(C)   an artist's manifesto

(D)   a lawful authority

(E)   a restaurant worker

20. The author probably uses the phrase "banging on the table" (lines 43-44) in order to

(A)   characterize his views on art as sometimes unreasonable

(B)   stress the urgency of his message

(C)   show that he is not above old-fashioned theatrics

(D)   assert his right for a turn to speak at last

(E)   distract the attention of art critics

21. In line 47, the word "frothy" most nearly means

(A)   frivolous

(B)   aerated

(C)   effervescent

(D)   carbonated

(E)   foamy

22. The phrase "kitchens at midnight, after parties" (lines 55-56) refers to the

(A)   food served at art openings

(B)   debates with university professors

(C)   concepts in art history

(D)   informal discussions about art

(E)   working conditions in schools

23. According to the author, "most people" (line 56) would consider the traditional view of art

(A)   idealistic

(B)   elitist

(C)   unethical

(D)   naive

(E)   unfamiliar

24. The primary purpose of the last paragraph is to

(A)   question whether only certain kinds of art are legitimate

(B)   show that the production of art is an unnatural activity

(C)   indicate that two activities have a complementary purpose

(D)   account for the appeal of both art and criticism

(E)   place divergent interpretations of art into historical perspective

DRILL 6 (12 minutes)

Questions 14-24 are based on the following passage.

The following excerpt is from a book about attempts to discover a reliable method for accurately determining a boat's east-west position in the open sea.

As a child, I learned the difference between latitude and longitude. The latitude lines—or parallels—stay parallel to each other as they girdle the globe from the
Line Equator to the poles in a series of shrinking concentric
5 rings. The meridians of longitude go the other way: they loop from the North Pole to the South and back again in great circles of the same size, so they all converge at the ends of the earth.

Any sailor worth his salt can gauge his latitude by
10 the length of the day, or by the height of the sun or other known guide stars above the horizon. Christopher Columbus followed a straight path across the Atlantic when he "sailed the parallel" on his 1492 journey. Determining longitude in the open sea, however, is a
15 problem that had stumped some of the wisest minds of the world for the better part of history. To learn one's longitude, one needs to know what time it is aboard ship and also the time at another place of known longitude—*simultaneously*. The two times enable the navigator
20 to convert the hour difference into a geographical separation. Precise knowledge of the hour in two different places at once—so easily accessible today from any pair of cheap wristwatches—was unattainable up to and including the era of pendulum clocks. On the
25 deck of a rolling ship, such clocks would slow down, or speed up, or stop running altogether. Normal changes in temperature encountered en route from a cold country of origin to a tropical trade zone thinned or thickened a clock's lubricating oil, and made its metal parts
30 expand or contract with disastrous results. A change in barometric pressure, or the subtle variations in the Earth's gravity from one latitude to another, could also cause a clock to gain or lose time.

For lack of a practical method of determining
35 longitude, every great captain in the Age of Exploration became lost at sea despite the best available charts and compasses. Vasco da Gama, Ferdinand Magellan, and Sir Francis Drake all reached their destinations by forces attributed to good luck or the grace of God.
40 As more sailing vessels set out to conquer or explore new territories, to wage war, or to ferry gold and commodities between foreign lands, the wealth of nations floated upon the oceans. Because no ship could reliably establish her whereabouts, untold numbers of
45 sailors died when their destinations suddenly loomed out of the sea and took them by surprise.

The quest for a solution to the longitude problem persisted over four centuries and across Europe.

Renowned astronomers approached the longitude
50 challenge by appealing to the clockwork universe: Galileo Galilei, Christiaan Huygens, Sir Isaac Newton, and Edmond Halley all entreated the moon and stars for help. Palatial observatories were founded at Paris, London, and Berlin for the express purpose of
55 determining longitude by the heavens. Meanwhile, lesser minds devised schemes that depended on the yelps of dogs, or the cannon blasts of signal ships strategically anchored—somehow—on the open ocean.

As time passed, the search for a solution to the
60 longitude problem assumed legendary proportions. The governments of the great maritime nations offered jackpot purses for a workable method. The British Parliament, in its Longitude Act of 1714, set the highest bounty of all: naming a prize worth several million
65 dollars in today's currency for a "Practicable and Useful" means of determining longitude.

English clockmaker John Harrison, a mechanical genius who pioneered the science of portable precision timekeeping, devoted his life to this quest. Without
70 formal education or apprenticeship to any watchmaker, Harrison nevertheless constructed a series of virtually friction-free clocks that required no lubrication and no cleaning, that were made from materials impervious to rust, and that kept their moving parts perfectly
75 balanced in relation to one another, regardless of how the world pitched or tossed about them. He did away with the pendulum, and he combined different metals inside his works in such a way that when one component expanded or contracted with changes in temperature, the
80 other counteracted the change and kept the clock's rate constant. Harrison had accomplished what Newton had feared was impossible: he invented a clock that would carry the true time like an eternal flame from home port to any remote corner of the world.

85 A man of simple birth, Harrison crossed swords with the leading lights of his day. He made a special enemy of the Reverend Nevil Maskelyne, the royal astronomer, who contested Harrison's claim to the coveted prize money, and whose tactics can be described
90 only as foul play. Harrison's every success was parried by the scientific elite, who distrusted his magic box. The commissioners in charge of the longitude prize—including Maskelyne—continually changed the contest rules to favor the chances of astronomers over the likes
95 of Harrison and his fellow "mechanics." But the utility and accuracy of Harrison's approach triumphed in the end. An aged, exhausted Harrison, taken under the wing of King George III, ultimately claimed his rightful monetary award in 1773—after forty struggling years
100 of political intrigue, international warfare, academic backbiting, scientific revolution, and economic upheaval.

14. The function of the first paragraph (lines 1-8) is to

(A) draw a distinction
(B) offer an opinion
(C) demonstrate a method
(D) test a phenomenon
(E) put forth a theory

15. The discussion in lines 21-33 suggests that before Harrison's invention, the chief drawback to using clocks at sea was that timepieces of the time were too

(A) unwieldy
(B) unreliable
(C) mechanical
(D) ponderous
(E) inexpensive

16. In line 35, the author refers to "every great captain" in order to

(A) point out that skilled navigators were sometimes unable to calculate their positions at seas
(B) praise the ingenuity of some of history's most famous explorers
(C) show that these captains were too superstitious to trust maps and compasses
(D) demonstrate that the longitude problem primarily affected large ships
(E) indicate that no one was immune from the violence that plagued high seas

17. The author uses the phrase "the wealth ... oceans" (lines 42-43) in order to emphasize

(A) the need for divine inspiration
(B) skills of accomplished sailors
(C) importance of accurate navigation
(D) prosperity of western nations
(E) desire for material things

18. The author lists the series of names in lines 51-52 in order to

(A) lend an air of authority to the author's choice of topic
(B) demonstrate that astronomers had difficulty predicting the movements of the sun
(C) create the impression that astronomers were likely to solve the challenge of longitude
(D) argue that modern astronomy rose as a result of the quest to solve the navigation problem
(E) put the magnitude of a dilemma in perspective

19. As used in line 54, the word "express" most nearly means

(A) sole
(B) known
(C) conspicuous
(D) quick
(E) rapid

20. It is implied that the author views the plots discussed in lines 55-58 ("Meanwhile...ocean") as

(A) impractical
(B) visionary
(C) tentative
(D) ingenious
(E) mysterious

21. In line 76, "the world" most likely refers to

(A) scientific disputes
(B) nations at war
(C) the movement of a ship at sea
(D) the movement of a clock's components
(E) the movement of stars in the sky

22. In lines 67-84, the author suggests that Harrison's timepieces were most notable for their

(A) silence
(B) popularity
(C) portability
(D) simplicity
(E) cost

23. The phrase "crossed swords with" (lines 85-86) most nearly means

(A) inspired
(B) condemned
(C) joined with
(D) competed with
(E) attracted the attention of

24. The attitude with which the commissioners in charge of the longitude contest (lines 90-95) viewed Harrison and his efforts can best be described as

(A) inquisitive
(B) appreciative
(C) ambivalent
(D) conciliatory
(E) dismissive

DRILL 7 (13 minutes)

Questions 13-24 are based on the following passage.

The following passages address the issue of how historians should write about history. Passage 1 discusses the work of two twentieth-century British historians. Passage 2 considers an essay by an American historian.

Passage 1

In 1955, the British historian Geoffrey Elton published his critically acclaimed monograph *England Under the Tudors.* Elton, a traditionalist in the mold of
Line   Leopold von Ranke, was primarily interested in how a
5   handful of visionary leaders had transformed the British monarchy into an efficient bureaucratic system. While Elton's writings on British history are still admired by a select group of professional scholars, Elton himself is more widely remembered for his role in a spirited and
10   long-running debate with fellow historian E.H. Carr.

Elton, like other traditional historians, believed that history was made by great and powerful leaders—kings, generals, and prime ministers. For Carr, however, history was the product of vast social forces, set in motion by
15   the actions of ordinary people. He argued that men such as Napoleon and Bismarck did not play a major role in shaping history; rather, they were simply swept along by social forces over which they had little control. Carr derided those historians who focused exclusively on the
20   actions of powerful individuals, famously remarking that "millions had crossed the Rubicon*, but only Julius Caesar's crossing is considered noteworthy by historians."

Today, the overwhelming majority of professional
25   historians have followed the path of Carr, rather than that of Elton. They tend to view Elton's style—with its polished narratives, literary devices, and obsession with individual figures—as out of step with the spirit of a democratic age. For these historians, the practice of
30   history begins with an exhaustive study of the facts of daily life. They draw from records left in private cellars, town halls, and police stations. They study marriage licenses, rental agreements, even old restaurant menus. Wherever paper has accumulated, they believe, they will
35   find the real life of real people.

Of course, the traditionalist historians have not all disappeared. A few of them, in fact, have achieved notable popular success by writing accessible, novelistic works about Great American Heroes such as George
40   Washington or John Adams. These books regularly make *The New York Times* best-seller list: readers love a good thriller, and their consciences are salved by picking up tidbits of history that they should have learned in high school. But while the general public is soothed
45   and comforted by such easily readable fare, these works

do little to advance our understanding of history. The historian should seek to broaden our understanding of the past by providing a rich and detailed portrait of how people actually lived; only then can we understand how
50   these peoples' lives have relevance for our own. The historian's work is no longer furthered by rehashing the lives of the famous few, for in history, the crowd is what matters. And what shapes the crowd are not singular individuals, who matter little, but rather the overall
55   conditions of life.

Passage 2

In her essay "The Domestication of Politics," the historian Paula Baker seeks to go beyond the historian's traditional focus on powerful and influential individuals by studying the lives of ordinary citizens. In particular,
60   Baker focuses on the role that ordinary women, such as wives, mothers, and working women, played in shaping political events in nineteenth-century America.

This approach to writing about history has been sharply criticized by certain scholars, who believe that
65   history is shaped by those who govern nations, command armies, or control vast fortunes. For these scholars, men like Abraham Lincoln, Ulysses H. Grant, and Andrew Carnegie were the true forces behind the great historical events of the nineteenth century. What irritates these
70   historians most about Baker is her insistent focus on the lives of ordinary women, for how could nineteenth century American women, who did not even have the legal right to vote, much less hold political office, have influenced American politics?

75   Baker's response is that women in the nineteenth century, denied the privilege of voting or holding office, responded by forming societies devoted to combating social problems such as temperance and poverty. It was the efforts of thousands of anonymous women
80   that gave these social issues national prominence and forced politicians to take these issues seriously. Thus, nineteenth century women pioneered the political practice of campaigning on behalf of particular issues, rather than for a political party or candidate, a practice
85   that would have momentous consequences for twentieth-century politics.

Baker's method has an important advantage over the traditional historian's focus on influential persons: it is able to show how important historical events
90   are set in motion, sometimes decades earlier, by the collective action of ordinary individuals. This is Baker's contribution to the writing of history—she reminds us that a historian must do more than simply chronicle the lives of famous individuals. The aim of the historian is
95   to lay bare the great social trends that often originate in the mundane lives of everyday people.

*A river in northern Italy.

13. The authors of the two passages are most similar in their

(A) admiration for scholarly debate
(B) idealization of great historical figures
(C) preference for modern over ancient history
(D) interest in clarifying the purpose of writing about history
(E) emphasis on narrative structures and literary techniques

14. The author of Passage 2 would most likely consider which of the following questions most useful in determining the relevance of Elton's *England Under the Tudors*?

(A) Does it vividly portray the major political events of the time?
(B) Does it correctly identify the most influential members of Tudor society?
(C) Does it identify underlying patterns in the activities of ordinary persons?
(D) Does it make archaic ways of living appealing to modern readers?
(E) Does it use modern techniques of historical analysis?

15. In line 8, the word "select" most nearly means

(A) limited
(B) influential
(C) chosen
(D) antiquated
(E) delicate

16. Paula Baker (Passage 2) would most likely challenge Elton's belief about history (lines 11-13, Passage 1) by arguing that the

(A) contributions of average citizens are often overestimated
(B) impact of those who lack political power may be significant
(C) biographical details of major figures may be unfamiliar to modern readers
(D) importance of female historians has been overlooked by male scholars
(E) skills needed to write about history take years to develop

17. Carr (Passage 1) most likely refers to "Julius Caesar's crossing" in order to

(A) suggest that much of what is learned in school is irrelevant
(B) show that a powerful leader was respected by his subjects
(C) bemoan the lack of standard in modern scholarship
(D) criticize an instance of unimaginative thinking
(E) characterize an approach as overly narrow

18. The author of Passage 1 implies that the "overwhelming majority" (line 24) views Elton's approach to writing about history as .

(A) anachronistic
(B) facetious
(C) original
(D) pragmatic
(E) irreverent

19. For which of the following qualities would "these historians" (line 29) most likely praise Baker's article "The Domestication of Politics" (Passage 2) ?

(A) Its imaginative interpretation of familiar historical events
(B) Its refreshing appeal to non-specialists who are interested in history
(C) Its thorough examination of documents that detail people's activities
(D) Its accurate depiction of the lives of distinguished persons
(E) Its skillful use of narrative techniques and literary devices

20. The author of Passage 1 most probably uses the words "soothed" and "comforted" to reflect his overall

(A) contempt for the way history is taught in most schools
(B) disdain for readers of certain popular works about history
(C) mistrust of historians who falsify crucial historical details
(D) satisfaction about the universal appeal of American history
(E) appreciation for the accessible style of certain writers

21. The "scholars" (line 64, Passage 2) are most similar in attitude to

(A) the author of Passage 1
(B) the author of Passage 2
(C) Elton (Passage 1)
(D) Carr (Passage 1)
(E) Baker (Passage 2)

22. Lines 63-74 of Passage 2 suggest that Baker's critics view her work as

(A) indifferent to ethical concerns
(B) riddled with historical inaccuracies
(C) marred by frivolous and pointless digressions
(D) concerned with issues of marginal importance
(E) insensitive to women and minorities

23. The last paragraph of Passage 2 suggests that Baker's approach

(A) revolutionizes a moribund field
(B) addresses a historical injustice
(C) contradicts a prevailing viewpoint
(D) evokes nostalgia for the past
(E) provides a broad perspective

24. The authors of both passages imply that a historian should primarily be concerned with

(A) academic reputations
(B) important legislation
(C) controversial figures
(D) oppressed minorities
(E) general tendencies

 © TPR Education IP Holdings, LLC

TIMED DRILLS—SELF-ANALYSIS

1. From the previous timed drills, the question types that I regularly answered correctly were the following:

2. The question types that I regularly answered incorrectly were the following:

3. New vocabulary words that I learned from the previous timed drills are as follows:

4. I marked reference windows in all of the drills. True / False

5. Whenever possible, I predicted the answer to Reading Comprehension questions. True / False

6. I used POE answer choice labels for all questions. True / False

DRILL 8 (13 minutes)

Questions 13-24 are based on the following passage.

The following passage discusses three women who achieved distinction in a male-dominated science.

At the beginning of the twentieth century, the leading American astronomical observatories were small factories for the production of knowledge. Like
Line many businesses of the day, they were governed by
5 autocratic directors. Work was specialized, with some people building instruments, others observing, and still others reducing data for publication. These last workers, the "computers" as they were called, increasingly were women.

10   One of the first American women hired as a "computer" was Maria Mitchell, who began doing calculations for the UB Nautical Almanac Office in 1849. Mitchell was already well-known for discovering a comet in 1847. She did her calculations at home, not in
15 the well-regulated environment of an observatory. None of the colleges that had telescopes accepted women and the existing American observatories employed only men.

    Like most American astronomers of her day, Mitchell eventually found employment beyond the chores of
20 computing. Mid-nineteenth century American educators gave astronomy a prominent place in their curricula. In the early 1860s, when Matthew Vassar decided to establish a women's college offering educations equivalent to those of the best men's colleges, he
25 naturally planned to hire an astronomer and build an observatory. Maria Mitchell was his choice for the post. Thus, at the age of 47, Mitchell assumed a scientific position that took her outside the home and required her to speak in public. By the 1870s, Mitchell's interests
30 included the general status of women. Her activities did not lead to any major changes in the position of women in science, but they demonstrated her conviction that women not only could but should make larger contributions to science.

35   By the turn of the century several observatories had permanent staffs of computers working at one location. Preeminent among these workers was Annie Jump Cannon of the Harvard College Observatory, who would eventually classify the spectra of literally hundreds
40 of thousands of stars and receive both national and international recognition. In 1925, when the anatomist Florence Sabin was nominated to the National Academy of Sciences, Cannon also was mentioned as a possible nominee. Some leading astronomers were not
45 enthusiastic about the idea. However, E. B. Wilson of the Harvard School of Public Health pointed out that the botanists in the academy placed great value on the systematic work of describing and classifying plants. He found it unfortunate that the astronomers seemed to
50 value interpretation so much more than the observation on which it was based. Despite Wilson's urgings, Cannon was never elected to the academy. The computer's work, no matter how well performed, did not qualify her to join the ranks of elite American astronomers.

55   During the period between the World Wars, observatory staff came to include not only computers and observers but also astronomers who were as well-educated and widely published as the directors themselves. At this point, autocratic government would
60 no longer suffice. The new breed of astronomers included some women, such as Cecilia Payne of the Harvard College Observatory. At the same time, complex machines increasingly performed routine work in both observatories and factories. Those who operated
65 the machines, while not strictly segregated by sex as the human computers of earlier days had sometimes been, were not necessarily considered part of the astronomical community. Thus, in astronomy as in other sciences, the path to a research career came to be more
70 narrowly defined by advanced degrees and other formal credentials.

    The experiences of astronomers preceding World War II encouraged their independence and gave even computers a new sense of value in their skills. By 1946,
75 the Observatory Council, a group consisting of Harvard faculty astronomers and Cecilia Payne, began meeting regularly to review observatory business. At the same time, astronomers increasingly applied individually to government agencies for research funding. Thus, the
80 director came to share authority not only with other staff, but with entirely separate institutions. However productive it continued to be, the Harvard observatory was no longer comparable to a nineteenth-century factory.

85   Women of Payne's education and demonstrated achievements in theoretical astrophysics did not fit neatly into contemporary American observatories. Payne strongly felt the disadvantages of working at an institution where she lacked the recognition accorded
90 other faculty members; in addition, she was expected to shape her research around the programs of the observatory and received a much smaller salary than did male astronomers of equal standing. Indeed, on several occasions she warned women who considered pursuing
95 careers in astronomy that they should do so only if nothing else would satisfy them, for nothing else was probably what they would get. It was an era when several organizations designed to encourage scientific careers for women had foundered. Payne's celebrity, however,
100 was eventually enhanced not only by her books and research papers, but also through occasional newspaper articles, public lectures, and a textbook based on the astronomy course she taught at Radcliffe in the 1950s.

She also wrote an autobiography which was published
105 posthumously.

Payne's achievements, along with those of women
astronomers before and after her, undoubtedly deserve
attention and celebration. At the same time, it is sad to
note how strictly women have been confined to roles that
110 promote efficient production of results and demonstrate
the authority of more powerful and influential male
astronomers. One wonders what both astronomy and
those who practiced it have lost.

13. In line 5, the employees of observatories that
were run by "autocratic directors" were most
likely

(A) renowned astronomers
(B) specialized workers
(C) computer operators
(D) women scientists
(E) astrophysicists

14. The word "computers" is used in line 8 to mean

(A) the machines that calculated astronomical
data
(B) women who built instruments in
observatories
(C) women who edited papers to be published
(D) factory-built astronomical instruments
(E) women who performed calculations and
compiled data

15. The comment that Maria Mitchell's "activities
did not lead to any major changes in the position
of women in science" (lines 30-32) is offered by
the author in order to point out that

(A) Mitchell had no influence in the scientific
community
(B) despite Mitchell's efforts, the status of women
scientists still needed improvement
(C) Mitchell should have done her calculations at
an observatory, not at home
(D) women made few contributions to science
(E) women scientists were not being promoted to
management positions

16. The passage suggests that a major difference
between the botanists and astronomers in the
National Academy of Sciences was

(A) the degree to which each group valued
observation and classification
(B) that astronomers valued interpretation while
botanists did not
(C) that the astronomers refused to elect women
to the academy
(D) that the botanists were less systematic in their
work than were the astronomers
(E) the degree of international recognition
received by each group

17. According to the fourth paragraph (lines 35-54),
E. B. Wilson recommended that

(A) Annie Jump Cannon be nominated to the
National Academy of Sciences
(B) botanists place less value on the work of
classifying plants
(C) astronomers place more value on the work of
interpretation
(D) women be allowed to teach astronomy at the
college level
(E) women astronomers learn how to classify
plants

18. The author uses the phrase "new breed" in line
60 in order to refer to

(A) astronomers who operated complex
machines in observatories
(B) observatory directors who published
scientific articles
(C) astronomers who overthrew the autocratic
directors
(D) computers and observers who worked in
observatories
(E) astronomers whose reputations were on par
with those of the observatory directors

19. One major difference that occurred between the
World Wars in observatories was in the shift from

(A) a majority of women employees to an even
distribution of men and women
(B) systematic work to specialized work
(C) observing comets to classifying stellar
spectra
(D) the use of human computers to the use of
complex machines for routine work
(E) autocratic to segregated management

20. The author would most strongly agree with which of the following statements about women who have pursued research careers since World War II?

(A) Most of them have done more routine work than did women a century ago.

(B) They have become well-educated, widely published astronomers.

(C) Many have been overqualified, therefore unable to fit neatly into the institutions where they have worked.

(D) Only a few have not been considered part of the astronomical community.

(E) Many have gone to graduate school and earned doctorates.

21. The author primarily uses Cecilia Payne's warning in lines 93-97 to

(A) convince women not to pursue astronomical careers

(B) show Payne's concern that women would not be paid equally if they decided to become astronomers

(C) indicate that scientific careers are unsatisfying for women

(D) illustrate Payne's frustration over the lack of opportunities and recognition accorded to women astronomers

(E) predict that women would not be successful unless they joined organizations designed to encourage scientific careers

22. The word "celebration" is used in line 108 to mean

(A) a holiday

(B) observation

(C) praise

(D) a ceremony

(E) ritualization

23. The three women astronomers discussed in the passage were used by the author to illustrate

(A) how women worked better away from the regulated environment of the observatory

(B) that the work women did in the field of astronomy was not worthy of attention

(C) both the achievements and the frustrations of women astronomers

(D) that women have only pursued astronomy since 1847

(E) that computers eventually received as much renown as did observatory directors

24. In the final paragraph (lines 106-113), the author has assumed all of the following EXCEPT

(A) Other women besides the three discussed in the passage have made contributions to the field of astronomy

(B) Most women have allowed their scientific roles to be restricted in order to balance family and career demands

(C) Some women astronomers have been less influential than their male colleagues

(D) Astronomy and astronomers might be better off if women astronomers had not been confined to narrow roles in the past

(E) Confining the roles of women astronomers helped to perpetuate the authority of male astronomers

VOCABULARY

HIT PARADE

WHEN VOCABULARY LEARNING GOES BAD

Having a strong vocabulary will get you far on the verbal parts of the SAT, but it takes more than a few obscene flashcards to master what you need to know!

MATH

WRITING

READING

VOCABULARY

WEEK 1

Are You Talkin' to Me?

candid
                                          KAN did
completely honest, straightforward

Candace's candidness overwhelmed her business colleagues, who were not used to such honesty.

conjecture
                                          kun JEK chur
inference; guesswork

At this point, Kimaya's hypothesis about single-cell biorhythms is still conjecture: She doesn't have conclusive evidence.

didactic
                                          die DAK tik
instructive

The tapes were entertaining and didactic; they both amused and instructed children.

effusive
                                          ef YOO siv
showing excessive emotion; overflowing

Accepting his Oscar for Best Supporting Sound Editor, Ben delivered the most effusive speech in Academy Awards history: he cried, he hugged people, he blew kisses to the audience, and then he cried some more.

euphemism
                                          YOO fuh miz um
a mild, indirect, or vague term substituting for a harsh, blunt, or offensive term

"To pass away" is a common euphemism for dying.

extrapolate
                                          ek STRAP uh layt
to infer or estimate by extending or projecting known information

Seeing the wrecked bike and his daughter's skinned knees, Heath extrapolated that she had had a biking accident.

incoherent
                                          in ko HAIR unt
lacking cohesion or connection

Maury's sentences were so incoherent that nobody understood a word.

insinuate
                                          in SIN yoo ayt
to introduce or communicate stealthily

Sean insinuated that Grace stole the arsenic, but he never came out and said it.

loquacious   low KWAY shus

very talkative

I'm not eloquent, so I'll just come out and say it: Bobby is loquacious and will talk, and talk, and talk.

lucid   LOO sid

easily understood; clear

Our teacher provides lucid explanations of even the most difficult concepts so that we can all understand them.

rhetoric   RET uh rik

the art of using language effectively and persuasively

Since they are expected to make speeches, most politicians and lawyers are well-versed in the art of rhetoric.

What's Up, Teach?

acumen   AK yoo men

quickness, accuracy, and keenness of judgment or insight

Judge Ackerman's legal acumen was so well regarded that he was nicknamed the "Solomon of the South."

adroit   uh DROYT

dexterous; deft

An adroit balloon-animal artist, Adrianna became popular at children's parties.

ascertain   as er TAYN

to find out, as through investigation or experimentation

The private investigator had long suspected my dog; before long, he ascertained that Toto was indeed the murderer.

astute   uh STOOT

shrewd; clever

Stewart is financially astute; he invests wisely and never falls for scams.

circumspect   SER kum spekt

careful; prudent; discreet

Ned's circumspect manner makes him a wise appointment to the diplomatic corps.

MATH

WRITING

READING

VOCABULARY

disseminate　　　　　　　　　　　　dis SEM uh nayt

to scatter widely, as in sowing seed

> The news about Dave's embarrassing moment at the party disseminated quickly through the school; by the end of the day, everyone knew what had happened.

erudition　　　　　　　　　　　　er yuh DISH un

deep, extensive learning

> Professor Rudy's erudition was such that she could answer any question her students put to her.

pedantic　　　　　　　　　　　　puh DAN tik

excessively concerned with book learning and formal rules

> Pedro's pedantic tendencies prompted him to remind us constantly of all the grammatical rules we were breaking.

perspicacious　　　　　　　　　　　　per spih KAY shus

shrewd; clear-sighted

> Persephone's perspicacious mind had solved so many cases that the popular private investigator was able to retire.

pragmatic　　　　　　　　　　　　prag MAT ik

practical

> Never one for wild and unrealistic schemes, Matt took a pragmatic approach to research.

precocious　　　　　　　　　　　　pre KO shus

exhibiting unusually early intellectual aptitude or maturity

> Bobby Fisher's precocious intellect made him one of the world's best chess players before he could even drive.

prolific　　　　　　　　　　　　PRO liff ick

very productive; producing great quantities

> Charles Harold St. John Hamilton was the world's most prolific author; it is estimated he wrote the equivalent of 1,000 novels.

prospectus　　　　　　　　　　　　pro SPEK tus

formal proposal

> Before writing my thesis, I had to submit a detailed prospectus to the department for approval.

rudimentary   roo duh MEN tuh ree
> *basic; elementary; in the earliest stages of development*
>> Josh's rudimentary golf skills were easily overpowered by Tiger Woods' amazing performance on the green.

When the Going Gets Tough

abstruse   ab STROOS
> *difficult to understand*
>> Abby found her professor's lecture on non-Euclidian geometry abstruse; she doubted anyone else in class understood it either.

callous   KAL us
> *emotionally hardened; unfeeling*
>> Callie's callous remark about her friend's cluttered room really hurt his feelings.

convoluted   kon vo LOO tid
> *intricate; complex*
>> The directions were so convoluted that we became hopelessly lost.

disaffected   DIS a fek ted
> *having lost faith or loyalty; discontent*
>> The disaffected cat trainer finally quit his job when he realized you just can't train cats, no matter how much you yell at them.

enigma   en IG ma
> *a puzzle, mystery, or riddle*
>> The emu was an enigma; you could never tell what it was thinking.

inscrutable   in SKROOT uh bul
> *difficult to fathom or understand; impenetrable*
>> The ancient poet's handwriting was so inscrutable that even the most prominent Latin scholars could not read the manuscript.

reticent   RET uh sint
> *inclined to keep silent; reserved*
>> Rosanna's reticent behavior caused the interviewer to think her incapable of conversing with other students.

staid   STAYD
> *unemotional; serious*
>> Mr. Estado was well known for his staid demeanor; he stayed calm even when everyone else celebrated the team's amazing victory.

Cultural Artifacts

arcane   ar KAYN
> *known or understood by only a few*
>> The dusty archive includes an arcane treasure trove of nautical charts from the Age of Discovery.

assimilate   uh SIM uh layt
> *to absorb or become absorbed; to make or become similar*
>> Keisha assimilated so quickly to her new school that she was named head of the social committee a month after enrolling.

autonomy   aw TAHN uh mee
> *independence; self-determination*
>> Candice gained autonomy upon moving out of her parents' house and into her own apartment.

cosmopolitan   koz mo PAHL i tun
> *worldly; widely sophisticated*
>> Inga was surprisingly cosmopolitan considering that she had never left her tiny hometown in Norway.

derivative (n)   duh RIV uh tiv
> *something that comes from another source*
>> *Special Victims Unit* and *Criminal Intent* are derivatives of the original *Law and Order* drama series.

esoteric   es oh TAIR ik
> *intended for or understood by only a small group*
>> Esme's play is extremely esoteric; someone not raised in Estonia would find it difficult to follow.

gaffe   GAF
> *a clumsy social error; a faux pas*
>> Geoff committed the gaffe of telling his date that he'd gone out with her sister the night before.

idiosyncrasy   ID ee oh SINK ruh see

characteristic peculiar to an individual or group

> She had many idiosyncrasies, one of which was washing her socks in the dishwasher.

insular   IN suh ler

isolated; narrow or provincial

> The family was so insular that no one else could get near them.

orthodox   OR thuh doks

adhering to the traditional and established, especially in religion

> My father held an orthodox view of baseball; he believed that the field should be outside and made of real grass.

potentate   PO tun tayt

one who has the power and position to rule over others; monarch

> An omnipotent potentate is a person to be reckoned with; great power in the hands of a great leader is a powerful combination.

Cast Out

castigate   KAS tih gayt

to scold, rebuke, or harshly criticize

> Mr. Castile preferred not to castigate student misbehavior publicly; instead, he would quietly send the troublemaker to the principal's office.

censure   SEN shur

to issue official blame

> In recent years the FCC has censured networks for the provocative antics of Super Bowl halftime acts; what goes on during the game, however, usually escapes the organization's notice.

denounce   duh NOWN(T)S

to condemn openly

> In many powerful speeches throughout his lifetime, Martin Luther King, Jr. denounced racism as immoral.

reclusive   ree KLOO siv

seeking or preferring seclusion or isolation

> Our neighbors were quite reclusive, hardly ever emerging from behind the closed doors of their home.

relinquish   ree LING kwish
> *to retire from; give up or abandon*

Ricky relinquished his career in order to search for the source of the world's best relish.

renounce   ree NOWN(T)S
> *to give up (a title, for example), especially by formal announcement*

Nancy renounced her given name and began selling records under the moniker "Boedicia."

vituperative   vie TOOP ur uh tiv
> *marked by harshly abusive condemnation*

The vituperative speech was so cruel that the members left feeling completely abused.

There's No Way Around It

circumscribe   SER kum skryb
> *to draw a circle around; to restrict*

The archeologist circumscribed the excavation area on the map.

contiguous   kun TIG yoo us
> *sharing an edge or boundary; touching*

The continental United States consists of 48 contiguous states.

WEEK 2

I'll Be the Judge of That!

conciliatory   kon SIL ee uh tor ee
appeasing; soothing; showing willingness to reconcile

> After arguing endlessly with them for weeks, Connie switched to a more conciliatory tone with her parents once prom season arrived.

credible   KRED uh bul
capable of being believed; plausible

> The shocking but credible report of mice in the kitchen kept Eddie up all night.

exonerate   eg ZON er ayt
to free from blame

> Xena was exonerated of all charges.

incontrovertible   in kahn truh VERT uh bul
indisputable; not open to question

> The videotape of the robbery provided incontrovertible evidence against the suspect—he was obviously guilty.

indict   in DITE
to officially charge with wrongdoing or a crime

> President Nixon's aides were indicted during the Watergate scandal.

litigious   luh TIJ us
prone to engage in lawsuits

> Letitia was a litigious little girl; at one point, she tried to sue her dog.

partisan (adj)   PAR tiz un
devoted to or biased in support of a party, group, or cause

> Today's partisan politics are so antagonistic that it's difficult to reach a successful compromise on any issue.

parity   PA ruh tee
equality, as in amount, status, or value (antonym: disparity)

> The judges at the Olympics must score each athlete's performance with parity; such impartial treatment is hard since one always wants to root for one's own country.

rectitude   REK ti tood
moral uprightness; righteousness

Thanks to his unerring sense of fairness and justice, Viktor was a model of moral rectitude; his hometown even erected a statue in his honor.

remiss   ree MISS
lax in attending to duty; negligent

Cassie was remiss in fulfilling her Miss America duties; she didn't even come close to ending world hunger.

repudiate   ree PYOO dee ayt
to reject the validity or authority of

I repudiated the teacher's arguments about Empress Wu Zetian's reputation by showing him that the reports of her cruelty were from unreliable sources.

sanctimonious   sank ti MO nee us
feigning piety or righteousness

The sanctimonious scholar had actually been plagiarizing other people's work for years.

scrupulous   SKROO pyoo lus
principled, having a strong sense of right and wrong; conscientious and exacting

Evan's scrupulous behavior began to annoy his friends when he called the cops on them for toilet papering their teacher's house.

solicitous   so LIS it us
concerned

The parents asked solicitous questions about the college admissions officer's family.

substantiate   sub STAN shee ayt
to support with proof or evidence; verify

The argument was substantiated by clear facts and hard evidence.

veracity   vuh RA si tee
adherence to the truth; truthfulness

Since Vera was known for her veracity, it came as a complete shock when her family found out she'd lied on her application.

vindicate   VIN dih kayt
to free from blame

Mrs. Layton was finally vindicated after her husband admitted to the crime.

Flattery Will Get You Nowhere

cajole   kuh JOL
to urge with repeated appeals, teasing, or flattery

The sweet-talking senior cajoled an impressionable junior into seeing *The Lord of the Rings* for the tenth time.

chicanery   chik AY ner ee
trickery

The candidate accused his debate opponent of resorting to cheap chicanery to sway the electorate.

obsequious   ob SEEK wee us
fawning and servile

Kevin was so obsequious that even his teachers were embarrassed; as a result, his sucking up rarely led to better grades.

sycophant   SIK uh fent
insincere, obsequious flatterer

Siggie is such a sycophant; he slyly sucks up to his teachers and reaps the rewards of his behavior.

One Person Can Change the World

altruism   AL troo iz im
unselfish concern for the welfare of others; selflessness

Alta, a model of altruism, gave her movie ticket to someone who needed it more.

eminent   EM uh nent
distinguished; prominent

Emeril Lagasse is one of the most eminent chefs working today; every TV watcher knows how well he is known and highly regarded.

empathetic   em puh THET ik
identifying with and understanding of another's situation, feelings, and motives

Emily is one of my most empathetic friends; she can always relate to my emotions.

extol   ek STOL
to praise highly

Tollivan extolled the virtues of the troll while his teacher looked on amazed.

laudatory   LAW duh tor ee
full of praise

The principal's speech was laudatory, congratulating the students on their SAT scores.

magnanimous   mag NAN uh mus
courageously or generously noble in mind and heart

The magnanimous prince cared deeply for his country and its people.

philanthropic   fil un THROP ik
humanitarian; benevolent; relating to monetary generosity

Phil was a philanthropic soul, always catering to the needy and the underprivileged.

reciprocate   ree SIP ro kayt
to mutually take or give; to respond in kind

The chef reciprocated his rival's respect; they admired each other so much that they even traded recipes.

Get Rid of It

defunct   duh FUNKT
no longer existing or functioning

The theory that the world was flat became defunct when Magellan sailed to the West and didn't fall off the earth.

eradicate   er RAD i kayt
to get rid of as if by tearing it up by the roots; abolish

Radcliffe did her best to eradicate the radishes from her farm.

quell   KWEL
to put down forcibly; suppress

Nell quelled the fight over the quiche by throwing it out the window—she had long given up on reasoning with her sisters.

raze   RAYZ
to level to the ground; demolish

It is difficult to raze a city building without demolishing other structures around it.

squelch   SKWELCH
to crush as if by trampling; squash

Sam wanted to keep squash as pets, but Quentin squelched the idea.

supplant   suh PLANT

to usurp the place of, especially through intrigue or underhanded tactics

> The ants prepared to supplant the roaches as the dominant insect in the kitchen; their plan was to take the roaches by surprise and drive them out.

stymie   STY mee

to thwart or stump

> Stan was stymied by the Sudoku puzzle; he just couldn't solve it.

If You Can't Say Anything Nice

abase   uh BAYS

to lower in rank, prestige, or esteem

> Bayard's withering restaurant review was an attempt to abase his former friend, the owner.

deride   duh RIDE

to mock contemptuously

> Derrick was derided for wearing two different colored socks, but he couldn't help it—it was laundry day.

derogatory   duh RAH guh tor ee

insulting or intended to insult

> The unethical politician didn't just attack his opponent's views; he also made derogatory remarks about the other candidate's family and personal hygiene.

disparage   dis PAR uj

to speak of negatively; to belittle

> Wanda disparaged Glen by calling him a cheat and a liar.

effrontery   eh FRON ter ee

brazen boldness; presumptuousness

> The attorney's effrontery in asking such personal questions so shocked Esther that she immediately ran from the office.

ignominy   IG nuh mi nee

great personal dishonor or humiliation; disgraceful conduct

> Ignacio felt great ignominy after the scandal broke.

MATH

WRITING

READING

·VOCABULARY·

impugn   im PYOON
> *to attack as false or questionable*

Instead of taking the high road, the candidate impugned his opponent's character.

mar   MAR
> *to damage, especially in a disfiguring way*

The perfect day was marred by the arrival of storm clouds.

pejorative (adj)   puh JOR uh tiv
> *disparaging, belittling, insulting*

Teachers should refrain from using pejorative terms such as "numbskull" and "jackass" to refer to other teachers.

vex   VEKS
> *to annoy or bother; to perplex*

Bex's mom was vexed when Bex was very vague about her whereabouts for the evening.

vindictive   vin DIK tiv
> *disposed to seek revenge; revengeful; spiteful*

Vincenzo was very vindictive; when someone hurt him, he responded by vigorously plotting revenge.

WEEK 3

Overkill

bombastic   bom BAS tik

given to pompous speech or writing

> The principal's bombastic speech bombed in the eyes of the students; it only furthered their impression of him as a pompous jerk.

ebullience   eh BOO li ents

intense enthusiasm

> A sense of ebullience swept over the lacrosse fans when their team won the game.

exorbitant   eg ZOR bit int

exceeding all bounds, as of custom or fairness

> I wanted to buy a Porsche, but the price was exorbitant; instead, I purchased a used mail truck.

exuberant   eg ZOO bur ent

full of unrestrained enthusiasm or joy

> William was exuberant when he found out that he'd gotten into the college of his choice.

embellish   em BELL ish

to ornament or decorate; to exaggerate

> One can never trust that Anwar's stories are realistic; his details are almost always embellished so that his experiences sound more interesting than they are in reality.

flagrant   FLAY grent

extremely or deliberately shocking or noticeable

> Burning the flag shows flagrant disrespect for the country.

gratuitous   gruh TOO uh tus

given freely; unearned; unnecessary

> The film was full of gratuitous sex and violence not essential to the story.

lavish (adj)   LAV ish

extravagant

> Lavanya's wedding was a lavish affair.

lugubrious   luh GOO bree yus
mournful, dismal, or gloomy, especially to an exaggerated or ludicrous degree
Lucas's lugubrious eulogy for his pet lobster quickly became ridiculous.

opulent   OP yoo lent
displaying great wealth
The ophthalmologist's opulent home was the envy of his friends; the crystal chandeliers, marble floors, and teak furniture must have cost a fortune.

ornate   or NAYT
elaborately decorated
The wood carvings were so ornate that you could examine them many times and still notice things you had not seen before.

penchant   PEN chent
a strong inclination or liking
Penny's penchant for chocolate-covered ants led her to munch on them all day.

redundant   ree DUN dint
needlessly repetitive
The author's speech was terribly redundant, repeating the same phrases, saying the same thing over and over, and constantly reiterating the same point.

ubiquitous   yoo BIK wit us
being or seeming to be everywhere at the same time; omnipresent
Kenny had a ubiquitous little sister; wherever he turned, there she was.

Through Someone Else's Eyes

vicarious   vie KA ree us
felt or undergone as if one were taking part in the experience or feelings of another
Stan, who was never athletic but loved sports, lived vicariously through his brother, a professional basketball player.

vignette   vin YET
a short scene or story
The poodle vignette in my new film expresses the true meaning of Valentine's Day.

Lots 'n' Lots

amalgam   uh MAL gum

a combination of diverse elements; a mixture

> The song was an amalgam of many different styles, from blues to hip-hop to folk.

inundate   IN un dayt

to overwhelm as if with a flood; to swamp

> The day after the ad ran, Martha was inundated with phone calls.

multifarious   mul ti FAYR ee us

diverse; various

> The multifarious achievements of Leonardo da Vinci—which range from architecture and painting to philosophy and science—are unparalleled in our century.

multiplicity   mul tuh PLI sit ee

state of being various or manifold; a great number

> A multiplicity of views is essential to a healthy multicultural democracy.

It's Getting Better All the Time

alleviate   uh LEE vee ayt

to ease a pain or burden

> Alvin meditated to alleviate the pain from the headache he got after taking the SAT.

beneficial   ben uh FISH ul

producing or promoting a favorable result; helpful

> According to my doctor, tea's beneficial effects may include reducing anxiety.

cathartic   kuh THAR tik

relaxing after an emotional outburst

> Cathy found that yelling at her idiotic coworkers for a while had a cathartic effect, and she was able to calmly go back to work.

curative   KYUR uh tiv

able to heal or cure

> The aloe had a curative effect on my sunburn; within hours, the flaking had stopped.

palliative   PAL lee uh tiv

relieving or soothing the symptoms of a disease or disorder without effecting a cure

> Watching professional polo on TV became a palliative for the screaming child; it was the only thing that would quiet him.

therapeutic   thair uh PYOO tik

having or exhibiting healing powers

> The therapeutic air of the Mediterranean Sea cured Thomas of his asthma.

Model Behavior

complement (n)   KOM plem ent

something that completes, goes with, or brings to perfection

> The lovely computer is the perfect complement to the modern furnishings in Abby's apartment.

epitome   ep IT o mee

a representative or example of a type

> She is the epitome of selflessness; no matter how much or little she has, she always gives to others.

felicitous   fuh LIH sih tus

admirably suited; apt

> Jamie Foxx made a felicitous speech when he won his Oscar.

Liar, Liar, Pants on Fire

belie   bee LIE

to misrepresent

> He smiled in order to belie his hostility.

debunk   dee BUNK

to expose untruths, shams, or exaggerated claims

> The university administration debunked the myth that bunk beds are only for children by installing them in every dorm on campus.

dubious   DOO bee us

doubtful; of unlikely authenticity

> Jerry's dubious claim that he could fly like Superman didn't win him any summer job offers.

duplicitous   doo PLIS uh tus

deliberately deceptive

> The duplicitous man duplicated dollars and gave the counterfeits to unsuspecting vendors.

fabricate   FAB ruh kayt

to make up in order to deceive

> Fabio fabricated the story that he used to play drums for Metallica; he has never actually held a drumstick in his life.

fallacy   FAL uh see

a false notion

> The idea that there is only one college for you is a fallacy.

mendacious   men DAY shus

lying; untruthful

> John's mendacious statements on the stand sealed his fate; he was found guilty of lying to the court about his role in the crime.

specious   SPEE shus

having the ring of truth or plausibility but actually false

> Susie's specious argument seemed to make sense, but when I looked more closely, it was clearly illogical.

Sittin' on the Fence

ambiguous   am BIG yoo us

open to more than one interpretation

> Big's eyes were an ambiguous color: in some lights, brown, and in others, green.

ambivalent   am BIV uh lint

simultaneously feeling opposing feelings; uncertain

> Amy felt ambivalent about her dance class: on one hand, she enjoyed the exercise; but on the other, the choice of dances bored her.

apathetic   ap uh THET ik

feeling or showing little emotion

> The apathetic students didn't even bother to vote for class president.

capricious　　　　　　　　　　　　　　kuh PREE shus

impulsive and unpredictable

The referee's capricious behavior angered the players; he would call a foul for minor contact, but ignore elbowing and kicking.

equivocal　　　　　　　　　　　　　　e KWIV uh kul

open to two or more interpretations and often intended to mislead; ambiguous (antonym: unequivocal)

The politician made so many equivocal statements during the scandal that no one could be sure of what, if anything, he had admitted to having done.

erratic　　　　　　　　　　　　　　e RAT ik

markedly inconsistent

Erroll's erratic behavior made it difficult for his friends to predict what he would do in a given moment.

impetuous　　　　　　　　　　　　　im PET choo us

suddenly and forcefully energetic or emotional; impulsive and passionate

Mr. Limpet was so impetuous that we never knew what he would do next.

impetus　　　　　　　　　　　　　IM pit us

an impelling force or stimulus

A looming deadline provided Imelda with the impetus she needed to finish her research paper.

sporadic　　　　　　　　　　　　　spo RAD ik

occurring at irregular intervals; having no pattern or order in time

Storms in Florida are sporadic; it's hard to predict when they're going to occur.

vacillate　　　　　　　　　　　　　VA sil ayt

to sway from one side to the other; oscillate

The cook vacillated between favoring chicken and preferring fish; he just couldn't decide which to prepare.

whimsical　　　　　　　　　　　　　WIM zi kul

characterized by whim; unpredictable

Egbert rarely behaved as expected; indeed, he was a whimsical soul whose every decision was anybody's guess.

I Just Can't Take It Anymore

flag (v)   FLAG
    to decline in vigor or strength; to tire; to droop

      After several few days climbing mountains in pouring rain, our enthusiasm for the hiking trip began to flag.

jaded   JAY did
    worn out; wearied

      Jade's experiences had jaded her; she no longer believed that the junk stacked in her garage was going to make her rich.

MATH

WRITING

READING

VOCABULARY

WEEK 4

She's Crafty

clandestine   klan DEST in

done secretively, especially to deceive; surreptitious

> I met the secret agent in an alleyway, where she handed me the plans for the clandestine operation.

ingenuous   in JEN yoo us

lacking in cunning, guile, or worldliness (antonym: disingenuous)

> Janine was so ingenuous that it was too easy for her friends to dupe her.

subterfuge   SUB ter fyoozh

a deceptive stratagem or device

> The submarine pilots were trained in the art of subterfuge; they were excellent at faking out their enemies.

surreptitious   sir up TISH us

secretive; sneaky

> Sara drank the cough syrup surreptitiously because she didn't want anyone to know that she was sick.

Just a Little Bit

dearth   DERTH

scarce supply; lack

> There was a dearth of money in my piggy bank; it collected dust, not bills.

modicum   MAHD ik um

a small, moderate, or token amount

> A modicum of effort may result in a small score improvement; in order to improve significantly, however, you must study as often as possible.

paucity   PAW sit ee

smallness in number; scarcity

> The struggling city had a paucity of resources and therefore a high level of poverty.

MATH

WRITING

READING

VOCABULARY

squander SKWAN der

to spend wastefully

Carrie squandered her savings on shoes and wasn't able to buy her apartment.

temperate TEM per ut

moderate; restrained (antonym: intemperate)

Temperate climates rarely experience extremes in temperature.

tenuous TEN yoo us

having little substance or strength; shaky

Her grasp on reality is tenuous at best; she's not even sure what year it is.

I Will Survive

diligent DIL uh jint

marked by painstaking effort; hardworking

With diligent effort, they were able to finish the model airplane in record time.

maverick MAV rik

one who is independent and resists adherence to a group

In the movie *Top Gun,* Tom Cruise played a maverick who often broke rules and did things his own way.

mercenary MUR sin air ee

motivated solely by a desire for money or material gain (when used as an adjective); a professional soldier (when used as a noun)

During the war, Mercer was a mercenary; he'd fight for whichever side paid him the most for his services.

obstinate OB stin it

stubbornly attached to an opinion or a course of action

Despite Jeremy's broken leg, his parents were obstinate; they steadfastly refused to buy him an Xbox.

proliferate pro LIF er ayt

to grow or increase rapidly

Because fax machines, pagers, and cell phones have proliferated in recent years, many new area codes have been created to handle the demand for phone numbers.

tenacity   te NAS uh tee
    persistence

    With his overwhelming tenacity, Clark was finally able to interview Brad Pitt for the school newspaper.

vigilant   VIJ uh lent
    on the alert; watchful

    The participants of the candlelight vigil were vigilant, as they had heard that the fraternity across the street was planning to egg them.

Connect the Dots

extraneous   ek STRAY nee us
    irrelevant; inessential

    The book, though interesting, had so much extraneous information that it was hard to keep track of the important points.

juxtapose   JUK stuh pohz
    to place side by side, especially for comparison or contrast

    Separately the pictures look identical, but if you juxtapose them, you can see the differences.

novel (adj)   NOV il
    fresh; original; new

    It was a novel idea, the sort of thing no one had tried before.

superfluous   soo PUR floo us
    extra; unnecessary

    If there is sugar in your tea, honey would be superfluous.

synergy   SIN er jee
    combined action or operation

    The synergy of hydrogen and oxygen creates water.

tangential   tan JEN chul
    merely touching or slightly connected; only superficially relevant

    Though Abby's paper was well written, its thesis was so tangential to its proof that her teacher couldn't give her a good grade.

I Write the Songs

aesthetic   es THET ik
having to do with the appreciation of beauty

>   Aesthetic considerations determined the arrangement of paintings at the museum;
>   as long as art looked good together, it didn't matter who had painted it.

aural   AW rul
of or related to the ear or the sense of hearing

>   It should come as no surprise that musicians prefer aural to visual learning.

cacophony   kuh KAH fuh nee
discordant, unpleasant noise

>   Brian had to shield his ears from the awful cacophony produced by the punk
>   band on stage.

dirge   DERJ
a funeral hymn or lament

>   The dirge was so beautiful that everyone cried, even those who hadn't known
>   the deceased.

eclectic   ee KLEK tik
made up of a variety of sources or styles

>   Lou's taste in music is quite eclectic; he listens to everything from rap to polka.

incongruous   in KAHN groo us
lacking in harmony; incompatible

>   My chicken and jello soup experiment failed; the tastes were just too
>   incongruous.

sonorous   SAHN ur us
producing a deep or full sound

>   My father's sonorous snoring keeps me up all night unless I close my door and
>   wear earplugs.

strident   STRY dent
loud, harsh, grating, or shrill

>   The strident shouting kept the neighbors awake all night.

© TPR Education IP Holdings, LLC

Dude, This Sucks!

debacle   duh BAHK ul
disastrous or ludicrous defeat or failure; fiasco

> Jim's interview was a complete debacle; he accidentally locked himself in the bathroom, sneezed on the interviewer multiple times, and knocked over the president of the company.

debilitate   duh BIL i tayt
impair the strength of; weaken

> Deb ran the New York City marathon without proper training; the experience left her debilitated for weeks.

tumultuous   tum UL choo us
noisy and disorderly

> The tumultuous applause was so deafening that the pianist couldn't hear the singer.

It's All in the Timing

anachronistic   ah nak ruh NIS tik
the representation of something as existing or happening in the wrong time period

> I noticed an anachronism in the museum's ancient Rome display: a digital clock ticking behind a statue of Venus.

archaic   ar KAY ik
characteristic of an earlier time; antiquated; old

> "How dost thou?" is an archaic way of saying "How are you?"

dilatory   DIL uh tor ee
habitually late

> Always waiting until the last moment to leave home in the morning, Dylan was a dilatory student.

ephemeral   uh FEM er ul
lasting for only a brief time

> The importance of SAT scores is truly ephemeral; when you are applying, they are crucial, but once you get into college, no one cares how well you did.

redolent   RED uh lint
> *fragrant; aromatic; suggestive*
>> The aroma of apple pie wafted into my room, redolent of weekends spent baking with my grandmother.

temporal   TEM per ul
> *of, relating to, or limited by time*
>> One's enjoyment of a Starbucks mocha latte is bound by temporal limitations; all too soon, the latte is gone.

Who Can It Be Now?

onerous   O ner us
> *troublesome or oppressive; burdensome*
>> The onerous task was so difficult that Ona thought she'd never get through it.

portent   POR tent
> *indication of something important or calamitous about to occur; omen*
>> A red morning sky is a terrible portent for all sailors—it means that stormy seas are ahead.

prescience   PREH shens
> *knowledge of actions or events before they occur; foreknowledge; foresight*
>> Preetha's prescience was such that people wondered if she was psychic; how else could she know so much about the future?

Boooring!

austere   aw STEER
> *without decoration; strict*
>> The gray walls and bare floors of his monastery cell provided an even more austere setting than Brother Austen had hoped for.

banal   buh NAL
> *drearily commonplace; predictable; trite*
>> The poet's imagery is so banal that I think she cribbed her work from *Poetry for Dummies.*

hackneyed   HAK need

worn out through overuse; trite

All Hal could offer in the way of advice were hackneyed old phrases that I'd already heard a hundred times before.

insipid   in SIP id

uninteresting; unchallenging; lacking taste or savor

That insipid movie was so predictable that I walked out.

prosaic   pro ZAY ik

unimaginative; dull (antonym: poetic)

Rebecca made a prosaic mosaic consisting of identical, undecorated tiles.

soporific   sah puh RIF ik

inducing or tending to induce sleep

The congressman's speech was so soporific that even his cat was yawning.

vapid   VAP id

lacking liveliness, animation, or interest; dull

Valerie's date was so vapid that she thought he was sleeping with his eyes open.

WEEK 5

It All Changes So Fast

brevity   BRE vi tee

the quality or state of being brief in duration

Brevity = briefness. (You can't get any shorter than that!)

expedient   ek SPEE dee ent

appropriate to a purpose; convenient; speedy

It was more expedient to use Federal Express than to use the post office.

transient   TRAN zhent

passing quickly in time or space

Jack Dawson enjoyed his transient lifestyle; with nothing but the clothes on his back and the air in his lungs, he was free to travel wherever he wanted.

Full On

augment   awg MENT

to make greater, as in size, extent, or quantity; to supplement

> The model Angele Franju is rumored to have augmented her studies in chemistry with a minor in German literature.

bolster   BOWL ster

to hearten, support, or prop up

> The class bolstered Amelia's confidence; she had no idea she already knew so much.

burgeon   BER jun

to grow and flourish

> The burgeoning Burgess family required a new house because its old one only had one bedroom.

copious   KO pee us

plentiful; having a large quantity

> She took copious notes during class, using up five large notebooks.

distend   dis TEND

to swell out or expand from internal pressure, as when overly full

> The balloon distended as it was filled with helium, much like Mike's stomach after Mike ate an entire turkey on Thanksgiving.

grandiose   gran dee OHS

great in scope or intent; grand

> The party was a grandiose affair; hundreds of richly dressed guests danced the night away.

prodigious   pruh DIJ us

enormous

> Steven Spielberg's prodigious talent has made Spielberg the most successful film producer and director of our time.

profundity   pro FUN di tee

great depth of intellect, feeling, or meaning

> The actor's profundity surprised the director, who had heard that he was a bit of an airhead.

redouble   ree DUB ul
to make twice as great; to double

Rita redoubled her efforts to become president of her class by campaigning twice as hard as before.

scintillating   SIN til ay ting
brilliant

The writer's scintillating narrative diverted Isabel's attention away from her other guests.

Don't Make Waves

averse   uh VERS
strongly disinclined

Ava proved so averse to homework that she would break out in hives at the mere mention of it.

conspicuous   kun SPIK yoo us
easy to notice; obvious (antonym: inconspicuous)

The red tuxedo was conspicuous among all the classic black ones. What was he thinking?

demure   duh MYUR
modest and reserved

Muriel was the most demure girl in the class, always sitting quietly in the back of the room and downplaying any compliments she received.

diffidence   DIF uh dins
timidity or shyness

Lea's diffident nature often prevented her from speaking out in class.

docile   DAHS i ul
submissive to instruction; willing to be taught

The SAT class was so docile that the teacher wondered if she was in the right room.

innocuous   in NAHK yoo us
having no adverse effect; harmless

The plants were as innocuous as they looked; we suffered no ill effects from eating their leaves.

placid   PLAS id
> calm or quiet; undisturbed

> Lake Placid was the place to go for those in need of a quiet vacation.

quiescent   kwee ES sint
> quiet, still, or at rest; inactive

> Quinn's quiescent behavior made him an ideal roommate.

Do You Agree?

concord   KON kord
> agreement (antonym: discord)

> The class was in concord about the necessity to perform *Hamlet,* rather than *King Lear,* in the spring show.

concur   kun KUR
> to agree

> The board concurred that the con artist who had stolen their money had to be convicted.

dogmatic   dog MAT ik
> stubbornly attached to insufficiently proven beliefs

> Avik was dogmatic in his belief that the power lines were giving his dog headaches.

fastidious   fas TID ee us
> carefully attentive to detail; difficult to please

> Kelly, always so fastidious, dramatically edited our group's report.

intransigence   in TRAN zi jents
> refusal to moderate a position or to compromise

> Jeff was so intransigent in his views that it was impossible to have a rational debate with him.

jocular   JOK yoo ler
> characterized by or given to joking

> Yung-Ji's jocular disposition helped him gain popularity.

meticulous   muh TIK yoo lus

extremely careful and precise

Since Kelly was so meticulous, we asked her to proofread our group's report.

Officer Friendly

affable   AF uh bul

easygoing; friendly

My mom always said that the key to being affable is the ability to make others laugh.

alacrity   uh LAK ruh tee

promptness in response; cheerful readiness; eagerness

I was so happy when I got the acceptance letter from the University of Alaska that I sprinted home with great alacrity to share the good news.

amiable   AY mee uh bul

friendly; agreeable; good-natured

Mr. Amis was so amiable that he let us call him "Big A."

benign   be NINE

kind and gentle

Uncle Ben is a benign and friendly man who is always willing to help.

sanguine   SAN gwin

cheerfully confident; optimistic

Harold's sanguine temperament kept him cheerful, even through somber times.

Nasty Boys

belligerent   buh LIH jer int

eager to fight; hostile or aggressive

The prosecutor was reprimanded for his belligerent cross-examination of the witness, who had dissolved into tears.

cantankerous   kan TANK er us

ill-tempered and quarrelsome; disagreeable

The dog hid under the tank as a result of the cat's cantankerous disposition.

MATH

WRITING

READING

VOCABULARY

contentious　　　　　　　　　　　kun TEN shus

quarrelsome

The contentious debate over science class content is increasingly making the news.

deleterious　　　　　　　　　　　dil uh TER ee us

having a harmful effect

It was only once he started his test that Murray realized the deleterious effects of one too many Red Bulls; he couldn't concentrate and his hands were shaking so much he could barely write.

exacerbate　　　　　　　　　　　eg ZA ser bayt

to increase the severity, violence, or bitterness of; aggravate

Alan's procrastination problems were exacerbated by the monkeys who kept throwing bananas at him while he tried to concentrate.

flippant　　　　　　　　　　　FLIP ent

disrespectfully humorous or casual

Flap's flippant remarks to the teacher got him sent to the principal's office.

insolent　　　　　　　　　　　IN suh lint

insulting in manner or speech

The insolent prime minister stuck her tongue out at the queen.

nefarious　　　　　　　　　　　nuh FAYR ee us

flagrantly wicked; vicious

Dorothy's kindness and bravery triumphed over the nefarious antics of the Wicked Witch of the West.

pernicious　　　　　　　　　　　per NISH us

extremely or irrevocably harmful; deadly

The fertilizer's pernicious effects were not immediately obvious, but researchers became suspicious when all their petunias died.

rancorous　　　　　　　　　　　RANK er us

marked by bitter, deep-seated ill-will

They had such a rancorous relationship that no one could believe that they had ever gotten along.

repugnant　　　　　　　　　　　ree PUG nent

arousing disgust or aversion; offensive or repulsive

The pug's behavior at the dog park was repugnant, causing other dogs to avoid him altogether.

supercilious   SUPE er sil lee us

disdainful; haughty; arrogant

The supercilious nobleman traveled through the town with a haughty expression, sneering at the peasants as he was carried past them.

Earth, Wind, and Fire

arboreal   ar BOR ee ul

relating to or resembling a tree or trees

The Rocky Mountain National Forest will celebrate its arboreal splendor with an Arbor Day concert.

invocation (n)   in vo KAY shun

a call (usually upon a higher power) for assistance, support, or inspiration

The group invoked the god of war as their protector on the field of battle.

stratify   STRAT i fy

to layer or separate into layers

Jonas studied the stratified bedrock and was able to see which time periods went with which layers.

variegated   VAR ee ih gay tid

having streaks, marks, or patches of a different color or colors; varicolored

The wood's markings were so variegated that Mr. Vargas assumed they had been painted on.

verdant   VUR dent

green with vegetation

The garden was verdant after the rain.

HIT PARADE ALPHABETICAL LIST

abase	to lower in rank, prestige, or esteem
abstruse	difficult to understand
acumen	quickness, accuracy, and keenness of judgment or insight
adroit	dexterous; deft
aesthetic	having to do with the appreciation of beauty
affable	easygoing; friendly
alacrity	cheerful willingness; eagerness
alleviate	to ease a pain or a burden
altruism	unselfish concern for the welfare of others; selflessness
amalgam	a combination of diverse elements; a mixture
ambiguous	open to more than one interpretation
ambivalent	simultaneously feeling opposing feelings; uncertain
amiable	friendly and agreeable in disposition; good-natured and likable
anachronistic	the representation of someone as existing or something as happening in other than chronological, proper, or historical order
apathetic	feeling or showing little emotion
arboreal	relating to or resembling a tree
arcane	known or understood by only a few
archaic	characteristic of an earlier period; old-fashioned
ascertain	to discover with certainty, as through examination or experimentation
assimilate	incorporated and absorbed into the mind; made similar; caused to resemble
astute	shrewd; clever
augment	to make (something already developed or well under way) greater, as in size, extent, or quantity
aural	of, relating to, or perceived by the ear
austere	without decoration; strict
autonomy	independence; self-determination; self-government or the right of self-government
averse	strongly disinclined
banal	drearily commonplace and often predictable; trite
belie	to picture falsely; misrepresent
belligerent	inclined or eager to fight; hostile or aggressive
beneficial	producing or promoting a favorable result; advantageous
benign	kind and gentle
bolster	to buoy up or hearten; to support or prop up
bombastic	given to pompous speech or writing
brevity	the quality or state of being brief in duration

burgeon	to grow and flourish; to put forth new buds, leaves, or greenery; sprout
cacophony	jarring, discordant sound; dissonance
cajole	to urge with gentle and repeated appeals, teasing, or flattery
callous	emotionally hardened; unfeeling
candid	characterized by openness and sincerity of expression; unreservedly straightforward
cantankerous	ill-tempered and quarrelsome; disagreeable
capricious	impulsive and unpredictable
castigate	to inflict severe punishment on
cathartic	causing relaxation after an emotional outburst
censure	to criticize severely; blame
chicanery	a trick; deception by trickery
circumscribe	to draw a circle around; to restrict
circumspect	heedful of circumstances and potential consequences; prudent
clandestine	done secretively, especially to deceive; surreptitious
complement	something that completes, makes up a whole, or brings to perfection
conciliatory	appeasing; soothing; pleasant
concord	agreement (antonym: discord)
concur	to agree; to be of the same opinion
conjecture	inference or judgment based on inconclusive or incomplete evidence; guesswork
conspicuous	easy to notice; obvious (antonym: inconspicuous)
contentious	quarrelsome
contiguous	sharing an edge or boundary; touching
convoluted	intricate; complex
copious	plentiful; having a large quantity
cosmopolitan	so sophisticated as to be at home in all parts of the world or conversant with many spheres of interest; pertinent or common to the whole world
credible	capable of being believed; plausible
curative	something that cures; a remedy
dearth	a scarce supply; a lack
debacle	a sudden, disastrous collapse, downfall, or defeat; a rout
debilitate	to sap the strength or energy of; enervate
debunk	to expose or ridicule falseness, shams, or exaggerated claims
defunct	having ceased to exist or live
deleterious	having a harmful effect
demure	modest and reserved in manner or behavior
denounce	to condemn openly as being evil or reprehensible
deride	to speak of or treat with contemptuous mirth

MATH

WRITING

READING

VOCABULARY

derivative	a by-product
derogatory	tending or intending to belittle
didactic	intended to instruct
diffidence	timidity or shyness
dilatory	habitually late
diligent	marked by painstaking effort; hard-working
dirge	a funeral hymn or lament
disaffected	having lost faith or loyalty; discontent
disparage	to speak of in a slighting way or negatively; to belittle
disseminate	to scatter widely, as in sowing seed
distend	to swell out or expand from or as if from internal pressure
docile	ready and willing to be taught; teachable
dogmatic	stubbornly adhering to insufficiently proved beliefs
dubious	doubtful; of unlikely authenticity
duplicitous	given to or marked by deliberate deceptiveness in behavior or speech
ebullience	intense enthusiasm
eclectic	made up of a variety of sources or styles
effrontery	brazen boldness; presumptuousness
effusive	showing excessive emotion; overflowing
embellish	to make beautiful by ornamenting; to decorate
eminent	distinguished; prominent
empathetic	identification with and understanding of another's situation, feelings, and motives
enigma	one that is puzzling, ambiguous, or inexplicable; a riddle
ephemeral	lasting for only a brief time
epitome	a representative or example of a class or type
equivocal	open to two or more interpretations and often intended to mislead; ambiguous (antonym: unequivocal)
eradicate	to get rid of as if by tearing it up by the roots; abolish
erratic	having no fixed or regular course; wandering
erudition	deep, extensive learning
esoteric	intended for or understood by only a particular group
euphemism	the act or an example of substituting a mild, indirect, or vague term for one considered harsh, blunt, or offensive
exacerbate	to increase the severity, violence, or bitterness of; aggravate
exonerate	to free from blame
exorbitant	exceeding all bounds, as of custom or fairness
expedient	appropriate to a purpose; speedy
extol	to praise highly

extraneous	irrelevant
extrapolate	to infer or estimate by extending or projecting known information
exuberant	full of unrestrained enthusiasm or joy
fabricate	to make in order to deceive
fallacy	a false notion
fastidious	possessing careful attention to detail; difficult to please
felicitous	admirably suited; apt
flag (v.)	to decline in vigor or strength; to hang limply; droop
flagrant	extremely or deliberately shocking or noticeable
flippant	marked by disrespectful levity or casualness; pert
gaffe	a clumsy social error; a faux pas
grandiose	characterized by greatness of scope or intent; grand
gratuitous	given freely; unearned; unwarranted
hackneyed	worn-out through overuse; trite
idiosyncrasy	a structural or behavioral characteristic peculiar to an individual or group
ignominy	great personal dishonor or humiliation
impetuous	characterized by sudden and forceful energy or emotion; impulsive and passionate
impetus	an impelling force; an impulse
impugn	to attack as false or questionable
incoherent	lacking cohesion, connection, or harmony
incongruous	lacking in harmony; incompatible
incontrovertible	indisputable; not open to question
indict	to accuse of wrongdoing; charge
ingenuous	lacking in cunning, guile, or worldliness; artless (antonym: disingenuous)
innocuous	having no adverse effect; harmless
inscrutable	difficult to fathom or understand; impenetrable
insinuate	to introduce or otherwise convey gradually and insidiously
insipid	uninteresting; unchallenging
insolent	insulting in manner or speech
insular	suggestive of the isolated life of an island; narrow or provincial
intransigence	refusing to moderate a position, especially an extreme position; uncompromising
inundate	to overwhelm as if with a flood; to swamp
invocation	to call on (a higher power) for assistance, support, or inspiration
jaded	worn out; wearied
jocular	characterized by or given to joking
juxtapose	to place side by side, especially for comparison or contrast
laudatory	giving praise

MATH

WRITING

READING

VOCABULARY

lavish	characterized by or produced with extravagance and abundance
litigious	tending to engage in lawsuits
loquacious	very talkative
lucid	easily understood; clear
lugubrious	mournful, dismal, or gloomy, especially to an exaggerated or ludicrous degree
magnanimous	courageously noble in mind and heart
mar	to inflict damage, especially disfiguring damage, on
maverick	one who is independent and resists adherence to a group
mendacious	lying; untruthful
mercenary	motivated solely by a desire for monetary or material gain (adjective); a professional soldier (noun)
meticulous	extremely careful and precise
modicum	a small, moderate, or token amount
multifarious	having great variety; diverse
multiplicity	the state of being various or manifold
nefarious	infamous by way of being extremely wicked
novel	fresh; original; new
obsequious	full of or exhibiting servile compliance; fawning
obstinate	stubbornly adhering to an opinion or a course of action
onerous	troublesome or oppressive; burdensome
opulent	exhibiting a display of great wealth
ornate	elaborately decorated
orthodox	adhering to the accepted or traditional and established faith, especially in religion
palliative	relieving or soothing the symptoms of a disease or disorder without effecting a cure
parity	equality, as in amount, status, or value (antonym: disparity)
partisan	devoted to or biased in support of a party, group, or cause
paucity	smallness of number; fewness
pedantic	characterized by a narrow, often ostentatious concern for book learning and formal rules
pejorative	describing words or phrases that belittle or speak negatively of someone
penchant	a definite liking; a strong inclination
pernicious	tending to cause death or serious injury; deadly
perspicacious	having or showing penetrating mental discernment; clear-sighted
philanthropic	humanitarian; benevolent
placid	calm or quiet; undisturbed by tumult or disorder
portent	an indication of something important or calamitous about to occur; an omen
potentate	one who has the power and position to rule over others; a monarch

MATH

WRITING

READING

VOCABULARY

pragmatic	practical
precocious	manifesting or characterized by unusually early development or maturity, especially in mental aptitude
prescience	knowledge of actions or events before they occur; foresight
prodigious	enormous
profundity	great depth of intellect, feeling, or meaning
proliferate	to grow or increase rapidly
prolific	very productive; producing great quantities
prosaic	unimaginative; dull
prospectus	a formal summary of a proposed venture or project
quell	to put down forcibly; suppress
quiescent	being quiet, still, or at rest; inactive
rancorous	hateful; marked by deep seated ill-will
raze	to level to the ground; demolish
reciprocate	to mutually take or give
reclusive	seeking or preferring seclusion or isolation
rectitude	moral uprightness; righteousness
redolent	having or emitting fragrance; aromatic; suggestive, reminiscent
redouble	to become twice as great
redundant	needlessly wordy or repetitive in expression
relinquish	to retire from; give up or abandon
remiss	lax in attending to duty; negligent
renounce	to give up (a title, for example), especially by formal announcement
repudiate	to reject the validity or authority of
repugnant	arousing disgust or aversion; offensive or repulsive
reticent	inclined to keep one's thoughts, feelings, and personal affairs to oneself
rhetoric	the art of using language effectively and persuasively
rudimentary	of or relating to basic facts or principles; elementary; being in the earliest stages of development
sanctimonious	feigning piety or righteousness
sanguine	of a healthy reddish color; ruddy; cheerfully confident; optimistic
scintillating	brilliant
scrupulous	principled, having a strong sense of right and wrong; conscientious and exacting
solicitous	anxious or concerned
sonorous	producing a deep or full sound
soporific	inducing or tending to induce sleep
specious	having the ring of truth or plausibility but actually not true
sporadic	occurring at irregular intervals; having no pattern or order in time
squander	to spend wastefully or extravagantly; dissipate

squelch	to crush by or as if by trampling; squash
staid	unemotional; serious
stratify	to form, arrange, or deposit in layers
strident	loud, harsh, grating, or shrill; discordant
stymie	to thwart; stump
substantiate	to support with proof or evidence; verify
subterfuge	a deceptive stratagem or device
supercilious	disdainful; haughty; arrogant
superfluous	extra; unnecessary
supplant	to usurp the place of, especially through intrigue or underhanded tactics
surreptitious	done by secretive means
sycophant	a servile self-seeker who attempts to win favor by flattering influential people
synergy	the interaction of two or more agents or forces so that their combined effect is greater than the sum of their individual effects
tangential	merely touching or slightly connected; only superficially relevant
temperate	moderate in degree or quality; restrained (antonym: intemperate)
temporal	of, relating to, or limited by time
tenacity	persistence
tenuous	having little substance or strength; shaky
therapeutic	having or exhibiting healing powers
transient	passing away with time; passing from one place to another
tumultuous	noisy and disorderly
ubiquitous	being or seeming to be everywhere at the same time; omnipresent
vacillate	to sway from one side to the other; oscillate
vapid	lacking liveliness, animation, or interest; dull
variegated	having streaks, marks, or patches of a different color or colors; varicolored
veracity	adherence to the truth; truthfulness
verdant	green with vegetation; covered with green growth
vex	to annoy or bother; to perplex
vicarious	felt or undergone as if one were taking part in the experience or feelings of another
vigilant	on the alert; watchful
vignette	a short scene or incident, as from a movie
vindicate	to free from blame
vindictive	disposed to seek revenge; revengeful; spiteful
vituperative	using, containing, or marked by harshly abusive censure
whimsical	subject to erratic behavior; unpredictable

MATH

WRITING

READING

VOCABULARY

MORE VOCABULARY

MASTER ROOT LIST

a-	negative prefix	duc/dul-	lead
ab-	away from/negative prefix	dys-	faulty, bad
ac/acr-	sharp	e/ex/ej-	out, outward
ad/at-	to, toward	en/em-	into
amb-	go/walk	epi-	upon
ambi-	both/mixed	equ/equi-	equal
ami/amo-	love	esce-	becoming
an/anti-	against	eu-	good, pleasant
andr-	human, male	extr-	outside, beyond, additional
anim-	life, spirit	fac/fic/fig-	do, make
ante-	before	fer/ferr-	strong, iron-like
anthr-	human	fid-	faithful
apt/ept-	skill, ability	fort-	strong
arbo-	tree	fract-	break, split
arch-	rule, over	frat-	brother
aud-	sound	fren-	highly energetic
auto-	self	gen-	birth, creation, kind, type
bell/belli-	war	geo-	earth
ben/bono-	good	gno/kno-	know
bi-	two	grand-	big
bio/bios-	life	graph-	write
bra-	arm	grat-	grateful
carn-	meat, flesh	gress-	step
cent-	hundred	gust-	taste
chron-	time	gyn-	female
circ/circu-	around	hemi-	half, split part
cis/cise-	cut	her/hes-	stick (on)
cli-	lean	herb-	plant
clu/clo/cla	close, shut	hetero-	different, mixed
co/com/con	with, together	hex/sex-	six
contr-	against	homo-	same
cred-	believe	hyd/hydr-	water
culp-	blame	hyper-	over, beyond
cur/cour-	run (a course)	hypo-	under, insufficient
de-	away from/opposite, of	il-	not
dec/deci-	ten	im-	not, into
dent-	teeth	in-	not, into
derm-	skin	inter-	between
desc-	down	intra-	within
dext-	dexterity, ability	itis-	inflammation, infection
di-	two, apart, split	ium-	place, building of
dic/dict-	say, tell	jeu/ju-	play, youthful
dign/dain-	worth	jaun-	yellow
digt-	finger, digit	lab/labo-	work
dis-	apart from, not	laud-	praise
domi-	rule over	lav-	wash
dorm-	sleep	lev-	rise

log/loqui-	to speak
lu/luc/lum-	light
mag/magna-	great
mal-	bad
man/manu-	hand
mar/mer-	sea
matr-	mother
met/meter	measure
meta	more, beyond
mic/micro-	tiny
mill-	thousand
mis-	wrong, bad
mit-	send
mob/mobi-	moving
mor/mort-	death
morph-	change (shape)
mut-	change, alter
nat/natu-	natural, birth
neg-	negative
neo/nov-	new
noct-	night
nom/nym-	name
non/not-	negative prefix
nounce-	call
nox/nec-	harmful
ob-	against
olfac-	smell
ology-	study of
omni-	all, every
ory-	place of
pac/pax/plac-	peace, pleasing
pan	all, everywhere
par	equal
para-	beyond
path-	feeling, emotion
patr-	father
pen/pend-	weight
pent-	five
peri-	around
pet/pec-	small
phil-	love, high regard
phob-	fear
phon-	sound
pod/ped-	foot
pon/pos-	place, put
port-	carry
post-	after
poten-	power, influence
pre-	before
pro-	for

prox-	near
pseudo-	false
pug-	fighting
quad-	four
qui-	quiet
quint-	five
re-	again
schi-	split
sci/scien	knowledge
scop-	see
scrib/scrip-	write
sec/sequ-	follow, come after
sed/sid-	sit, be still
solo-	alone
son/soni-	sound
soro-	sister
spec/spic-	see, look
sta/sti-	still, unmoving
sua-	smooth
sub-	under
super-	beyond, greater than
syn/sym-	bring together
tact-	touch
tech/techn-	tools
tele-	at a distance
temp-	time
ten/tend-	hold
terr-	earth, ground
tox-	harmful, poisonous
tract-	pull
trans-	across
trep-	fear, anxiety
tri-	three
un-	not
uni/uno-	one
us/ut-	use
val/vale-	value, feel
vend-	sell
ver/vera/veri-	true
verd-	green
verge-	boundary, together
verse-	turn
vete-	experienced
vi/vit/viv-	alive
vid/vis-	see
voc-	call, talk
vor-	eat, consume

TOO MUCH IS NEVER ENOUGH: THE MONSTER LIST

So you've mastered all 250 words in the Hit Parade, have you? If so, onward and upward! Here is a list of an additional 400+ words that have appeared on SATs in the past three years. While they are less common than the Hit Parade words, these words—once mastered—will give you an even bigger leg up on the SAT.

abate	calumny	demagogue	felicitous
aberration	capacious	demurral	fiasco
abjure	catalyst	denigrated	finagle
abridge	cavort	denude	flotilla
acrid	chicanery	depravity	flourish
acrimony	chronic	depreciatory	foible
adept	circuitous	derelict	foppish
affectation	circumvent	dilapidated	fortitude
aghast	cloying	dilettante	founder
agnostic	coerced	din	frivolous
allocate	cogent	disarming	fulsome
anomaly	commodity	disincline	furtiveness
antipathy	compendious	disinterested	futile
antiseptic	complacence	disjointed	gaffe
antithesis	complicity	dispatch	gaiety
apportionment	condone	dispensation	gait
approbation	conferred	disperse	gallantry
appropriate (v.)	conflagration	disputation	galled
apt	congenial	distillation	galvanize
arable	conglomeration	divisive	garish
archipelago	conjure	doctrinaire	garner
arid	conscript	doggerel	garrulous
ascetic	consonance	dormant	gaunt
aspersion	contiguous	dour	gibe
atrophy	convergence	effacement	gregarious
attenuate	convivial	empirical	guileless
audacious	corollary	encumbrance	haranguing
avant-garde	corpulence	endemic	harbinger
avarice	corroborate	enervated	hermetic
averse	courtier	epitaph	heterogeneity
balm	culpability	equanimity	histrionic
baneful	cumulative	equivocal	holistic
barrage	curtail	eschew	hubris
bellicose	dalliance	excise	iconoclast
benefactor	daunting	exculpate	illicit
benevolent	decorous	exemplar	immaterial
blandish	decried	expedient	immutable
blatant	defamation	expropriation	imperious
brandish	deferment	facetious	impervious
bravado	deleterious	facile	impetus
buttress	delineation	faction	imprudent
cadent	deluge	feign	inane

inchoate
incisive
inconspicuous
incredulous
indigence
indigenous
indiscriminate
indolence
indomitable
induction
industrious
ineffable
inexorable
infamous
infelicity
ingenious
ingénue
innate
insidious
insolvent
instigation
insurrection
intermittent
interpolated
invective
invidious
iridescent
irreproachable
irresolute
itinerant
knave
labyrinth
laconic
lament
languid
latency
lethargic
libelous
lilt
lionize
lithe
lurid
machination
magisterial
malevolence
malicious
malign
manifesto
mediate

mélange
mire
mirth
miser
missive
mitigate
monotonous
motley
mundane
munificent
myopic
naïveté
nebulous
negate
nominal
nonchalance
notoriety
obstreperous
obtuse
occlusion
odoriferous
officious
opacity
oscillate
ossified
ostensible
ostentation
pallid
panacea
pander
panoramic
paradigm
paragon
parity
pathos
patronage
pedagogical
pedestrian
pensiveness
penurious
peripheral
perjure
perpetuate
perquisite
petulant
phlegmatic
pillory
placebo
plasticity

plaudit
plebian
plenitude
pluralistic
polarize
portent
posthumous
potentate
precarious
precedent
precept
precipitous
preclude
predilection
preeminent
premeditated
preponderance
prerogative
prescience
prevaricate
prodigious
profligate
profusion
propensity
punctilious
pundit
pungency
quagmire
quandary
querulous
quixotic
rambunctious
rapport
rapture
raucous
recalcitrant
recessive
recommence
recrimination
redoubtable
refute
relegate
remuneration
reparation
repartee
repertory
reprieve
requite
resolute

respite
resplendent
retraction
retroactive
risqué
rousing
ruffian
sacrosanct
sagacious
salient
sallow
salutary
salvo
sate
savant
scarce
scourge
scuttle
seditious
sedulous
serpentine
sibilant
slander
solace
somber
sophomoric
spate
spurious
spurned
squalid
stark
staunch
stoic
stolid
subversive
succinct
succulent
sullen
sumptuous
supple
surfeit
surmise
tacit
tactile
tangible
taut
teem
temper
tempest

MATH

WRITING

READING

VOCABULARY

temporal
temporize
tenet
terse
thwart
toady
topography
tortuous
touchstone
tractable
transitory
treacle
tremulous
trenchant
tribulation
trove

truculence
tryst
turpitude
ubiquitous
unalloyed
unctuous
unflagging
unscrupulous
unstinting
urbane
usurp
valor
vehemence
venal
verbatim
verdant

virtuoso
virulence
vitiate
vivacious
vociferous
voluminous
voracious
wane
warrant
wary
watershed
wax
wheedle
winnow
wistful
zenith

THE SAT: INSIDER INFO AND GAME DAY PREPARATIONS

YOUR ANSWERS ON THE SAT

We can learn a lot of important things by looking at a real SAT answer key.

Overall

Insider Info: Every question is assigned a difficulty level from 1 (easiest) to 5 (hardest). Order of difficulty exists on all sections of the test except for Reading passages (Reading section) and Improving Paragraphs (Writing section), though questions in these sections still are ranked on the 1–5 difficulty scale. There is a balanced distribution of answer choices. It is extremely rare for the same answer choice to show up five times in a row. Even four in a row is uncommon, but possible.

What we learn from this: Always be aware of question number and your location on the test. POOD matters greatly, because there are occasional "speed bumps" in the OOD.

Reading

Insider Info: Average time allowed per question (without skipping)—approximately 1 minute. Sentence Completions follow an order of difficulty. Reading passages do not. Most Reading questions are of medium difficulty.

What we learn from this: Expect Sentence Completions to get harder as you progress, though you may find that the first question starts at a medium level. POOD in Reading will allow you to dodge the timesuckers and tough questions.

Math

Insider Info: Average time allowed per question (without skipping)—1 minute, 15 seconds. Order of difficulty is consistent, and it is very important to note that, in the section that contains Grid In questions, question #8 is hard, but #9 is easy. Grid In answers are mostly "reasonable"; about 7 of the ten answers are integers.

What we learn from this: Awareness of your location on the test is crucial on the Math section with 18 questions, ten of which are Grid Ins. Most students should skip questions 7 and 8 initially and do them last, along with 17 and 18. Grid In answers are often integers, and are never negative. Strange decimal answers (ones without simple fractional equivilants) should be double-checked. An answer of .04367211 on the SAT is likely wrong.

Writing

Insider Info: Average time allowed per question (without skipping)—approximately 43 seconds. Order of difficulty exists within each distinct question type (Improving Sentences and Error IDs). And similar to the Grid-In Math sections, the OOD starts over at easy when you move from Error ID to Improving Sentences. OOD does not exist in the Improving Paragraphs portion. The last 5 Error IDs are often quite hard. For Error ID, this test had 6 answers of (E), No error. Typically there would be 3 or 4 without error, so 6 is unusual, but not shocking. The Improving Paragraphs on this test were a little harder than usual. Usually these are predominantly of medium difficulty.

What we learn from this: Order of difficulty exists and should influence student decisions on the long Writing section, especially on questions 9-11 (Improving Sentences) and questions 25-29 (Error ID), where the questions will likely be difficult. Also, don't be afraid to say that the sentence is correct as written.

SAT Advice

DAY BEFORE THE TEST

Chill Out

Do not cram the night before the test. Though this actually may work (sometimes) for a history test, it is pointless on the SAT, which actually tests no facts. You should prepare as much as possible in the months and weeks leading up to the test, but the day before the test is a time to relax and take it easy. Eat a good dinner. Watch a DVD with friends and go to bed early. Be well rested.

DAY OF TEST

Wake Up

The SAT is a test of stamina. It is almost four hours of work and at least five hours in the testing center. You must wake up fully. Stretch. Shower. Breathe in and out. Walk the dog. Treat the SAT as you would a job interview. Be ready and alert.

Exercise

Do sit-ups or push-ups. Run on the treadmill. Do jumping jacks. Exercising for 10-15 minutes will get your heart pumping and your blood racing. THIS will truly wake you up instead of relying on a shower or breakfast.

Breakfast

You must have it. Brains use energy. Feed your brain. Avoid pure sugar and go for protein, which keeps you full longer. Granola is better than a glazed doughnut. Even if you don't normally have a big breakfast, force yourself to have something simple. It will be at least 6 hours until you get another chance to eat a regular meal.

DO NOT consume excessive amounts of anything unusual on the morning of the SAT. This includes: caffeine, sugar, and prescription drugs. Many students have foolishly tried to get a "sugar rush" or consumed excessive coffee for the same caffeine effect. This is not smart for many reasons. Don't do it. If you normally have a cup of tea every morning, fine, but seven cups...bad idea. Outside of the shaking and twitching, your bladder will hate you. The general rule: Do not, on the morning of a very important test, do anything you've never done before in terms of food and drink.

Arrival at Testing Center

Know where you are going the night before the test. You must know exactly where the center is, especially if you have never been there before. A test trip a couple days before the big day is a good idea. Arrival time is usually 7:45 AM. Show up close to that, but not too early. You likely will not start your test until after 8:30 AM. Also, expect many other students to be arriving at the same time. It may be very crowded at your site.

Bring with You:

Mandatory
- **Admission ticket**: printed from CollegeBoard.com
- **Photo ID**: from school or state
- **Calculator**: with fresh batteries
- **5 sharpened pencils**: they might not be provided
- **Watch on wrist**: phones are not allowed on desk during test and small digital timers may also be forbidden

Recommended
- **Jacket/layered clothing**: to put on or take off as needed
- **Nutritious, simple food**: energy bar or small sandwich on break (for 5 minute break)
- **Small drink**: cannot be kept on desk (for 5 minute break)
- **Gum**: studies show it helps your score (but chew quietly)
- **Book/magazine/mp3 player**: to entertain yourself if there is a delay

WHAT TO EXPECT FROM YOUR PROCTOR

Overall

Proctors and proctoring vary greatly from site to site and room to room within sites. Do not expect your proctor to be either good or bad. You never know what you'll get. Some are experienced. Some know nothing. Some follow the rules very carefully. Some make things up and skip instructions.

Start of Test

Reporting time for the day of test is 7:45 AM for most SAT sites. However, many sites are not organized and students may actually begin section 1 of the SAT as early as 8:15 or as late as 9:15. Expect delays and a lot of boring rules and filling in bubbles before you begin.

Pencils and Calculators

Bring your own pencils. They are usually, but not always, provided by the proctors. In fact, bring 5 sharp pencils to be safe. Technically, the SAT rules say you can't use mechanical pencils, but proctors do not always enforce that, so you may want to bring back ups just in case. Calculators are NOT provided, so bring one. Technically, you can do all the math without a calculator, but there are problems on which the little machine can help. Load it up with fresh batteries the night before your test.

Cheating

Cheating includes moving forward to new sections or backwards to completed sections. Obviously, communicating with other students or sharing answers is cheating, but these are so foolish that we're sure you wouldn't even think of behaving like that. In any testing room, there will be several distinct forms of the same test. This means you may take the same exact test as others in your room, but your sections might be in a different order. **Don't cheat.**

Timing

You must watch the time yourself. Proctors can hurt you by shorting you on time (and yes, some give too much time). Proctors often give 5-minute warnings near the end of each section, but **don't count on it**. Some sites and schools have very old non-digital clocks that proctors don't watch carefully. You must double-check all the timing. If you get shorted, mention it right away so that it does not happen on subsequent sections and the proctor knows that you are watching too. One extra minute can mean one extra question, which can mean more points. Also, phones are NOT allowed on the desk at any time during the test, so you will NOT be able to use your phone as a clock (or a calculator). Additionally, calculators (some of which have clocks) are ONLY allowed on your desk during math sections. The moral of the story: Wear a watch.

Breaks

Proctors must give you three breaks. They come after section 2 (5 minutes), section 4 (5 minutes) and section 6 (5 minutes). For the first and third break, your proctor may start the exam again even if you have not returned. Some proctors allow students 5 minutes for the second break. Do not let your proctor skip breaks. And use them! Always stand and leave the room if only for a sip of water. Never remain in your seat and nap. Get up. It makes a difference.

In the words of Bob Marley: Get up, stand up.

Food and Drinks

No food or drinks are allowed on your desk. However, you are permitted to eat and drink in hallway during breaks. SAT rules permit it. We encourage you to eat a small snack. Keep it simple. The test is long. Stay alert and maintain your energy. It's likely that you won't be done until after 1:00 P.M.

Proctor Types

Your proctor may be vigilant like a prison warden or half asleep and reading the newspaper in the corner. Either way, be sure you are aware of the time yourself and stay focused. Open the test immediately when permitted and work up until the very last minute when the proctor says "put your pencils down." You don't get any points for finishing a section before everyone else. Actually, rushing will cost you points.

Other Items

Proctors usually keep testing rooms quiet, but you may encounter some distractions. You must be able to ignore some small things, including: sniffling students, buzzing lights, noises outside building, conversation in hallway, ticking clocks, tapping feet of nervous students, and clanging radiators. If any of these distractions becomes severe, report it to the proctor and attempt to fix the issue. But most of the above noises could be part of a regular testing experience that you will have deal with and ignore. Do not expect perfection from your "real" testing experience.

Testing Problems

If anything dramatic happens during your test that severely affects your concentration or the timing of the test, you must report it to the proctor before leaving the site. Treat it as a complaint that you must file with the proctor. Try to get names and numbers of other students in the room who can corroborate your tale of woe. If you wait until returning home to contact the College Board, they will treat the complaint less seriously than one that is reported on site by several students.

COMMON SAT MYTHS

If you sign your name, you get 600 points.   The truth: Minimum score on each SAT section is 200. You don't "get" 600 points. It's not possible to score lower.

If you fill in all five answers on every question, you get a perfect score.   The truth: If you fill in more than one answer on any question, you receive zero points for that question.

SAT Essay graders will grade you on facts, spelling, punctuation, and grammar.   The truth: Though the above details are important, your SAT essay score is more influenced by a clear thesis statement, strong supporting examples, and a solid structure.

If you don't know, guess answer choice (C).   The truth: Every single answer shows up an equal number of times. By the end of the test, you will have an equal amount of A, B, C, D, and E answers.

There is a "better" curve on certain SAT testing days throughout the year.   The truth: If you analyze the scoring grids for all released real SATs, you will find that there is little to no difference in the scaled scores from test to test. This includes Saturday and Sunday administrations. We've checked.

You need to be "good at grammar" to do well on the SAT Writing section.   The truth: The SAT tests only a few grammar rules over and over. You need to know the few they test consistently.

You need to be really good at math to do well on the SAT.   The truth: The SAT does not test any math concepts beyond algebra. No trigonometry or calculus or advanced geometry exists on the test. The exam focuses on concepts you learned from 7th to 9th grade. The most important skill in the math section is reading comprehension! Half the battle is figuring out what the question is asking and making sure you give that answer.

You need to be a great reader to do well on the SAT Reading section.   The truth: You need to be able to read selectively and quickly. You never need to know anything from the real world that isn't mentioned in the passages they give you. All your correct answers will be supported by information that you can point to on the page.

The SAT measures intelligence.   The truth: The one thing the SAT tests better than anything else is your ability to take the SAT. It is not an IQ test and never was.

A great SAT score gets you into great schools.   The truth: Standardized test scores are only one part of your admission to college. Every year, the top colleges reject students with excellent SAT scores. Academic performance in school and the personal element of your application (extra curricular activities, personal statement, teacher recommendations) matter as well.

PACING REVIEWS

PACING REVIEW FOR DIAG #2

Now that your second diagnostic test is coming up soon, it's a good idea to revisit the pacing strategy that we discussed the first day of class.

Your scores from the first practice test: Critical Reading: _____

                                                 Grammar: _____

                                                 Math: _____

Your goal for the second practice test: Critical Reading: _____

                                                 Grammar: _____

                                                 Math: _____

CRITICAL READING PACING CHART

To get: (scaled score)	You need to earn: (raw points)	Attempt approximately this many questions			
		24 question section	24 question section	19 question section	Total # of questions to attempt
300	5	6	6	3	15
350	9	8	8	4	20
400	16	11	11	8	30
450	23	14	14	10	38
500	31	16	16	11	43
550	40	19	19	13	51
600	46	22	22	16	60
650	53	23	23	17	63
700	59	23	23	18	64
750	63	all	all	all	67
800	67	all	all	all	67

How many **you** are going to do   _____   _____   _____   _____

Your Total

GRAMMAR PACING CHART

To get: (scaled score)	You need: (raw points)	Answer this many questions		Total # of questions to attempt
		35-question section	14-question section	
35	10	10	5	15
40	16	13	7	20
45	22	18	8	26
50	28	22	9	31
55	33	26	10	36
60	38	27	11	38
65	42	31	all	45
70	45	all	all	49
75	47	all	all	49
80	49	all	all	49

How many **you** are going to do   _____   _____   _____

Your Total

MATH PACING CHART

To get: (scaled score)	You need to earn: (raw points)	So attempt this many questions				Total # of questions to attempt
		20 question MC	8 question MC	Grid-Ins	16 question MC	
350	8	6	2	2	2	12
400	13	7	3	3	4	17
450	20	9	4	4	6	23
500	27	11	5	5	8	29
550	33	14	6	6	10	36
600	39	16	6	7	13	42
650	45	18	7	8	14	48
700	49	19	7	9	15	50
750	52	all	all	all	all	54
800	54	all	all	all	all	54

How many **you** are going to do   _____   _____   _____   _____   _____

Your Total

PACING REVIEW FOR DIAG #3

Now that your third diagnostic test is coming up soon, let's readjust your pacing strategy.

Your scores from the second practice test: Critical Reading: _____

                                        Grammar: _____

                                        Math: _____

Your goal for the third practice test: Critical Reading: _____

                                          Grammar: _____

                                          Math: _____

CRITICAL READING PACING CHART

To get: (scaled score)	You need to earn: (raw points)	Attempt approximately this many questions			
		24 question section	24 question section	19 question section	Total # of questions to attempt
300	5	6	6	3	15
350	9	8	8	4	20
400	16	11	11	8	30
450	23	14	14	10	38
500	31	16	16	11	43
550	40	19	19	13	51
600	46	22	22	16	60
650	53	23	23	17	63
700	59	23	23	18	64
750	63	all	all	all	67
800	67	all	all	all	67

How many **you** are going to do   _____   _____   _____   _____

Your Total

GRAMMAR PACING CHART

To get: (scaled score)	You need: (raw points)	Answer this many questions		Total # of questions to attempt
		35-question section	14-question section	
35	10	10	5	15
40	16	13	7	20
45	22	18	8	26
50	28	22	9	31
55	33	26	10	36
60	38	27	11	38
65	42	31	all	45
70	45	all	all	49
75	47	all	all	49
80	49	all	all	49

How many **you** are going to do   _____   _____

Your Total

MATH PACING CHART

To get: (scaled score)	You need to earn: (raw points)	So attempt this many questions				Total # of questions to attempt
		20 question MC	8 question MC	Grid-Ins	16 question MC	
350	8	6	2	2	2	12
400	13	7	3	3	4	17
450	20	9	4	4	6	23
500	27	11	5	5	8	29
550	33	14	6	6	10	36
600	39	16	6	7	13	42
650	45	18	7	8	14	48
700	49	19	7	9	15	50
750	52	all	all	all	all	54
800	54	all	all	all	all	54

How many **you** are going to do   _____   _____   _____   _____

Your Total

PACING REVIEW FOR DIAG #4

Now that your fourth diagnostic test is coming up soon, let's readjust your pacing strategy.

Your scores from the third practice test:

Critical Reading: ____

Grammar: ____

Math: ____

Your goal for the fourth practice test:

Critical Reading: ____

Grammar: ____

Math: ____

CRITICAL READING PACING CHART

To get: (scaled score)	You need to earn: (raw points)	Attempt approximately this many questions			Total # of questions to attempt
		24 question section	24 question section	19 question section	
300	5	6	6	3	15
350	9	8	8	4	20
400	16	11	11	8	30
450	23	14	14	10	38
500	31	16	16	11	43
550	40	19	19	13	51
600	46	22	22	16	60
650	53	23	23	17	63
700	59	23	23	18	64
750	63	all	all	all	67
800	67	all	all	all	67

How many **you** are going to do _____ _____ _____ _____

Your Total

GRAMMAR PACING CHART

To get: (scaled score)	You need: (raw points)	Answer this many questions		Total # of questions to attempt
		35-question section	14-question section	
35	10	10	5	15
40	16	13	7	20
45	22	18	8	26
50	28	22	9	31
55	33	26	10	36
60	38	27	11	38
65	42	31	all	45
70	45	all	all	49
75	47	all	all	49
80	49	all	all	49

How many **you** are going to do　　　————————　————————　————————

Your Total

MATH PACING CHART

To get: (scaled score)	You need to earn: (raw points)	So attempt this many questions				Total # of questions to attempt
		20 question MC	8 question MC	Grid-Ins	16 question MC	
350	8	6	2	2	2	12
400	13	7	3	3	4	17
450	20	9	4	4	6	23
500	27	11	5	5	8	29
550	33	14	6	6	10	36
600	39	16	6	7	13	42
650	45	18	7	8	14	48
700	49	19	7	9	15	50
750	52	all	all	all	all	54
800	54	all	all	all	all	54

How many **you** are going to do　　　————　————　————————　————————　————

Your Total

© TPR Education IP Holdings, LLC | **557**

PRACTICE QUESTIONS ANSWER KEY

MATH PRACTICE ANSWER KEY

No More Algebra

Plugging In

3. E
6. E
6. C
7. E
8. E
9. A
10. A
10. D
10. C
11. C
13. D
14. D
15. D
17. D
18. B
19. D
20. E

Plugging In Your Own Number

10. C
11. D
18. C

Plugging In on Geometry

8. A
10. E
12. D
12. C
13. C

Grid Ins

9. 1/25
10. 25
11. 7/3
12. 50
13. 5, 6, or 7
14. 8
15. 20
16. 3/24

Fundamentals

Properties of Numbers

1. E
2. B
3. D
4. D
4. B
4. B
4. E
4. B
5. A
6. D
9. D
9. D
11. C
14. C
15. D
15. 11 or 66
18. C
19. E

Fractions and Decimals

3. E
4. D
5. D
6. E
7. C
12. D

Equations and Inequalities

2. B
3. E
4. E
5. C
7. A
9. D
10. A
10. E
11. B
11. D
11. C
12. C
13. C
18. A

Geometry

Geometry Basics

2. C
2. C
3. C
3. E
5. E
6. D
7. A
7. B
8. E
8. A
9. D
10. B
10. C
12. C
14. B
14. $7 < x < 13$
18. B
20. D

Parallel Lines

4. D
5. B
10. B

Circles

10. C
13. E
14. D
14. C
16. $\dfrac{1}{8}$

Coordinate Geometry

7. B
8. D
11. D
13. C
16. B
16. B
17. 2 or 26

Overlapping Figures

9. D
12. E
14. A
15. D
16. B
16. B
19. B
19. B
20. D

More Ways To Plug In

Plugging in the Answers

2. B
5. D
6. A
6. B
7. B
7. E
8. C
9. C
9. A
9. A
10. E
12. D
12. A
13. C
14. A
15. D
17. B
20. B

Must Be

4. C
5. E
10. B
12. A
16. A
18. D

Arithmetic

Average, Median, & Mode

3. C
4. C
5. C
6. B
7. C
8. D
9. D
10. B
10. D
11. 700
11. B
12. E
13. C
15. 95
20. A

All About Percents

2. C
5. D
8. D
9. D
10. 64
11. 40
11. C
12. E
13. D
14. B
16. 23
16. A

 © TPR Education IP Holdings, LLC

Ratios and Variation

2. A
4. D
6. E
8. C
9. 9.5
10. E
11. C
12. E
13. 168
14. B
17. A
18. 12
18. 12
19. B

Probability

10. B
13. B
13. $\frac{2}{3}$ or $\frac{4}{6}$
16. B
17. D
18. D
19. A

Geometric Probability

9. C
13. B
14. E
15. B

How Many Different...

8. D
9. E
14. A
17. D
18. 960

Patterns and Sequences

5. B
8. C
11. B
13. B
16. D
18. C
19. D
19. D

Functions & Graphs

Funky Roots and Exponents

6. B
8. D
9. A
13. B
14. B
17. A

Quadratics

4. B
6. D
7. A
8. A
9. D
14. 3
19. D

Rational and Radical Equations

3. E
6. B
7. B
9. D
10. B
11. E
13. B
14. 3
15. 4
18. D
20. E

Functions and Expressions

7. B
11. D
15. D
16. 3
20. E

Slope

8. B
9. C
10. B
12. B
14. C
18. E
20. B

Linear and Quadratic Functions

13. D
13. C
13. B
14. A
16. B
16. D
17. B

Behavior of Graphs

3. D
11. A
13. A
15. E
16. D
18. 0
18. 16
19. A
20. D

POOD Review

14. A
11. D
14. B
9. D
17. B
15. A
16. D
18. D
19. E
20. D

Content Review Practice

Working with Equations

i. 3

ii. $\dfrac{7}{4}$

iii. 56

1. D
2. A
3. C
3. C
4. E
4. A
10. A
14. E

Simultaneous Equations

8. A
11. C
12. B
13. E
14. E
14. B
15. C

Exponents and Roots

2. B
3. D
3. D
3. C
3. C
4. E
5. D
6. D
6. D
6. C
7. C
8. D
9. C
10. D
10. D
14. E
18. C
18. 15

Sets

4. B
6. A
12. 2
14. D
16. E

Right Triangles

9. B
11. C
13. B
16. D

Trig? Who Needs It?

8. D
11. C
14. C
14. C
14. A
18. 5

Four or More Sides?

5. C
8. 180
13. A
14. B
16. D

Using Data

18. B
5. C
7. D
13. D
18. B
18. $\dfrac{9}{15}$ or .6
12. C

 © TPR Education IP Holdings, LLC

WRITING PRACTICE ANSWER KEY

Essay Preview

You're the Grader!

Be sure to ask your instructor to explain why each of these essays deserved the scores they received.

Essay	Score
Essay A:	5
Essay B:	4 or 5
Essay C:	4 or 5
Essay D:	6
Essay E:	4
Essay F:	3
Essay G:	5
Essay H:	6
Essay I:	2

Improving Sentences

Prepositions

6. E
7. B
19. B
21. B

Pronoun Agreement Drill

1. one
2. his
3. her
4. it
5. it's
6. her
7. one
8. he is
9. he
10. she
11. they
12. me
13. we

Identify the Pronoun Errors

12. A
13. D
14. A
22. B
24. C
25. B
26. B
29. E

Subject-Verb Agreement Drill

1. are…ways
2. concentration… has
3. neither…is
4. plots and… style…make
5. understanding…is
6. Sensationalism…is
7. Smoking…is
8. either…is
9. both…require
10. Each…is

Improving Sentences Drill 1

1. B
2. A
3. C
4. C
5. A
5. C
6. E
7. C
7. B
8. A
8. D
8. B
9. B
9. E
10. D
10. B
10. C
11. C
12. B
13. E
14. E

Improving Sentences Drill 2

1. A
2. B
3. C
4. D
5. C
6. B
7. D
8. C
9. E
10. B
11. A
12. E
13. E
14. A

Error IDs

Idiom Drill 1

1. to
2. of
3. of
4. from
5. over or with
6. no preposition
7. as
8. to
9. for
10. as
11. no preposition
12. to
13. to
14. to
15. as
16. by
17. so too

Idiom Drill 2

1. but also
2. as
3. and
4. and
5. and
6. or
7. nor
8. whether
9. that
10. than
11. to…to…that… than
12. than
13. to…as…as
14. as

Pronouns: Practice

1. correct—object of a preposition = object case
2. It was he—He posted that comment.
3. correct—reflexive pronouns are used only after its related subjective pronoun (e.g., I = myself; he = himself)
4. correct—than they (have). Subject case is required.
5. Kelly can yodel better than he (can). Subject case is required.
6. correct—I shall email it to him/her/whom = object case
7. correct—You can count on…me to save the world.
8. It's I = It is I
9. correct—object of a preposition = object case

Pronoun Patrol

1. I
2. me
3. they
4. We
5. my
6. her
7. He
8. my…him
9. hers
10. herself
11. Our…our
12. me
13. whom
14. us
15. themselves

Diction Errors

allusion: an indirect reference	**illusion**: an erroneous perception
implicate: to connect incriminatingly	**imply**: to indicate indirectly
perspective: a mental outlook or view	**prospective**: something likely to happen
describe: to convey an impression of	**ascribe**: to attribute to a certain cause
deduce: to conclude through reasoning	**induce**: to bring about or cause
consciousness: the state of being conscious	**conscience**: your source of moral judgment
compliment: an expression of praise	**complement**: something that completes
elude: to escape or avoid	**allude**: to refer to indirectly
desirous: having or expressing desire for something	**desirable**: advisable; recommendable; worthwhile
principal: head of a school	**principle**: fundamental basis for conduct
accept: to receive or to agree to	**except**: excluding
indict: to charge with a crime; accuse	**induct**: to introduce; to install in a new office
declined: to deny consent to	**descended**: to move down
precede: to come before	**proceed**: to carry on and move forward
affect: to act on or cause a change	**effect**: something that is caused, a consequence

 © TPR Education IP Holdings, LLC

Error ID Drill 1

12. C (verb tense)
13. D (verb parallelism)
14. C (verb parallelism)
15. A (S/V agreement)
16. D (verb parallelism)
17. D (verb parallelism)
18. E (pronoun case)
19. B (S/V agreement)
20. B (S/V agreement)
21. C (S/V agreement)
22. E (verb tense)
23. D (redundancy)
24. B (S/V agreement)
25. C (verb tense)
26. C (idiom)
27. E (S/V agreement)
28. A (pronoun case)
29. D (subjunctive)

Error ID Drill 2

12. D (verb parallelism)
13. B (adjective/adverb)
14. E (verb parallelism)
15. D (verb parallelism)
16. A (adjective/adverb)
17. C (pronoun ambiguity)
18. E (pronoun agreement)
19. C (pronoun case)
20. A (pronoun case)
21. E (subjunctive)
22. E (diction)
23. C (parallelism)
24. D (verb parallelism)
25. D (idiom)
26. B (noun agreement)
27. C (redundancy)
28. C (S/V agreement)
29. A (diction)

Error ID Drill 3

12. D (verb parallelism)
13. C (verb tense)
14. A (pronoun ambiguity)
15. E (verb tense/idiom)
16. A (faulty comparison)
17. C (pronoun agreement)
18. A (S/V agreement)
19. E (comparative)
20. A (where/when)
21. C (conjunction)
22. C (conjunction)
23. D (pronoun ambiguity)
24. B (diction)
25. D (pronoun agreement)
26. D (diction)
27. A (colon)
28. D (idiom)
29. B (faulty comparison)

Error ID Drill 4

12. A (adjective/adverb)
13. B (verb tense)
14. D (redundancy)
15. E (conjunction)
16. B (conjunction)
17. C (diction)
18. B (where/when)
19. C (verb parallelism)
20. E (pronoun case)
21. A (verb tense)
22. E (idiom)
23. D (conjunction)
24. B (diction)
25. C (S/V agreement)
26. A (pronoun agreement)
27. D (faulty comparison)
28. D (parallelism)
29. C (where/when)

Error ID Drill 5

12. D (verb parallelism)
13. E (subjunctive)
14. B (who/which)
15. B (conjunction)
16. C (redundancy)
17. B (less/fewer)
18. E (comparison)
19. C (pronoun usage)
20. B (adjective/adverb)
21. C (comparative/ superlative)
22. D (idiom/parallelism)
23. C (between/among)
24. D (S/V agreement)
25. D (pronoun case)
26. A (misplaced modifier)
27. D (pronoun ambiguity)
28. A (amount/number)
29. A (noun agreement)

Error ID Drill 6

12. A (adjective/adverb)
13. A (verb tense)
14. C (S/V agreement)
15. D (verb parallelism)
16. D (verb tense)
17. C (verb parallelism)
18. E (idiom/diction)
19. D (diction)
20. D (faulty comparison)
21. C (where/when)
22. D (verb tense)
23. B (where/when)
24. D (faulty comparison)
25. B (S/V agreement)
26. B (pronoun case/ comparison)
27. E (idiom)
28. B (idiom)
29. E (subjunctive)

Improving Paragraphs

Down to Two Drill

1. C
2. B
3. E
4. B
5. A

Improving Paragraphs 1

30. D
31. D
32. D
33. B
34. B
35. C

Improving Paragraphs 2

30. B
31. D
32. A
33. E
34. A
35. A

Improving Paragraphs 3

30. D
31. A
32. B
33. E
34. C
35. C

READING HOMEWORK ANSWER KEY

Sentence Completions

Warm Up!
1. bad
1. primitive, poor
1. innate, hereditary
2. rarely or long ago
3. slipped or stopped or slowed
3. common
3. dangerous
4. addressed; returned to
4. perfectionist
5. championed
5. reluctantly
6. stability, order
6. suddenly; on its way
7. biased or too kind
7. after death
7. brutal
8. consensus
8. imbued; injected

One Blank at a Time
1. A
2. C
3. B
4. B
5. B
6. C

Sentence Completion Drill 1
1. C
2. B
3. A
4. E
5. A
6. C
7. C
8. B

Sentence Completion Drill 2
1. C
2. B
3. B
4. B
5. E

Sentence Completion Drill 3
1. C
2. E
3. D
4. D
5. C
6. D
7. C
8. B

Sentence Completion Drill 4
1. C
2. D
3. B
4. A
5. D
6. C
7. C
8. D

Sentence Completion Drill 5
1. B
2. E
3. A
4. B
5. D
6. B
7. D
8. A

Sentence Completion Drill 6
1. B
2. A
3. B
4. B
5. E
6. A
7. B
8. D

Sentence Completion Drill 7
1. D
2. A
3. D
4. A
5. E
6. E
7. C
8. E

Sentence Completion Drill 8
1. D
2. C
3. D
4. C
5. A
6. D
7. E
8. C

Sentence Completion Drill 9
1. A
2. E
3. D
4. A
5. D
6. E
7. C
8. C

Timed Drills

Sentence Completion Drill 10

1. A
2. E
3. B
4. A
5. C
6. B

Sentence Completion Drill 11

1. D
2. D
3. C
4. B
5. B

Sentence Completion Drill 12

1. E
2. C
3. B
4. D
5. B

Sentence Completion Drill 13

1. A
2. A
3. E
4. C
5. E

Drill 1

18. C
19. B
20. D
21. D
22. E
23. A
24. A

Drill 2

16. C
17. A
18. D
19. D
20. C
21. C
22. C
23. B
24. D

Drill 3

10. B
11. A
12. C
13. E
14. D

Drill 4

9. B
10. A
11. E
12. B

Drill 5

13. E
14. A
15. D
16. D
17. E
18. D
19. B
20. B
21. A
22. D
23. E
24. C

Drill 6

14. A
15. B
16. A
17. C
18. E
19. A
20. A
21. C
22. C
23. D
24. E

Drill 7

13. D
14. C
15. A
16. B
17. E
18. A
19. C
20. B
21. C
22. D
23. E
24. E

Drill 8

13. B
14. E
15. B
16. A
17. A
18. E
19. D
20. E
21. D
22. C
23. C
24. B

HOMEWORK PLANNER

SAT HOMEWORK PLANNER

Homework from...	...is due (write the date!)	Manual assignment	Additional assignment

SAT HOMEWORK PLANNER

Homework from...	...is due (write the date!)	Manual assignment	Additional assignment

euphemism	didactic	conjecture	candid
lucid	insinuate	incoherent	extrapolate
ascertain	adroit	acumen	rhetoric
erudition	disseminate	circumspect	astute
pragmatic	perspicacious	pedantic	husbandry

mild or vague substitute for harsh or offensive term	instructive	inference; guesswork	completely honest
clear	to introduce or communicate sneakily	lacking cohesion or connection	to infer from known information
to find out	dexterous, deft	accuracy, keenness	art of using language persuasively
extensive learning	to scatter widely; to spread	careful, discreet	shrewd
practical	shrewd, clear-sighted	concerned with book learning and rules	the application of scientific principles to agriculture, especially to animal breeding

abstruse	rudimentary	prospectus	precocious
inscrutable	enigma	convoluted	callous
assimilate	arcane	staid	reticent
entourage	derivative	cosmopolitan	autonomy
insular	idiosyncrasy	gaffe	esoteric

difficult to understand	difficult to understand	to make or become absorbed	group of attendants or associates	isolated
basic	mystery	known by only a few	something that comes from another source	characteristic peculiar to an individual or group
proposal	complex	serious	worldly	clumsy social error
exhibiting early ability, especially intelligence	unfeeling	reserved	independence	understood by only a small group

censure (v.)	castigate	potentate	orthodox
renounce	relinquish	reclusive	denounce
conciliatory	contiguous	circumscribe	vituperative
indict	incontrovertible	exonerate	credible
rectitude	parity	partisan (adj.)	litigious

to issue official blame	to scold	monarch	adhering to the traditional and established
to give up, especially by formal announcement	give up or retire from	preferring isolation	to condemn openly
appeasing, soothing	sharing an edge or boundary	draw a circle around; restrict	marked by harshly abusive condemnation
to officially charge with wrongdoing	indisputable	to free from blame	capable of being believed
being morally correct in judgment	equality	biased in support of a party, group, or cause	prone to engage in lawsuits

remiss	repudiate	sanctimonious	scrupulous
solicitous	sophistry	substantiate	veracity
vindicate	cajole	chicanery	obsequious
sycophant	altruism	eminent	empathetic
extol	laudatory	magnanimous	philanthropic

principled	thinking you are better than others	to reject the validity of	slacking off; lax in performing duties
truthfulness	to support with proof or evidence	a believable but false argument	concerned
attempting to please to a great degree	trickery	to urge with teasing or flattery	to free from blame
understanding of another's feelings	distinguished, prominent	selflessness	flatterer
humanitarian	noble	full of praise	to praise highly